Pearson New International Edition

Intercultural Business Communication
Lillian Chaney Jeanette Martin
Sixth Edition

Pearson Education Limited
Edinburgh Gate
Harlow
Essex CM20 2JE
England and Associated Companies throughout the world

Visit us on the World Wide Web at: www.pearsoned.co.uk

© Pearson Education Limited 2014

PEARSON®   ISBN 10: 1-292-03966-3
ISBN 13: 978-1-292-03966-4

British Library Cataloguing-in-Publication Data
A catalogue record for this book is available from the British Library

ARP Impression 98
Printed in Great Britain by Clays Ltd, St Ives plc

Table of Contents

The Nature of Intercultural Communication

Objectives

Upon completion of this chapter, you will

- understand such terms as intercultural, international, intracultural, multicultural, and ethnocentric.
- recognize how communication barriers affect intercultural communication.
- understand the differences between norms, rules, roles, and networks.
- distinguish between subcultures and subgroups.
- understand the concepts of business globalization, glocalization, and grobalization.
- differentiate between ethnocentric, polycentric, regiocentric, and geocentric management orientations.

The number of North Americans who work for foreign employers and the number of foreign companies who have built plants in the United States are increasing. Evidence that the world is becoming more cosmopolitan can be seen in the number of international businesses, such as Coca-Cola, McDonald's, Sony, and Honda, which are common around the world. The new economic bonanza is apparent in the universal appreciation of food such as sushi, fashion such as jeans, and music such as U.S. jazz and rock. Because of the global boom, more and more business will involve international activities, which require the ability to communicate across cultures.

Because communication is an element of culture, it has often been said that communication and culture are inseparable. As Alfred G. Smith (1966) wrote in his preface to *Communication and Culture,* "Culture is a code we learn and share, and learning and sharing require communication. Communication requires coding and symbols that must be learned and shared." Godwin C. Chu (1977) observed that every cultural pattern and every single act of social

From Chapter 1 of *Intercultural Business Communication*, Sixth Edition. Lillian H. Chaney, Jeanette S. Martin.

behavior involves communication. To be understood, the two must be studied together. Culture cannot be known with a study of communication, and communication can only be understood with an understanding of the culture it supports.

To gain a better understanding of the field of intercultural communication, knowledge of frequently used terms is important. Such terms as intercultural, international, and multicultural are often used interchangeably; however, certain distinctions should be made.

Edward T. Hall first used the term intercultural communication in 1959. Hall was one of the first researchers to differentiate cultures on the basis of how communications are sent and received. Hall defined **intercultural communication** as communication between persons of different cultures.

Intercultural business communication is a relatively new term in the business world and is defined as communication within and between businesses that involves people from more than one culture. Although we generally think of the United States as one culture, a great deal of cultural diversity exists. For example, between the 2000 and 2010 census, the Hispanic population increased 43%. Hispanics are currently 16% of the U.S. population, Whites are 64%, African Americans 14%, Asians 5%, American Indians and Alaskan Natives 0.9%, Native Hawaiians and other Pacific Islanders 0.2%, and others 0.9%. The Asian and Latin American populations grew as expected during the last decade. Many U.S. citizens communicate interculturally almost daily because communication occurs between people of different cultural backgrounds (U.S. Census Bureau News, 2011).

Susumu Yoshida, Managing Director of Sumitomo Chemical Asia Pte Ltd., in his address to a group of international business executives in Kyoto, Japan, June 19, 2002, said: "We are on the threshold of globalization. The world economy is 'borderless' and markets are becoming essentially one. Corporations are looking at the free flow of goods and services, capital, and human resources, as well as information, as the pathway to growth. Hence, the corporate strategy of going global is no longer a choice but rather a 'must' for survival.... A lack of effective intercultural communication skills often causes misunderstandings. This leads to irritation and even distrust between the parties concerned. More often than not, problems arise from differences in communication styles." (Yoshida, 2002, pp. 708, 710).

Global business communication is becoming a common term to replace international or intercultural business communication when speaking of communication between businesses from different countries. This is due in part to the fact that international is assumed to be on a government level rather than on a secular level. In addition, intercultural can take place within a country between people of different cultural backgrounds and not necessarily between people from different countries. The term global business communication describes the process more accurately (Association for Business Communication Conference Panel, 2010).

As contact occurs between cultures, diffusion takes place. **Diffusion** is the process by which the two cultures learn and adapt materials and adopt practices from each other. This practice is exemplified by how Columbus joined the Old and New Worlds. The Old World gave the New World horses, cows, sheep, chickens, honeybees, coffee, wheat, cabbage, lettuce, bananas, olives, tulips, and daisies. The New World gave the Old World turkeys, sugarcane, corn, sweet potatoes, tomatoes, pumpkins, pineapples, petunias, poinsettias, and daily baths. With the increased globalization of the economy and interaction of different cultures, the concept of a world culture has emerged. A **world culture** is the idea that as traditional barriers among people of differing cultures break down, emphasizing the commonality of human needs, one culture will emerge, a new culture to which all people will adhere. So why study intercultural business communication? Because it addresses procedural, substantive, and informational global problems, intercultural business communication allows you to work on the procedural issues of country-to-country contacts, diplomacy, and legal contexts. You can then become involved with the substantive, cultural level and become sensitized to differences. You can also gather information to make decisions when you are in an intercultural environment. The United States continues to welcome a large number of immigrants each year and has been referred to as a melting-pot society. **Melting pot** means a sociocultural assimilation of people of differing backgrounds and nationalities; the term implies losing ethnic differences and forming one large society or **macroculture**. Although the idea of everyone's being the same may sound ideal, the problem with this concept is that many U.S. citizens want to maintain their ethnic-cultural heritage. Rather than being one melting-pot society, therefore, the reality is that many U.S. cities are made up of neighborhoods of people with a common heritage who strive to retain their original culture and language. In San Francisco, a visit to Chinatown with its signs in Chinese and people speaking Chinese verifies this reality. Many street signs in other U.S. cities, such as New York, Miami, and Honolulu, are in another language in addition to English. The result has not been the melding of various cultures into one cultural group as idealists believed would happen. Because cultures exist within cultures (**microcultures**), communication problems often result. In reality, the United States is a salad bowl of cultures rather than a melting pot. Although some choose assimilation, others choose separation. Thus, the assumption that America is a cultural melting pot, which assumes assimilation, is no longer valid ("Differences," 1996).

Intracultural communication is defined as communication between and among members of the same culture. Generally, people who are of the same race, political persuasion, and religion or who share the same interests communicate intraculturally. Having the same beliefs, values, and constructs facilitates communication and defines a particular culture (Lustig & Koester, 1998). However, because of distance, cultural differences may exist within a culture, such as differences in the pace of life and regional speech patterns between residents of New York City and Jackson, Mississippi. Distance is also a factor in the differences in the dialects of the people of other cultures, such as in northern and southern Japan.

The terms intercultural communication and international communication should not be used interchangeably. Intercultural communication, as stated previously, involves communication between people of different cultures. **International communication** takes place between nations and governments rather than individuals; it is formal and ritualized. The dialogue at the United Nations, for example, is international communication.

Because all international business activity involves communication, knowledge of intercultural communication and international business communication is important to prepare you to compete successfully in international environments. In fact, upward mobility and promotion in tomorrow's corporate world may depend on your knowledge of intercultural business communication.

GLOBALIZATION, GLOCALIZATION, AND GROBALIZATION

Globalization

Although globalization has come to the world, most of the world's businesses are not globalized. Business **globalization** is the spread of ways of life across the world both socially and in business (Ritzer, 2003). International firms have subsidiaries or components in other countries; however, control of the foreign operations is maintained at the home-country headquarters. Multinational firms allow their foreign operations to exist as domestic organizations. Most firms are global, either sourcing, producing, or exporting. Many times, the product may also be partially or completely manufactured somewhere other than the United States. In the past, some U.S. corporations have been largely insulated from globalization because of a strong domestic market and an absence of foreign competitors. However, this trend is changing as foreign corporations enter the U.S. market.

The personnel of an organization must have a global mindset for the firm to succeed in the international marketplace. Evans, Doz, and Laurent (1990) found that successful multinational corporations do not submerge the individuality of different cultures completely in the corporate culture, that intercultural contact can promote a determination not to adjust to other cultures, and that new management theory and practice can be presented only to individuals who are culturally able and willing to accept it. Rhinesmith (1996) states, "The corporate culture contains the values, norms of behavior, systems, policies, and procedures through which the organization adapts to the complexity of the global arena" (p. 14). Successful corporations have found that the values, beliefs, and behaviors of the parent corporation do not need to be the beliefs, values, and behaviors of the offices in other cultures. Hofstede's (2004) study of IBM determined that managers had to adjust the corporate management philosophy to fit the beliefs, values, and behaviors of the country in which they were working. Companies with franchises abroad have had to make certain adjustments to accommodate the tastes and preferences of individual countries; for example, Tex-Mex cuisine is prepared kosher in Israel. According to Rhinesmith (1996), "Diversity—both domestic and international—will be the engine that drives the creative energy of the corporation of the twenty-first century. Successful global managers will be those who are able to manage this diversity for the innovative and competitive edge of their corporations" (p. 5). Evans, Doz, and Laurent (1990) state that the five elements critical to building a successful corporate culture are (1) a clear and simple mission statement, (2) the vision of the chief executive officer, (3) company-controlled management education, (4) project-oriented management training programs, and (5) emphasis on the processes of global corporate culture (p. 118).

Lopez-Vasquez, director of multicultural affairs at the Oregon Health Sciences University and a consultant with IEC Enterprises, Decatur, Georgia, believes that well-meaning managers who become supervisors of Hispanic workers often make the mistake of attempting to adopt a "color-blind" approach. "The cultural disparities are obvious," he says.

Lopez-Vasquez argues for what he calls "essential treatment" for Hispanic employees. "I suggest that companies recognize that today it's essential to take steps to recruit and retain Hispanics, because Hispanics in the United States represent a fast-growing market and because Central and South America are key areas for success in international markets," he says. (Staa, 1998, p. 8)

Although the United States depends on foreign economic opportunities, multinational firms have had problems with U.S. citizens working in foreign assignments. The failures to adapt included differences in lifestyle, language, and business philosophy as well as problems with finances, government, cultural shock, housing, food, gender, and family. Ruch (1989) found that the ability to blend with the host culture and explain one's own culture is more important than product, price, or quality advantages. Although many of the people sent on foreign assignments know their U.S. market, they are unable to accept another culture on that culture's terms even for short periods.

Glocalization

The term **glocalization** refers to "the interpenetration of the global and the local, resulting in unique outcomes in different geographic areas" (Robertson, 2001, in Ritzer, 2003, p. 193). As the world grows more pluralistic, glocalization looks at the uniformity and differences between areas of the world. The degree to which a society chooses to adapt indicates the degree of glocalization that is happening. Globalization can cause glocalization that is nationalistic or cosmopolitan. How globalization of an item is embraced determines the degree of glocalization that happens to the community. Advertising and providing products are not seen as coercive; they allow the new society to receive information with which to accept or reject a product.

Grobalization

Grobalization, according to Ritzer (2003), "focuses on the imperialistic ambitions of nations, corporations, organizations, and the like and their desire, indeed need, to impose themselves on various geographic areas" (p. 194). Because of the drive for profits to grow, once an organization has saturated one market, it must reach out (globalize) in order to continue the profit's growth. This expands not only the profits of the organization but also the culture, the efficiencies, the capitalistic economic system, and the consumption patterns to a new group of people (Ritzer, 2003).

As the term grobalization relates to culture, it is an expansion of common codes and practices from one location to another. In other words, it is the imposition of an organization on a new culture. What the locals do with the imposition is the glocalization of the imposition, which involves their acceptance, adaptation, or rejection. Glocalization is the interaction of the old way of doing things with the new. Many times this process results in a replacement of the way things were done previously. Sometimes the process develops into a cultural hybrid, but it does bring change and reaction from the new culture that is being infiltrated. With glocalization, the different cultures in the world are becoming more alike. Individuals locally have the ability to adapt, innovate, and maneuver; and social processes may range from entrenchment to the old ways of doing things in the culture to embracing of the new. With grobalization, the world is becoming the same; individuals have little control of the changes that are happening to their cultures. Social processes are one-directional because they affect and make a new culture; they do not uphold the old culture (Ritzer, 2003).

Although we travel to experience the differences between us and people of other cultures socially, culturally, climatically, scenically, and architecturally, it is becoming more difficult because of globalization, glocalization, and grobalization to see the differences—with the exception of climate and scenery. Multinational corporations have had a significant role in this convergence process. While a global strategy for a product means economies of scale, many companies find that where cultural differences are strong, a multidomestic strategy that takes into consideration the cultural differences is necessary in order to expand their markets (Marsden, 2008).

CULTURE

Whereas communication is a process, **culture** is the structure through which the communication is formulated and interpreted. Culture deals with the way people live. When cultures interact, adaptation must take place for the cultures to communicate effectively. With intercultural business communication, being aware of each culture's symbols, how they are the same, and how they are different is important.

Dimensions of Culture

To communicate effectively in the intercultural business environment, knowing all the cultural factors that affect the situation is essential. The graphical representation of culture in Figure 1 has three primary dimensions—language, physical, and psychological (Borden, 1991, p. 171).

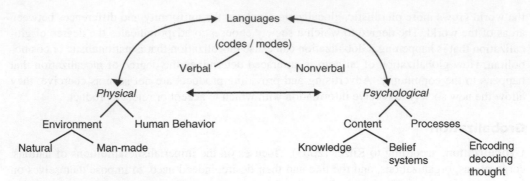

FIGURE 1 Dimensions of Culture

*Adapted from *American ways* (3rd ed.) by Gary Althen with Janet Bennett, 2011, Boston, MA: Intercultural Press, Inc. Used by permission.

The language, physical, and psychological dimensions of culture are interdependent. As we are born into a society, no one dimension is more important than the others. The individual dimensions develop in harmony with each other.

First, the language dimension is used to communicate with other people who have similar values and beliefs. Second, the physical dimension relates to the physical reality of our environment and the cultural activities of the people. The physical dimension is measured objectively. Third, the psychological dimension relates to our knowledge, beliefs, and mental activities. The psychological dimension is measured subjectively. Although we can alter these characteristics and our way of communicating with others, we must first understand our own personal dimensions and understand why we are the way we are.

Culture is learned through perception. Perceptions are formed in various ways: where we are born and raised, the language we learn, the people and environment with which we live, and the psychological stimuli we encounter. No two individuals view the external world the same because no two individuals receive exactly the same stimuli or share the same physical sensory receptors. Because we know only what we have personally perceived and cannot know for sure what someone else has perceived, intercultural communication involving different cultures becomes particularly difficult (Singer, 1998).

Another way to describe culture is by using the cultural metaphor, which has six dimensions (Gannon, Locke, Amit, Pino, & Kristof-Brown, 2005):

1. What do members of a society assume about the nature of people? Specifically, are people good, bad, or a mixture?
2. What do members of society assume about the relationship between a person and nature? Specifically, should we live in harmony with nature or subjugate it?
3. What do members of society assume about the relationship between people? Specifically, should a person act in an individual manner, or should he or she consider the group before taking action (individualism to groupism or collectivism in terms of such issues as making decisions, conformity, etc.)?
4. What is the primary mode of activity in a given society? Is it being or accepting the status quo, enjoying the current situation, and going with the flow of things? Or is it changing things to make them better by setting specific goals and accomplishing them within specific schedules?

5. What is the conception of space in a given society? Specifically, is space considered private in that meetings are held in private and people respect an individual's need for space by avoiding close physical encounters? Or is space viewed as public? That is, everyone participates in meetings and decision making, emotions are expressed publicly, and people stand in close proximity to one another?

6. What is the society's dominant temporal orientation: past, present, or future?

Gannon et al. (2005) use this system to separate cultures into seven groups: authority-ranking cultures; equality-matching cultures; market-pricing cultures; cleft national cultures; torn national cultures; same metaphor, different meanings cultures; and the base culture and its diffusion across borders. The authority-ranking cultures include Thailand, Japan, India, Bedouins of Saudi Arabia, Turkey, Brazil, Poland, and South Korea. The equality-matching cultures include Germany, Sweden, Ireland, Canada, Denmark, and France. The market-pricing cultures include the United States and Britain. Cleft national cultures include Malaysia, Nigeria, Israel, Italy, and Belgium. The torn national cultures include Mexico and Russia. The same metaphor, different meanings cultures are Spain and Portugal. The base culture and its diffusion across borders include China and Singapore.

Using a cultural intelligence approach to studying culture suggests that different cultures structure knowledge differently and that these differences determine aspects of behavior and communication such as information that is accepted as a proof for an opinion or argument, the syntax of the information, and the topics that are considered appropriate to discuss. In order for people to be culturally intelligent, they must have cognitive flexibility and metacognition across different cross-cultural settings, the behavioral ability to interact interculturally, and the motivation to do so. Some people are able to communicate interculturally easier than others (Earley, Murnieks, & Mosakowski, 2007).

If you find that a particular cultural attitude is constant across cultures, then you do not have to be concerned about that particular cultural trait. However, if you find that a particular cultural attitude varies for specific cultures, you should consider the effect it will have on communications with cultures that possess this attitude. A **cultural symbol** is a word or object that represents something in the culture. Cultural symbol variability may be included in social cognitive processes such as information processing, persuasive strategy selection, conflict management styles, personality, social relations, and self-perceptions as well as habits, norms, rules, roles, networks, language, and environment. All the factors interact and influence each other. To communicate effectively in the intercultural business environment, it is important to know all the cultural factors that affect the situation.

Stereotypes of U.S. Culture

Stereotypes, perceptions about certain groups of people or nationalities, exist with U.S. persons and those of other cultures. Although stereotyping is a guide to a national culture, it does not work well with individuals, particularly those who have worked in international business or who have lived or studied abroad. Individuals generally differ from their national culture in some aspects (Lewis, 2006).

In *American Ways*, Althen and Bennett* (2011) describe typical U.S. businesspersons as people who tend to do the following:

- Be informal in their relationships.
- Be rather formal in their business attire (suits for men and dresses or suits for women); however, many firms are becoming more relaxed in their dress codes or have a casual day when employees can dress less formally.

---

*Adapted from *American Ways* (3rd ed.) by Gary Althen with Janet Bennett, 2011, Boston, MA: Intercultural Press, Inc. Used by permission.

- Be workaholics because they spend more time working than they do with their families or social engagements; U.S. executives tend to put in long hours at the office.
- Embarrass foreign businesspeople by doing manual labor (e.g., mowing their own lawns) or tasks that would be done by the lower class or servants in their country.
- Be overly concerned with time, money, and appointments; people of other cultures interpret the need of U.S. businesspeople to begin meetings on time and start business discussions immediately as an indication that they are unfriendly, impersonal, and cold.
- Make decisions on hard, objective facts rather than on personal feelings, social relationships, or political advantage.
- Consider contracts and the written word as very important and to be taken very seriously.
- Be aware of the status differences within the organization; however, generally no display of superiority or inferiority is made, which tends to make rank-conscious foreigners very uneasy.
- Be mobile; they rarely work for one company all their lives, which is very different from many countries in the world.
- Convey superiority in their actions because they feel the United States is a superior nation.

Althen and Bennett (2011) stereotyped U.S. persons as workaholics; they added these stereotypes of persons in the United States: arrogant, loud, friendly, impatient, generous, and monolingual. These descriptions, admittedly, are stereotypes.

ENCULTURATION

Enculturation is the socialization process you go through to adapt to your society. When you grow up in one culture, you learn one way of classifying, coding, prioritizing, and justifying reality. Cultural information that you are willing to share with outsiders is considered **frontstage culture**, while cultural information that is concealed from outsiders is considered **backstage culture**. An example of frontstage culture is a sales representative who loudly announces, "We got the Hunter Fan account." This information is readily shared. An example of backstage culture is the sales representative who conceals the fact that his child is mentally retarded. Frontstage and backstage cultures vary by culture and by individuals within the culture because some people are inherently more open than others. As a representative of your company, you need to learn what the culture with which you are working considers acceptable frontstage information that can be shared and what is considered backstage information that is not to be shared with others.

Datan, Rodeheaver, and Hughes (1987) use the concept of scripts to explain the cognitive imprinting that happens during enculturation:

Individuals experience events in their lives as "scenes"—organized wholes combining people, places, time, actions, and in particular, affects that amplify these experiences and provide a sense of urgency about understanding them. Out of early scenes, the individual develops sets of rules for interpreting, evaluating, producing, predicting, or controlling future scenes. These rules—"scripts"—are initially innate but are supplemented and replaced by learned scripts. Higher-order scripts are created when scenes are combined and instilled with fresh affect— "psychological magnification." ... The order in personality development, then, derives from the individual's need to impose order—the script—on the critical events, or scenes, in life. And, finally, scripts that initially arise from scenes begin to give rise to scenes instead, as the individual's construction of experience affects experience itself. (p. 164)

Examples of such scripts are the inability of the Japanese to say the word "no" directly but instead to say that "it would be difficult," and the difficulty for someone of a strong Christian background to lie to save face when lying is never condoned for a Christian.

ACCULTURATION

People do not want to abandon their past; therefore, they acculturate new ideas into their existing culture. **Acculturation** is the process of adjusting and adapting to a new and different culture (Hazuda, Stern, & Hoffner, 1988). If people of two different cultures absorb a significant number of each others' cultural differences and have a number of similarities, **cultural synergy** takes place with the two cultures merging to form a stronger overriding culture. Corporate cultures are examples of the synergy of diverse cultures.

A manager, to be productive and creative, must make his or her workers realize that the corporation is more important than individual differences. Differences are not to be suppressed but instead managed to maximize the group's productivity and creativity. Hofstede's (2004) work shows that what motivates a worker in one country may or may not be important to a worker in another country. For corporations to get the most from their people, they must have managers who can work effectively with many cultural groups.

People who learn more than one culture are **multicultural** and can move between two cultures very comfortably. An example of multicultural persons is the royal Grimaldi family of Monaco. Princess Grace was a U.S. citizen and married Prince Ranier of Monaco. The Grimaldi children were raised in Monaco; however, because of the time they spent in the United States, they were acculturated to this country. Although acculturation increases the interconnectedness of cultures, differences are sources of potential problems. All differences will probably not be absorbed by either culture.

Acculturation has four dimensions: integration, separation, assimilation, and deculturation. When a minority moves into a majority culture, he or she will choose one of these modes either consciously or subconsciously. Although as a majority culture we may feel that assimilation is the correct acculturation process, the individual may not feel that this fits his or her needs. Assimilation takes place when individuals are absorbed into their new culture and withdraw from their old culture. Integration takes place when individuals become an integral part of the new culture while maintaining their cultural integrity. Separation happens when individuals keep their culture and stay independent of the new culture. Deculturation occurs when individuals lose their original culture and do not accept the new culture, leading to confusion and anxiety (Alkhazraji, 1997). The acculturation mode that an individual chooses is governed by the individual's views and desired ways of life.

ETHNOCENTRISM

Ethnocentrism is the belief that your own cultural background, including ways of analyzing problems, values, beliefs, language, and verbal and nonverbal communication, is correct. Ethnocentrists believe that their culture is the central culture and that other cultures are incorrect, defective, or quaint. When we evaluate others, we do it through our self-reference criterion because it is what we know. Fisher (1997) in his research refers to ethnocentrism as mindsets.

Mindsets are ways of being that allow us to see, perceive, and reason through our own cultural awareness. Mindsets are learned by growing up in a particular culture. We learn to be open or closed to others and their way of living; however, these mindsets can be altered. Mindsets include the psychological and cultural factors that make us individuals and make us different or similar. We are predisposed because of enculturation to perceive and reason according to our cultural upbringing. Our reactions to situations are preprogrammed until we decide to change. Every culture in the world has a different mindset, and every individual within that culture has a variance to that mindset (Chaney & Martin, 2005).

The U.S. mindset includes the concept that the American way is best. ("American" as used in the United States is an example of ethnocentrism because the term "American" actually refers to all the people in North, South, and Central American countries.) Although this is mainly a U.S. concept, people who are born in smaller countries feel the same about their own country—that *it* is the best place to live. The belief that one's own culture is best is a natural phenomenon common to all cultures. Although it is natural to be ethnocentric and have a particular mindset, we need to look at other mindsets from the perspective of the people who hold them before we judge them as good or bad. However, we must be careful about generalizing about other cultures or making assumptions about how they view the United States.

The term Ugly American was derived from the behavior of U.S. travelers observed by persons in other cultures who judged them inconsiderate of the culture they were visiting. This term came from the 1958 book by William Lederer and Eugene Burdick and the subsequent 1963 movie by the same name. The book and movie depict an incompetent, ignorant U.S. ambassador in a fictional Southeast Asian country. The term quickly caught on to describe rude, self-centered people who have no sensitivity for those who are different from them. In reality, most U.S. Americans, when traveling to other countries, do not fit this stereotype of the Ugly American. They want to understand people of other cultures but are simply uninformed (Bosrock, 1995).

NORMS, RULES, ROLES, AND NETWORKS

Norms, rules, roles, and networks are situational factors that influence encoding and decoding of both verbal and nonverbal messages within a culture. They are unwritten guidelines people within the cultural group follow. **Norms** are culturally ingrained principles of correct and incorrect behaviors that, if broken, carry a form of overt or covert penalty. **Rules** are formed to clarify cloudy areas of norms. The U.S. Supreme Court is an excellent example of an organization that looks at the intent of a rule and determines how strongly or loosely it should be followed. A **role** includes the behavioral expectations of a position within a culture and is affected by norms and rules. **Networks** are formed with personal ties and involve an exchange of assistance. Networks and the need to belong are the basis of friendships and subgroups (Chaney & Martin, 2005). An example of a political network is the exchange of votes between U.S. legislators needed to support their projects.

What makes a norm, rule, role, or network in one society can be very different for another society because we do not all share the same backgrounds or systems.

SUBCULTURES AND SUBGROUPS

Subcultures are groups of people possessing characteristic traits that set apart and distinguish them from others within a larger society or macroculture. The U.S. macroculture, which comprises 64% of the population, is White. The largest U.S. subcultures include Hispanics (or Latinos) (16%), African Americans (14%), Asians (5%), Native Hawaiians and other Pacific Islanders (0.2%), and Native Americans and Alaskan Natives (0.9%) (U.S. Census Bureau, 2011). In addition to ethnicity and race, subcultures in the United States may be categorized by age, religion, and sexual preferences. Examples of subcultures (or microcultures) in the United States include teenagers, baby boomers, millennials, GenX, African Americans, Catholics, disabled individuals, and trade associations. All these groups have similarities to the macroculture but also have some differences. To meet the definition of a subculture, the following three criteria should be met:

- The group members are self-identifiable; that is, group members want to be considered a part of the group.
- Group members exhibit behavior that is characteristic of the group.
- The macroculture recognizes the group as a subculture and has given it a name; for example, senior citizens (Klopf & McCroskey, 2007). A term used more recently for subcultures is "cocultures," because of the possible implication that members of "subcultures" or "nondominant groups" are perhaps inferior (Samovar, Porter, & McDaniel, 2009).

Intercultural business communication necessitates working with subcultures. The subcultures form a diversity of ethnic identities with which managers must learn to work harmoniously. Women are one such subculture. As Adler (1993) states, "Although women represent over 50% of the world's population, in no country do women represent half, or even close to half, of the corporate managers" (p. 3). In some Middle East, Far East, and South American countries, business is male oriented. Because North American women have progressed in the business world faster than their counterparts in most other countries of the world, they may expect to automatically be accepted by men who would be offended by women in business in their own culture. Although men in some countries are still apprehensive about conducting business with women, Bosrock (1995) states that "regardless of the attitude toward women in a given country, most women are treated politely. Much of the resistance to women in business is directed at local women, not Westerners" (p. 109). Even in Asian and South American cultures where women are traditionally seen as nurturers of the family, attitudes are changing. Many employers now are less concerned with gender than performance (Bosrock, 1994, 1997). Women sent abroad have a very high success rate. A self-report showed that 97% of the female expatriate managers were successful; a much higher percentage than reported by male expatriates (Adler, 1993).

Subgroups, although also part of the macroculture, are groups with which the macroculture does not agree and with which it has problems communicating. Members of these groups often engage in communication behavior that is distinctively different from that of the dominant culture. Examples of subgroups include youth gangs, prostitutes, saboteurs, embezzlers, and other groups that have unique experiences and/or characteristics not sanctioned by the macroculture (Dodd, 1997). The vocabularies of subgroup members make it difficult for members of the macroculture and subcultures to understand the intended meanings of the words used by subgroup members (Samovar et al., 2009).

CULTURAL INTELLIGENCE

Cultural intelligence, according to Peterson (2004), is the ability to exhibit certain behaviors, including skills and qualities, which are culturally tuned to the attitudes and values of others. Cultural intelligence involves the areas of linguistic intelligence, spatial intelligence, intrapersonal intelligence, and interpersonal intelligence. Although speaking a second language is not essential to **linguistic intelligence**, it is helpful to learn about the customer's native language when conducting business internationally. In addition, using international business English can increase effectiveness when communicating with persons of other cultures. **Spatial intelligence** is an important aspect of cultural intelligence; it involves the way space is used during greetings and introductions, as well as during meetings and other encounters. **Intrapersonal intelligence** involves an awareness of one's own cultural style in order to make behavioral adjustments to international counterparts. **Interpersonal intelligence** includes the ability to understand other people and their motivations. Peterson (2004) recognized psychologist Howard Gardner's theory of multiple intelligences and summarized succinctly the preceding four categories of cultural intelligence: "To interact well with people from other cultures, it helps to (a) speak a bit of their language, (b) know how closely to stand (and other nonverbal behavior), (c) know about your own cultural style, and (d) know how your cultural style meshes with those of others" (p. 95).

COMMUNICATION BARRIERS

When encountering someone from another culture, communication barriers are often created when the behavior of the other person differs from our own. **Communication barriers** are obstacles to effective communication. An example of such a barrier is the head nod. The nod indicates understanding in the United States, but in Japan it means only that the person is listening. By understanding intercultural communication, we can break down barriers and pave the way for mutual understanding and respect.

The following are barriers to communication:

- **Physical**—time, environment, comfort and needs, and physical medium (e.g., telephone and letter)
- **Cultural**—ethnic, religious, and social differences
- **Perceptual**—viewing what is said from your own mindset
- **Motivational**—the listener's mental inertia
- **Experiential**—lack of similar life happenings
- **Emotional**—personal feelings of the listener
- **Linguistic**—different languages spoken by the speaker and listener or use of a vocabulary beyond the comprehension of the listener
- **Nonverbal**—nonword messages
- **Competition**—the listener's ability to do other things rather than hear the communication

Several cultural iceberg models exist. What you do not see culturally can be a barrier to your ability to communicate effectively and complete your agenda. As shown in Figure 2, the values that are below the "waterline" represent those on which behaviors are based; however, we respond to the surface values that we can sense. To truly understand a culture, we must explore the behaviors below the waterline. The common elements of trust, sincerity, and integrity are necessary to building successful business relationships when cultural differences exist (Funakawa, 1997).

INTERCULTURAL CONSTRUCTS

Borden (1991) lists seven constructs that individuals must possess if they are going to succeed interculturally. The degree to which we can understand intercultural communication depends on the degree to which the following are true:

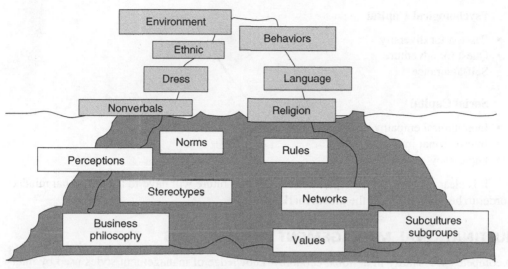

FIGURE 2   Cultural Iceberg

- We are aware that our intent to communicate, either as communicator or communicatee, may result in only expressive behavior or information gathering, respectively.
- Our cybernetic (self-concept) in one culture can operate independently of our cybernetic in another culture.
- We are competent in the languages of other cultures.
- We are able to work within the constraints (personal, situational, and cultural) of the human communication system established by the communication from other cultures.
- We are culturally literate in our own and other cultures.
- We know the position of our culture and other cultures on the four universal dimensions of values and their interaction with the cultural orientation model.
- We know the cultural orientation of our culture and other cultures on the associative–abstractive, particularistic–universalistic, and closed-minded/open-minded dimensions and can use it as the first approximation of the cognitive style of the communicants (pp. 210–213).

GLOBAL MINDSETS

In order for managers to be successful interculturally, they will need to develop a global mindset. The Thunderbird Global Mindset Project involved interviews with 215 international executives in the triad. The interviews identified the following attributes as needed by successful intercultural managers (Javidan, Hough, & Bullough, 2010):

Intellectual Capital

- Global business savvy
- Cognitive complexity
- Cosmopolitan outlook

Psychological Capital

- Passion for diversity
- Quest for adventure
- Self-assurance

Social Capital

- Intercultural empathy
- Interpersonal impact
- Diplomacy

It is clear to see that the corporate leaders of the future will have to have a global mindset in order to be competitive in the global marketplace.

MULTINATIONAL MANAGEMENT ORIENTATIONS

To compete successfully in a global economy, knowledge of management styles used by international corporations is also important. With the emergence of the concept of world culture has come a heightened awareness of the interdependence of nations and the need to break cultural barriers and find ways to work harmoniously with people of all cultures.

Multinational firms, those located in more than one nation, generally will follow either an ethnocentric, polycentric, geocentric, or regiocentric form of management. Multinational firms such as Sony, Quaker Oats, ExxonMobil, Robert Bosch, and Nissan may follow a single management style at all global locations or may use various styles of management to increase productivity while maintaining worker morale. All multinational or global corporations are **transnational**, which means they cross the borders of countries in conducting their business (Moran & Stripp, 1991).

Not all these management styles consider the diversity of cultures working within them, nor are they managed to take advantage of the surprises that surface in multinational management. As Rhinesmith (1996) has stated, global managers have a mindset that allows them to take advantage of and manage the complexity, adaptability, teams, uncertainty, and learning that the global organization requires. Because people are the most critical factors for an organization to succeed globally, they are also the restraining factor in the firm's capability to survive and grow. Human resource development personnel must be involved in the education and changing of the mindsets. The global mindset differs from the domestic mindset, as illustrated in Table 1 (Rhinesmith, 1996, p. 27).

TABLE 1 Comparison of Domestic and Global Mindsets

Domestic Mindset	Global Mindset
Functional expertise	Bigger, broader picture
Prioritization	Balance of contradictions
Structure	Process
Individual responsibility	Teamwork and diversity
No surprises	Change as opportunity
Trained against surprises	Openness to surprises

Source: From *A manager's guide to globalization* (p. 27) by S. H. Rhinesmith, 1996, Homewood. IL: Richard D. Irwin. Inc. Used with publisher's permission.

The person who can manage a domestic operation does not necessarily have the competencies to manage a global operation. People who have a global mindset tend to live life in many ways that may be physically, intellectually, emotionally, or spiritually different, depending on the culture with which they are interacting.

When a firm is located in one country and all its sales are in the same country, **ethnocentric management** practices are employed. Ethnocentric management does not account for cultural differences in the workforce. All workers will be treated the same. Many times the management practices employed rely on one person's views of how the organization should be run. Some domestic corporations financed abroad that purchase goods abroad for resale at home or buy technology abroad still need to think globally because of their international activities (Moran & Stripp, 1991). For example, U.S. car manufacturers complained that their cars were not selling in Japan. These manufacturers, however, had not changed the position of the steering wheel from the left to the right for driving on the opposite side of the road from the United States, and they had not downsized their cars in consideration of the limited space available to park cars in Japan. When a company expands internationally, it must consider the consumers who are targeted to buy its products.

Werner G. Hennecker (Pegasus Gold): "We run our business on a certain set of standards, regardless of whether we're in the United States or Kazakhstan. Our in-house environmental policy is much more stringent than that required by any of the areas in which we operate, but it's inviolate. It's been interesting getting people in some parts of the world that haven't worried much about environmental issues to focus on them. Our solution was to base a large part of our bonus program on employees' avoidance of environmental incidents." (Donlon, 1996, p. 3)

Polycentric management practices consider the culture of the country in which the firm is located. The people in charge consider the cultural needs of the workers in the area in which the firm is located. A melting-pot effect may seem to exist because the majority's culture is considered in management decisions. In the United States, you see this particularly in small firms. Leaving the polycentric management practices behind is part of the problem employees have when they move to a foreign country to work because they were comfortable with the old management style (Moran & Stripp, 1991).

Regiocentric management considers the region rather than the country in which the firm is located, realizing that countries can and often do have many different cultural backgrounds. The regional theory acknowledges that in the United States all areas are not the same. For example, different management strategies are required for running a production facility in Michigan with high unionization and a facility in Mississippi with low unionization and different ethnic bases. Management strategies consider the diversity of the workforce (Moran & Stripp, 1991). Unions tend to keep the workers from interacting directly with management. Many firms now want to use Total Quality Management (TQM), which utilizes interaction between workers and management. Saturn automotive built their plant in Springfield, Tennessee, because they could start the plant without a union and implement TQM. Although Saturn now has a workforce that is unionized, the union works with management; and the quality and sales of the Saturn automobile have been better than any other General Motors' product.

Shepard: "We've also developed a program called Aegon University, in which we put managers in their 30s and 40s from different countries into a dormitory setting and bring in

> international executives to speak to them. Even more important, this gives them the opportunity to network individually. They are building an e-mail system among the graduates of Aegon University that lets them share practices they think might work across borders in addition to potential customers that operate globally in the pension business." (Donlon, 1996, p. 4)

Geocentric management requires a common framework across countries with enough freedom for individual locations to operate regionally to meet the cultural needs of the workers. Geocentric refers to the synergy of ideas from different countries of operation. The most successful multinational corporations use integrated geocentric management. Corporations have common control practices that the individual locations are free to modify. Recognizing the management style used is helpful to competing successfully in a global economy (Moran & Stripp, 1991).

> Claude I. Taylor (Air Canada): "When we first started to go international, we had Canadians everywhere. We found that didn't work, because they weren't accepted and they didn't understand the local culture. That meant we had two levels of labor problems: We had a management problem and a contract problem.
>
> Today, we're expanding rapidly in the United States, and we have the odd Canadian in there part-time. But our philosophy for outside markets is to bring foreigners—from France, Germany, Hong Kong, and South Korea, for example—into Canada for six months, indoctrinate them about what we do, and then send them back." (Donlon, 1996, p. 3)

The ability of different cultures to communicate successfully in a business environment, to assimilate their cultures and conduct business, and to do this either within the United States or abroad is the emphasis of intercultural business communication. Different cultures do present communication problems; differing business practices and negotiation strategies pose additional problems. Intercultural business communication involves a knowledge and understanding of other cultures, including their subcultures, subgroups, and standards of behavior. With the emergence of the concept of a world culture has come a heightened awareness of the interdependence of nations and the need to break the cultural barriers to find ways to work harmoniously with people of all cultures.

Bosrock (1995) offers the following "Ten Commandments for Going International":

1. Be well prepared.
2. Ask questions, be observant, and listen.
3. Make an effort; trying and making a mistake is better than not trying at all.
4. When problems develop, assume the main cause is miscommunication.
5. Be patient; accomplishing your goals in another country/culture usually requires more time and effort.
6. Assume the best about people; most people act on the basis of their learned values and traditions.
7. Be sincere.
8. Maintain a sense of humor.
9. Make an effort to be likable; when people like you, they will forgive your mistakes.
10. Smile.

Terms

Acculturation
Backstage culture
Communication barriers
Cultural intelligence
Cultural symbol
Cultural synergy
Culture
Diffusion
Enculturation
Ethnocentric management
Ethnocentrism
Frontstage culture
Geocentric management
Global business
  communication
Globalization

Glocalization
Grobalization
Intercultural business
  communication
Intercultural
  communication
International
  communication
Interpersonal intelligence
Intracultural
  communication
Intrapersonal intelligence
Linguistic intelligence
Macroculture
Melting pot
Microculture

Mindsets
Multicultural
Multinational firm
Networks
Norms
Polycentric management
Regiocentric
  management
Roles
Rules
Spatial intelligence
Stereotypes
Subculture
Subgroup
Transnational
World culture

Exercise 1

Instructions: Match the following terms with their definition.

_____ 1. Belief that your own culture is superior	**A.** Acculturation
_____ 2. The socialization process we go through to learn a culture	**B.** Backstage culture
_____ 3. A sociocultural assimilation	**C.** Enculturation
_____ 4. Cultural information concealed from outsiders	**D.** Ethnocentrism
_____ 5. Absorption of new ideas into existing culture	**E.** Frontstage culture
_____ 6. Between members of same culture	**F.** Intercultural
_____ 7. Between persons of different cultures	**G.** International
_____ 8. Between nations and governments	**H.** Intracultural
_____ 9. Groups having traits differing from the macroculture	**I.** Melting pot
_____ 10. Culturally ingrained principles of correct/ incorrect behavior	**J.** Norms
	K. Subcultures

Questions and Cases for Discussion

1. The United States has long been called a melting pot. What does this term mean?
2. What does it mean for a firm to be global?
3. Give examples of how products have been globalized.
4. Explain the differences between norms, roles, rules, and networks.
5. Define a subculture and give examples of U.S. subcultures.
6. What is cultural synergy?
7. Distinguish between intercultural communication and intracultural communication.
8. Identify the dimensions of culture.
9. Identify types of barriers to communication.
10. Are business cultures necessarily aligned to national cultures?

CASES

The following procedure is recommended for analyzing the cases: (a) read the case carefully, paying attention to details; (b) read the questions at the end of the case; (c) reread the case, taking notes on or highlighting the details needed for answering the questions; (d) identify relevant facts, underlying assumptions, and critical issues of the case; (e) list possible answers to the questions; and (f) select the most logical response to the question. Your professor may ask that you submit answers to the case questions in writing.

Case 1

At a reception for a U.S. political candidate, the guests appear to be divided into groups. People in some groups are all African American, others are Latin American, and others are Asian. Explain the cultural phenomena that are operating at this political gathering.

Case 2

The U.S. automotive manufacturers have complained about Japanese automotive imports and that the U.S. car firms are locked out of the Japanese market. The Japanese have countered that the U.S. firms have not done their homework; they offer cars that are too big or are not fuel-efficient. Although U.S. car sales have decreased in the United States, Japanese car sales have increased. Japanese manufacturers have begun to assemble cars in the United States; many U.S. firms are moving part of their operations to Mexico. Discuss the implications to these firms as they globalize.

Case 3

In 1979, the shah of Iran was admitted to the United States for medical reasons. The Iranians reacted by holding all diplomatic personnel hostage in the embassy in Iran. The secretary of state was Henry Kissinger, and the president was Jimmy Carter. The United States took the position that the Iranians should not be upset with the shah's being allowed into the United States for the humanitarian reason of medical need. The shah had been a friend to the United States and the United States to the shah; therefore, the U.S. government felt a certain obligation to the shah. The revolution in Iran was based on Islamic religious assumptions. Give two position statements, one using the mindset of the United States and the second using the mindset of Iran to show how and why each viewed its position as correct. Is objectivity difficult to maintain when writing the Iran position statement?

Case 4

The United States has globalized faster than it has paid attention to mindsets that differ from the U.S. mindset. The world is connected by news satellites that have allowed the Iraq War to be viewed as it has unfolded—the world literally has watched the war happen. Explain how the world and public opinion has been affected by mass media. Include how world negotiations have changed for governments, diplomats, politicians, and businesses.

Case 5

It is commonly said that most countries' industrial leaders do not have the mindset necessary to be successful in all the three industrial triads in the world (North American, Asian, and European). For example, some U.S. companies have pulled out of China. Explain how the different multinational management orientations would be difficult for people from each of these triads to use in the other two triads in order to be successful.

Activities

1. Clip a story from the local newspaper that is related to some aspect of intercultural communication, such as problems encountered by persons of other cultures in the acculturation process or problems between subgroups; give a short report to the class.
2. Ask a member of the class who is from another culture to discuss how cultural norms and rules in his or her culture differ from those in the United States.
3. Invite a member of the business community who conducts business globally to address problems encountered when dealing with representatives of other cultures whose form of management (ethnocentric, polycentric, geocentric, or regiocentric) may be different from that in the United States.
4. Interview a foreign student on roles of women and children in his or her culture. In a report to the class, make comparisons between these roles and those in the United States.
5. Write a one-page proposal for improving relationships between U.S. students and students from other cultures in your school.
6. Analyze a multinational corporation's annual report and determine where it is producing and selling goods and what the profit margins of those goods are compared to other multinational firms.

References

Adler, N. J. (1993). Competitive frontiers: Women managers in triad. *International Studies of Management and Organization, 23*(2), 3–23.

Alkhazraji, K. M. (1997). *Immigrants and cultural adaptation in the American workplace.* New York: Garland.

Althen, G., with Bennett, J. (2011). *American ways* (3rd ed.). Boston, MA: Intercultural Press.

Association for Business Communication Panel on Global Business Communication. (2010, October). Montreal, Canada.

Borden, G. A. (1991). *Cultural orientation: An approach to understanding intercultural communication.* Upper Saddle River, NJ: Prentice Hall.

Bosrock, M. M. (1994). *Put your best foot forward: Asia.* St. Paul, MN: International Education Systems.

Bosrock, M. M. (1995). *Put your best foot forward: Europe.* St. Paul, MN: International Education Systems.

Bosrock, M. M. (1997). *Put your best foot forward: South America.* St. Paul, MN: International Education Systems.

Chaney, L. H., & Martin, J. S. (2005). Intercultural communication: Bridging cultural differences. In S. O'Brien (Ed.), *Communication for a global society, 2005 NBEA Yearbook* (pp. 100–114). Reston, VA: National Business Education Association.

Chu, G. C. (1977). *Radical change through communication in Mao's China.* Honolulu: University Press of Hawaii.

Datan, N., Rodeheaver, D., & Hughes, F. (1987). Adult development and aging. *Annual Review of Psychology, 38*, 153–180.

Differences between sexes are shrinking. (1996). *USA Today, 124*(2608), p. 10.

Dodd, C. H. (1997). *Dynamics of intercultural communication* (5th ed.). New York: McGraw-Hill.

Donlon, J. P. (1996, September). Managing across borders. *Chief Executive, 117*, 58–68.

Earley, P. C., Murnieks, C., & Mosakowski, E. (2007). Cultural intelligence and the global mindset. In M. Javidan, R. M. Steers, & M. A. Hitt (Eds.), *The global mindset* (Vol. 19). Oxford, England: Elsevier.

Evans, P., Doz, Y., & Laurent, A. (Eds.). (1990). *Human resource management in international firms: Change, globalization, innovation.* New York: St. Martin's.

Fisher, G. (1997). *Mindsets* (2nd ed.). Yarmouth, ME: Intercultural Press.

Funakawa, A. (1997). *Transcultural management: A new approach for global organizations.* San Francisco, CA: Jossey-Bass.

Gannon, M. J., Locke, E. A., Amit, G., Pino, A., & Kristof-Brown, A. L. (2005). Cultural metaphors as frames of reference for nations: A six-country study. *International Studies of Management & Organization, 35*(4), 37–47.

Hazuda, H. P., Stern, M. P., & Hoffner, S. M. (1988). Acculturation and assimilation among Mexican Americans: Sales and population-based data. *Social Science Quarterly, 69,* 687–706.

Hofstede, G. (2004). *Cultures and organizations* (2nd ed.). London: McGraw-Hill.

Klopf, D. W., & McCroskey, J. C. (2007). *Intercultural encounters* (4th ed.). Boston, MA: Pearson.

Javidan, M., Hough, L., & Bullough, A. (2010). *Conceptualizing and measuring global mindset: Development of the Global Mindset Inventory.* Glendale, AZ: Thunderbird School of Global Management. Retrieved from http://www.thunderbird.edu/knowledge_network/ctrs_excellence/global_mindset_leadership_institute/development_of_the_global_mindset_inventory.htm

Lewis, R. D. (2006). *When cultures collide: Leading across cultures.* Boston, MA: Nicholas Brealey International.

Lustig, M. W., & Koester, J. (1998). *Intercultural competence.* New York: Addison Wesley.

Marsden, A. (2008, May). Integrated management. *Financial Management,* 50.

Moran, R. T., & Stripp, W. G. (1991). *Dynamics of successful international business negotiations.* Houston, TX: Gulf.

Peterson, B. (2004). *Cultural intelligence: A guide to working with people from other cultures.* Yarmouth, ME: Intercultural Press.

Rhinesmith, S. H. (1996). *A manager's guide to globalization: Six skills for success in a changing world.* New York: McGraw-Hill.

Ritzer, G. (2003). Rethinking globalization: Glocalization/grobalization and something/nothing. *Sociological Theory, 21*(3), 193–201.

Ruch, W. V. (1989). *International handbook of corporate communication.* Jefferson, NC: McFarland.

Samovar, L. A., Porter, R. E., & McDaniel, E. R. (2009). *Communication between cultures* (7th ed.). Belmont, CA: Thomson Learning.

Singer, M. R. (1998). *Perception & identity in intercultural communication.* Yarmouth, ME: Intercultural Press.

Staa, D. (1998). No need for inter-American cultural clash. *Management Review, 87*(1), 8.

Smith, A. G. (1966). *Communication and culture: Readings in the codes of human interaction.* New York: Holt, Rinehart & Winston.

U.S. Census Bureau. (2011). Foreign trade statistics, top trading partners. Retrieved January 17, 2012, from http://www.census.gov/foreign-trade/statistics/highlights/top/top1012yr.html

U.S. Census Bureau News. (2011). 2010 census shows America's diversity [Released March 24, 2011]. Retrieved January 17, 2012, from http://2010.census.gov/news/releases/operations/cb11-cn125.html

Yoshida, S. (2002). Globalization and issues of intercultural communications. *Vital Speeches of the Day, 68*(22), 708–712.

Glossary

Acculturation is the process of adapting to a new and different culture.

Backstage culture is cultural information that is concealed from outsiders.

Communication barriers are obstacles to effective communication.

Cultural intelligence is the ability to exhibit certain behaviors that are culturally tuned to the attitudes and values of others.

Cultural symbol is a word or object that represents something in the culture.

Cultural synergy occurs when people of different cultures absorb a significant number of cultural differences from the other culture and have a number of similarities that merge to form a stronger overriding culture.

Culture is the structure through which the communication is formulated and interpreted; deals with the way people live.

Diffusion is the process by which two cultures learn and adapt materials and adopt practices from each other.

Enculturation refers to adapting to the cultural patterns of a person's society.

Ethnocentric management occurs when a firm is located in one country and all its sales are also in the same country; does not account for cultural differences in the workforce.

Ethnocentrism is the belief that your own cultural background, including ways of analyzing problems, language, verbal communication, and nonverbal communication, is correct.

Frontstage culture refers to cultural information that you are willing to share with outsiders.

Geocentric management is a type of management that requires a common framework with enough freedom for individual locations to operate regionally to meet the cultural needs of the workers; a synergy of ideas from different countries of operation.

Global business communication is communication between businesses from different countries.

Globalization is the capability of a corporation to take a product and market it anywhere in the world.

Glocalization is the interpenetration of local and global; the result is geographically unique outcomes.

Grobalization is an emphasis on the imperialistic ambitions of companies and countries and their need to impose themselves on certain geographic areas.

Intercultural business communication refers to communication within and between businesses that involves people from more than one culture.

Intercultural communication is communication between persons of different cultures.

International communication is communication between nations and governments rather than individuals; quite formal and ritualized.

Interpersonal intelligence includes the ability to understand other people and their motivations.

Intracultural communication refers to communication between members of the same culture.

Intrapersonal intelligence involves an awareness of a person's own cultural style in order to make behavioral adjustments with international counterparts.

Linguistic intelligence is an aspect of intelligence that includes learning about international customers' native languages.

Macroculture is the larger society or culture.

Melting pot is a sociocultural assimilation of people of differing backgrounds and nationalities; being or becoming the same.

Microculture is a subculture; a group of people possessing characteristic traits that distinguish them from others within the macroculture or larger culture.

Mindsets refer to a way of being that allows you to see and perceive things through your own filters.

Multicultural refers to learning more than one culture and being able to move between two cultures comfortably.

Multinational firm is a corporation with operations and subsidiaries in many foreign countries.

Networks are formed with personal ties and involve an exchange of assistance.

Norms are culturally ingrained principles of correct and incorrect behaviors that, if broken, carry a form of overt or covert penalty.

Polycentric management is a type of management that considers the culture of the country in which the firm is located.

Regiocentric management is a type of management that considers the region rather than the country in which the firm is located, realizing that countries can and often have many different cultural backgrounds.

Roles include the behavioral expectations of a position within a culture and are affected by norms and rules.

Rules are formed to clarify cloudy areas of norms.

Spatial intelligence involves the way space is used during meetings and other encounters.

Stereotypes are perceptions about certain groups of people or nationalities.

Subculture is a group of people possessing characteristic traits that set apart and distinguish it from others within a larger society (or macroculture).

Subgroups refer to groups of people possessing characteristic traits that set apart and distinguish them from others within a larger society/culture (or macroculture); groups with which the macroculture does not agree and has problems communicating.

Transnational refers to corporations that cross the borders of countries in conducting their business.

World culture involves the breaking down of traditional barriers among people of differing cultures, emphasizing the commonality of human needs.

Answers to Exercises

Matching

1. D
2. C
3. I
4. B
5. A

6. H
7. F
8. G
9. K
10. J

Universal Systems

Objectives

Upon completion of this chapter, you will

- increase your understanding of systems that are universal to all cultural groups and their relationship to communicating and negotiating in a global setting.
- understand the role that economic and political systems play in communicating interculturally in business settings.
- see the relationship between educational systems and global communication.
- gain insight into social systems and hierarchies that affect effective intercultural business communication.

Cultural systems have an impact on multicultural communication. **Cultural universals** are formed out of the common problems of all cultures. The following systems are found in all cultures: economic systems, political systems, educational systems, marriage and family systems, and social hierarchies and interaction. Knowing how cultural systems in the United States differ from those of other cultures can enhance communication effectiveness when conducting business with persons of other cultures. Although these systems are universal to all cultures, different cultures may deal with an issue in a significantly different way. In communicating interculturally, the variabilities are equally as important as the similarities.

ECONOMIC SYSTEMS

A culture develops an economic system to meet the material needs of its people. The way in which the products that meet the material needs of the people are produced, distributed, and consumed is referred to as the **economic system**. All societies not only work out ways of producing or procuring goods but must also determine the procedure for distributing them.

From Chapter 2 of *Intercultural Business Communication*, Sixth Edition. Lillian H. Chaney, Jeanette S. Martin. Copyright © 2014 by Pearson Education, Inc. All rights reserved.

The different economic systems in the world today include capitalism, socialism, agrarianism, and barter. The United States and Japan are capitalistic, Sweden and China are socialistic, Belize and Cambodia are agrarian, and Laos and the Marshall Islands barter. The relationship between the public and private sectors and which sector dominates may make some economic systems a blend of the first three systems. No single correct economic system exists. The U.S. method of distributing goods is based on the capacity to pay, although such countries as Cuba distribute goods according to need.

ECONOMIC "-ISMS"

- **Socialism**—You have two cows. The government takes one and gives it to your neighbor.
- **Communism**—You have two cows. The government takes both of them and gives you part of the milk.
- **Capitalism**—You have two cows. You sell one of them and buy a bull.
- **Fascism**—You have two cows. The government takes both cows and sells you the milk.
- **Bureaucracy**—You have two cows. The government takes both of them, shoots one, milks the other, and then pours the milk down the drain.
- **Democracy**—Everyone has two cows. A vote is taken, the loser cries discrimination, the lawyers sue (on a contingency basis), and the government takes at least 39% (Zenzone, 2012).

In addition to identifying the type of economic system a country follows, it is also important to understand other aspects of the country's economy, including **imports** (goods brought into the country) and **exports** (goods sent out of the country). This knowledge may prove useful in the negotiation process. The top 10 countries to which the United States exports, according to the U.S. Census Bureau figures for 2010, are Canada, Mexico, China, Japan, United Kingdom, Germany, South Korea, Brazil, the Netherlands, and Singapore. South Africa was 58 and Nigeria 44 from the African continent. The Scandinavian countries and their positions as U.S. trading partners are Sweden, 41; Norway, 48; Finland, 55; and Denmark, 57. Latin American countries that are in the top 50 U.S. trading partners are Brazil, 8; Chile, 24; Dominican Republic, 35; Ecuador, 39; Guatemala, 43; Honduras, 42; Mexico, 2; Panama, 37; Peru, 33; and Venezuela, 25.

The world's economy is changing. The OECD (Organization for Economic Cooperation and Development) follows the world economies and is dedicated to democracy and the market economy. Thirty-four member nations include Australia, Austria, Belgium, Canada, Chile, Czech Republic, Denmark, Estonia, Finland, France, Germany, Greece, Hungary, Iceland, Ireland, Israel, Italy, Japan, South Korea, Luxembourg, Mexico, the Netherlands, New Zealand, Norway, Poland, Portugal, Slovak Republic, Slovenia, Spain, Sweden, Switzerland, Turkey, United Kingdom, and the United States. The countries they are currently watching are the BRIC countries of Brazil, Russia, India, and China and the CISA countries of China, India, and South Africa (OECD, 2010). Forecasts are that in less than 40 years Brazil, Russia, India, and China's economies will be bigger than those of the G6 (Antkiewicz & Whalley, 2005; Wilson & Purushothaman, 2003). In 2005, BRIC's foreign exchange reserves were 40% of the world's total foreign exchange reserves. China is the fastest growing exporter, and its imports are also increasing significantly. From 1996 to 2006, Africa's exports to China grew by 1,200%, reaching $25 billion in 2006. As Western markets mature, the BRIC and CISA countries will also experience growth. The countries where foreign investments are currently being made are ranked as follows: China (first), India (second), United States (third), Russia (fourth), Brazil (fifth), and Mexico (sixth). The trend of sending remittances back to their home country families is strongest among people from India, China, Mexico, Philippines, Brazil, Egypt, and Nigeria. India's remittances for 2004 were $21.7 billion, China's $21.3 billion, and Mexico's $18.1 billion (Shaw, Cooper, & Antkiewicz, 2007).

A brief description of the economic systems of the United States and 17 countries with which the United States conducts international business follows. Also included are other details of the economies of these countries (*CIA Factbook*, 2012; *CultureGrams*, 2010; *Human Development Reports*, 2011; Shaw et al., 2007; U.S. Census Bureau, 2011). The GDP (Gross Domestic Product) per capita figures are given as the purchasing price parity to the U.S. dollar. (The GDP is the value of goods and services earned per capita). The HDI (Human Development Index) measures poverty, literacy, education, life expectancy, and similar factors. The unemployment numbers are for 2010.

Australia

Vast mineral deposit exports and beef and sheep production keep Australia strong. The GDP for Australia was $41,000, and the unemployment rate was 5.2% in 2010. Australia is second in the United Nations' HDI rankings. Australia was the United States' 15th largest trading partner in 2010. The currency is the Australian dollar (AUD).

Brazil

Brazil's economy is the largest in South America and among the world's largest. The distribution of income is very unequal; about 20% of the population lives in poverty. Brazil had an annual GDP per capita of $10,800 in 2010. Unemployment ranges from high in larger cities to moderate in other areas; in 2010, unemployment was 6.7%. Brazil's HDI ranking is 84 of 187 countries. Brazil is a major producer of bananas, coffee, and oranges. Brazil also produces sugarcane; however, much of it is used to produce ethyl alcohol, which is used to provide fuel for about a third of Brazil's automobiles. Exports include automobiles and parts, metals, textiles, and minerals. Brazil was America's 10th largest trading partner in 2010. The *real* (BRL) is the unit of currency.

Canada

Canada's economy is very strong. The economy is capitalistic with socialistic controls in the areas of health care and the retirement system. Manufacturing, mining, fishing, farming, and food processing drive the economy. Canada's real GDP per capita as of 2010 was $39,400. (Dollars in text are U.S. dollars unless otherwise specified.) Unemployment was 8% as of 2010. The HDI rank for Canada is 6 out of 187 countries. Canada is a world leader in the production of gold, uranium, silver, oil, natural gas, agricultural products, wood pulp, timber, and copper. Canada exports wheat, barley, oats, and other agricultural products. Tourism is an important source of revenue in recent years. Canada exports more products to the United States than it imports. They were the top U.S. trading partner in 2010.

In 1993, Canada joined Mexico and the United States in signing NAFTA, which provides expanded markets for goods. The unit of currency is the Canadian dollar, also called the *loonie* by Canadians. Canada continues to be one of the largest trading partners of the United States.

China

The Chinese government is supporting the growth of the private sector. Half of China's population is employed in agriculture. China leads the world in the production of rice, tobacco, corn, barley, soybeans, and peanuts. It produces manufactured goods, oil, minerals, coal, and steel. The real GDP was $7,600 in 2010; China's HDI ranking is 101 out of 187 countries. The unemployment rate was 6.1%. The economy has grown quickly since the 1990s. China was the third largest trading partner of the United States in 2010. Foreign investment is largest in China due to the low-wage labor. A large deficit budget threatens the social security systems that are in place. The currency is the *renminbi*; the standard unit is the *yuan* (¥).

France

France was the eleventh largest trading partner of the United States in 2010. The French standard of living is high, with an average annual real GDP per capita of $33,100 in 2010. Unemployment is 9.3%. The HDI ranking for France is 20 out of 187 countries. France is a major producer of such products as wine, milk, butter, cheese, barley, and wheat. The principal exports are machinery and transport equipment, steel products, and agricultural goods. The *euro* (€) is the unit of currency.

Germany

Germany is one of the largest economies in Europe and in the world, behind the United States and Japan. The German economy is based on principles of free enterprise and private ownership; however, government and business work together closely. The former communist system of East Germany is now being changed; emphasis is now on deciding what is best for the economy of the unified Germany. Germany had an average annual real GDP per capita of $35,700 in 2010. The HDI ranking for Germany is 9 out of 187 countries. Germany's main exports are cars, steel, aluminum, televisions, and other manufactured goods, making it one of the largest exporters in the world. Germany was the United States' sixth largest trading partner in 2010. Germany's unemployment rate is 8.4%. The *euro* (€) is the unit of currency.

India

India's economy includes farming, handicrafts, modern industries, and support services. India has a large number of well-educated people proficient in the English language who are being used by software services companies. India is ranked second in foreign investment due to technology, research and development, and business processing. India is more compatible with the established global economy because of its having been part of the British commonwealth. India's growth inhibitors are high illiteracy, bureaucratic red tape, weak infrastructure, and fiscal deficit. GDP in India was $3,500, and the unemployment rate was 10% in 2010. India is ranked 134 out of 187 countries in the HDI rankings. India was the 17th largest trading partner of the United States in 2010. The *rupee* (INR) is the unit of currency.

Iraq

Many nations from which the old regime of Iraq had borrowed money have forgiven Iraq for those debts. Iraq's GDP was approximately $3,800 in 2010, and the unemployment rate was 15.3% in 2009. Iraq was the 29th largest trading partner of the United States in 2010. The HDI ranking is not available. The currency is the New Iraq dollar (NID).

Japan

Japan's economy is a capitalistic/free-market one based on manufacturing, fishing, and exporting. Except for fish, Japan must import more than half of its food supply. Japan must also import most of its raw materials for manufacturing, and more than 95% of exports are manufactured goods.

Japan is one of the world's most productive nations. The average annual real GDP per capita was $34,000 in 2010. The unemployment rate is 5%. The HDI rank for Japan is 12 out of 187 countries. Machinery, electronics, engineering, textiles, and chemicals are major industries in Japan. Japan exports much more to the United States than it imports; this trade imbalance is a source of friction between Japan and the United States. Japan was the fourth largest trading partner of the United States in 2010. The *yen* (¥) is Japan's currency.

Mexico

In Mexico, the oil industry, agriculture, tourism, and *maquiladoras* (Mexican assembly facilities often near a major U.S. market) employ most of the working people. The government is attracting foreign investments, privatizing state-owned companies, and deregulating trade to combat unemployment, high inflation, and debt.

U.S. companies such as General Motors, Sam's Wholesale Clubs, Hunter Fan, and Blockbuster Video have shown their faith in Mexico's economic stability by investing billions of dollars there. Export industries have been growing since 1993 with the passage of NAFTA with the United States and Canada. NAFTA resulted in lowered trade barriers and led to an increase in *maquiladoras*. Mexico was the United States' second largest trading partner in 2010. Mexico's unemployment rate was 5.4% in 2010. However, 10% of the population lacks education and economic opportunities. Mexico's HDI ranking is 57 of 187 countries. Mining and petroleum are the two most important industries, but tourism is a source of employment for many people. Mexico exports oil, coffee, agricultural products, and engines. Mexico is also a major supplier of marijuana despite costly efforts to curb the drug trade. Real GDP per capita is $13,900. The unit of currency is the Mexican *peso* (MXN).

The Netherlands

The Netherlands has an open economy dependent on foreign trade. The economy has stable industrial relations; the Netherlands is a major European transportation hub. Industries include food processing, chemicals, petroleum refining, and electrical machinery. The GDP for the Netherlands is $40,300, and unemployment is 5.5%. The Netherlands was the United States' ninth largest trading partner in 2010. The Netherlands is ranked 3 out of 187 on the HDI rankings. The Netherlands uses the *euro* (€) as its currency.

New Zealand

New Zealand is an industrialized, free-market economy that competes globally. GDP in New Zealand is $27,700, and unemployment is 6.5%. New Zealand imports a lot of agricultural products. New Zealand is ranked 5 out of 187 in the HDI rankings. New Zealand was the 52nd largest trading partner of the United States in 2010. Australia and New Zealand have a free trade agreement called Closer Economic Relations (CER). The currency is the New Zealand dollar (NZD).

Singapore

Although Singapore is the smallest country in Southeast Asia, it has a highly developed and successful free-market economy. Singapore's GDP is $62,100. Singapore ranks 26 out of 187 in the HDI rankings. The unemployment rate is 2.2%. Electronics and manufacturing are the main sources of exports. The recession from 2001 to 2003 caused a slump in the technology sector. Singapore is Southeast Asia's financial and high-tech hub. Singapore was the United States' 10th largest trading partner in 2010. The currency is the Singapore dollar (SGD).

South Korea

The late 1990s proved detrimental to the South Korean economy. Strikes, a large budget deficit, political scandals, bankruptcies, and competition from other countries and corporations affected the economy. The South Korean economy largely depends on international trade. The real GDP is $30,000 per capita. The unemployment rate is 3.7%. The HDI rank for South Korea is 15 out of 187 countries. South Korea was the United States' seventh largest trading partner in 2010. The currency of South Korea is the *won* (KPW).

Taiwan

Taiwan is a major exporter of textiles, electronics, machinery, metals, timber products, and high-technology items. Taiwan has a large middle class and a highly skilled labor force. Unemployment is currently at 5.2%. The real GDP is $35,700 per capita. Taiwan was the United States' 13th largest trading partner in 2010. China is Taiwan's largest trading partner. The currency is the New Taiwan dollar (NT$).

United Arab Emirates

The United Arab Emirates' (UAE) real GDP per capita is $49,600, with an unemployment rate of 2.4%. The HDI rank for UAE is 30. The UAE was the United States' 21st largest trading partner in 2010. The currency of UAE is the Emirati *dirham* (AED).

United Kingdom (England, Scotland, Wales, and Northern Ireland)

Consisting of the island of Great Britain and Northern Ireland, the United Kingdom (UK) has one of the largest economies in Europe. The United Kingdom's economy is based on capitalism; however, many sectors of the economy were nationalized or socialized between 1945 and 1980. Since the 1980s, some of the sectors have been privatized, and less industry regulation has been encouraged. The United Kingdom is still a major industrial power in the world. The United Kingdom does most of its trading with the European Union. The average annual real GDP per capita is $34,800. Unemployment was about 7.8%. Exports include manufactured goods, crude oil, and consumer goods. The natural resources of the United Kingdom include oil, natural gas, iron ore, and salt. The United Kingdom is 28 out of 187 countries in the HDI rankings. The pound sterling (£) is the unit of currency. The United Kingdom was the fifth largest trading partner of the United States in 2010.

United States

The U.S. economic system is capitalistic with socialistic overtones. Free-market principles tempered by government regulations operate the economy. In addition, the United States is a financial center with an economy that affects the world. The U.S. capitalistic system is affected by inflation (brought about by the change from an industrially oriented economy to a service and technical economy), unemployment, and the economy of other countries as many U.S. corporations have become multinational. The 2010 trade deficit was $345.8 billion (U.S. Census Bureau, 2011). Direct foreign investments by other countries into the United States was $ 2.674 trillion; direct foreign investments by the United States abroad was $ 3.817 trillion in 2010 (*CIA Factbook*, 2012).

The economy in the United States is the largest and most technically advanced in the world, with an average real gross domestic product (GDP) per capita in 2010 of $47,200. Unemployment in the United States in 2010 was 9.6%. U.S. exports include capital goods, cars, consumer goods, food, and machinery. Tourism is important to many state economies. U.S. citizens believe that materialism is an important aspect of life. This materialism encourages replacement of possessions. Much of this purchasing is done with credit cards, and credit card debt is very high. The HDI ranking for the United States is 4 out of the 187 countries ranked.

The United States is part of the North American Free Trade Agreement (NAFTA), which is expanding markets, services, and manufacturing between the United States, Canada, and Mexico. The unit of currency is the U.S. dollar ($).

POLITICAL SYSTEMS

The **political system** is the governing system of the country, which can be based on dictatorship, inherited rights, elected procedures, consensus, or conquest. A person's age, economic expertise, or marital status may be considered when selecting people for political positions in some countries. In other countries, oratory skills and the ability to sway public opinion may be factors. Group members may even select a political leader because they believe the person to have supernatural powers. A description of a few political systems follows (*CIA Factbook*, 2012).

Australia

Australia, which is a bicameral federal parliamentary state, has six federated states, plus the Australian Capital Territory and the Northern Territory. The Queen of England is the head of state, but she is represented by an Australian governor-general. The prime minister and the federal Parliament (76 Senators, 150 House of Representatives) are elected by those over 18 years of age. Failure to vote in federal and state elections may result in a fine. The major parties are the Australian Labour Party, the Liberal Party, and the National Party.

Brazil

Brazil is a federative republic made up of 26 states and one federal district, Brasilia. Each state has its own elected governor and legislative body. The president is head of state and government. Presidents, governors, and mayors may run for two consecutive terms. The National Congress consists of a 513-seat Chamber of Deputies and an 81-seat Federal Senate. The country is considered a stable democracy. Voting is compulsory for citizens between the ages of 19 and 70 but optional for those between the ages of 16 and 18 and those above 70.

Canada

Canada is officially a confederation with a parliamentary democracy, a system partially patterned after that of Great Britain and the United States. The Parliament includes up to 105 senators, who are appointed, as well as 308 members of the House of Commons, who are elected.

The leader of the majority party in the House of Commons is automatically the prime minister. The central government has power in the areas of national health insurance, trade, the military, and development. The country is divided into provinces; each province controls its region. The Queen of England is represented by a governor-general. The voting age is 18.

China

The National People's Congress elects the president and vice president for a five-year term, and they are eligible for a second term. The legislative branch of National People's Congress is elected by the regional or provincial People's Congresses and the People's Liberation Army to serve a five-year term. The national policies of the People's Republic of China are determined by a 20-member Politburo and a 7-member Standing Committee. The only legal party is the Chinese Communist Party (CCP). The president of the country is the general secretary of the CCP. The National People's Congress has 2,987 locally elected members.

Hong Kong is a self-governing region of China. The Hong Kong's chief executive is advised by 15 executive councilors and 60 legislative councilors. Hong Kong has 36 representatives to China's national legislature.

France

The French Republic has 22 regions divided into 96 departments. The president serves as the head of state and as the executive head of the government for a five-year term. The president from the majority party in the National Assembly appoints the prime minister. The National Assembly has 577 members who are elected for a five-year term. The Senate has 348 members who serve a six-year term and who are elected by the Electoral College. The voting age is 18.

Germany

Germany is a federal republic. Germany's president is elected by members of the federal and state legislatures for up to two five-year terms. The chancellor is the head of the government and is elected by the lower house of Parliament, the Federal Assembly, for a four-year term. The legislature has two houses, the Federal Council (*Bundesrat*) and the Federal Assembly (*Bundestag*). There are 16 states in the country, and each has its own legislature and autonomy in many matters. State governments elect 69 members to the *Bundesrat*, and 614 members of the *Bundestag* are elected by popular vote. The voting age is 18.

India

India is a federal republic that has 28 states and 7 union territories. India has a president, prime minister, and the parliament. An Electoral College elects the president for a five-year term. The members of the majority party in the parliament choose the prime minister. The parliament has two houses: the *Rajya Sabha* (the Council of States) and the *Lok Sabha* (the House of the People). The *Rajya Sabha* has 250 members, and the *Lok Sabha* has 543 elected members. The voting age is 18.

Iraq

Iraq is a parliamentary democracy with executive, legislative, and judicial branches. The 325 members of the Council of Representatives of which 317 are elected by popular vote and 8 seats are reserved for minorities. The Council of Representatives elects the presidency council. The voting age is 18.

Japan

Japan, a constitutional monarchy, has an emperor with no governing power as its head of state. The prime minister (who heads the government) and his cabinet make up the executive branch. Legislative power rests with the *Diet*, a 242-seat House of Councilors (or upper house) and the 480-seat House of Representatives (or lower house). The 47 prefectures or provinces have governors who are elected by the people. The voting age is 20.

Mexico

Mexico has a federal republic with the president elected by all voters over 18 years of age for a six-year term. Mexico has 31 states and one federal district. The legislature is made up of a 128-seat Senate and a 500-seat Chamber of Deputies. Although voting is compulsory, it is not enforced. Technically, the 31 states of Mexico are autonomous; however, the federal government in the areas of education, security, and national industries heavily controls them.

The Netherlands

The governing structure of the Netherlands is a constitutional monarchy. The Netherlands has a queen, prime minister, and Council of State. The country has a 75-seat upper house called the First Chamber and a 150-seat lower house called the Second Chamber; they are all elected by those who are 18 or older.

New Zealand

New Zealand is a democratic parliamentary monarchy with the Queen of England as head of state. A governor-general represents the Queen. The prime minister and a 120-seat House of Representatives are elected by those 18 years of age or older.

Singapore

Singapore is a democratic republic that has a president who is elected by popular vote for a six-year term and a prime minister who is appointed by the president and parliament. The parliament is made up of 93 members of whom 84 are elected and 9 are appointed by the president. The voting age is 21, and all citizens are required to vote in national elections.

South Korea

The Republic of South Korea elects most members of government. The State Council includes the president and the prime minister (whom the president appoints). The president is elected by popular vote for a five-year term. The National Assembly has 299 members who serve a four-year term and are elected. The voting age is 19.

Taiwan

Taiwan is a multiparty democracy. The government consists of a president, who is elected by popular vote for a four-year term and can be reelected for a second term, and a unicameral legislature called the Yuan. The Yuan has 113 seats; people who occupy these seats are elected by specific groups of people directly. The president appoints the premier, who is the head of the government. The voting age is 20.

United Arab Emirates

The UAE is a federation of seven emirates. The Federal Supreme Council made up of seven emirate rulers elect the president and vice president for a five-year term, and there is no term limit. The Federal National Council has 40 seats; half of the seats are appointed and half are elected through the Electoral College which has 6,689 members.

United Kingdom (England, Scotland, Wales, and Northern Ireland)

The United Kingdom is ruled by a constitutional monarchy with a parliament. Although the monarch (Queen Elizabeth II) is the head of state, elected officials govern through Parliament. Britain has no written constitution. The main legislative body is the 646-member House of Commons, 529 of whom are from England; they serve a five-year term. Members are elected by citizens over the age of 18. The party with the most members in Parliament governs; that party's leader becomes the prime minister, who, along with the cabinet, governs as the executive body. The 92-member House of Lords makes up Parliament's upper chamber. Scotland, Wales, and Northern Island established their own governments in 1999; these governments had limited powers in such areas as education and health.

United States

The U.S. political system is a democratic federal government, with individual states having designated rights. The president is elected by the Electoral College, and other positions are voted on by the people. Congress, which is dominated by the Democratic and Republican parties, has two houses: the 435-seat House of Representatives and the 100-seat Senate. U.S. citizens tend to be very proud of their political system yet may not be well informed about politics. However, U.S. citizens do not like their system to be criticized. The voting age is 18.

Since the bombing of the World Trade Centers and the Pentagon on September 11, 2001, U.S. Americans tend to embody what to many is a curious combination of admiration for their political system in general and disdain for its particular operations. They criticize their leaders but do not want foreigners to do so. They think about politics as a separable aspect of life, one they can choose to ignore. Since 9/11, there has been a strong resurgence of patriotism in the United States. This resurgence has again raised the question of separation of church and state in the country.

The United States has a separate judicial branch of government. Lobbyists are very influential groups in regard to government policies.

WORLD ECONOMICS

Companies worldwide have become increasingly affected by economic, political, and competitive pressures from companies in other countries. Although it is well known that the automobile, steel, textile, and electronic industries face worldwide competition, it may not be as well known that many small- and medium-sized firms also have to compete in world markets (Nath, 1988).

The United States maintained a substantial technological lead after World War II during the 1950s, 1960s, and the beginning of the 1970s. Today this competitive edge is gone, and the macroeconomy of the world affects the performance of U.S. industry. Many U.S. industries were not prepared for this change in the macroeconomy, and the U.S. government had to provide temporary protection for industries and negotiate with foreign firms to limit their exports to the United States. In addition, the Department of Justice relaxed antitrust rules, thus allowing more joint ventures. When a particular industry is caught in the growing complexity of global economics, many smaller firms, regions, and communities may face adverse economic times. Although U.S. companies are facing intensive foreign competition, the groundwork has been laid to increase productivity, reduce capacity requirements, and increase flexibility, making the United States able to compete in the long run.

During the 1980s and 1990s, the inflow of foreign funds was due to high interest rates in the United States, the value of the dollar, stock prices of U.S. firms, and the formation of joint ventures. The influx of foreign investments has made it difficult to distinguish a U.S. firm from a foreign firm. Many companies now have no allegiance to a given nation but are truly multinational firms in their thinking and actions. The actions multinational firms take are in the best interest of their corporation rather than the best interest of their originating country. If a corporation can manufacture a product cheaper in another country, it will do so by closing the current plant and opening a new plant in another country. Many product lines are produced almost entirely outside the United States today, including televisions, camcorders, electronic components, tires, and clothing. Some firms have had to move abroad to compete with the imports. With wages being very high in the United States compared to many other locations in the world, firms could no longer entice U.S. citizens to buy their U.S.-produced products.

The multinational firm also has to deal with a very complex political environment. A successful domestic company learns and operates within the existing political situation. A company that moves into the international environment must learn how to manage and predict politics in other nations. The multinational firm deals successfully with many diverse and conflicting political environments. Some people are concerned that because of the size, wealth, resources, and knowledge of some multinational companies, the organization will become political bodies themselves. In many countries, the multinational firm exercises power that parallels that of the country's government. For example, in the Middle East, corporations within the oil cartels exert power that equals that of the government. Some multinational managers view the world as a single marketplace, ignoring national boundaries. The multinational company may well be an agent of change in the future.

Multinational companies also must be concerned with supernationalism, international politics, and international relations of the nations in which they operate. Decrees by such organizations as the United Nations, the European Union, and NAFTA are only a few examples of **supernationalism** today. Regionalism and economic interdependency are common in international politics, and it is projected that more regional trade agreements will be formed in the near future.

Companies also have to be concerned with subnationalism and the strife and political havoc that can result. **Subnationalism** exists when a political body attempts to unite diverse people under one government. With the discarding of communism in Eastern Europe, one of the results has been that subnationals want their own countries and their own governments once again.

Nationalism, supernationalism, and subnationalism are all active forces that the multinational companies have to consider because such factors affect the politics and the economics of the areas of the world in which they operate. Although the form and content of the "-isms" may vary from region to region, the possibility of upheaval is something multinational companies must consider. A company must analyze the political environment's positive and negative aspects before it expands. Other economic differences that may need to be considered before doing business in another nation include chronic high inflation versus low inflation, developed banking systems versus primitive systems, agricultural economy versus an industrial economy versus a technological economy, low employee productivity versus high employee productivity, and favorable versus unfavorable balance of payments and currency exchange rates.

Note: CultureGrams, published by ProQuest CSA, provides additional information related to conducting business in a number of countries. The four-page *CultureGram* for each country covers a variety of topics, such as greetings, visiting, eating, gestures, people, lifestyle, land and climate, history, commerce, government, economy, education, transportation, communication, health, and information for the traveler. Another source of information is the *CIA Factbook,* which is available online and covers land, government, and economic data.

EDUCATIONAL SYSTEMS

The educational system of a country may be formal, informal, or a combination of the two. People in societies such as the Maoris of New Zealand and the Aleuts of Alaska still pass on a great deal of information concerning their cultural heritage by word of mouth; people in other societies, such as the United States and Canada, include most of their cultural heritage in textbooks. Other societies do some of both. However it is accomplished, every society has a way of passing on its cultural heritage. **Cultural heritage** is the body of customary beliefs, social norms, material traits, thoughts, speech, and the artistic and intellectual traditions of a society.

There are many different and legitimate ways of thinking; we in the West value one of these ways above all others—the one we call "logic," a linear system that has been with us since Socrates.... We have been taught to think linearly rather than comprehensively.... Given our linear, step-by-step, compartmentalized way of thinking, fostered by the schools and public media, it is impossible for our leaders to consider events comprehensively. (Hall, 1976, p. 255)

Because societies are different, formal education varies between countries. The types of educational training in business also vary between and within countries and may include liberal arts, technical training, and apprenticeships. Liberal arts training includes the humanities and considers learning important in its own right. Technical business training is generally narrowly focused along specialized lines such as marketing, management, finance, economics, accounting, or management information systems. A problem with technical training is that there is very little human training and thought given to the people part of the business process. The apprenticeship program offers students practical experience and theory.

As the population of Third World nations receives training beyond the secondary level, these nations become more developed and similar in their use of technologies (Victor, 1997). One of the arguments for NAFTA is that it will help Mexico train and educate its population and will prevent foreign companies from taking advantage of an illiterate workforce. NAFTA requires that a company going into Mexico from the United States or Canada provide the same safety standards within its plants as in its home country and contribute to water treatment facilities and sewage treatment plants. The costs of such standards make the advantages of a workforce willing to work for low wages deteriorate quickly.

Accessibility to education varies from country to country. Much of Europe operates on a two-track system in which, at approximately the age of 12, children are assigned to a vocational track or a university track. The United States, Japan, and the Russian Federation, however, have open access to the educational system for all children; the importance the family places on education, the child's ability, and the quality of the child's teachers all play an important role in how far a child will go in the educational system (Victor, 1997).

How people are expected to learn may be seen as a continuum that ranges from very involved in the learning process (much interaction between teachers and students) to little involvement (no interaction between teachers and students). In the Israeli kibbutz, for example, children are expected to react spontaneously, and the classrooms are noisy. Chinese classrooms, on the other hand, are silent because of the reverence paid to knowledge, truth, and wisdom (Samovar, Porter, & McDaniel, 2009).

The value of an education, after it is received, varies again from country to country. A description of educational systems in the United States and other selected countries is given in the following sections (*CultureGrams*, 2010). Many smaller and less-developed African and Latin American countries have some of the poorest literacy rates; however, the Scandinavian countries are all 99% literate for both males and females.

Australia

Australia has 99% literacy for males and females. Education is public and financed by federal funds. Australians have seven years of primary and five years of secondary education that are compulsory. A significant portion of the population goes on to the university to complete some higher education

Brazil

The Brazilian educational system consists of nine years of elementary education and three years of secondary education. About 40% of students entering school go on to the secondary level. Approximately half of secondary school graduates enter trade schools. Acceptance at Brazil's top universities requires passing entrance exams and a special college-preparation course. Brazil's literacy rate is 88% for males and 89% for females.

Canada

In Canada, the provinces are responsible for their educational system; however, all the provinces provide free and compulsory education for persons between the ages of 6 and 16. The literacy rate is 99%. In Newfoundland, primary and secondary educations are free but operated by different religious groups. In Quebec, the government supports school boards and directs school curricula for Catholic and Protestant schools. Although the government subsidizes a university education, students pay for tuition. About 40% of the population seeks university or technical training after high school.

China

Although 100% of children are enrolled in the first grade, the overall literacy rate in China is 92.2% (the male literacy rate is 96% and female is 88.5%). Children attend school six days a week. Students attend school for 12 years. Students have to pay their tuition or sign a contract with a state company who will sponsor them.

Hong Kong has a higher literacy rate of 94% overall (97% for males and 90% for females). Education is considered very important to success in Hong Kong, and entrance to the better secondary schools is very competitive.

France

France's educational system has several unique aspects. Education is free and compulsory for those between the ages of 6 and 16. The literacy rate is 99%. The Catholic schools, partially subsidized by the state, enroll 20% of the children. Secondary school begins at age 11 and continues through age 18. Secondary education is offered by *lycées* and colleges. The *lycée* is the equivalent of a U.S. junior college. On completing secondary school, students take a comprehensive exam for one of the 60 universities. Except for marketing schools, most university training is also free in France.

The French also consider the university from which someone graduates to be very important because it determines that person's position in society. Although positions in business and government are not limited to a few institutions, alumni of the *Grandes Écoles* are considered more favorably. The *Grandes Écoles* and the alumni of the *Grandes Écoles* control business in France; and to be successful in business dealings in France, people must network through alumni.

Germany

In the Federal Republic of Germany's educational system, people must determine their careers early in life. Education is free from kindergarten through the university level. School begins with preschool at age 4; however, school is mandatory from age 6 to 15. Literacy overall is 99%. People of Germany are required to choose between technical training and college training at the age of 13. The entrance exam to universities is very difficult; acceptance into the university can be gained only by passing a rigorous exam after finishing a college preparatory school.

India

In India, education is free and compulsory from 6 to 14 years of age. Girls tend to drop out of school early; in fact, only 20% graduate from secondary school and less than 10% enter higher education. India has more than 250 universities and 3,000 colleges. India's overall literacy is 61%; the literacy rate for males is 73.4% and for females 47.8%.

Iraq

The literacy rate in Iraq is 74.1% overall—84.1% for males and 64.2% for females. Males will spend 11 years in school, and females will spend 8 years in school. Religious education is important to the people of Iraq. Because major religious events reported in the Torah, Old Testament, New Testament, and Qu'ran happened in Iraq, it is an important historical location to Judaism, Christianity, and Islam.

Japan

The educational system in Japan is very competitive; entrance exams to private schools and universities are rigorous. Competition is keen for acceptance to the prestigious schools because graduating from these schools usually assures the person a position in a top corporation. Japan's literacy rate is 99%. Education for persons between the ages of 6 and 15 is generally free and compulsory; after age 15, tuition must be paid. Math and science are stressed. *Jukus* (cram schools) are utilized to prepare students for entrance exams.

In Japan, education is expected to be difficult and sometimes unpleasant.

> The story goes that an elderly Japanese college professor took a student's paper, rolled it, and hit the student over the head with it yelling, "It's no good!" When asked why he had done that rather than offering the student some suggestions for improving the paper, he replied, "If I told him what to do, that would be too easy, and he would forget. If I make him find it himself, he will always remember." (Dillon, 1990)

In addition, the heavy intellectual demand on the students occurs during the primary and secondary education years rather than in the college years. After high school, the students take a very competitive university entrance exam. Because the university a student graduates from determines the company for which he or she will work, the better the university, the better that person's life will be. A close allegiance (i.e., sense of loyalty) is maintained between graduating classes, employee careers, alma mater, and year of graduation.

Mexico

Mexico has compulsory and free education for persons between the ages of 6 and 15. Although the literacy rate reported is 91% overall (92% for males and 90% for females), figures on various subcultures, such as the Amerindian, vary. Following six years of primary education and three years of secondary education, students choose either a preuniversity education or a technical education program. College entrance exams are difficult; only one-third of the students pass the exam. A university degree takes from three to seven years to complete.

The Netherlands

In the Netherlands, school is free and compulsory from 5 to 16 years of age. Primary education ends at age 12; secondary school begins with two years of basic education followed by choosing between different types of high schools from prevocational to preuniversity. Higher education is subsidized in the Netherlands. Literacy rates overall and for males and females are all 99%.

New Zealand

Education is free and compulsory from ages 5 to 16 in New Zealand. Students who attend the university study for two years after the compulsory requirements are met. A rigorous exam is administered in the fifth year for university admission. More New Zealand women meet the qualifications than men and have a higher university admission rate. New Zealand has an over-all, male, and female literacy rate of 99%.

Singapore

In Singapore, school is compulsory for ages 6 to 16. At the end of primary school, students take an exit exam that places them in secondary school by ability and aptitude. Most Singaporeans graduate from a secondary school. Literacy among younger Singaporeans approaches 100%. Overall, the literacy rate is 97% for males and 89% for females.

South Korea

Education is one of the virtues of Confucianism and is valued by the Korean culture. School is compulsory from ages 6 to 12. Most students complete secondary school, which is very demanding. Entering a university takes a lot of intensive training; it is very difficult to pass the entrance exam. The adult literacy rate overall is 99% for males and females.

Taiwan

In Taiwan, school is free and compulsory from ages 6 to 15. Students take national exams to enter high school or senior vocational school. Entrance examinations for the university are very difficult, and students may study as long as a year before taking the exam. Many students go to universities abroad. The youth literacy rate approaches 100%. The adult literacy rate overall is 98% for males and 92% for females.

United Arab Emirates

In the UAE, all children are required to go to school from ages 6 to 12. In kindergarten the boys and girls go to school together; however, after that they are separated by gender for school. The literacy rate for males is 76.1% and for females 81.7% in the UAE. The progress through school is by examinations. The government covers the cost of a university education.

United Kingdom (England, Scotland, Wales, and Northern Ireland)

The United Kingdom has free and compulsory education for those between the ages of 5 and 16, and its literacy rate is 99%. The General Certificate of Secondary Education Exam is taken at age 16 to allow students to earn the General Certificate. At age 18, after earning the General Certificate of Education, students may attend one of more than 40 universities or attend one of the various professional schools. Members of the upper class tend to go to the elite educational institutions. Although it is possible for someone in the lower classes to attend such schools, primarily those with alumni connections attend the elite educational institutions. Therefore, a person's position in society determines educational opportunities.

Countries that do not have an entrenched formal educational infrastructure for all people tend to have two classes of people: the small, wealthy upper class and the lower class in which the majority live in poverty. The wealthy people who attend school and in many cases go to college abroad have a very different view of the world and their cultural heritage. The masses hold a strong allegiance to the cultural past. Depending on the country involved, the literacy level of the masses can vary widely. A person cannot take for granted that everyone can read, has knowledge of mathematics, or is familiar with technology. Many times what is important in one nation may be very unimportant in another nation (Victor, 1997).

Examples of cultures that place more emphasis on informal rather than formal education include Gambia, with 41% adult literacy and no universities; Mali, with a literacy rate of 27% for males and 12% for females—its first university was recently built in Bamako; and Bangladesh, with a literacy rate of 43%. Only 3% complete three or more years at a university, compared to almost 24% of U.S. citizens who complete degrees (*CultureGrams,* 2010).

United States

In the United States, education for those who are 5 to 16 years of age is compulsory and free. Although not highly competitive up to the secondary level, the U.S. educational system is somewhat competitive at the postsecondary level at such schools as Harvard, the Massachusetts Institute of Technology (MIT), and Yale, where intellectual demands may be rigorous. Because education is a state's right, competition between and within state educational systems may vary.

The literacy rate in the United States is 99%. However, variations exist by region, and functional illiteracy exists in the adult population. Even though graduating from certain prestigious institutions of higher learning may help in securing initial corporate positions, what a person does on the job determines the person's career and the companies for which the person will work. University ties then become less important.

Anybody can get into college in the United States, according to Malaysian students. Malaysians, remarking on the easy accessibility of American colleges and universities, compared U.S. schools unfavorably to those of the British who once ruled Malaysia and provided the model for their educational system. However, the Malaysians observed, "You Americans put men on the moon, so there must be something right about your system." (Althen, 2011, p. 89)

MARRIAGE AND FAMILY SYSTEMS

Marriage and family systems are made up of attitudes, beliefs, and practices related to marriage and the family that are held by people in a particular culture. To survive, all societies must procreate. Because human infants must depend on adults for their basic needs, cultures have defined how the young children in their culture will be reared and who is responsible for their care. Consequently, all cultures have devised rules concerning who can marry and have set procedures to be followed when people marry and raise families. Anthropologists have researched and categorized much of this information for us (Ferraro, 2010).

Although many ways of being a family exist, people tend to consider their own background first when they consider the concept of family. In many parts of the world, the concept of family is so strong that it is of paramount importance in each person's life. This is particularly true in the Japanese, Chinese, Spanish, African, Arabic, Indian, Italian, and Turkish cultures. In some cultures, the association of the family is so strong that sharing the family wealth with outsiders or protecting outsiders is an unknown concept. In the United States and parts of Europe, work and family life are often combined; business guests are invited to the home. The Japanese, Taiwanese, and people of many Arabic nations, on the other hand, would not invite business guests to their home.

The word family has very different connotations around the world. In the United States, the definition of a family encompasses the nuclear family and the extended family. The **nuclear family** consists of the father, mother, and children; the **extended family** consists of grandparents, uncles, aunts, and cousins (Samovar et al., 2009).

In many countries, the family may include second-, third-, and fourth-generation relationships. Arab families may have more than a hundred close relatives, and in Mexico even godparents are considered family. Family can mean your immediate biological family, or it can mean the entire culture. In some parts of the world, the children are reared and taught communally as in parts of Israel. Each community member takes part in raising and educating each child. The family unit, as the culture views "family," will help foster individual and/or group dependency (Victor, 1997).

In Italy, the most important affiliation is to the family, which is also responsible for a large number of self-employed people and small businesses. A necessity of Italian life is an affiliation with at least one prime interest group (such as a political party or trade union) in order to live and work. The ability to be hired and work in many countries depends on your relatives. Nepotism and favoritism are considered a way of life. However, in U.S. corporations, nepotism and favoritism are viewed with disfavor because the person being hired under such circumstances is often considered unqualified or corrupt. Corporations may need to adjust their views of family relationships to be successful in multinational business relationships (Victor, 1997).

Family systems originally evolved to meet the needs of the society; subsequently, the following forms developed: **polygyny**, one man with many wives; **polyandry**, one woman with many husbands; **monogamy**, one husband and wife; and **serial monogamy**, a number of different monogamous marriages (Dodd, 1997). See Figure 1.

FIGURE 1   Family Systems

Many Arabic countries and followers of Islam practice polygyny. The Arabic countries currently have the highest birthrate in the world; however, they also have a very small population base. In the UAE, 80% of the people who live there are not Emiratis. The UAE has had to import people to fill the jobs that are available; therefore, the government encourages men to have large families and many wives. Polyandry would help reduce the birthrate and has been practiced by many of the Polynesian nations. Monogamy is practiced in North America, South America, Asia, Europe, and parts of Africa. Serial monogamy is practiced where people are able to remarry after divorce or the death of a spouse; the United States practices serial monogamy.

Another aspect of family is establishing who is in control or who plays the role of the authority figure. Families can be **patriarchal** (father oriented) or **matriarchal** (mother oriented) (see Figure 2). Inheritance rights and the naming of children help determine whether a society is matriarchal or patriarchal (Dodd, 1997).

Jewish families are matriarchal because of the Judaic code of inheritance through the mother, although the father's name is used. Nationally, however, the Jewish are patriarchal.

FIGURE 2   Family Authority Figures

Christians and followers of Islam tend to be patriarchal, and the father's name is given to the children. Spanish women maintain their maiden name by hyphenating it to their married name; however, the Spanish culture is patriarchal. Many professional women in the United States are now retaining their maiden name when they marry.

A brief description of marriage and family customs in the United States and in other selected countries follows to give you an idea of how family structure and customs vary from culture to culture (*CultureGrams,* 2010).

Australia

In Australia, dating begins by age 15 and sometimes in small groups. The age to wed is 23 for women and 25 for men. Many couples are choosing to live together before or instead of marrying; however, church weddings are still common. Australian couples generally have two or three children, and extended families are not strong in Australia. Women comprise 40% of the workforce, and single-parent homes are becoming more common. Independence is valued; the elderly live in their own homes as long as they can.

Brazil

In Brazil, group dating begins at about age 14 with couples emerging later. While Brazilians have married young in the past, today many wait until they are older. Although families have traditionally been large, smaller families with one to three children are becoming more the norm. Families are important; unmarried children usually remain at home until they marry. When elderly parents are unable to live by themselves, they tend to live with their children rather than going to a nursing home.

Canada

The Canadian family system is similar to that of the United States in that dating begins before age 16. Many couples are choosing to live together. If they do marry, it is generally after 30 years of age. Frequently, both parents work outside the home. The average family size is two children; one-third of marriages end in divorce.

China

The family is more important than the individual to the Chinese. The elderly are highly respected and are taken care of by their children. Because boys are prized as heirs to the family name, there are currently more males in China. Young people do date, but they are discouraged from getting serious until men are 22 and women are 20. If they marry before these ages, they lose government benefits. College students cannot marry until after graduation. The women maintain their maiden name; however, the children receive the father's surname.

Hong Kong couples generally wait to marry until they have job security and can live by themselves. Even if women work outside the home, they are still responsible for the home. Usually they have only one or two children. They also have one of the lowest divorce rates in the world.

France

France tends to have an elitist attitude toward the family and who their children date. Dating begins around age 15. In France, social class, wealth, and educational level are important when choosing a spouse. The nuclear family is common in France; however, living together before or instead of marrying is also common. The average family has only one child, with many couples choosing to have no children. Many of the French have moved away from the extended family to work or study.

Germany

The German family system includes dating that is Dutch treat (each gender pays his or her own expenses). There is no word for dating in the German language. Marriage occurs generally after the age of 20, but Germans usually believe they must have some financial security prior to marriage. Living together before marriage is not unusual. The family is generally patriarchal, and one to two children are the norm. In the former East Germany, it is common for both parents to work, although in what was West Germany, it is less common for both parents to work.

India

Dating is not customary in India. Most marriages are arranged with the consent of the bride and groom. Weddings are great feasts and ceremonies. Families still tend to be large; middle- and upper-class families provide financially for their children until they finish their education and take a position. The family is patriarchal; the elderly are revered and taken care of by their children.

Iraq

In Iraq, women are much protected; dating is rare. Marriages are arranged with the bride and groom's consent. First cousins may marry. The groom pays a dowry to the family of the bride. Weddings are great feasts and ceremonies. Families tend to be large and include the extended family in activities. Several generations often live in one household.

Japan

In Japan, the family system is changing. In the past, most marriages were arranged; now, however, many of the young follow the custom of Western cultures and choose their own spouse. Dating begins around age 15, but the average age for marriage is 27 for men and a little younger for women. Men feel they must be financially secure before marriage, and they assume financial responsibility for the wedding. The family includes the extended family and has a strong sense of obligation and responsibility. A person's actions reflect strongly on the family as well as on the person. Although the father is the breadwinner, the mother runs the household. In the past, it was considered improper for women to work outside the home; however, many of the younger women have now chosen to have a career rather than marriage and a family. Families tend to be small with fewer than three children. Having a male heir is important in Japan as well as in most other Asian countries. The divorce rate is very low, and the marriages are monogamous.

Mexico

In the Mexican family system, dating is allowed; however, a boy often meets the girl at a prearranged place rather than picking her up at her home. Marriage follows the customary Catholic traditions. The Mexican family tends to be large by U.S. standards (more than three children), and family unity is very important. The divorce rate is low, so monogamous families are the norm. In the rural areas particularly, households include members of the extended family. Although the family is patriarchal, the mother runs the household. Family responsibilities take precedence over all other responsibilities.

The Netherlands

In the Netherlands, youth begin dating with group activities at 13–16 years of age. Couples often live together before marriage. Because couples pay for their own weddings, guests generally will give them money to cover the expenses. Children leave home at 18 years of age. Families are small and very close. The elderly usually live by themselves. Both parents tend to work outside the home.

New Zealand

Dating begins at 15 or 16 in New Zealand with group activities beginning at 12 years of age. Marriage comes in the late twenties, and many couples choose to live together first. The family generally has two children, and both parents work. The number of single parents is increasing. Many families are very close; however, these family ties are not as strong as they once were.

Singapore

In Singapore, dating is discouraged until a child is 17 years of age as it is seen as interfering with school studies. Marriage comes in the late twenties. Because there are many religions, a large variety of wedding ceremonies take place. Generally couples have only one or two children. The elderly tend to live with their children or close by, and it is the responsibility of the children to take care of the parents. Because many parents both work, they tend to share the household responsibilities or hire household help.

South Korea

In South Korea, the oldest son not only receives the greatest respect but also has the greatest responsibilities. Family hierarchies and genealogies are very important and determine who receives more respect within the family. Because of their studies, Korean youth rarely date seriously until college or when they begin working. In the rural areas, some marriages are still arranged; however, the parties involved do know each other.

Taiwan

Family is very close in Taiwan with elderly parents often living with their children. A strong sense of unity and obligation to other family members is part of the Taiwanese culture. Dating does not begin until people start their higher education because of the concentration on education. Marriage age is generally between 27 and 30.

United Arab Emirates

Although there are nuclear families in the UAE, the extended family is very important. Women have a central role in the family and can own property and businesses. Children live at home until they marry. The average family has five children. The government offers economic incentives to have children. Their children care for the elderly.

United Kingdom (England, Scotland, Wales, and Northern Ireland)

In the United Kingdom, dating begins around 13–16 years of age. People seem to be marrying later in life and having fewer children. The legal age to marry is 16, but most marry in their late twenties and will have one to two children. Single-parent families are becoming more common.

United States

Dating in the United States begins as early as age 13. The average age for marriage is 26 for men and 24 for women. In the United States, you will find a nuclear family, which consists of either monogamous or serial monogamous parents or single-parent families. The nuclear family generally maintains a close relationship with members of the extended family. The traditional family includes a mother, father, and one or more children. However, one out of three children is born out of wedlock. Some women are choosing not to marry the father of the baby or are using sperm banks if they prefer to be solely responsible for a child. Almost half of all women work, thus affecting decisions on family size. Many older members of the extended family live in private or government institutions rather than with their immediate families, partly because of the mobility of the family and changes in living conditions.

SOCIAL HIERARCHIES AND INTERACTION

Although human behavior is never totally controlled, society, through social order, limits its randomness. People learn through enculturation what is and is not proper social behavior. Generally, learning is introduced by the older family members to the younger family members; however, most of the social ideals arise in society in general and not in the family directly. Many times, there are family and nonfamily orientations. A good starting point to learn about another culture is from children's literature, television shows, and games that are enjoyed by the culture. The social structure of a society tends to be enduring and is shared by the members of the culture. Social values are changed very slowly when dealing with an entire society. As business becomes multinational and as people meet and deal with other ways of living, proper **social hierarchies** and **social interactions** are being tested. We either adapt or remain restricted in the cocoon of our own culture. If you are to communicate successfully in a multicultural environment, you must understand that different is simply different, not better or worse. The actions of the people of other cultures are correct for them.

The family functions at many levels within a society: they are the caregivers of the young and the old; they provide emotional support; they transmit culture; and they transmit identity. The family tells the children early in life who they are and with whom they should play. The family is part of a wider culture. As the Swedish proverb says, "Children act in the village as they have learned at home." The home is where we first learn about our culture. It is interesting that as governments change, the family unit continues to survive. The idea of family is one of the oldest and fundamental building blocks of human beings. Many cultures in the world consider the elderly the most important members of the family; these cultures include the Chinese, Japanese, Arabs, Mexicans, Malaysians, Filipinos, French, Native Americans, and African Americans (Samovar et al., 2009).

In examining social hierarchies and social interactions, we must consider the five sets of structures into which society can be divided: social reciprocity, group membership, intermediaries, formality, and property (Condon & Yousef, 1998).

Social reciprocity refers to the way in which formal and informal communications are handled. Someone who believes in independent social reciprocity tries to avoid commitment; under symmetrical-obligatory social reciprocity, people have an equal obligation. Under complementary-obligatory social reciprocity, people are forever indebted to others.

Group membership has two extremes: People can belong to many groups or very few groups, and there is a middle ground between the two. People belonging to many groups generally are not strongly associated with any of them and do not want to give up their personal freedom; likewise, people that belong to few groups for a long time may tend to subordinate themselves to the group. The people occupying the middle ground try to balance group affiliation and personal freedom.

The use of intermediaries in societies can tell you a great deal about the makeup of the society. **Intermediaries** are people who act as go-betweens with other people. If intermediaries are not used, society members are direct and independent. If intermediaries are always used, society members dislike confrontation and are very group oriented. In the middle, society members are sometimes direct and sometimes want someone else to intervene.

Formality is the degree of preciseness, regularity, or conformity expected within the society. Formality is particularly troublesome between cultures because even the most formal culture also has some informality and because the most informal culture has some formality. Selective formality, which is the middle ground between the two extremes, can be very different in various cultures.

The last structure is **property**, which is something that is or may be possessed. Property can be viewed as private, utilitarian, or community. U.S. Americans think of property as an extension of the self; Mexicans think of property ownership in relation to feelings and need. In the past, communist countries had community property. Native Americans also believed that land was community property. Even in private property cultures, there is common property, such as parks, land grant colleges, and hospitals. The three values of the five structures discussed are capitalism, socialism, and communism.

True equality does not exist in any country in the world because of power, wealth, and privilege, which exist in all countries. Although the United States considers equal opportunity important, the differences in children's lives make it clear that not all will grow up with an equal opportunity for wealth or position. Human beings do not choose their cultural interaction and social hierarchical foundations; they are born or adopted into them. Hierarchical divisions can be social classes, gender, ethnic groups, castes, or tribes. Although aristocracies or monarchies may not be active in many nations in the world, they still form a large network. Through this network, many members are still in positions to influence the public. Religion and legal systems are used in many cultures to enforce class distinctions.

No nation in the world treats women and men equally. The Human Development Index (HDI) was developed by the United Nations Development Program to measure individual purchasing power, health, and education for the population as a whole. Table 1 contains the rankings of overall HDI and the Inequality-adjusted Human Development Index (*Human Development Reports*, 2011). Laws, rules, or religion may preserve or dictate social interaction and the social hierarchies that may evolve within a given culture. All cultures have punishments that are administered when cultural norms are violated. Although punishment is universal, the scope of punishment for the same crime may vary significantly between cultures and include fines, incarceration, or death.

When working interculturally, you may need to adjust your approach to work to match that of people in the host country. Differences exist in such areas as speed and efficiency, time, rules of work, kinesics, friendships, work-role expectations, social acceptance, the showing of respect, correct body posture, knowledge, the showing of empathy, role behavior, management interaction, and ambiguity tolerance. By taking the time to learn about the characteristics of a culture, you show people your sincerity and friendship. Management skills that consider differences among cultures will solve business problems more successfully. Friendships in many cultures are necessary before any business is ever conducted. In fact, friendship and work may

TABLE 1 Rankings of Overall HDI and Inequality-Adjusted Human Development Index (IAI) in 34 Countries

Country	HDI	IAI	Country	HDI	IAI
Norway	1	1	France	20	16
Australia	2		Spain	23	17
The Netherlands	3	4	Italy	24	21
United States	4	22	Singapore	26	—
New Zealand	5		United Kingdom	28	19
Canada	6	12	Greece	29	25
Ireland	7	6	Mexico	57	55
Liechtenstein	8		Russian Federation	66	38
Germany	9	8	United Arab Emirates	30	
Sweden	10	3	Philippines	112	72
Switzerland	11	9	Paraguay	107	75
Japan	12		China	101	72
Hong Kong	13		Sri Lanka	97	57
South Korea		27	India	134	88
Belgium	18	15	Swaziland	140	93
Finland	22	11	South Africa	123	106

be interrelated. Examples of social hierarchies and interactions for selected cultures including the United States follow (*CultureGrams*, 2010; *Human Development Reports,* 2011; Samovar et al., 2009).

Australia

Australians value tolerance and fairness and enjoy owning property. They dislike aggression and pompous behaviors. They are very polite people and enjoy having fun. As a culture, they are very clean and active environmentalists.

Brazil

Separation of classes is a way of life in Brazil. People of the upper classes live separately from the working class. Family background and education are important; ethnic background is not. Brazilians are proud of their country; they are outgoing, friendly, and free spirited. They are creative in finding ways to solve problems.

Canada

Canadians view their society as separate from the United States and do not like being considered the same as people in the United States. French Canadians are very proud of the cultural heritage they maintain. Canadians are generally more formal than U.S. residents but are friendly and kind to guests. They tend to be quite social but conservative; etiquette is important to them.

China

The Chinese are a hospitable, yet reserved, people. According to the principle of *guanxi*, friends are committed to helping each other when the need arises. Maintaining family honor and social standing is important. Confucianism has an impact on the attitudes of the people and reinforces the biological and cultural mores that exist in China. Hong Kong also holds the Confucian standards as a way of life.

France

The French are hierarchical; there is a correct way to do things, and everything else would be incorrect. Success, according to the French, is measured by education, family, and finances. Friendships are not made easily, but once made, are important.

Germany

As an individualistic culture, Germans are also a hierarchical society. Germans display a strong internal discipline and culturally have a need for order and structure. In addition, they value honesty and thriftiness. Friendships are not developed quickly, but they are considered important.

Japan

The Japanese are concerned with social reciprocity, which can be seen in the importance of gift giving. Formality and conformity in life, work, and family are all important aspects of the social hierarchy of the society. The Japanese are quite social and devoted to their families, employers, and superiors. Friendships are not made easily but are made for life and not taken lightly. Loyalty and seeking fulfillment through the group rather than as an individual is important. The Japanese like to use intermediaries, particularly when trying to resolve negative situations in order to help everyone save face. Property is important but quite expensive because so many people live in such small geographic areas.

> Japanese men have a saying: "To have the best of all worlds is to have an American house, eat Chinese food, and have a Japanese wife. To have the worst of all worlds is to have a Japanese house, eat British food, and have an American wife."

Mexico

Mexicans view social reciprocity as important. Mexicans are good hosts and place great importance on being a good employer, a good employee, and a good friend. People of Mexico involve religion in their social interactions. Most Mexicans are Catholic and take their religion and religious celebrations seriously. Much of their life is informal with the exception of their religion. Their attitude toward property is an aspect of their social attitude of sharing. Property is viewed in a utilitarian way as belonging to those who need it. A possessive attitude toward property is infrequent.

The Netherlands

The Dutch tend to plan and schedule rather than be spontaneous. The Dutch respect privacy, honesty, and directness. Egalitarianism is a central part of the Dutch society. A strong need for order gives the society its hierarchical structure.

New Zealand

New Zealanders enjoy a relaxed and informal lifestyle. People of New Zealand are practical and self-reliant. They value home ownership. In addition, theirs is a multicultural and egalitarian society.

Singapore

In Singapore, the society is unique as it blends the traditional Asian values with Western values. Goals include a good career, a condominium, car, and money. Being able to afford material possessions is important since space is at a premium. Singaporeans have an ordered society that is enforced by law as well as culture.

South Korea

Confucianism permeates South Korean life. Status is determined by age, gender, education, family background, wealth, occupation, and political ideology. Social contacts determine success. South Koreans tend to be very friendly. Young people are much more materially oriented than their parents or grandparents. Genealogy and backgrounds are important and determine how people are treated in this hierarchical society.

Taiwan

The Taiwanese are friendly and generous. The Confucian ethics are seen throughout the society. Material possessions are important, but a good education is the most important possession. People of Taiwan are hard working and avoid criticism or frankness.

United Arab Emirates

For the people of the UAE, life has changed rapidly in the past 30 years in the business world. Social reciprocity is still important. Although the people are friendly and hospitable, their personal privacy is important. The social hierarchy has been maintained by formal and conservative traditions. Emiratis are devoted to their extended family and to their religion. *Shari'a* is the state law; and therefore, religion influences the life of the Emiratis.

United Kingdom (England, Scotland, Wales, and Northern Ireland)

Tradition and customs are important to the English, Welsh, and Irish. The English tend to be reserved and expect others to act accordingly. They are embarrassed by displays of emotion or excessive enthusiasm—unless it is at a cricket or *futbol* game. Politeness and humor are important in the United Kingdom; however, their sense of humor and sarcasm are quite different from that seen in the United States. In a study of television advertisements, Martin, Chaney, and Moore (2004) found that companies used a local advertising style when advertising in England and used more puns and satire than they did in advertisements in Japan or Mexico.

United States

In the United States, people like to believe they can rise above cultural bias and change their status; yet at the same time, many find security in the social hierarchy and social interaction patterns into which they were born. A common saying in the United States is, "The apple does not fall far from the tree." In the United States, wealth is related to social class. However, the U.S. society still admires achievement above all else. People who invent, discover, or "make it on their own" are widely admired. U.S. Americans enjoy socializing and are frank and outspoken; they will discuss most subjects except personal issues. They will tend to be informal, belong to very few groups, do not use intermediaries, and are possessive of property.

Terms

Cultural heritage	Marriage and	Property
Cultural universals	family systems	Serial monogamy
Economic systems	Matriarchal	Social hierarchies
Exports	Monogamy	Social interaction
Extended family	Nuclear family	Social reciprocity
Formality	Patriarchal	Subnationalism
Group membership	Political systems	Supernationalism
Imports	Polyandry	
Intermediaries	Polygyny	

Exercise 1

Instructions: Match the currencies on the right with their country on the left.

_____	1. Australia	A. dollar
_____	2. United Kingdom	B. drachma
_____	3. China	C. euro
_____	4. India	D. peso
_____	5. Japan	E. pound sterling
_____	6. Mexico	F. riyal
_____	7. France	G. rupee
_____	8. South Korea	H. won
_____	9. Saudi Arabia	I. yen
_____	10. Germany	J. yuan

Exercise 2

Instructions: Circle the T for true or the F for false.

1. T F Most countries have similar economic systems.
2. T F No true universal government body exists.
3. T F Political systems in England and Japan are dissimilar.
4. T F Multinational companies are responsible only to the country in which they are based.
5. T F Enculturation means learning about other cultures.
6. T F Educational systems throughout the world vary widely.
7. T F The university from which a person graduates is important in France.
8. T F A major family system in the United States is serial monogamy.
9. T F Islamic believers tend to be matriarchal.
10. T F Social reciprocity is relatively unimportant in Japan and Saudi Arabia.

Questions and Cases for Discussion

1. Define universal cultural systems and identify them.
2. Why do societies develop economic/political systems, and what do these systems do for the members of a society?
3. Compare the economic systems of Japan and Canada.
4. Compare the political systems of the United Kingdom and Mexico.
5. Discuss differences in educational systems in various cultures.
6. Explain how marriage and family systems in the United States are different from those of other cultures.

7. How important is social reciprocity in Mexico, Japan, and the United Arab Emirates?
8. What are intermediaries? In which countries are intermediaries used?
9. Explain cultural variations in the way property is viewed.
10. Explain what is meant by "equality" in the United States. Does the term mean the same thing in other countries?

CASES

The following procedure is recommended for analyzing the cases: (a) read the case carefully paying attention to details; (b) read the questions at the end of the case; (c) reread the case, taking notes on or highlighting the details needed for answering the questions; (d) identify relevant facts, underlying assumptions, and critical issues of the case; (e) list possible answers to the questions; and (f) select the most logical response to the question. Your professor may ask that you submit answers to the case questions in writing.

Case 1

Education is offered to everyone in the United States; however, 25% of the people who enter school as five-year-olds never graduate from high school. In Japan, the high school graduation rate is 95%, and in Germany and the United Kingdom it is equally as high. However, in countries such as Mexico and Third World nations, many people never complete the equivalent of a high school education. The percentage of people who attend college after high school varies from country to country as described in this chapter.

Currently, many nations are sending a large number of students to U.S. universities, and many foreign companies are giving grants to U.S.

"think tank" universities (such as MIT, Stanford, Chicago, and Harvard).

1. In light of this information, what do you see as the future role of U.S. universities in the world?
2. Is the fact that 25% of the U.S. population does not graduate from high school important in light of what is happening in other countries in the world?
3. Is the fact that so many foreign students are attending college in the United States positive or negative? What do you see as the long-term effects?

Case 2

Many Korean children and children of other nationalities have been adopted by U.S. Americans. Generally, these children were reared in homes where the parents were not of the nationality of the adopted child. Sometimes after the children become adults, they return to their native country to learn about people of their own ethnic heritage. Would language differences pose a problem? What cultural problems would these children have?

Case 3

Many of the former communist countries have changed their economic and political systems.

Examples are the Russian Federation, the former Czechoslovakia, and the former East Germany. What cultural changes will be necessary in their educational system to have a smooth transition?

Case 4

Because more and more firms are becoming multinational and must deal with a number of monetary systems, what is the feasibility of developing one monetary system (such as the *euro* in Europe) to do away with exchange rates? Do multinational firms have the capability to help bring about a world currency?

Case 5

Intercultural business communication takes on many roles in the world. One that the United States is currently living in is the Afghanistan situation. Many U.S. businesses have signed contracts to provide services in Afghanistan to the Afghanistan government or the U.S. military forces. The U.S. civilians who take these positions do so, for the most part, for the money because they are paid more than twice what they would be paid in the United States for the same type of work. If you chose to take one of these positions, what would you want to know, how would you prepare for the welcoming and/or the hatred you would experience, and what characteristics that you possess would be strengths or weaknesses? Do you feel that foreign workers in Afghanistan should train an Afghanistan person to replace them? What are the intercultural relationship problems in this current situation?

Activities

1. Interview an Asian or a Latin American student to learn about the educational system in his or her country and the relationship between educational training and positions in business and society. Be prepared to share your findings with the class.
2. Research the economic system of a country you would like to visit. Prepare a one-page summary for class discussion and submission to the instructor.
3. Research the marriage and family system of a country of your choice. In a one-page written summary, make comparisons with the family lifestyle in the United States.
4. Prepare a list of countries with patriarchal family systems and those with matriarchal family systems to better understand the role of women in various cultures.
5. List at least two countries that practice the following family systems: polygyny, polyandry, monogamy, and serial monogamy.

References

Althen, G., with Bennett, J. (2011). *American ways* (3rd ed.). Boston, MA: Intercultural Press.

Antkiewicz, A., & Whalley, J. (2005). Shifting economic power: From OECD to BRICSAM, mimeo.

CIA Factbook. (2012). Retrieved from http://www.cia.gov/library/publications/the-world-factbook/print/ca.html

Condon, J. C., & Yousef, F. (1998). *An introduction to intercultural communication.* Yarmouth, ME: Intercultural Press.

CultureGrams. (2010). Ann Arbor, MI: ProQuest CSA.

Dillon, L. S. (1990, May). The occidental tourist. *Training & Development Journal, 44,* 72–80.

Dodd, C. H. (1997). *Dynamics of intercultural communication.* New York: McGraw-Hill.

Ferraro, G. P. (2010). *The cultural dimension of international business* (6th ed.). Upper Saddle River, NJ: Prentice Hall.

Hall, E. (1976). *Beyond culture.* New York: Anchor Books.

Human Development Reports. (2011). Retrieved January 20, 2012, from http://hdr.undp.org/en/reports and http://hdr.undp.org/en/statistics/ihdi/

Martin, J. S., Chaney, L. H., & Moore, T. (2004). An assessment of the use of humor in advertising in England, Japan, and Mexico using award-winning advertisements. Paper presented at the International

Academy for Intercultural Research Conference, Taipei, Taiwan.

Nath, R. (Ed.). (1988). *Comparative management.* New York: Ballinger.

Organization for Economic Cooperation and Development (OECD). (2010). Retrieved January 19, 2012, from http://www.oecd.org.

Samovar, L. A., Porter, R. E., & McDaniel, E. R. (2009). *Communication between cultures* (7th ed.). Belmont, CA: Thomson Learning.

Shaw, T. M., Cooper, A. F., & Antkiewicz, A. (2007). Global and/or regional development at the start of the twenty-first century? China, India, and South Africa. *Third World Quarterly, 28*(7), 1255–1270.

U.S. Census Bureau. (2011). Exhibit 6a. Exports, Imports and Trade Balance by Country and Area, Not Seasonly Adjusted: 2010. Retrieved from http://www.census.gov/foreign-trade/Press-Release/current_press_release/ft900.pdf

Victor, D. A. (1997). *International business communication.* New York: HarperCollins.

Wilson, D., & Purushothaman, R. (2003). *Dreaming with the BRICs: The path to 2050.* New York: Goldman Sachs.

Zenzone Forum.com. (2012). Thread: 2 cows explain all political and economicisms. Retrieved from http://www.zenzoneforum.com/threads/18089-2-cows-explain-all-political-amp-economic

Glossary

Cultural heritage includes the values, ideals, and beliefs that a person inherits from his or her culture.

Cultural universals are formed out of the common problems all cultures have.

Economic system is the way in which the physiological needs of the people are produced, distributed, and consumed.

Exports are goods sent out of the country.

Extended family consists of grandparents, uncles, aunts, and cousins.

Formality refers to the degree of preciseness, regularity, or conformity expected within the society.

Group membership has two extremes: People can belong to many or to few groups. In addition, a middle area exists between the two extremes.

Imports refer to goods brought into the country.

Intermediaries are people who act as go-betweens with other people.

Marriage and family system refers to attitudes, beliefs, and practices related to marriage and the family held by people in various cultures; importance placed on marriage and the family in a society.

Matriarchal refers to a mother-oriented family.

Monogamy is a family system that includes one husband and one wife.

Nuclear family is a family consisting of the father, mother, and children.

Patriarchal refers to a father-oriented family.

Political system is the governing system that originates from dictatorship, inherited rights, election procedures, consensus, or conquest.

Polyandry refers to one woman with many husbands.

Polygyny is a family system consisting of one man with many wives.

Property is something that is or may be possessed.

Serial monogamy refers to a family system that includes a number of different monogamous marriages through divorce or death.

Social hierarchy refers to the structure of a culture.

Social interaction refers to what is acceptable and unacceptable communication between people in a culture.

Social reciprocity refers to the way formal and informal obligations are handled, ranging from the belief that people are forever indebted to others to those who feel no obligation to others.

Subnationalism exists when a political body attempts to unite diverse people under one government.

Supernationalism refers to extending authority over more than one nation.

Answers to Exercises

Matching		True/False	
1.	A	1.	F
2.	E	2.	T
3.	J	3.	F
4.	G	4.	F
5.	I	5.	F
6.	D	6.	T
7.	C	7.	T
8.	H	8.	T
9.	F	9.	F
10.	C	10.	F

Contrasting Cultural Values

Objectives

Upon completion of this chapter, you will

- appreciate the role that values play in communicating effectively with persons from other cultures.
- understand differences in word meanings among cultures.
- learn how attribution and perception play a role in cultural values.
- appreciate attitude differences toward men and women in various cultures.
- understand how attitudes toward work and ethics vary with the culture.
- learn how religious influences impact cultural values.
- understand how individualism and collectivism play a role in cultural values.

VALUES

Values form the core of a culture. **Values** are social principles, goals, or standards accepted by persons in a culture. They establish what is proper and improper behavior as well as what is normal and abnormal behavior. Values are learned by contacts with family members, teachers, and religious leaders. What people hear, read, and watch on television influences their value systems.

People in various cultures have different attitudes toward women, ethical standards, and work. Semantic differences and attributions affect cultural values as do religious influences. Because the U.S. workplace is becoming increasingly diverse culturally, managers need to be aware of the values of all workers. Managers are more likely to understand what motivates people of different cultures and to deal effectively with problem situations if they understand the cultural background of the person.

From Chapter 3 of *Intercultural Business Communication*, Sixth Edition. Lillian H. Chaney, Jeanette S. Martin. Copyright © 2014 by Pearson Education, Inc. All rights reserved.

Some values held by people in the United States are not shared by people in other cultures. In their book *American Ways*, Althen and Bennett (2011) identify a number of U.S. values and assumptions, including equality, informality, individualism, directness, and attitude toward the future, time, and work.

People in the United States may claim that all persons are equal and that no person is superior to another simply because of wealth, education, or social status. In reality, subtle distinctions are made within a group to acknowledge status differences, many of which are nonverbal. Because of this belief in equality, U.S. Americans are uncomfortable with certain displays of respect, such as bowing, that are common in some cultures. Although inequalities do exist, many women hold positions of power and influence in education, government, and industry.

People in the United States are also rather informal when compared to people of other cultures. They often dress more casually. In fact, it is not unusual to see the president of the United States dressed in casual attire. The posture of U.S. people is often informal; assuming a slouched stance or putting feet on a desk or chair is not uncommon. The speech of U.S. people is also rather informal; they often address people they hardly know by their first names.

Another quality that people in the United States value is directness. They prefer that people be open and get to the point. Such sayings as "What is the bottom line?" and "Put your cards on the table" illustrate the importance placed on directness in the United States. In some cultures, such as those found in Asia, people do not value directness. They will not reveal their emotions using the same nonverbal cues as Westerners; therefore, people in the United States have difficulty reading Asian body language (the reverse is also true). U.S. Americans generally believe that honesty and truthfulness are important unless the truth would hurt a person's feelings or unless they do not know the person well enough to be candid. They are less concerned with saving face than are people in Asia.

People in the United States value time; they study time-management principles to learn how to get more work done in a day. They are concerned with punctuality for work and appointments, and they study ways of working more efficiently. The success of the fast-food industry in the United States is directly related to eating on the run rather than wasting time lingering over meals. In other parts of the world, mealtime is very leisurely. In many South American countries, businesses close for two hours in the middle of the day for a long meal and a *siesta* (rest), but people often work into the evening.

The importance of time to different cultures is directly related to religious dogma. The Puritans who came to the United States were more concerned with wasting time and with planning for the future than about the past or present. Native Americans, African Americans, Latin Americans, and Asians, however, come from a different combination of religious biases and cultural differences and are occupied with the past and present. One of the reasons Deming's theory of management was adopted in Japan before it was adopted in the United States was the amount of time it takes to formulate group decisions as opposed to individual decisions. The Japanese have always been team oriented; therefore, it was easier for Deming to sell them on his theories.

People in the United States do not place as great an emphasis on history as do people of many other cultures; they look to the future and consider change to be desirable, particularly if they are Christians. In the Asian, Arabic, and Latin cultures, the past is revered. Their future is determined by fate or, in some religions, by the Almighty. People of the Islamic faith believe that if they work hard and pray, everything will be as Allah desires. They simply try to live in harmony with whatever changes occur, rather than seeking change, as is true in the U.S. culture. Table 1 contains contrasts of the priority of cultural leadership theories (CLT) of the different cluster groups in the House study (House, Hanges, Javidan, Dorfman, & Gupta, 2004, p. 682).

    A study of the chart reveals that while a culture may have some leadership characteristics that they share with another culture, no two cultures rank the leadership characteristics the same way.

TABLE 1 Ranking of Societal Clusters Using Absolute CLT (Cultural Leadership Theories) Scores

Charismatic/ Value Based	Team Oriented	Participative	Humane Oriented	Autonomous	Self-Protective
Higher	*Higher*	*Higher*	*Higher*	*Higher*	*Higher*
Anglo	L. America	Germanic E.	Southern Asia	E. Europe	Southern Asia
L. America		Nordic E.	Sub-Sahara Arabs	Germanic E.	Middle East
Southern Asia		Anglo	Anglo	Confucian A.	Confucian A.
Germanic E.				Southern Asia	E. Europe
Nordic E.				Nordic E.	
				Anglo	
				Middle East	
				L. Europe	
				Sub-Sahara Arabs	
				L. America	
Sub-Sahara Arabs	E. Europe	L. America	Confucian A.		L. America
L. Europe	Southern Asia	L. Europe	L. America		Sub-Sahara Arabs
E. Europe	Nordic E.	Sub-Sahara Arabs	Middle East		L. Europe
Confucian A.	Anglo		E. Europe		
	Sub-Sahara Arabs		Germanic E.		
	Germanic E.				
	Confucian A.				
Middle East	Middle East	E. Europe	L. Europe		Anglo
		Southern Asia	Nordic E.		Germanic E.
		Confucian A.			Nordic E.
		Middle East			
Lower	*Lower*	*Lower*	*Lower*	*Lower*	*Lower*
Charismatic/ Value Based	**Team Oriented**	**Participative**	**Humane Oriented**	**Autonomous**	**Self-Protective**

SEMANTIC DIFFERENCES

Semantics is the study of the meaning of words; it involves the way behavior is influenced by the use of words and nonverbal methods to communicate.

Words in the English language often have multiple meanings, some of which are contradictory. The word sanction, for example, may mean either to restrict a particular activity or to authorize it. Semantic differences are compounded when interacting with people of other cultures. Even when both speak the same language, a word may have a different meaning and implication in another culture.

Although England and Australia are English-speaking countries, words are often used in a different way in these countries from the way they are used in the United States. The word homely, for example, means "plain" in the United States although in England, it means friendly, warm, and comfortable. To the English, a sharp person is one who is devious and lacking in principles rather than one who is quick, smart, and clever, which is its meaning in the United States. The expression "quite good" has a different meaning to the English than to U.S. Americans. While the English interpretation is "less than good," the U.S. meaning is "very good." Australian English also holds some surprises for people in the United States. In Australia you would hear such terms as bloke for "man," lollies for "candy," and sandshoes for "sneakers."

A misunderstanding over the meaning of one word during an important meeting in World War II caused an argument between U.S. Americans and the British. The problem was caused by the British interpretation of the phrase "to table an item," which to them means to bring up the item for immediate consideration. The U.S. interpretation, on the other hand, was to shelve or postpone the subject.

Language problems are compounded when conducting business with people in non-English-speaking countries. Differences in the meanings of words are often lost in translation. Sometimes a word has no real counterpart in the other language, and the translator must select a word that he or she believes is similar to the meaning intended.

Semantic differences can be seen in the meaning of the word "stop" in the United States and in South America. A U.S. American while traveling in Bolivia observed that drivers rarely stopped at the red octagonal sign with the word *alto*, the Spanish word for "stop." A local Bolivian explained that in this country, the stop sign is more a recommendation than a traffic law.

Brand names for U.S. products have caused problems when translated into another language. For example, the Spanish translation of Ford Motor Company's Fiera truck means "ugly old woman," not a very flattering name for a vehicle. U.S. firms have had to exercise greater care when introducing products in non-English-speaking countries because of marketing errors made in the past when product names and slogans were translated into another language. When conversing with people of other cultures, be sure your meaning is clear by avoiding slang, contractions, and idioms; by paraphrasing what the other person has said; and by speaking slowly and distinctly.

ATTRIBUTION AND PERCEPTION

Attribution, or the ability to look at social behavior from another culture's view, can cause communication problems because known experiences from your own culture are used in explaining unknown behaviors of those in another culture. **Perception**, the learned meaning of sensory images, may involve learning a new reaction to an old learned stimulus.

> Dunkin' Donuts discontinued an ad featuring Rachael Ray, a celebrity on the Food Network, when it received complaints that the fringed black-and-white scarf Ms. Ray was wearing could be viewed as support for Muslim extremists and terrorists. (Fox News, 2008)

To lessen anxiety when communicating with someone of an unfamiliar culture, reducing uncertainty and increasing predictability about your own and the other person's behavior are important. According to **uncertainty-reduction theory**, people use uncertainty-reduction to determine who they can interact with or develop a relationship with based on similarities they find between their own attitudes, behaviors, and beliefs and those of others. People who have high uncertainty avoidance prefer to specialize, avoid conflict, want clear instructions, and do not want competition. Some ways to reduce uncertainty about other people include observing them, trying to get information about them, and interacting with them (Gudykunst, 1985).

Uncertainty avoidance can be used to determine whether people who have different convictions can be personal friends. People from countries with weak uncertainty avoidance are more likely to remain close friends in spite of differing opinions, although those in countries with strong uncertainty avoidance are less likely to remain friendly following open disagreements. Some key differences between weak and strong uncertainty avoidance societies in the workplace are noted in Table 2 (Hofstede & Hofstede, 2005).

Attribution training involves making people aware of their own cultural context and how it differs from the cultural context of the country to which they will travel. Measuring employees' attribution confidence and then training them to be cognizant of their personal differences with the assignment culture is often used to prepare employees for overseas assignments. Employees are given scenarios that summarize problems they may encounter while living in another country. Participants are then asked to select the one response considered correct from

TABLE 2 Uncertainty Avoidance

Weak Uncertainty Avoidance	Strong Uncertainty Avoidance
Shorter employment time with employers	Longer employment time with employers
Few rules expected	Emotional need for rules
Tolerance for ambiguity	Need for precision and formalization
Top managers concerned with strategy	Top managers concerned with daily operations
Focus on decision process	Focus on decision content
Better at invention, worse at implementation	Worse at invention, better at implementation

Source: Based on chart in *Cultures and Organizations* (p. 189) by G. Hofstede & G. J. Hofstede, 2005, London: McGraw-Hill Book Company.

the viewpoint of the native of the country being studied. With feedback from the trainer and exposure to numerous situations, participants are better able to understand cultural variations in behavior and look at the situation from the other culture's viewpoint.

ATTITUDES TOWARD WOMEN

Attitudes are our likes (or affinities) and dislikes (or aversions) to certain people, objects, or situations. Attitudes are rooted in our behavior and in our emotions (Moran, Harris, & Moran, 2011). Sometimes our personal attitudes may differ from those of the macroculture or dominant culture. For example, a U.S. American male may have the attitude that women belong in the home and not in the workplace. The attitude of the macroculture, however, is that women may choose to work or to stay home and take care of the family.

A society's attitudes toward women are influenced by cultural roots. In some cultures, such as the United States, women are supposed to have the same rights as men. In other countries, such as Libya and Kenya, women are considered subordinate to men. In fundamental Islamic cultures, women are allowed to work only with other women.

Although according to the Qur'an women must give consent to their marriage, are given inheritance, and have equal religious rights and responsibilities with men, Qur'an verses also depict men as superior to women. However, Muslim women cover themselves for protection from those who might hurt them. The Muslim proverb demonstrates this: "A woman is like a jewel: You don't expose it to thieves." Most women of Islamic faith embrace their religious traditions just as women of other faiths embrace theirs (Samovar, Porter, & McDaniel, 2009, p. 95).

Saudi Arabia is the only country in the world to ban women—both Saudi and foreign—from driving. The prohibition forces families to hire live-in drivers; those who cannot afford the $300 to $400 a month for a driver must rely on male relatives to drive them to work, school, shopping, or the doctor. (Al-Shihri, 2011)

This attitude toward a woman's role in society is carried into the workplace. In the United States, gender differences in the workplace are deemphasized. The women's rights movement has worked for such legislation as fair employment laws requiring that men and women must be given equal pay for equal work. Even though differences in pay still exist, treating men and women equally is expected in U.S. firms. The acceptance of women at higher levels is evidenced by the appointments of Sandra Day O'Connor and Ruth Bader Ginsburg to the U.S. Supreme Court and Hillary Rodham Clinton as U.S. Secretary of State. The number of women appointees to top national- and state-level positions continues to increase. In large corporations, the number of women executives is also on the increase. Women-owned businesses are making a significant contribution. In fact, in 2006 there were 7.7 million businesses owned by women in the United States generating $1.1 trillion in annual sales and employing 7.2 million people (National Numbers, 2006). Women in the United States own 10.73% of the businesses compared to 18.45% that are owned by men (Allen, Elam, Langowitz, & Dean, 2007).

Women in the United States earn 80 cents for every dollar men make, which is much better than the 59 cents to the dollar that women earned in the 1960s. The largest differences are for women with college degrees (Bravo, 2008). Compared to this U.S. trend, women in France own 3.16% of the businesses compared to 6.66% owned by men; in the United Kingdom 6.15% of females own businesses compared to 15% owned by men; and in Thailand 45.42% of businesses are owned by women compared to 51% that are owned by men. What is interesting is that the gender difference is more pronounced in high-income countries. Europe and low- and middle-income Asian countries show the largest gaps with Latin American and Caribbean low- and middle-income countries showing the largest business ownership by women. However, women entrepreneurs in high-income countries have more education than those in low- and middle-income countries (Allen et al., 2007).

According to Wilen (2000), the number of women in business continues to increase and companies are no longer focusing on international managers in terms of gender. More companies, such as DuPont and Procter & Gamble, were hiring women. More women are earning business undergraduate degrees and M.B.A.s than ever before. In certain situations, it has been found that women give a company a competitive advantage. Many times the largest hurdles for women are the misperceptions and sexist attitudes of managers in the United States rather than barriers in international business.

U.S. women have been socialized to be deferential and patient, which gives them an advantage over U.S. men when conducting business in Japan.

Recent studies have found that women adapt better than men in intercultural situations (Halsberger, 2007). Women manage adversity better and are often given "glass cliff" assignments that have a greater risk of failure and criticism than men do (Wilen, 2000). One problem for men and women are couples who have dual careers. Companies are beginning to recognize the special problems these couples face and are trying to give support to the spouse as well as to the employee in international assignments (Altman & Shortland, 2008).

Following the collapse of communism and the rise of the Pacific Rim, a New World order is emerging with a larger number of countries following the democratic system of government. With democracy come increased opportunities, especially for women and especially in government and politics.

In the United States, women hold top management positions in 20% of the businesses; Australia, 23%; the United Kingdom, 21%; Thailand, 38%; Poland, 32%; European Union, 30%; New Zealand, 27%; Denmark, 13%; the Netherlands, 15%; China, 31%; Philippines, 47%; the Russian Federation, 42%; India, 15%; and Japan, 7%. The Philippines had the highest number of women in senior management positions (Thornton, 2011). U.S. women in international assignments comprised 13–14% of the employees on international assignment in 1998 (Varma, Stroh, & Schmitt, 2001).

In many countries of the world, women are just beginning to be accepted at managerial levels. Progress in the advancement of women is slow in the Middle East. In such countries as Saudi Arabia, the Islamic belief in the subordination of women has impeded the progress of working women. Women in Mexican businesses are respected, but they are expected to compete on an equal footing with men and prove their competence. Although Mexican businesses have historically been male dominated, this seems to be changing as many Mexican businesswomen are now enjoying success at managerial levels.

With mounting global competitiveness, companies need to examine their current attitudes and practices toward women to ensure that they are making maximum use of their resources and that selection and promotion decisions are based solely on qualifications rather than along gender lines. Fortunately, people in many other countries, including those where women are not treated as equals, are beginning to change their sexist attitudes, and are less concerned with gender than performance.

Although some women in various countries may have received their first job opportunities from family or political connections, others advanced because of professional qualifications and job competence. Major problems that women in the workforce have faced, such as child-care and trying to combine a career and family, are common to all cultures. As more women are successful in managing multiple priorities and demands on their time and as they demonstrate that they are equally effective in high positions in business and politics, it will be easier for women in all cultures to advance to positions of prestige, importance, and responsibility. The following quote by the late mayor of Ottawa expresses the view held by many women in the workplace.

> Whatever women do, they must do twice as well as men to be thought half as good. Luckily, that is not difficult (Charlotte Whitton, 2010).

WORK ATTITUDES

Attitudes toward work are culturally diverse. The term **work attitudes** refers to how people of a culture view work. **Work**, defined as mental or physical activities directed to socially productive accomplishments, in some societies is associated with economic values, status and class, and cultural values.

People in the United States value work and tend to subscribe to the **work ethic**, which means that hard work is applauded and rewarded, although failure to work is viewed negatively and with disdain. U.S. Americans admire people who work hard and are motivated to achieve; they have an aversion to idleness and prefer people of action to people of ideas. This concept of the United States as a work-ethic society is sometimes referred to as the "Protestant ethic," which suggests that a person's work (or "calling") comes from God and that people demonstrate their worth to the Almighty and to themselves through their work. Proverbs such as "Blessed is he who has found his work" and "Satan finds mischief for idle hands" express the idea that in the United States, work is virtuous as well as respectable (Ferraro, 2010). Reward systems in many firms are based on an employee's achievement and willingness to work beyond a 40-hour week. U.S. senior-level executives often work 56 hours a week, far more than in many European countries. They take only 14 days of vacation a year, far fewer than in some countries in Europe, where people often close businesses for a month to go on vacation (Utroska, 1992). The average number of hours worked per week, per person for select countries, according to the International Labor Organization (ILO, 2010), is shown in Table 3.

TABLE 3 Working Hours per Week by Country (2009)

Country	Hours (Avg.)	Country	Hours (Avg.)
Singapore	46.3	Japan	40.7
India	46.9	United Kingdom	40.7
China	46.8	Germany	40.3
Mexico	44.5	The Netherlands	38.4
South Korea	43.4	New Zealand	38.3
United States	42.3	France	37.5
Switzerland	42.0	Canada	30.4
Brazil	41.3	—	—

This attitude toward work and responsibility to a job is ingrained from an early age in the United States. Parents teach their children about the American free enterprise system, which is based on the premise that you are the master of your own destiny, that you can be anything you want to be if you are willing to try hard enough, and that you will be rewarded for hard work. In contrast, people in the Islamic countries place great importance on the will of Allah and believe that planning for the future would conflict with religious beliefs.

To people in the United States, the job is almost an identification badge. A person's personal identity is associated with his or her occupation. Evidence of this identification with the job is shown when making introductions. People tend to include the person's occupation or job title along with the name; for example, "I'd like to present Betty Freeman, owner of the Health Hut" or "This is Jay Hunt, president of Southern Express." Success is not only measured by the job title but by the perception of what one earns; the implication is that the high income has probably resulted from the person's willingness to work 12- and 14-hour days, seven days a week.

People in the United States are action oriented; they are often unable to relax because they feel guilty doing nothing. People from other cultures have observed that U.S. Americans even work at relaxing. Television commercials in the United States often depict an activity as leisure—activities that persons in other cultures would consider manual labor such as gardening or washing the car. When they do take vacations, U.S. Americans are inclined to plan what they will do and where they will go so that the entire time is scheduled. Even those who participate in sports for recreation seem to try to make work out of it (Althen & Bennett, 2011).

A graduate student from India recounted his first experience at being invited to the home of a U.S. graduate student. When he arrived, his U.S. friend invited him into the house, where he was dressing his son while his wife was sweeping the patio. His friend then asked him to help with grilling the chicken outdoors. As the Indian student narrated the story in his intercultural communication class, he expressed surprise that his friend and his wife did all their own work. In his country, he had never swept a floor, cooked a meal, or dressed his children.

Unlike people in a number of countries, many people in the United States consider spending hours visiting a waste of time and may excuse themselves from a group because they say they need to get back to work. People in other countries view with both amazement and amusement this apparent obsession with work.

In much of Europe, attitudes toward work seem to be more relaxed. Many businesses close during the month of August when people go on vacation. Most Europeans do not work on weekends or holidays, as they believe this is time that should be spent with family or engaging in personal activities. The French, in particular, value their vacation time and prefer not to work overtime. They enjoy the longest vacations of any country in the world; French law dictates that employees receive a minimum of five weeks of vacation a year. German companies appear to be moving in this direction as well. Despite the extended free time, people of both France and Germany are very productive when they work. Australians, too, value free time; they say they work to get a vacation. Australians have the shortest working hours of any country in the world, and they enjoy taking frequent breaks throughout the day.

Although many people of the United States receive a two- or three-week vacation, the individual vacation time periods are staggered so that businesses will not be closed for an extended period. Upper-level management workers often do not take all their vacation time each year. Because of these attitudes toward work, the culture of the United States is referred to as a "live to work" culture in contrast to the cultures in countries such as Mexico that are "work to live" cultures.

The attitude of Japanese men toward work is very group oriented, and it plays a major role in their lives. They work Monday through Friday; 18-hour days are not unusual. Because of the long hours, relaxation does not include working around the house. Instead, they relax by watching television, playing computer games, browsing the Internet, drinking, or joining their friends at the local bar. However, this attitude appears to be changing as they become more westernized.

A study in Mexico of Mexican expatriate managers found that they could motivate the workforce through building community and allowing collective control versus paternalistic control to dictate the way the facility operated. They found that most problems were caused by intercultural misunderstandings (stereotypes) rather than by local cultural issues (Litrico, 2007).

ATTITUDES TOWARD ETHICS

Ethical standards are guidelines established to convey what is perceived to be correct or incorrect behavior by most people in a society. According to Ferrell and Gardiner (1991), ethical conduct "is something judged as proper or acceptable based on some standard of right and wrong" (p. 2). According to Borden (1991), being ethical means keeping your values in balance; if you compromise your values, you are being unethical. What it comes down to, according to Rabbi Dosick (2000), is that you have to determine what is right and what is wrong. Although there are sometimes penalties for doing both right and wrong, you have to be able to live with yourself and sleep at night.

When ethics is viewed in a global context, it is important to recognize that what is unethical in some cultures may not be considered unethical in others. Thus, managers who conduct business globally will want to be aware of the terms **ethical relativism** and **ethical universalism** in order to gain an appreciation for differing cultural views in what is considered right and wrong.

Those who believe in ethical relativism maintain that ethical principles vary with the culture. For example, in the United States, it is considered customary to care for the aged and infirmed either in the home of adult children or in special retirement/nursing homes for the elderly. On the other hand, the Inuit custom is for the elderly and infirmed to go away to die rather than be a burden on the tribe during a move to winter quarters. Those who believe in ethical universalism, however, believe that certain values are universal across cultures regardless of race, gender, culture, or religion. An example of ethical universalism is the United Nations' Universal Declaration of Human Rights (Klopf & McCroskey, 2007; Moran, Harris, & Moran, 2011). Three of the 30 articles included in the Declaration relate to intercultural communication and declare that all people are born free and equal in rights and dignity; have a right to freedom of religion, thought, and conscience; and have the right to freedom of expression and opinion (Samovar, Porter, & McDaniel, 2009).

In the United States, the dominant culture (macroculture) makes the determination of what is right or wrong. Even though nondominant groups (microcultures) may disagree with these standards for ethical/unethical behavior, their views are not a consideration; they must abide by the criteria established by the macroculture (Klopf & McCroskey, 2007).

Honesty and truth telling, according to beliefs of people in the U.S. macroculture, are important aspects of ethical behavior. When a clerk gives a customer too much change during a transaction, for example, the recipient is expected to be honest and point out the error. U.S. children are often told the story about young Abraham Lincoln who, as a clerk in a small dry-goods store, realized after the customer left that he had overcharged her. Lincoln reportedly walked two miles through the snow to return the overcharge of a penny. Dosick (2000) sums up feelings of people of the U.S. macroculture regarding honesty: "Dishonesty is dishonesty, and cheating is cheating, whether it involves a little or a lot. If you cheat, you defraud; you diminish yourself as a human being, and you violate the trust that others have in you. And eventually, you will pay" (p. 32). To emphasize the importance of always telling the truth, some U.S. parents even tell their children, "If you'll just tell me the truth, I won't punish you." Therefore, as adults, U.S. persons subscribe to the saying, "Always tell the truth; let your word be your bond, and let your honor be your word" (Dosick, 2000, p. 19).

People in some U.S. microcultures may have a different attitude toward honesty and truth telling; they may feel that clerks who give customers too much change should suffer the consequences. Further, people in some microcultures may condone lying in certain circumstances, such as lying about the condition of a house in order to make a sale. In addition, people in these microcultures may feel that saving face is more important than telling the truth. According to people in the U.S. macroculture, however, truth and honesty must take precedence over benefiting financially, making a sale, or causing offense.

Ethical standards are subject to change, even within a culture. In the United States, for example, slavery was considered moral at one time; however, it is no longer considered so.

Ethical standards should be addressed when conducting business with persons of other cultures, especially those whose standards of ethical behavior differ markedly from our own. Even though we carry our frame of reference and value system with us when conducting business internationally, we should also be aware that our values may differ from those of other countries. For example, in the United States, bribery and graft are illegal. In some of the Latin American countries, however, using gifts to assure success in sealing an agreement is an accepted way of conducting business.

A suggested approach to international business ethics includes the following:

- Identify in writing both individual and corporate ethical values; specify which values are rigid, such as honesty and integrity, and those that are flexible, such as taking into account another culture's values.
- Involve all employees in the development of a corporate code of ethics.
- Assure that all individuals understand the company's ethical values; have employees sign a statement periodically indicating that they have read and understand the corporate code of ethics.
- Monitor compliance with the code of ethics; establish consequences for breaching the code of ethics (Scevola, 2009).

Personal ethics or moral standards may differ from societal ethics. Your own standards of what is right and wrong may be more stringent than those of your society as a whole. Problems may occur when the reverse is true, that is, when your ethical standards are lower than those considered acceptable by society. Of course, your ethical standards must meet the minimum level of behavior identified by law as acceptable. It has been found that peer reporting of unethical behavior is affected by cultural attitudes and styles of communication. Cultural unfamiliarity affects the communication of seen unethical behaviors. Culturally diverse encounters have revealed different patterns of expression, modes of behavior, value sets, attitudes, and styles of communication within the same nation. Cultural diversity includes race, gender, sexual orientation, age, religion, socioeconomic backgrounds, and such. Some of the culturally diverse issues are personal, some are group, and some are corporate. Personal issues include prejudice, stereotyping, personality, values, and identity. Group issues include ethnocentrism and intergroup member conflicts, and corporate issues include acculturation, structural, informal integration, and institutional bias. It is important to understand that many levels of ethical differences exist; thus, a determination of what constitutes unethical behavior should take into consideration the cultural standards involved (King, 2000).

Although many U.S. Americans are inclined to believe that their standards of business ethics are shared by other countries, in reality, standards of business ethics are not universal. For example, the Islamic standard of ethics is based on participating in religious ceremonies, adhering to codes of sexual behavior, and honoring one's parents. This definition or interpretation of ethical standards is not shared by U.S. Americans. Another dimension of business ethics relates to what is commonly referred to as using "backdoor connections" for conducting business; using such connections is common, for example, in South Africa and Nigeria as well as in the People's Republic of China. In fact, the Chinese use informal relationships in allocating resources and making decisions. Another ethical problem U.S. firms face when conducting business abroad is the unorthodox accounting and taxation practices used in some countries. In such countries as Brazil and Spain, keeping three sets of accounting books as a means of avoiding taxes is common. These practices violate not only the ethical standards of U.S. businesspeople but also the U.S. law. Another ethical problem encountered by U.S. firms doing business in other countries is the nonsanctity of legal contracts. To U.S. businesspersons, "a card laid is a card played." To Chinese, Koreans, and Japanese, who emphasize long-term relationships, renegotiation is common. As a result, U.S. businesspersons are never sure when they have a final agreement. People of the United States also question the ethicality of certain activities such as taking a potential customer on a yachting trip or a weekend gambling outing, clearly intended to influence buying decisions (Engholm & Rowland, 1996). An increased concern for ethics has been seen in the United States because of blatant misconduct of persons in government and industry. Religious leaders have been convicted of fraud and Wall Street moguls found guilty of insider trading. An increase in ethical training is taking place in schools, so that the next generation will be better prepared to make appropriate decisions involving ethical behavior.

Religion also affects ethics. All religions are against murder, robbery, lying, and adultery. All religions also stress humility, charity, and veracity (Samovar et al., 2009). With these similar ethical principles, religion should be more of a unifying principle than a dividing one. However, religion is truly a way of life for many people in the world.

RELIGIOUS INFLUENCES

Religious influences have an impact on when and how business is conducted in international settings. In some cultures, such as those of North and South America, Australia, and Europe, lifestyle and religion are separate. In much of northern Africa and southern Asia, no distinction is made between lifestyle and religion because religion is a lifestyle. Businesspersons in these countries may seek the advice of religious leaders on business matters.

The United States has never had an official state church; religious observances rarely interfere with business. Although business is not conducted on such religious holidays as Christmas, no one feels obligated to participate in religious ceremonies or observe religious customs. Religion is a personal matter in the United States. Members of one family often hold different beliefs and belong to different denominations.

The United States subscribes to the doctrine of "separation of church and state." According to this doctrine, the government does not lend official support to any particular religion and may not interfere with a person's practicing any religion. A total of 85% of the population say they are religious. About 24% of the population is Roman Catholic; 51% is Protestant. Other Christian denominations make up about 3–5% of the total, while non-Christian groups also have substantial numbers in the United States (*CultureGrams,* 2010).

Some countries have officially recognized religions and participate in religious rituals that would affect business encounters. In Saudi Arabia, United Arab Emirates, Iran, and Iraq, for example, Islam is the official religion. Muslims observe the ritual of stopping work five times a day to pray. Meetings with people in Islamic countries should be sufficiently flexible to allow for this daily ritual, which is a way of life for Muslims. Conducting business during the month of Ramadan (which varies from year to year) is not recommended because Muslims are required to fast from dawn to sunset. Because of the impact of religion on all aspects of life in Islamic countries, businesspeople should learn about religious rituals and beliefs prior to conducting business there. The majority of Chinese people practice a combination of Confucianism, Taoism, and Buddhism (*CultureGrams,* 2010).

A newly admitted patient became agitated about the arrangement of his hospital room. He kept saying that his bed should be on the opposite wall. The nurse explained that this would be impossible because the oxygen and other needed equipment had been installed on this side of the room and the wires were not long enough to reach the other side. When the nurse learned that the patient was Muslim and needed to face the east toward Mecca to say his prayers five times a day, she arranged for him to be moved to another room that met his needs. (Dresser, 2005)

Fasting for the month of Ramadan means not eating anything—no gum, no water, not even medicine—although you are not asked to fast if you are sick. The virtue of fasting is that you feel what it is like to be hungry so you can empathize with the poor. In addition, you are not to hurt anyone during fasting; you are to be tolerant. If you hurt someone, then you have broken one of the pillars of fasting. Islam is about peace, not violence (Hammouri, 2008).

When working with people in countries that practice nonliterate religions (those that lack written precepts), an understanding of the logic of their beliefs is important. Some Native Hawaiians, for example, believe in curses and spirits; this belief should be accommodated. Witchcraft is practiced in such countries as Zaire; conducting business with people of these cultures may involve changing the sales and marketing techniques that you would ordinarily use.

Religious beliefs and practices affect business in many countries. Although both the United States and Italy are primarily Christian countries, religious holidays are more numerous in Italy than in the United States. Sri Lanka, for example, has 27 holidays. Religious beliefs also affect consumption patterns; for example, Hindus do not eat beef, and Muslims and Orthodox Jews do not eat pork. When conducting business internationally, religion must be considered.

Worldwide there are 1.3 billion Muslims: 270 million in Arab nations, 400 million in the rest of the Middle East, and 6 million in the United States, not including the Nation of Islam (excluded because they do not follow the five pillars) (Shabass, 2004). In many countries where Islam is practiced, it controls life, with all other parts of life taking a secondary role. Religion answers many questions for people such as what is life and death, how was the universe created, how did our society originate, how do we relate as individuals and members of a society, and what is our relationship to nature? Religion in many cases is the psychological welfare for individuals, helping them to understand what cannot be easily explained. Religion is responsible for many of the contrasting cultural values between people (Samovar et al., 2009).

INDIVIDUALISM AND COLLECTIVISM

Individualism refers to the attitude of valuing ourselves as separate individuals with responsibility for our own destinies and our own actions. Proponents of individualism believe that self-interest is an appropriate goal. **Collectivism** emphasizes common interests, conformity, cooperation, and interdependence (see Figure 1). Individualism and collectivism are the opposite ends of a continuum. Thus, we have to remember that some societies have factors near each end plus factors from the middle. It is impossible to put a society or an individual from a given society at one end of the continuum or the other because most people have attitudes that are associated with both ends of the continuum.

FIGURE 1 Individualism Versus Collectivism

Cultural values, whether they are of our culture or any other culture, are learned through shared activities or cultural practices and shared meanings or cultural interpretation. Because these components are cumulative, both within and between people in a culture, people who belong to a particular culture know how others will act. As people develop their values within a culture, they go through three tasks: relationship formation, knowledge acquisition, and autonomy/relatedness. Cultural learning evolves over a lifetime, over historical time, and over evolutionary time. The environment we are in, what society tells us is valued, and the values we develop based on cultural learning make each of us in the world unique. When someone tends toward the collectivistic or interdependent end of the continuum, he or she considers individual choice as less important than the group and social obligations and responsibilities. When someone leans toward the individualistic end of the spectrum, individual rights are very important and social obligations are of primary importance. Countries that are more collectivistic include China, Japan, India, Nigeria, Cameroon, and Puerto Rico. Values that are important to these cultures include responsibility, honesty, politeness, respect for elders and family, and looking to the society for the values to embrace. Germans, European Americans, and the Dutch all embrace individualism, which includes self-maximization, independence, creativity, curiosity, assertiveness, self-esteem, and education. Cultures where people are face-to-face, in smaller communities, or are in a subsistence economy tend to value tradition, and change comes very slowly because they are more collectivistic. Examples include Iraq, Iran, Afghanistan, and many of the smaller African nations. In major cities, with extended economies, you find more individualism. Criticisms of the individualistic/collectivistic paradigm include that the paradigm is too simplistically applied to countries and all people within a country, that the paradigm does not allow for both individualistic and collectivistic values to coexist in the same culture, that some values are valued by both individualistic and collectivistic cultures, and that qualitative and quantitative variability exists within the individualistic/collectivistic paradigm (Greenfield, Keller, Fuligni, & Maynard, 2003).

Hofstede originally studied the IBM Corporation in 53 countries and determined the dimensions on which countries' business cultures differed. Using statistical analysis and theoretical reasoning, Hofstede developed five dimensions, which he labeled power distance, uncertainty avoidance, collectivism versus individualism, femininity versus masculinity, and long-term versus short-term cultures. The countries were then ranked according to their scores (Hofstede & Hofstede, 2005). This study was the first of its kind, and the data were collected in the late 1970s from 50 countries in one organization; he wrote his first book in 1980. Since then, many more women are working in corporations than in the 1970s, more countries are involved in international business, and cultural changes have taken place during this time period; therefore, it is necessary to look at the Hofstede study data in relation to new studies that are being completed, such as the GLOBE study headed by House et al. (2004).

The United States ranked first in individualism in the Hofstede study, followed by Australia, Great Britain, Canada, and the Netherlands. Countries that ranked lowest on individualism included Colombia, Venezuela, Panama, Ecuador, and Guatemala (Hofstede & Hofstede, 2005).

People from the United States place great importance on individuality and self-reliance. Well-known phrases typically used by parents to convey this emphasis on self-reliance include "Do your own thing," "You made your bed, now lie in it," and "You'd better look out for yourself; no one else will." U.S. Americans have been conditioned from childhood to think for themselves, to express their ideas and opinions, and to make their own choices; they are taught to consider themselves as individuals who are responsible for their own actions as well as for their own destinies. Parents start training their children early in this way of thinking; they offer them choices of food, clothes, and toys and usually accommodate their preferences. When the choice does not work out, the child then experiences the results of the decision. The goal of parents is to bring up a self-reliant, responsible person by the age of 18. When children move out of their parents' home at that age and are completely self-supporting, parents feel successful. Children who still live with their parents past the age of 18 or 20 are viewed as immature and unable to live independently. The value U.S. Americans place on individualism, self-reliance, and independence is perceived by persons of different cultures as being self-centered with little consideration for other people (Althen & Bennett, 2011). This emphasis on individuality carries over into college/university choices as well as job choices that may take children away from friends and family members. Although individualism and the value placed on the family as an important unit are often associated, evidence shows that this relationship may not always exist. Costa Ricans, for example, have individualistic tendencies but they also value the extended family structure. Examining cultures within cultures is, therefore, important.

In other cultures, such as the Japanese, emphasis is placed on the group approach rather than on the individual approach to all aspects of life. The Chinese and Malaysians also value the group approach and the family. Their concern with following family traditions and with respecting the opinions of their parents is perceived as a sign of weakness and indecisiveness by U.S. Americans.

The GLOBE study found individualism/collectivism to have multiple levels within the two constructs. They discovered an in-group collectivism and institutional collectivism. The institutional scale showed societal variability that was not captured by the in-group scale (House et al., 2004).

The Power Distance Index is concerned with inequality within a society and how the country distinguishes between inequalities. The inequality can be of power, wealth, status, and social position, as well as physical and intellectual differences. In the business world, it concerns whether the employee and boss prefer a dependent or independent relationship with each other.

The index measures the extent to which the weaker members expect and accept the unequal distribution of power (Hofstede & Hofstede, 2005). The GLOBE study found that strong power distance was associated with male-dominated societies. In addition, they found that where power distance was strong, it was also most disliked (House et al., 2004).

The Masculinity and Femininity Index concerns how a society views assertiveness versus modesty. It is a relative construct rather than a biological distinction being made between countries. Although the terms masculinity and femininity are derived from what is considered important in life to the two genders (masculine includes earnings, recognition, advancement, and challenge; feminine includes manager, cooperation, living area, and employment security), the country's dimensional position and equality of the genders in the workplace have no relationship with each other (Hofstede & Hofstede, 2005). The GLOBE study on the gender egalitarianism of a country is probably more appropriate for intercultural business communication because it discusses the implications of the differences in gender egalitarianism. Societies that believe men and women are suited for similar positions are more gender egalitarian than societies that believe the roles for men and women should be different. The GLOBE study found that the cultural value of gender egalitarianism affected the type of leadership dimensions of charisma, participatory, or self-protectionist. In societies where men and women are more gender egalitarian, they rate the leadership dimensions more similarly (House et al., 2004).

The Uncertainty Avoidance Index measures the threat of ambiguity and unknown situations. Does a person embrace the unknown or does he or she become anxious concerning the unknown? Countries in which people have a strong uncertainty avoidance behavior tend to have a lot of laws and rules specifying correct behaviors as opposed to the countries with weak uncertainty avoidance behavior in which people only want rules when they are absolutely necessary (Hofstede & Hofstede, 2005). In the GLOBE study, uncertainty avoidance was defined as the tendency toward orderliness, consistency, structure, and regulation. The study found that uncertainty avoidance may be related to societal, economic, and organizational values such as innovation, perception of risk, per capita cash holdings, and growth. Higher uncertainty avoidance values were found where there was higher team orientation, humane orientation, self-protective leadership, and lower participative and charismatic leadership values (House et al., 2004).

The difference in a country's orientation to long-term or short-term goals can affect business. A long-term orientation is concerned with the future, perseverance, thrift, hard work, learning, openness, accountability, and self-discipline. A short-term orientation is concerned with the bottom line, control systems, respecting tradition, preserving face, and fulfilling social obligations (Hofstede & Hofstede, 2005). The GLOBE study calls this future orientation. They found that all cultures value future orientation whether or not they practice it except for Denmark. Countries that had weak future practices aspire to having stronger future orientation. Lack of visionary leadership or government control seems to indicate weaker future orientation practices. The Hofstede and GLOBE scales showed no relationship to each other (House et al., 2004).

A brief description of selected cultural values of 10 countries with which the United States conducts most of its international business follows (Bosrock, 1994, 1995a, 1995b; Country Studies, 2008; *CultureGrams,* 2010; Hofstede & Hofstede, 2005).

Brazil

Many Brazilian women work outside the home, especially those who live in the larger cities. While women hold upper-management positions, they are rarely found in the top positions of large firms. Women are found in positions in government, including members of Brazil's Supreme Court, as well as in education, medicine, and journalism. While Brazil has no official religion, about

70% of the population is Roman Catholic. In fact, Brazil is said to be the largest Roman Catholic country. Approximately 20% of the population is evangelical, nearly half of whom belong to the Assembly of God. Brazilians tend to think that the group is more important than the individual. Brazil ranks 39th, tied with Arab countries, on Hofstede's individualism index.

Canada

In Canada, women are accepted in business and government and are well represented. As in the United States, businesswomen feel free to invite businessmen to lunch or dinner; the one who extends the invitation usually pays. The two largest religious groups are Catholicism and Protestantism, but people of British descent are mostly Protestant. Canada also has significant numbers of Muslims, Buddhists, Hindus, and Sikhs. Canada, like the United States, believes in the separation of church and state. Canada is a work-oriented culture; both parents often work outside the home. Canada is a highly individualistic society; the country tied with the Netherlands and Hungary for fourth place in Hofstede's ranking of individualistic countries.

China

In China, the official government position is that citizens should be atheists. The Chinese constitution guarantees religious freedom with certain limitations. Many religions are practiced, including Buddhism, Taoism, Islam, and Christianity. Confucianism, a philosophy and a way of life, is practiced by the majority of the Chinese. China is a collectivistic society. Both women and men are employed in the economy. However, women generally do not have the highest positions in the economy although purportedly women are equal to men. Hofstede ranks China as 56th, tied with Bangladesh, Singapore, Thailand, Vietnam, and West Africa in the ranking of individualistic countries.

Hong Kong's religious philosophies include Taoism, Confucianism, and Buddhism; only 10% of the population is Christian. Laws protect religious freedom. Both men and women are employed in the economy. The people in Hong Kong tend to be less conservative than the rest of China.

Germany

Although East German women have always worked, West German women have been catching up for the past 30 years. West German women have had more traditional family values, and more of them are now pursuing university degrees and careers (Country Studies, 2008). Although sex discrimination is unlawful in Germany, cases are rarely pursued. A businesswoman should feel free to invite a German businessman to dinner and pay the bill without incident.

About 34% of the German people are Protestant, and 34% are Roman Catholic. Muslims are 4%. Although a number of other religions are active in Germany, almost 28% of the people have no official religious affiliation. In Hofstede's ranking of individualistic countries, Germany ranked 18th.

Japan

Women are highly visible in today's Japanese business world, comprising about 50% of the workforce. However, the majority hold lower-level staff positions, with only 10.1% in management positions (Fackler, 2007). Japanese women have made progress in the areas of government, advertising, publishing, and such technical fields as engineering. The possibility of their making significant advances to the higher levels of management in the near future is unlikely because traditionally the Japanese power structure has always been male dominated. Many families of Japanese people practice a combination of Buddhism and Shinto. Only about 1% of the Japanese are Christian. Japan is not an individualistic culture; in Hofstede's ranking of individualistic societies, the country was tied with Argentina and Morocco for 33rd place. The Japanese traditionally place the welfare of the group above the welfare of the individual. They respect age and value ambition, education, hard work, loyalty, and politeness.

Mexico

The role of women in Mexican society is changing. In the past, very few women entered business and politics. Now, however, Mexican women are holding more important positions in business and politics and are visible in the professions as dentists, doctors, lawyers, and teachers. Women were 23.5% of the workforce in 2006 (Nolan, 2007). Although men control the Mexican society, women control the men. Foreign businesswomen are not advised to invite Mexican businessmen to dinner because a man and woman dining alone suggests that they are romantically involved. The predominant religion (practiced by 89% of Mexicans) is Catholicism; small percentages are of Protestant and Jewish faith. Although the Catholic Church has little political influence, it does play an important role in the Mexican culture. Mexico is not considered an individualistic culture; the country was ranked 46th and tied with Bulgaria and Romania in Hofstede's ranking of individualistic countries. However, Mexicans have a sense of individualism in certain areas. For example, they try very hard to distinguish themselves from other Mexicans as they are aware of how they are perceived personally. Mexicans also value the family and personal relationships.

The Netherlands

Women are egalitarian in the Netherlands. The Netherlands is one of the leading nations in Europe for work equality between the genders. The religions practiced in the Netherlands are Roman Catholic (31%); Protestant, which is largely Dutch Reformed (21%); Muslim (4.4%); and other religions that make up about 3% of the population. The role of religion has diminished, and there is a strong separation of church and state. Although the Dutch are known for their liberalism, it is not a topic of polite conversation. The Netherlands ranks fourth, tied with Canada and Hungary, on Hofstede's individualism index.

Singapore

The population is 77% Chinese, 14% Malay, and 8% Indian. Religion may be more important than race in social relationships. The religious breakdown in Singapore is 43% Buddhist, 9% Taoist, 14% Muslim, 15% Christian, 15% atheists or agnostics, 4% Hindu, and 15% are other. Singaporeans are collectivistic.

South Korea

Women are not considered equal to men in South Korea; there is still a separation of female and male roles. In South Korea, 50% of the population is Christian, but Confucianism permeates the culture. Interactions are determined by a person's status and relationship with others. South Korea ranked 63rd in Hofstede's study on individualism and collectivism.

United Kingdom (England, Scotland, Wales, and Northern Ireland)

Although British women have made progress in the workplace, they have not fared as well as women in the United States and Canada. In 2008, the women of the United Kingdom (UK) made up 16.7% of the members of the House of Commons; in the United States, 15.2% of the House of Representatives seats and 18% of the Senate seats were held by women. According to 2008 figures, 19.5% of British barristers (lawyers) were women, while 30% of U.S. lawyers were women. England's state religion is the Church of England (Anglican Church) headed by the Queen. Although it no longer has political power, the Church has had much influence on England throughout its history. Other religions represented in the United Kingdom include Roman Catholic, Protestant (Presbyterian and Methodist), and Judaism. The Church of Wales is also an Anglican church with its own archbishop, and the Church of Scotland is a Presbyterian church. Northern Ireland is 44% Catholic. Three percent of United Kingdom's population is Muslim, 1% is Hindu, 0.7% is Sikh, and 0.5% is Jewish. Many in the United Kingdom claim no religious affiliation, and of those who do claim a religious affiliation, few are regular at church services. The United Kingdom is a very individualistic society; it is ranked third in Hofstede's ranking of individualistic countries.

United States

U.S. women are considered equal to men in the workplace, despite continued salary differences; women currently earn about 80 cents for every dollar that men are paid. Women hold leadership positions in government, business, and education. The United States has no official church. About 80% of the U.S. citizens are Christians; over half of the population is Protestant (primarily Baptists, Methodists, and Lutherans). A fourth of the population is Roman Catholic. Jews, Muslims, and Buddhists are other religious groups. Religion has little effect on business because of the government provision for the separation of church and state. The United States is an individualistic country; it ranks first on Hofstede's individualism index.

Terms

Attitudes	Ethical universalism	Values
Attribution	Individualism	Work
Attribution training	Perception	Work attitudes
Collectivism	Semantics	Work ethic
Ethical relativism	Uncertainty-reduction	
Ethical standards	theory	

Exercise 1

Instructions: Circle T for true or F for false.

1. T F Values are learned; they are not innate.
2. T F In the United States, the family is a top priority.
3. T F A characteristic valued by U.S. persons is directness.
4. T F People in Asian cultures value history.
5. T F Semantic differences between cultures that speak the same language are rare.
6. T F The word "yes" means the same in all languages.
7. T F Women in management are treated similarly in all cultures.

8. T F Japan has a well-enforced equal employment law preventing discrimination against women.
9. T F The U.S. society is considered to have a strong work ethic.
10. T F Ethical standards are culture specific.

Questions and Cases for Discussion

1. Explain how values are formed.
2. In what ways are the values of persons in the United States different from those of persons in other cultures?
3. Explain how semantic differences can affect intercultural communication. Give some examples.
4. Explain what is meant by the term attribution.
5. How are attitudes toward women culturally different? In what countries are women and men treated equally in the workplace?
6. Explain the differences between work attitudes in the United States and other countries. Are your personal work attitudes typical of the U.S. culture or another culture?
7. How are attitudes toward ethics in the United States different from those in Latin America?
8. What role does religion play in conducting business in the United States and Saudi Arabia?
9. Explain individualism and collectivism. Give examples of cultures that are primarily individualistic and those that are primarily collectivistic.
10. Explain the difference between ethical relativism and ethical universalism and give examples of each term.

CASES

The following procedure is recommended for analyzing the cases: (a) read the case carefully paying attention to details; (b) read the questions at the end of the case; (c) reread the case, taking notes on or highlighting the details needed for answering the questions; (d) identify relevant facts, underlying assumptions, and critical issues of the case; (e) list possible answers to the questions; and (f) select the most logical response to the question. Your professor may ask that you submit answers to the case questions in writing.

Case 1

Ching Lee was transferred by his Asian firm to assume a managerial position in a large automobile production plant in the United States. In his first report to his supervisor, he expressed concern that U.S. workers were not giving him the proper respect. What behaviors by U.S. workers could have led Ching Lee to draw this conclusion?

Case 2

A U.S. firm sent its senior-level manager, Laura Green, to negotiate a contract for a chain of fast-food restaurants in Saudi Arabia. What cultural attitudes and behaviors related to gender should she expect to encounter?

Case 3

When Brandon Hunt was sent to Mexico to oversee a production facility for his company, he became concerned over what he perceived to be a lack of seriousness about work on the part of Mexican workers. Employees were frequently late for work, left early, or did not come in at all. When questioned, employees explained that they had to help members of their family with their problems. Explain the apparent differences in U.S. American and Mexican attitudes toward work.

Case 4

When Disney opened its $4.4 billion Euro Disneyland outside Paris, concerns over the park's impact on French culture were expressed. To begin with, the French dedicate Sundays only to family outings. In addition, they are unaccustomed to snacking and eat promptly at 12:30, which creates bottlenecks at parks and restaurants. Disney learned that French employees objected to providing the friendly greetings and smiles expected of all amusement park workers. They then hired multilingual employees from all over Europe because Disney's goal was to attract people from all countries of Europe. A complaint of European investors was that rigid U.S. management style did not take into account the values and customs of the people it intended to attract. For example, Europeans often bring their own lunches and do not spend money at the park's gourmet restaurants and hotels. The park initially lost money after it opened in 1992. Discuss the course of action Disney could take to accommodate the values and customs of the people it hopes to attract.

Case 5

A mission of several U.S. businesspeople visited Taiwan. After meeting with the high-level officials of the Taiwanese firm, one of the U.S. people stated that although the U.S. firm members were received with courtesy and listened intently to comments, the U.S. group members unanimously agreed that they did not have a clear understanding of the points the Taiwanese wanted to make. They also shared the impression that the atmosphere was chilly during the meeting and that the Taiwanese appeared arrogant. During the meeting, as reported in the local Taiwanese paper the next day, the Taiwanese extended their utmost courtesy, were good listeners, did not strongly push their own views, and felt the U.S. group appreciated the fact they had not been aggressive. What went wrong? How is silence being used and confused in this situation? How do the differences in individualism and collectivism affect this situation?

Activities

1. Ask one person from each of the groups listed in this question: "What is your attitude toward work?" Report their responses to the class.
    a. blue-collar worker
    b. business professional
    c. educator
    d. high school student
    e. college student
2. Clip an article from the local newspaper related to ethics in business; summarize the article for class members.
3. Ask a professor or student from another culture to speak to the class on attitudes toward women in his or her culture.
4. Prepare a list of women in your state who have achieved high-ranking positions in either government or business. List the special qualifications these women possess that make them qualified for their positions. Prepare a similar list of women in high-ranking positions in another country of your choice.
5. Prepare a list of words (other than those mentioned in the chapter) that have different meanings in other areas of the United States or in other English-speaking countries.
6. Interview a U.S. student and an international student. Ask each student to rate the following values on a scale of 1 to 5 with 1 representing of *little or no importance* and 5 representing *very important:* individualism, leisure, independence, family, equality, teams, freedom, privacy, work, respect for the elderly, efficient use of time, directness, formality, competitiveness, and materialism. Summarize similarities and differences in response of students from the two cultures.

References

Allen, I. E., Elam, A., Langowitz, N., & Dean, M. (2007). *2007 Report on women and entrepreneurship.* Babson College: The Center for Women's Leadership. Retrieved July 11, 2008, from http://www.gemconsortium.org

Al-Shihri, A. (2011, May 22). Saudi woman detained for defying driving ban. *Press Register,* 12A.

Althen, G., with Bennett, J. (2011). *American ways* (3rd ed.). Boston, MA: Intercultural Press, Inc.

Altman, Y., & Shortland, S. (2008). Women and international assignments: Taking stock—a 25-year review. *Human Resource Management, 47*(2), 199–216.

Borden, G. A. (1991). *Cultural orientation: An approach to understanding intercultural communication.* Upper Saddle River, NJ: Prentice Hall.

Bosrock, M. M. (1994). *Put your best foot forward: Asia.* St. Paul, MN: International Education System.

Bosrock, M. M. (1995a). *Put your best foot forward: Europe.* St. Paul, MN: International Education System.

Bosrock, M. M. (1995b). *Put your best foot forward: Mexico/Canada.* St. Paul, MN: International Education System.

Bravo, E. (2008, June 18). *Why U.S. women earn so little money: The wage gap isn't getting any better.* Retrieved July 10, 2008, from http://www.thewip.net

Country Studies. (2008). *Women in society.* Retrieved July 10, 2008, from http://countrystudies.us/germany/91.htm

CultureGrams, USA, Canada, Brazil, China, Germany, Mexico, Japan, United Kingdom, Singapore, South Korea, Netherlands. (2010). Ann Arbor, MI: ProQuest CSA.

Dosick, W. (2000). *The business bible.* Woodstock, VT: Jewish Lights Publishing.

Engholm, C., & Rowland, D. (1996). *International excellence.* New York: Kodansha International.

Fackler, M. (2007, August 6). Career women in Japan find a blocked path. *New York Times.* Retrieved July 10, 2008, from http://www.nytimes.com/2007/08/06/world/asia/06equal.html

Ferraro, G. P. (2010). *The cultural dimension of international business* (6th ed.). Upper Saddle River, NJ: Prentice Hall.

Ferrell, O. C., & Gardiner, G. (1991). *In pursuit of ethics: Tough choices in the world of work.* Springfield, IL: Smith Collins.

Fox News. (2008, May 29). *Dunkin' donuts pulls Rachael Ray ad over 'terror' symbolism.* Associated Press. Retrieved May 29, 2008, from http://foxnews.com/printer_friendly_story/0,3566,359501,00.html

Greenfield, P. M., Keller, H., Fuligni, A., & Maynard, A. (2003). Cultural pathways through universal development. *Annual Review of Psychology, 54,* 461–490.

Gudykunst, W. B. (1985). The influence of cultural similarity, type of relationship, and self-monitoring on uncertainty reduction processes. *Communication Monographs, 52,* 203–217.

Halsberger, A. (2007). Gender differences in expatriate adjustment. Paper presented at the Academy of Management Annual Conference, Philadelphia, PA.

Hammouri, O. (2008, January 22). Questions and answers. *The Daily Mississippian,* pp. 1, 4.

Hofstede, G., & Hofstede, G. J. (2005). *Cultures and organizations.* London: McGraw-Hill.

House, R. J., Hanges, P. J., Javidan, M., Dorfman, P. W., & Gupta, V. (2004). *Culture, leadership, and organizations: The GLOBE study of 62 societies.* Thousand Oaks, CA: Sage.

International Labor Organization (ILO). (2009). *Yearbook of labour statistics 2009, 68th issue.* Geneva, Switzerland: ILO Publications.

King, G., III. (2000). The implications of differences in cultural attitudes and styles of communication on peer reporting behaviour. *Cross Cultural Management: An International Journal, 7*(2), 11–17.

Klopf, D. W., & McCroskey, J. C. (2007). *Intercultural communication encounters.* Boston, MA: Pearson.

Litrico, J. B. (2007). Beyond paternalism: Cross-cultural perspectives on the functioning of a Mexican production plant. *Journal of Business Ethics, 7*(1), 53–63.

Moran, R. T., Harris, P. R., & Moran, S. V. (2011). *Managing cultural differences: Global leadership strategies for cross-cultural business success* (8th ed.). Burlington, MA: Butterworth-Heinemann.

National Numbers. (2006). Retrieved July 10, 2008, from http://www.cfwbr.org/national/index.php

Nolan, J. L. (2007). *Observations on women in the workplace in Mexico.* Retrieved July 10, 2008, from http://www.associatedcontent.com/article/77440/observations_on_women_in_the_workplace.html

Samovar, L. A., Porter, R. E., & McDaniel, E. R. (2009). *Communication between cultures* (7th ed.). Belmont, CA: Wadsworth/Thomson Learning.

Shabass, A. (2004, July 7–8). *Content and strategies for teaching about the Arab World and Islam.* Workshop.

Scevola, C. (2009, December 16). The role of ethics in international business. *CS&P Fiduciaire.*

Thornton, G. (2011). *Women in senior management around the world.* Retrieved January 2012, from http://www.20-first.com/784-0-women-in-senior-management-around-the-world.html

Utroska, D. R. (1992, November). Management in Europe: More than just etiquette. *Management Review, 81,* 21–24.

Varma, A., Stroh, L. K., & Schmitt, L. B. (2001). Women and international assignments: The impact of supervisor–subordinate relationships. *Journal of World Business, 36*(4). Retrieved September 25, 2002, from Ebscohost database.

Whitton, C. (2010, October 19). *Top 25 empowerment quotations for women.* Retrieved September 14, 2012, from http://livingempowered.areavoices.com/2010/10/top-25-empowerment-quotations-for-women

Wilen, T. (2000). *International business: A basic guide for women.* US: Xlibris.

Glossary

Attitudes are likes (or affinities) and dislikes (or aversions) to certain people, objects, or situations.

Attribution is something seen as belonging to or representing something or someone.

Attribution training focuses on explanations of behavior from the point of view of a person in the host country.

Collectivism is the political principle of centralized social and economic control.

Ethical relativism is the belief that ethical principles vary with the culture.

Ethical standards are guidelines established to convey what is perceived to be correct or incorrect behavior by most people in a society.

Ethical universalism is the belief that certain values are universal across cultures regardless of race, gender, culture, or religion.

Individualism is the pursuit of individual rather than common or collective interests.

Perception is awareness or comprehension through the senses.

Semantics is the study of the ways behavior is influenced by the words and other symbols used to communicate.

Uncertainty-reduction theory refers to the creation of proactive predictions and retroactive explanations about our own behavior, beliefs, and attitudes, and those of others.

Values are beliefs and attitudes held by a culture.

Work refers to mental or physical activities directed to socially productive accomplishments.

Work attitudes are how people of a culture view work.

Work ethic refers to the attitude that work is applauded and rewarded, although failure to work is viewed negatively.

Answers to Exercises

True/False

1. T
2. F
3. T
4. T
5. F

6. F
7. F
8. F
9. T
10. T

Cultural Shock

Objectives

Upon completion of this chapter, you will

- understand the nature of cultural shock and its relationship to success in overseas assignments.
- be able to identify the typical stages of cultural shock.
- learn ways to alleviate cultural shock, including careful selection of persons for overseas assignments and predeparture training.
- understand the role of cultural stress, social alienation, social class and poverty–wealth extremes, financial matters, and relationships in dealing with cultural shock.
- understand how the extent to which persons in the host culture reveal their private selves may contribute to cultural shock.

Cultural shock (commonly called culture shock) is the trauma you experience when you move into a culture different from your home culture. Cultural shock is a communication problem that involves the frustrations of not understanding the verbal and nonverbal communication of the host culture, its customs, and its value systems (Samovar, Porter, & McDaniel, 2009). Frustrations may include lack of food, unacceptable standards of cleanliness, different bathroom facilities (see Figure 1), and fear for personal safety. Black, Gregersen, Mendenhall, and Stroh (1999) add another dimension to cultural shock. They suggest that the disruption of people's routines, which may range from getting up, eating breakfast, and going to work, creates a high degree of uncertainty that is very stressful. The more our routines are disrupted, the greater the level of anxiety and frustration. In addition, most people like predictability; for instance, they want the security of knowing how a hamburger at their favorite fast-food restaurant is going to taste. The English saying, "That song is best esteemed with

FIGURE 1 Cultural Shock Can Result from Bathrooms with Different Fixtures or Arrangements

which our ears are most acquainted," states the facts simply; we like to feel comfortable and be familiar with our surroundings. It is no surprise that cultural shock can cause so many problems with a person's comfort level. Losing our familiar signs, customs, norms, and behaviors can be very disturbing.

A woman in her mid-fifties was attending an intensive Spanish language school in Mexico and developed all the typical signs of cultural shock. She finished her five-week course and went home to find a position teaching English as a second language. Her new position was in Albania. She reported to friends that she was happy she had experienced cultural shock in a nonjob situation because when she started to feel the same things in Albania she was able to understand and work through the cultural differences. She enjoyed Albania so much she signed up for a second tour.

In a survey of 188 students from two Mid-South universities who had traveled or lived abroad, the greatest degree of cultural shock was reported in the lack of modern conveniences and standards of cleanliness. Other types of cultural shock showing statistical significance included attitudes toward women, nonverbal communication, clothing/business dress, family and marriage practices, housing, climate, educational system, financial problems, and values and ethical standards (Chaney & Martin, 1993). The absence of conveniences (such as telephones that work, running water available 24 hours a day, or buses that run on time), which are taken for granted in the United States, is an additional source of frustration. People with strong religious ties may feel spiritually adrift without a church of their faith. In the absence of bounty of U.S. shopping malls, supermarkets, and multiple television sets, depression may result. In addition to depression, people who experience cultural shock can become homesick, eat or drink compulsively, and even develop physical ailments. Unexplained anger and aggression toward people in the host culture are also reactions associated with cultural shock (Samovar et al., 2009).

On her first day of teaching at the local university in La Paz, Bolivia, shortly after her arrival from Atlanta, Georgia, Katherine Montague asked directions to the ladies' room. On entering, she observed three males using urinals and made a hasty retreat. Her U.S. colleagues explained that all restrooms were unisex; Katherine decided to take a taxi to her hotel.

Cultural shock has received increased attention by researchers only in the past two decades. However, Jack London, in his story "In a Far Country," which was published in 1900, stressed that a visitor to another culture should be prepared to acquire new customs and abandon old ideals. He suggested that sojourners (people who visit or reside temporarily in another country) should find pleasure in the unfamiliar because those who could not fit into the new culture would either return home or "die" of both psychological and physical ailments. More than a hundred years later, London's advice is still sound (Lewis & Jungman, 1986).

Engholm (1991) has identified a special kind of cultural shock experienced by U.S. travelers—**AsiaShock**. Engholm identifies the five progressive stages of AsiaShock:

1. Frustration with the culture, which includes the language, the food, and the local customs.
2. Unwillingness to understand the rationale behind the local ways of doing things; people of the United States quickly label a cultural behavior as backward and inefficient without trying to understand the rational basis for the behavior.
3. Ethnocentricity; people of the United States often label Asians as dishonest because they seem to say one thing and do another, failing to realize that Asians consider their behavior to be face saving rather than dishonest.
4. Racism, including the unflattering labeling of all Asians into such groups as Japs and coolies.
5. Avoidance of the culture; people of the United States tend to form their own clubs at which they commiserate about the difficulty of doing business in Asia rather than intermingling with the people of the culture.

Cultural shock can be costly to a firm because it often results in the premature return of U.S. businesspeople working overseas. Some research shows that employees sent to work in foreign countries do not fail because they lack technical or professional competence but because they lack the ability to understand and adapt to another culture's way of life. Estimates on early return of U.S. expatriate managers reported by Ferraro (1990) ranged from 45 to 85%. More recent surveys report lower early return rates that range from 4 to 8% (Harzing, 2002). When companies implement measures to combat cultural shock, such as conducting training programs for sojourners, the early return rate drops to less than 2%.

A family spent eight years in Saudi Arabia while the husband, an engineer, worked for Aramco. The youngest son had been born in Saudi Arabia. On moving back to the United States, the son, who was eight years old, went with his parents to buy a car. When the mother got in the car to drive home, the boy exclaimed, "But you can't drive a car, Mother!" He had never seen a woman drive in his entire life. Of course, his parents quickly explained that in the United States driving customs and laws are different from those in Saudi Arabia.

Some companies have used short-term stays of two to three months to determine an employee's potential for tolerating the culture. Sometimes these short-term projects are designed to prepare the person for a longer stay later. On other occasions, these brief trips are simply ways to use the talents of technical professionals who would be unwilling to go in the first place if it meant disrupting the professional advancement of a career-oriented spouse. Short trips are also cost-effective as the need to move the family is reduced or eliminated. Although the degree and type of cultural shock experienced by people who travel to another country for a short stay may be similar to the shock experienced by those who plan an extended visit, the strategies for coping during the short-term visit may differ.

Cultural shock and missing your way of life can cause you to give up free trips. A mid-level U.S. executive was in Taiwan for four weeks. The company policy was that if you were in the Far East for more than three weeks, you could take an all-expense paid trip to Hong Kong at the end of the third week. The executive chose to work through the weekend and the next week so he could finish early and go home.

Brislin (1981) identifies these five strategies used for coping with the new culture during short visits:

- **Unacceptance of the host culture**—The traveler simply behaves as he or she would in the home culture. No effort is made to learn the language or the customs of the host culture.
- **Substitution**—The traveler learns the appropriate responses or behaviors in the host culture and substitutes these responses or behaviors for the ones he or she would ordinarily use in the home culture.
- **Addition**—The person adds the behavior of the host culture when in the presence of the nationals but maintains the home culture behavior when with others of the same culture.
- **Synthesis**—This strategy integrates or combines elements of the two cultures, such as combining the dress of the United States and the Philippines.
- **Resynthesis**—The integration of ideas not found in either culture. An example of this strategy would be a U.S. traveler in China who chooses to eat neither American nor Chinese food but prefers Italian food.

STAGES OF CULTURAL SHOCK

Cultural shock generally goes through five stages: excitement or initial euphoria, crisis or disenchantment, adjustment, acceptance, and reentry. Cultural shock has been visualized as being represented by a **U-curve**, with the top of the left side of the curve representing the positive beginning, the crisis stage starts down the left side to the base of the U, the adjustment phase starts at the base of the curve, then acceptance moves up the right side of the curve, and reentry into the original culture is at the top of the right side of the curve (Davis & Krapels, 2005). The **W-curve** theory, a theory that explains the adaptation of the reentry phase, explains that reentry actually takes the form of a second U-curve, with a repetition of the stages experienced during initial adjustment to the foreign culture. By combining these two curves, a "W" is formed. For some sojourners, the reentry phase when returning to the home culture is equally as stressful as initial adjustment to a new culture (Klopf & McCroskey, 2007; Schmidt, Conaway, Easton, & Wardrope, 2007).

The first stage is excitement and fascination with the new culture, which can last only a few days or several months. During this time, everything is new and different; you are fascinated with the food and the people. Sometimes this stage is referred to as the "honeymoon" stage, during which your enthusiasm for the new culture causes you to overlook minor problems, such as having to drink bottled water and the absence of central heating or air conditioning (Black et al., 1999).

During the second stage, the crisis or disenchantment period, the "honeymoon" is over; your excitement has turned to disappointment as you encounter more and more differences between your own culture and the new culture. Problems with transportation, unfamiliar foods, and people who do not speak English now seem overwhelming. The practice of bargaining over the purchase price of everything, an exercise that was originally amusing, is now a constant source of irritation. Emotions of homesickness, irritation, anger, confusion, resentment, helplessness, and depression occur during the second stage. People at this stage often cope with the situation by making disparaging remarks about the culture; it is sometimes referred to as the "fight-back" technique. Others deal with this stage by leaving, either physically, emotionally, or psychologically. Those who remain may withdraw from people in the culture, refuse to learn the language, and develop coping behaviors of excessive drinking or drug use. Some individuals actually deny differences and will speak in glowing terms of the new culture. This second stage can last from a few weeks to several months.

In the third stage, the adjustment phase, you begin to accept the new culture or you return home. Those who stay will try new foods and make adjustments in behavior to accommodate the shopping lines and the long waits for public transportation. You begin to see the humor in situations and realize that a change in attitude toward the host culture will make the stay abroad more rewarding.

In the fourth phase, the acceptance or adaptation phase, you feel at home in the new culture, become involved in activities of the culture, cultivate friendships among the nationals, and feel comfortable in social situations with people from the host culture. You learn the language and may adopt the new culture's style of doing things. You even learn to enjoy some customs such as afternoon tea and the midday siesta that you will miss when you return to the home country.

The final phase is reentry shock, which can be almost as traumatic as the initial adjustment to a new culture, particularly after an extended stay abroad. Many individuals are shocked at the fact that they feel the same emotional, psychological, and physical reactions they did when they entered the new culture. **Reentry shock** is experienced on returning to the home country and may follow the stages identified earlier: initial euphoria, crisis or disenchantment, adjustment, and acceptance or adaptation. You would at first be happy to be back in your own country but then become disenchanted as you realize that your friends are not really interested in hearing about your experiences abroad, your standard of living goes down, and you are unable to use such new skills as a foreign language or bargaining in the market. You then move into the adjustment stage as you become familiar with new technology and appreciate the abundance and variety of foods and clothing and the improved standards of cleanliness. You finally move into the acceptance stage when you feel comfortable with the mores of the home culture and find yourself returning to many of your earlier views and behaviors (Klopf & McCroskey, 2007).

A former student from the United Arab Emirates called his U.S. professor to ask for information on purchasing property on the North Carolina coast. He explained that he was homesick for the United States and had decided to bring his family here every summer. After spending 15 years in the United States earning his bachelor, M.B.A., and Ph.D. degrees with only occasional visits back to his home country, he was experiencing reentry shock. (He made the readjustment and did not buy the North Carolina property.)

Although reentry shock is typically shorter than the first four stages of cultural shock in a new culture, expatriates who have made a good adjustment to the host culture may go through a rather long period of adjustment, lasting six months or more, when they are confronted with the changes that have taken place in their absence. Some of these changes are work related; expatriates may feel "demoted" when they return to middle-management positions without the bonuses, perks, and professional contacts they enjoyed abroad. In other situations, changes have taken place in the home country, including politics and styles of clothing, which require readjustment. In research conducted by Chaney and Martin (1993), the four types of reentry shock experienced by college students who had traveled abroad that were statistically significant were readjusting to lifestyle, readjusting to changes in social life, readjusting to changes in standard of living, and reestablishing friendships.

Research on repatriation revealed that meeting the job expectations of the person returning to the United States was very important. Therefore, it is imperative that employers put returning expatriates into realistic positions upon their return. The feelings of alienation and isolation can cause more trauma because returnees have the expectation that they will be returning to a familiar environment (Stroh, Gregersen, & Black, 2000). Other causes of cultural dissonance for the returnee include personnel changes, new company policies and procedures, different performance evaluation methods, different benefits and compensation, and different job responsibilities (O'Sullivan, 2002).

Some reentry problems are personal in nature. Many repatriates have changed; they have acquired a broadened view of the world and have undergone changes in values and attitudes. Personal problems may include unsuccessful attempts to renew personal and professional relationships as the realization sets in that their former friends do not share their enthusiasm for their overseas experiences and accomplishments. They must then make new friends who share this common experience. Children of expatriates encounter similar readjustment problems as their former friends have made new ones and they find that the education they received abroad is sufficiently different to cause problems when returning to schools in the United States.

Because reentry shock is a natural part of cultural shock, multinational corporations must provide training for repatriates to ensure that the transition to the home culture is a favorable experience. In the absence of such training, you can do much to counteract reentry shock by sharing your feelings (not your experiences) with sympathetic family members and friends, particularly those who have lived abroad. Correspond regularly with members of the home culture; ask questions concerning changes that are taking place. Subscribe to the home newspaper to stay abreast of current events. Keep in touch with professional organizations and other groups with which you may want to affiliate. Many repatriates have found that maintaining ties with the home culture cushions the shock associated with reentry (Dodd, 1997; Dodd & Montalvo, 1987; Klopf, 2000).

ALLEVIATING CULTURAL SHOCK

Many multinational firms find that cultural shock can be alleviated by selecting employees for overseas assignments who possess certain personal and professional qualifications. Another method of easing cultural shock is to conduct training programs for employees prior to overseas deployment (Krapels, 1993). Employees who have been given feedback on how they are doing and who have been developed to their maximum potential will be more satisfied with their assignments.

Selecting Overseas Personnel

Careful selection of persons for overseas assignments is important to enhance the chances for a successful sojourn. Personal qualifications needed when working in an unfamiliar culture include adaptability, flexibility, empathy, and tolerance. Good interpersonal skills and high self-esteem are also important.

The ability to react to different and often unpredictable situations with little apparent irritation shows a tolerance for ambiguity. Ambiguities are inherent in intercultural communication; many people, situations, rules, and attitudes make little sense. Much confusion results from being in another culture. Maintaining a high degree of tolerance and flexibility is essential. When companies recruit at colleges, they are looking for candidates who already have such qualifications as language proficiency and overseas experience. Many recruiters think that tolerance can be developed but that adaptability is difficult to develop; they prefer, therefore, to hire persons who have already acquired this trait through living abroad (Geber, 1992; McEnery & DesHarnais, 1990). Adaptability screening reduces costly turnover. Harvey (1985) suggests the use of the following questions to determine a candidate's adaptability:

- Is the person cooperative, agreeable, and sensitive to others?
- Is the candidate open to the opinions of others?
- How does the person react to new situations, and what effort does he or she make to understand and appreciate differences?
- Does the candidate understand his or her own culturally derived values?
- Is the candidate sensitive and aware of the values of other cultures?
- How does the person react to criticism?
- How well does the candidate understand the U.S. government system?
- Will the candidate be able to make and develop contacts with counterparts in the foreign culture?
- Is the candidate patient when dealing with problem situations?
- Is the candidate resilient when faced with adverse situations?

By using such questions as these, interviewers are better able to determine a candidate's suitability for the overseas assignment as well as the person's motivation for wanting to work abroad.

The ability to see the environment from the perspective of the host nationals is an indication of empathy. Bennett's concept of empathy recommends replacing the Golden Rule "do unto others as you would have them do unto you" with the **Platinum Rule** "do unto others as they would have done unto them." You can still maintain your own cultural identity but be able to interpret the new culture through the eyes of the national (Broome, 1991).

Professional qualifications include knowledge of business practices in the host culture and technical competence. Some companies consider language skills crucial. When the destination is the Far East, many companies believe some language training prior to departure is needed. When the use of English is pervasive in a country, proficiency in the host language may not be necessary. In any case, language knowledge seems to give an expatriate an extra chance of succeeding in the host culture. In addition to language knowledge, understanding the educational, political, economic, and social systems of a country is considered important (Tung, 1981).

An individual's success or failure is tied to qualities such as self-efficacy, prior international experience, age, cross-cultural fluency, interpersonal skills, flexibility, cultural sensitivity, and adaptability. **Self-efficacy** is an individual's self-image and confidence to adapt and function in a new environment. A sojourner's attitudes concerning personal safety, security, strength, and self-sufficiency correlate with a high self-efficacy. Bicultural individuals adapt better than monocultural individuals. Prior international experience is associated with a person's ability to adjust to a new culture. Bicultural people tend to be more cross-culturally fluent, culturally sensitive, and adaptable. Adaptive traits include anticipatory adjustments, psychological adjustments, and sociocultural adjustments. If what is anticipated actually happens, psychological uncertainty is reduced, so overlap between the two cultures can be very helpful in adaptation. The ability to understand new cultural behaviors, which is a personality characteristic, can reduce psychological adjustments. Sociocultural adjustments are helped if the host country people see the sojourner as a positive rather than a negative addition. Sociocultural training is very important to the success of this adaptation (Davis & Krapels, 2005).

Providing Predeparture Training for Host Country

An effective approach to cross-cultural training is to first explore how people adjust to new cultures. Learning principles that affect the success of training programs for global managers can be broken down into three steps: observing and emulating behaviors of persons in the host culture, retaining what has been learned, and experimenting with the new behavior until it becomes comfortable. For example, in the Philippines, social get-togethers are important in getting people of a company to feel comfortable together and to develop camaraderie that spills over into the workplace. These festive occasions, which often include cooking together, singing, dancing, and storytelling, serve an important function in employer/employee relations. Attending and participating are important; those who do not participate are viewed as cold and aloof. After observing such social events, U.S. managers who want to be successful in the host culture would then sponsor similar social outings to demonstrate their desire to become part of the new culture (Black, Gregersen, & Mendenhall, 1992).

Because of the reported lack of intercultural training by U.S. multinational companies, acculturation problems have affected the overall success rate of businesspersons in foreign countries. Research conducted by Krapels (1993) involving 102 international businesspersons representing 35 international Mid-South companies determined that 46% of the firms participating offered some type of predeparture training; however, only one firm had a formal training program in place. Because early return rates drop significantly when training programs are implemented, many multinational firms are now experimenting with a variety of training programs. Some companies are trying to boost tolerance of another culture by including trainees from overseas locations in their U.S.-based training programs. Other firms conduct training sessions overseas and send U.S. managers to these courses to provide training in the host culture at the same time that some exposure to the culture occurs. Still other companies incorporate cross-cultural awareness into their regular management training courses.

Advances in communication technology are now being used in intercultural training. For example, a major international firm uses global videoconferencing to train employees and their families at more than 200 sites around the world. Global educational networks with various universities are being developed to train executives who are going abroad. Computers are being used to enhance training effectiveness. Computer-aided training or learning has immense potential for multicultural education because it cuts across traditional language barriers (Moran, Harris, & Moran, 2011). Research indicates that such instruction not only encourages one-to-one learning but can save 30% of the time of more traditional methods. Regardless of the type of training offered, companies realize that success is limited to the extent that there is no substitute for actually living in another culture.

Approaches to intercultural training may be grouped as follows:

- The **intellectual model** is also called the classroom model. Participants are given facts about the host country using a variety of instructional methods, such as lectures, group discussions, and videotapes. This model, which is used most frequently, is based on the belief that cognitive understanding is necessary for performing effectively abroad. This training method is popular in the military as well as in business and educational institutions. Reasons for the popularity of the intellectual model are that staffing is relatively easy and participants are familiar with this approach. A limitation of this approach is that the knowledge gained may not coincide with what is actually needed when a person lives abroad. In other words, the person has learned facts and generalizations about the culture that do not take into account everyday happenings that the person experiences when living in the culture. The model teaches for knowledge and is not based on experience; it does not develop problem-solving skills or flexible attitudes.

- The **area training model**, also called the simulation model, emphasizes affective goals, culture-specific content, and experiential processes. This approach is centered on the trainee rather than the trainer, requires trainee involvement in the learning process, and emphasizes problem solving rather than acquiring information. Through field trips or such simulations as Bafa Bafa (in which participants are divided into two cultures, Alpha and Beta), trainees learn the rules of their culture and interact with members of the other culture. Critics of this approach point out that because it is a simulation, this type of training may still be dissimilar from the actual experience abroad. In addition, those who desire to have more knowledge about the culture (the focus of the intellectual model) would consider the dissimilarity from reality a drawback of this approach.
- The **self-awareness model**, also called the human relations model, is based on the assumption that the trainee with self-understanding will adapt to the new culture better and will therefore be more effective in the overseas assignment. To accomplish desired outcomes, trainers use role play or the sensitivity or Training (T-) Group approach. The **sensitivity training**, or **T-Group**, movement, popular in the late 1960s and 1970s, has not received much attention in recent years. This approach involved training exercises in which people are told in a group setting by others why their behavior is inappropriate, such as that they are perceived as arrogant, dogmatic, or judgmental. This training approach was controversial at best. Although some may have perceived the feedback as helpful, others were uncomfortable exploring their feelings and emotions and viewed it as threatening. Some critics of this approach point out that the American T-Group is based on U.S. values of directness, openness, and equality. Further, this approach does not give participants a framework of conceptual knowledge for analyzing future situations. In addition, cultural relativity and differences in values are not addressed.
- The **cultural awareness model** emphasizes cultural insight, and like the self-awareness model, stresses affective goals and an experiential process. In this approach, participants go from recognizing their own values to contrasting their values with those of other cultures using a variety of techniques, including realistic role-playing. This approach, although not as familiar to trainees as the intellectual approach, more nearly approximates interactions participants would experience in the new culture (Moran et al., 2011).
- The **interaction approach** is based on participants' interacting with people in the host country, either nationals or U.S. persons who have been in the host country for an extended time (Moran et al., 2011).
- The **multidimensional approach** is based on the concept that using any single training approach is not as effective as using an approach that attempts to combine cognitive, affective, and behavioral aspects of training. Critics of this approach say that integrating approaches is overly ambitious. However, advocates maintain that the integrated approach, balancing content with process, affective learning with cognitive, and culture specific with culture general, will better prepare participants for a successful overseas experience (Bennett, 1986).

Providing Feedback and Rewards

Global managers need feedback and rewards just as managers in the home culture do. The appraisal and reward system is different from the home system because people in overseas assignments have to be evaluated and rewarded in a way that takes into account the values of persons in the host culture and the expectations of the particular assignment. The evaluation criteria must be made clear. Areas typically included are leadership ability, interpersonal skills, negotiation skills, customer service, communication skills, and achievement of organizational objectives. For international managers, a key factor to be evaluated often includes profits, but in some countries, the main goal might be to build a presence in the country. In that case, making contacts and building close personal relationships with key officials in the host country are important. Another consideration in appraising overseas managers is who should do the evaluating. Many companies use a rating team headed by a senior human resources management executive. Persons who may be involved in the appraisal process include on-site superiors, peer managers, subordinates, and clients. The team leader might be expected to prepare an appraisal on the global manager every six months (Black et al., 1992).

Reward systems for global managers include special allowances for housing/utilities/furnishings, cost of living, hardship, education, home leave, relocation, medical, car and driver, club memberships, and taxes. The main objective of whatever reward system is used is to attract and retain quality employees. Rewards are especially important in overseas assignments because employees need to be compensated for what they are leaving behind: favorite foods, recreation, family and friends, educational opportunities, and health care. In addition, reward systems used for global managers need to take into consideration the idea of equity—the ratio between what they contribute and what they receive. A manager in the host country who is supposed to be on the same level as the U.S. manager often sees a disparity between what the two contribute and receive; this situation can cause friction and add to feelings of inequity between expatriate managers and local managers. Managers/government employees from the same country but not the same company/government agency also can experience feelings of dissatisfaction based on equity. One spouse of a U.S. expatriate complained that her husband's firm did everything "on the cheap," including housing allowances, bonuses, and home-leave airfares (economy class only), while their friends in other companies received higher housing allowances and bonuses and flew business class (Black et al., 1992).

Developing Employees to Their Maximum Potential

In the past, insufficient attention has been given to reacclimating global managers, specifically in planning for the return of managers who have been in foreign posts for some time. As a result, many managers become dissatisfied with their positions upon their return to their U.S. firm and leave the company. In fact, an estimated 20% of managers leave the firm within a year following repatriation. When you consider the firm's investment in the success of its global managers, the importance of focusing on repatriation becomes clear. Plans for successful repatriation adjustment should begin before the manager leaves the host country; the company should make clear the reason for the new assignment, what new skills and knowledge will be learned, and how the employee will contribute to the company's development upon his or her return. In addition, human resources department personnel should begin initial preparations for the manager's return at least six months prior to repatriation by providing home-country information and contacts. Other recommendations for successful repatriation include providing appropriate compensation for transition expenses, allowing sufficient time to move and get settled before reporting to work, assisting in the location of proper housing, and showing appreciation to the entire family for their contributions to the company during their overseas assignment (Black et al., 1992).

A U.S. expatriate made this observation on returning to his home in Dallas from an assignment in Caracas:

I was really looking forward to coming home, but now I don't feel like I belong. Before I left, I had a large corner office in my company; now I share an office with two other managers. Most people don't even know who I am. My wife isn't happy. In Caracas, our life was very social; we were invited to all the best parties. She had a cook, maid, seamstress, gardener, and nanny. Here she has no friends and no household help.

ASPECTS OF CULTURAL SHOCK

Aspects of cultural shock include cultural stress, social alienation, social class and poverty/ wealth extremes, financial matters, and relationships and family considerations. In addition, differences between the extent to which persons in the host and home cultures reveal their private selves may cause acculturation problems, particularly in communication.

Cultural Stress

Entering an unfamiliar culture is stressful; in fact, transitions of any type are both psychologically and physically stressful. The stress of getting ready for the move, of unpacking and getting settled upon arrival, and of adjusting to new foods can be so stressful that people become physically ill. Problems with housing, climate, services, or communication in another language bring additional stress.

Expatriates learn to use a variety of coping skills to alleviate stress. Unfortunately, some coping behaviors are negative. Taking drugs or drinking alcohol may provide a temporary superficial relief to the stressful situation but avoids dealing with the real source of stress. Another negative coping method, using food to alleviate stress, may create weight-gain problems. Positive techniques include diversions such as taking up a hobby or learning a new skill, planning family events, sharing problems with friends and family members, and changing one's mental outlook. Physical coping mechanisms, such as exercise and meditation, are useful in alleviating stress, as are spiritual techniques such as volunteering to help others and religious worship.

Some companies have found that providing prospective expatriates with a mentor who has worked in the host country can help reduce anxiety about adjustments that may be necessary in the new culture. Providing a second mentor located in the host country can reduce stress associated with learning acceptable behavior in the new culture and help avoid serious business and social blunders.

To alleviate culture stress, prepare for the second culture by reading up on the country, studying the language, and becoming aware of customs and traditions in the culture. Maintaining a sense of humor is very important in dealing with cultural stress.

Social Alienation

An aspect of cultural shock that can have adverse effects upon the newcomer to a culture is social alienation and the feelings of loneliness associated with being isolated from friends and the home culture. Feelings of alienation may be delayed somewhat because concern over such basic matters as housing, transportation, and work may buffer these feelings initially. As the months pass, however, you may feel more isolated as you experience numerous cultural differences, such as what is considered an appropriate topic of social conversation. The concern of people in the United States with fitness, exercise, and healthful eating is not shared by persons of many cultures; such topics, therefore, are inappropriate for conversation. You may also feel uncomfortable during political discussions because persons of other cultures cannot understand the logic behind such decisions as voting for a presidential candidate who is inexperienced in the international arena rather than for a seasoned politician who is respected in the international community.

Making an effort to become familiar with the nuances of the culture and cultivating friendships with persons from the home culture as well as the host culture can alleviate feelings of alienation. Enrolling in language classes and including host nationals in social events can cushion the shock of the new culture and pave the way toward a better understanding and appreciation of the people and their culture.

Social Class and Poverty/Wealth Extremes

In many developing countries, no "middle class" exists. Social classes and extremes in poverty and wealth are readily apparent.

The mention of social class in the United States is greeted with uncertain responses because many U.S. citizens prefer to believe that no social class exists in the United States. Class distinctions do exist in the United States, but they are so complicated and subtle that visitors from other countries often miss the nuances and even the existence of a class structure. Therefore, the official propaganda of social equality is a myth. According to people in the lower stratum, class is related to the amount of money you have. People in the middle stratum acknowledge that money has something to do with it but believe that the kind of work you do and your education are almost as important. People in the top stratum believe that your tastes, values, style, and behavior indicate your class, regardless of your education, occupation, or money (Fussell, 1983). Because U.S. personnel are accustomed to perpetuating this "fable of equality," the obvious existence of social class in other societies may make U.S. Americans uncomfortable. In cultures with virtually no middle class, U.S. persons are usually forced into the upper class of the host culture and may, at least temporarily, feel ill at ease in a social role in which numerous servants are the norm and distinctions are made between acceptable and unacceptable friends.

The informality of U.S. Americans, such as greeting strangers on the street with "Hi!" and calling people they scarcely know by their first names, is a source of cultural shock for many visitors to the United States. In many cultures, starting a conversation with a stranger in a shop or on a bus is considered unacceptable; in the United States, this behavior is commonplace. Foreigners are also often shocked to discover that not all U.S. Americans are wealthy and well educated—that we have large numbers of homeless persons and people who have not graduated from high school.

The poverty of the lower class in other cultures often makes U.S. Americans so uncomfortable that they feel compelled to help but may do so in socially unacceptable ways, such as paying a gardener twice the usual rate simply because the person is poor. Mentors in the host culture can be very helpful in advising U.S. persons regarding acceptable ways of dealing with poverty/wealth extremes and with gaining an insight into the class structure of the culture.

Financial Matters

Because adapting to a new culture and reentering the home culture involves financial adjustments, companies should provide financial counseling to both expatriates and repatriates. Although the focus is a little different, the primary consideration is the same: optimum use of the financial resources available.

Financial counseling for expatriates includes such information as cost and availability of housing, banking practices (including exchange rates), use of credit cards and checks, and costs of schooling for employees with families. Because substantial salary increases are often related to an employee's willingness to relocate, these increases should be discussed in terms of real purchasing power. Expenses related to a higher standard of living that many expatriates enjoy would include hiring domestic help and investing in appropriate formal attire. Customs in purchasing, such as bargaining in the market, should be addressed as well as the additional marketing expenses, which may include paying someone to guard your car while you shop, paying someone else to carry parcels, and paying another person to find fresh eggs or meat that are available only on the black market. Buying goods in grams rather than pounds is an additional purchasing consideration. Other costs include the added expenses of securing goods, such as the cost of tailor-made clothes in the absence of locally available ready-to-wear clothing.

By providing counseling before home-country reentry, the company is acknowledging that financial problems will occur and is demonstrating a willingness to help with these problems. One financial problem relates to the loss of buying power; on returning to the United States, the decrease can be about 30% in net disposable income. The focus of financial counseling for repatriates includes costs involved in relocating in a stateside home, accompanying adjustments to a lower salary, and the loss of perquisites. Because the loss of elite status is often difficult to accept, counseling should include the positive side of the changes, such as less money will be spent on clothes. To ease the transition financially, some companies provide a relocation pay supplement. Others grant annual leave in advance of the return to allow time for house hunting and related problems. Another expense that is receiving increased attention is the cost of providing counseling for family members, particularly children whose adolescence is delayed. Because repatriated children are usually retarded three to four years socially, counseling is often needed to help them work through this transition of readjusting to the home culture (Bird & Dunbar, 1991).

RELATIONSHIPS AND FAMILY CONSIDERATIONS

Problems with relationships, such as the failure of the spouse and other family members to adapt to the new culture, are a major factor in the early return of expatriates. Family and personal issues can be disruptive to acculturation, especially for families with children ages 3–5 and 14–16 (Harvey, 1985). The 3–5-year-olds often have emotional problems being uprooted from familiar surroundings; the 14–16-year-olds may have problems ranging from adapting socially to adjusting to a different educational system. Adolescents in particular need social continuity and often feel resentment toward their parents for uprooting them. Care must be taken to prepare children for the move by discussing openly their anxieties and fears and by providing them with information concerning expected changes in their lives. Being separated from family members and friends in the United States may cause loneliness for all involved. In addition, the spouse is experiencing his or her own problems in adjusting to an alien work environment and is unable to provide the time and emotional support needed during this difficult period of adjustment.

Two-career families in which one spouse (usually the wife) gives up a career to accompany the relocated spouse pose special adjustment problems. Job opportunities in the new culture may be nonexistent, and resentment and boredom may lead to family conflict. Adding unhappy children and an unhappy spouse to the stress of the new job in a foreign culture increases the probability of an early return to the home culture (Harvey, 1985).

Companies that provide training for employees prior to departure rarely include the family in such training. Because adjustment problems often involve the family, difficulties could be avoided in many cases by including family members in predeparture training.

PUBLIC AND PRIVATE SELF

People in various cultures differ with respect to how much of the inner self is shared with others. A method of considering a person's inner world is through the **Johari Window**, which includes "panes" that represent the self that is known and unknown to a person and the self that is known and unknown to others. The Johari Window (Luft, 1984), named for its creators, Joseph and Harrington, is shown in Figure 2.

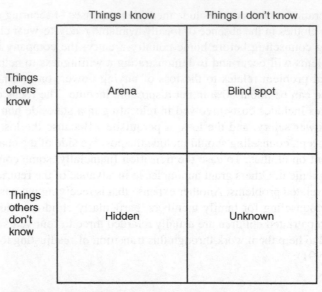

FIGURE 2   The Johari Window   *Source:* Data from *Group Processes: An Introduction to Group Dynamics* by Joseph Luft. Copyright © 1963, 1970, 1984, Palo Alto, CA: Mayfield Publishing Company. Used with permission.

The first window pane is information that is shared; it includes what is known both to the person and to others. This information may be limited to a few facts that the person chooses to share, such as occupation or telephone number, or it may include numerous facts and opinions that are shared with a large audience. The second pane represents what is known to others but not to the person; it represents the person's blind area. This may include motives that others are able to discern but that the person cannot see. The third pane represents what is known to the person but is unknown to others. Information that a person chooses not to disclose to others may range from a past indiscretion to aspects of his or her family life, such as marital status. The fourth pane is that aspect of the person's inner self that is unknown both to others and to the person. This may be information that is embedded deeply in the person's subconscious to the extent that neither the person nor others know of its existence.

The major dimensions of the Johari Window (what is known to self and to others) can be translated into a person's public self and private self. The public self may include information about a person's work, family, and interests or opinions on political and social issues. In some cultures, such as the Japanese, the public self is relatively small, although the private self is relatively large. People of the United States use a style of communication that includes a larger public self with the private self being relatively small. U.S. citizens readily express their opinions and reveal their attitudes and feelings to a larger extent than do persons from the Asian cultures. U.S. Americans use a variety of communication channels, including greater verbalization and greater use of nonverbal communication, such as touch. They conceal less than the Japanese and communicate on a wide range of topics. The Japanese offer fewer opinions and feelings and have fewer physical contacts. People of the United States have less rigid boundaries between the public and private selves; they use more spontaneous forms of communication and fewer ritualized ones. Because of this larger public self, U.S. Americans are sometimes criticized by persons of other cultures as being too outgoing and friendly, too explicit, and too analytical (Barnlund, 1975).

Obstacles to effective communication may be overcome to some degree by becoming knowledgeable about the communication styles of other cultures and by compromising between the two styles. When communicating with the Japanese, for example, U.S. Americans should avoid prying questions, observe formalities and rituals, respect the use of silence, maintain harmony, and understand that evasiveness is a natural part of their communication process.

Cultural shock is a reality that must be addressed by firms doing business abroad. The subject must be openly explained and understood. By admitting the existence of cultural shock and explaining how it may affect individuals, the shock loses some of its intensity; and adapting to the new culture is less traumatic.

The length of cultural shock/reentry shock will depend on such factors as personal resiliency, the length of the assignment, and the effort you put forth prior to departure to learn about the host culture.

Terms

Area training model	Interaction approach	Self-awareness model
AsiaShock	Johari Window	Self-efficacy
Cultural awareness model	Multidimensional approach	Sensitivity training T-group
Cultural shock	Platinum Rule	U-curve
Intellectual model	Reentry shock	W-curve

Exercise 1

Instructions: Circle the appropriate number to indicate the types and degree of cultural shock (either positive or negative) you experienced when entering a foreign culture.

Type of Cultural Shock	High Degree				Low Degree	None
1. Attitudes toward time	5	4	3	2	1	0
2. Attitudes toward women	5	4	3	2	1	0
3. Gestures, eye contact, and other nonverbal messages	5	4	3	2	1	0
4. Climate	5	4	3	2	1	0
5. Clothing/business dress	5	4	3	2	1	0
6. Customs, traditions, and beliefs	5	4	3	2	1	0
7. Educational system	5	4	3	2	1	0
8. Family and marriage practices	5	4	3	2	1	0
9. Financial problems	5	4	3	2	1	0
10. Food and diet	5	4	3	2	1	0

(continued)

(continued)

Type of Cultural Shock	High Degree				Low Degree	None
11. Housing	5	4	3	2	1	0
12. Lack of modern conveniences	5	4	3	2	1	0
13. Social class/poverty/wealth extremes	5	4	3	2	1	0
14. Social alienation (absence of people of same culture)	5	4	3	2	1	0
15. Standards of cleanliness	5	4	3	2	1	0
16. Transportation	5	4	3	2	1	0
17. Values and ethical standards	5	4	3	2	1	0
18. Work habits and practices	5	4	3	2	1	0

Exercise 2

Instructions: Circle T for true or F for false.

1. T F During the second stage of cultural shock, many sojourners develop such coping behaviors as drug and alcohol abuse.
2. T F Cultural shock can be alleviated by careful selection of employees for overseas assignments.
3. T F The Platinum Rule states: "Do unto others before they do unto you."
4. T F The intellectual or classroom approach to intercultural training is basically fact-oriented training.
5. T F Cultural stress can have both psychological and physical consequences.
6. T F A source of shock to foreigners is the discovery that not all U.S. citizens are well educated.
7. T F A source of cultural shock for many U.S. persons living abroad is the financial burden of the required higher standard of living.
8. T F A major factor in the early return of expatriates is family problems.
9. T F The Johari Window represents how you see the world.
10. T F Children of repatriates experience less reentry shock than do adults.

Questions and Cases for Discussion

1. Explain what is meant by the term cultural shock.
2. Identify and discuss the stages of cultural shock.
3. How can multinational firms alleviate cultural shock?
4. Identify and describe the approaches to intercultural training offered by multinational firms.
5. Identify types of cultural stress that may confront persons who are living abroad.
6. Identify positive coping skills that may be used to alleviate stress.
7. How can social class and poverty/wealth extremes be sources of cultural shock for U.S. Americans in overseas assignments?
8. What types of financial adjustments may be associated with cultural shock?
9. Explain how the Johari Window is related to cultural shock.
10. What types of reentry problems are often encountered by persons returning to the home culture? How can reentry shock be alleviated?

CASES

The following procedure is recommended for analyzing the cases: (a) read the case carefully paying attention to details; (b) read the questions at the end of the case; (c) reread the case, taking notes on or highlighting the details needed for answering the questions; (d) identify relevant facts, underlying assumptions, and critical issues of the case; (e) list possible answers to the questions; and (f) select the most logical response to the question. Your professor may ask that you submit answers to the case questions in writing.

Case 1

Larry was sent to Japan to represent his company and wanted to make a good impression on his Japanese hosts. He immediately asked them to call him by his first name and told several humorous stories intended to break the ice. He brought along gifts containing his company's logo and asked about the state of the Japanese economy. Larry got the impression that things were not going well and that he may have behaved inappropriately. What advice would you give him?

Case 2

Karl, his wife, and five-year-old son were completing a three-year assignment in Brazil and were scheduled to return to the United States in a month. Karl would return to work at the home office in Chicago. What should Karl and his family do to lessen the shock of returning to their home culture?

Case 3

Frank's company was planning to enter the Mexican market and had sent him to meet with Juan, the manager of the firm with which they planned to establish a partnership. They agreed to meet for lunch at 2 P.M. at a restaurant in Mexico City. At 2:30, Frank, thinking he had misunderstood the time or place, was leaving when he encountered Juan, who did not apologize for being late. Juan then ordered a special brandy for them and proceeded

to talk about the local museums, churches, and other points of interest. Frank indicated that he did not have time to visit local sites and was anxious to discuss their proposed business partnership. When the brandy arrived, Frank declined, saying he did not drink alcoholic beverages during the day. Each time Frank tried to turn the discussion to business, Juan immediately changed the subject to other topics, including inquiring about Frank's family and personal life. At the end of the two-hour lunch, no business had been discussed. Frank returned to the United States the following day and reported to his supervisor that the Mexican firm apparently had no interest in the proposed partnership. How could Frank have better prepared himself for the cultural shock he experienced?

Case 4

Janice Davis, a marketing representative for a U.S. firm, was looking forward to her assignment in Japan because she had visited the country on one occasion. However, her anticipation quickly turned to frustration. Because all store signs were in Japanese, she didn't know where to buy even a broom. Directions and instructions for using appliances were in Japanese. How could Janice have better prepared herself for the cultural shock she experienced?

Case 5

An international team is being organized. The members of the team are from Germany, Mexico, the Netherlands, and the United States. The main language of the group is English. The German member criticized the Mexican member for not being committed to the project because the Mexican had arrived late for the first meeting. What does commitment mean to each of these cultures? As they started working on the project, they discovered that some of the members had goals that were separate from the project goals. How would task- and group-maintenance functions differ between an international team of workers and a single country? What prejudices might these members have against other members of the group? Given what you know about these four cultures and any other cultural materials you may have, discuss the situation. Why were the members acting

as they did? What would everyone need to know as a member of an international team? How would exploring each other's beliefs, norms, and values at the initial meeting of the team affect the group?

Activities

1. For persons who have traveled or lived in a foreign country for a time, discuss the degree of reentry shock experienced upon returning to the home country in the following areas:
   a. Reestablishing friendships
   b. Readjusting to lifestyle
   c. Readjusting to job
   d. Changes in social life
   e. Changes in standard of living
2. Assume that you have just been made manager of your company's plants in Egypt. Prepare a list of the types of cultural shock you would expect to encounter.
3. After a year in Kenya, you are being returned to your U.S. office. List the types of reentry shock you would expect to experience.

4. You are reviewing applications of persons in your firm who have expressed an interest in an overseas assignment. List the special qualifications you would look for in deciding which three to interview.
5. Conduct an online search to determine what training films or materials are available for predeparture intercultural training of businesspersons.
6. Interview a person who has lived in a country other than the United States. Ask the person to identify the major types of cultural shock he or she experienced upon arrival in the country and what techniques were used for coping with cultural shock. Prepare a one-page summary of the interview and share your findings with the class.

References

Barnlund, D. C. (1975). *Public and private self in Japan and the United States*. Yarmouth, ME: Intercultural Press.

Bennett, J. M. (1986). Modes of cross-cultural training: Conceptualizing cross-cultural training as education. *International Journal of Intercultural Relations, 10*(2), 117–134.

Bird, A., & Dunbar, R. (1991, Spring). Getting the job done over there: Improving expatriate productivity. *National Productivity Review, 10*(2), 145–156.

Black, J. S., Gregersen, H. B., & Mendenhall, M. E. (1992). *Global assignments: Successfully expatriating and repatriating international managers*. San Francisco, CA: Jossey-Bass.

Black, J. S., Gregersen, H. B., Mendenhall, M. E., & Stroh, L. K. (1999). *Globalizing people through international assignments*. Reading, MA: Addison-Wesley Publishing.

Brislin, R. W. (1981). *Cross-cultural encounters: Face-to-face interaction*. New York: Pergamon.

Broome, B. J. (1991). Building shared meaning: Implications of a relational approach to empathy for teaching intercultural communication. *Communication Education, 40*(7), 236–249.

Chaney, L. H., & Martin, J. S. (1993, October). *Cultural shock: An intercultural communication problem*. Paper presented at the Annual Convention of the Association for Business Communication, Montreal, Quebec, Canada.

Davis, B., & Krapels, R. H. (2005). Culture shock and reverse culture shock: Developing coping skills. In S. O'Brien (Ed.), *Communication for a global society, 2005 NBEA Yearbook* (pp. 115–131). Reston, VA: National Business Education Association.

Dodd, C. H. (1997). *Dynamics of intercultural communication* (5th ed.). New York: McGraw Hill.

Dodd, C. H., & Montalvo, F. F. (Eds.). (1987). *Intercultural skills for multicultural societies*. Washington, DC: Sietar International.

Engholm, C. (1991). *When business east meets business west*. New York: John Wiley & Sons, Inc.

Ferraro, G. P. (1990). *The cultural dimension of international business*. Upper Saddle River, NJ: Prentice Hall.

Fussell, P. (1983). *Class*. New York: Ballantine.

Geber, B. (1992, July). The care and breeding of global managers. *Training, 29*, 33–37.

Harvey, M. G. (1985, Spring). The executive family: An overlooked variable in international assignments. *Columbia Journal of World Business, 20*, 84–92.

Harzing, A. W. (2002, February). Are our referencing errors undermining our scholarship and credibility? The case of expatriate failure rates. *Journal of Organizational Behavior, 23*(1), 127–148.

Klopf, D. W. (2000). *Intercultural encounters* (5th ed.). Englewood, CO: Morton.

Klopf, D. W., & McCroskey, J. C. (2007). *Intercultural communication encounters*. Boston, MA: Pearson Education.

Krapels, R. H. (1993). *Predeparture intercultural communication preparation provided international business managers and professionals and perceived characteristics of intercultural training needs*. Unpublished doctoral dissertation, Memphis State University, Memphis, Tennessee.

Lewis, T. J., & Jungman, R. E. (Eds.). (1986). *On being foreign; culture shock in short fiction*. Yarmouth, ME: Intercultural Press.

Luft, J. (1984). *Group processes: An introduction to group dynamics*. Palo Alto, CA: Mayfield Publishing Company.

McEnery, J., & DesHarnais, G. (1990, April). Culture shock. *Training and Development Journal, 44*, 43–47.

Moran, R. T., Harris, P. R., & Moran, S. V. (2011). *Managing cultural differences* (8th ed.). Burlington, MA: Butterworth-Heinemann.

O'Sullivan, S. L. (2002). The protean approach to managing repatriation transitions. *International Journal of Manpower, 23*(7), 597–616.

Samovar, L. A., Porter, R. E., & McDaniel, E. R. (2009). *Communication between cultures* (7th ed.). Belmont, CA: Thomson Learning.

Schmidt, W. V., Conaway, R. N., Easton, S. S., & Wardrope, W. J. (2007). *Communicating globally*. Los Angeles, CA: Sage.

Stroh, L. K., Gregersen, H. B., & Black, J. S. (2000). Triumphs and tragedies: Expectations and commitments upon repatriation. *The International Journal of Human Resource Management, 11*(4), 681–697.

Tung, R. (1981, Spring). Selection and training of personnel for overseas assignments. *Columbia Journal of World Business, 16*(1), 68–78.

Glossary

Area training model is also called the simulation model; an approach to intercultural training that emphasizes affective goals, culture-specific content, and experiential processes.

AsiaShock is a special kind of cultural shock experienced by U.S. people when traveling to Asian countries.

Cultural awareness model includes a comparison of values and behaviors of people in the home country and the host country.

Cultural shock is the trauma a person experiences when he or she moves into a culture different from his or her home culture; a communication problem that involves the frustrations that accompany a lack of understanding of the verbal and nonverbal communication of the host culture, its customs, and value systems.

Intellectual model is an approach to intercultural training, also called the classroom model, in which participants are given facts about the host country using a variety of instructional methods, such as lectures, group discussions, and videotapes.

Interaction approach refers to interaction with people in the host country, either nationals or U.S. persons who have been in the host country for some time.

Johari Window is a way of looking at a person's inner world (named for its creators, Joseph and Harrington). It includes panes that represent the self that is known and unknown to a person and the self that is known and unknown to others.

Multidimensional approach is an approach to intercultural training based on the concept that using any single approach is not as effective as using an approach that attempts to combine cognitive, affective, and behavioral aspects of training.

Platinum Rule is "do unto others as they would have done unto them."

Reentry shock sometimes called reverse cultural shock, refers to problems with readjustment to the home culture.

Self-awareness model is an approach to intercultural training also called the human relations model; it is based on the assumption that the trainee with self-understanding will understand the new culture better and will therefore be more effective in the overseas assignment.

Self-efficacy is an individual's self-image and confidence to be able to adapt and function in a new environment.

Sensitivity training is one element used in the self-awareness approach to intercultural training; includes training exercises in which people are told in a group setting why their behavior is inappropriate.

T-group is a group used in sensitivity training in which people are told why their behavior is inappropriate.

U-curve is a theory related to stages of cultural shock that visualizes the top of the left side of the curve representing the positive beginning, the crisis stage starting down the left side to the base of the U, the adjustment phase starting at the base of the curve, then acceptance moving up the right side of the curve, and reentry into the original culture being at the top of the right side of the curve.

W-curve is a theory of cultural shock that explains the adaptation or reentry phase–explaining that reentry actually takes the form of a second U-curve (thus forming a "W") with a repetition of the stages experienced during initial adjustment to the foreign culture.

Answers to Exercises

True/False

1. T
2. T
3. F
4. T
5. T
6. T
7. T
8. T
9. F
10. F

Language

From Chapter 5 of *Intercultural Business Communication*, Sixth Edition. Lillian H. Chaney, Jeanette S. Martin.
Copyright © 2014 by Pearson Education, Inc. All rights reserved.

Language

Objectives

Upon completion of this chapter, you will

- understand how language affects intercultural business communication.
- be aware of problems associated with language diversity.
- understand number usage differences that may have an impact on intercultural written communication.
- understand how language construction, thought, perception, and culture are linked.
- understand the limits of using a second language.
- be aware that language differences exist even when people speak the same language.
- understand the importance of accurate translation and interpretation to intercultural communication.
- understand how to use parables and proverbs as insights into the culture.
- understand the concepts of the Sapir–Whorf and Bernstein hypotheses.

Successful communication with someone from another culture involves understanding a common language. Without this shared language, communication problems may occur when a third party, the translator or interpreter, attempts to convey both the verbal and nonverbal intent of a message.

Although Chinese is the language spoken by the largest number of native speakers with English ranking second, English is considered the language of international business. However, you may fit in and be able to develop rapport if you are fluent in another person's language. Because so many variations exist in the English language (Australian English, British English, Caribbean English, Indian English, African English, and Irish English), messages are often misunderstood even when both parties speak this language with its many accents, dialects, and regional peculiarities. Unfamiliar accents may present barriers to effective communication (Gilsdorf, 2002).

People who speak English as a second language retain much of their foreign accent. Those for whom Spanish is a first language and English the second language, for example, often pronounce vowels as they are pronounced in the Spanish language. For example, "e" is pronounced as "a" and "i" is pronounced as "e." They may also pronounce certain consonants as they would in Spanish, such as "j" is pronounced as "h" ("Hoolian" for "Julian"). When the wrong syllable is accented (such as dév-eloped rather than de-véloped), understanding is difficult.

A Chinese restaurant, which was located in a part of town mainly inhabited by Mexicans, employed primarily Chinese workers who did not speak or understand Spanish. When a Mexican customer ordered *arroz* (Spanish for rice), the Chinese server thought the customer was requesting a rose; the server directed the customer to a florist located nearby. (Hodge, 2000, p. 153)

Language holds us together as groups, differentiates us into groups, and controls the way we shape concepts, how we think, how we perceive, and how we judge others. When we understand how important and complex that a culture's native language is, it is easier to see why in a country such as India, English is the official language. The Indian people do, however, use more than 100 native languages or dialects for communication within their microcultures.

Women and men, at least in the United States, have different modes of discourse. Women engage in "rapport talk" and men in "report talk." Women seek connections and agreement and are more cooperative in discussions. Men tend to be more individualistic and controlling in their conversations. When women and men have conversations, the men talk and interrupt women more often and focus on their topics rather than listening to the women (Tannen, 2001). In addition, women are more personal, understanding, and sympathetic than men. They also use more verbal hedges (I feel, I think) and more qualifying terms (perhaps, possibly) than men. Women, however, have a more difficult time handling professional criticism objectively than men. Women hold their anger for days, while men behave the next day as though they have forgotten what was said. Women are inclined to apologize more frequently than men do. When women say "I'm sorry," they mean they are sorry that the event happened rather than apologizing for something they did. Men apologize when they are criticized only when absolutely necessary (James & Peltier, 1998; Samovar, Porter, & McDaniel, 2009). Many languages are spoken differently by the men and women of the same culture. For example, in Japanese, the women speak with a softer intonation than men do.

The closest concepts to common worldwide languages are numbers and music. Unlike mathematicians, businesspeople must be sensitive to the nuances of a language. This is important to assure understanding when communicating with people whose first language differs from their own or even with those whose language is the same as their own. Language is only part of communication. How the language is used in relationship to nonverbal communication and the beliefs and values of the culture is also very important.

Sociolinguistics refers to the effects of social and cultural differences upon a language. People reveal class differences by their accent, phrasing, and word usage. According to Fussell (1983), U.S. Americans with good educational backgrounds and relatively high incomes speak in a similar manner regardless of where they live in the country. People who use such terms as ain't (is/are not), reckon (suppose), and afeared (afraid) are considered uneducated.

How strongly group members feel about themselves and their membership in the group determines how members of a group talk to people in other groups. If a group views itself as a vital ethnolinguistic group (a group that views itself as culturally different from the main group and has developed its own language or dialect), they are more likely to maintain their distinctive linguistics in a multilingual setting. The more important a language is viewed to be, the more important the group using the language is in terms of economic, social, and language status. Because people in other cultures also reveal their class level by their accent, pronunciation, and word usage, when selecting an interpreter, be sure to determine whether the person is experienced in the regional and sociolinguistic groups with whom you are dealing.

HIGH- AND LOW-CONTEXT LANGUAGE

The concept of high- and low-context language has been researched by Hall and Hall (1990). A **high-context language** transmits very little in the explicit message; instead, the nonverbal and cultural aspects of what is not said are very important. In high-context cultures (Latin Americans, Arabs, Japanese, Chinese, and Koreans), people must read between the lines to understand the intended meaning of the message. Silence is often used to communicate in high-context cultures. Communication is indirect, rather than direct. When conflict occurs, it should be handled subtly and discreetly (Samovar et al., 2009). Bernstein (in Funakawa, 1997) calls the speech coding system of high-context languages restricted code. The spoken statement reflects the social relationship and the relationship's shared assumptions.

The U.S. language and culture, on the other hand, are examples of low-context communication. (Germans, Scandinavians, and Swiss are also low context.) In a **low-context language** and culture, the message is explicit; it may be given in more than one way to ensure understanding by the receiver. In low-context languages, a person states what is expected or wanted. High-context languages tend to be indirect and nonverbal, whereas low-context languages tend to be direct and verbal. Because people of low-context cultures favor directness, they are likely to consider high-context communication a waste of time. An awareness of how high- and low-context cultures approach conflict is important; U.S. Americans, for example, will raise their voices, speak rapidly, and express clearly what is on their minds. People of China, on the other hand, will be less open and will use body language, silence, and pauses to convey messages (Samovar et al., 2009). The speech system used in low-context cultures is elaborated code. Low-context cultures require verbal elaboration due to fewer shared assumptions (Bernstein, in Funakawa, 1997).

In both low- and high-context societies, if there is perceived disagreement between the verbal and nonverbal message, the nonverbal signals are relied on, rather than what is actually said. However, in high-context cultures, the nonverbal signals are much more subtle and elusive to the untrained senses. An example of high-context communication is the way the Japanese indicate no. The Japanese say "yes" for no but indicate whether "yes" is yes or really no by the context, tone, time taken to answer, and facial and body expressions. This use of high-context communication can be very confusing to the uninitiated, nonsensitive intercultural businessperson. In the United States, which is a low-context society, "no" means no. Group-oriented, collectivistic cultures tend to use high-context languages; individualistic cultures tend to use low-context languages.

LANGUAGE DIVERSITY

Achieving successful communication is difficult because of the diversity of dialects and accents within a language. In the United States, currently more than 311 languages and dialects are spoken; 162 of these languages are indigenous with 149 being languages that are used by immigrants. About 17.9% of the population speaks a native language other than English in the home with 82.1% using English only (Languages, 2008).

The diversity between languages and within the same language is arbitrary. Words in themselves have no meaning; meanings were assigned at some point by people in a culture. For example, the word "business" in the United States connotes how we choose to make and exchange commodities. In other languages, people assign other sounds to mean business, such as *shobai, bijinesu, shigoto, entreprise, comercio,* and *negocios.* In English, synonyms for business also exist, such as commerce, trade, and enterprise.

The diversity of languages causes problems both for managers and applicants for jobs. What is the correct way of assessing English-language skills of job applicants? Managers must ask themselves how important correct English-language skill is in this position. Perhaps the ability to speak and write English well is not essential for job performance; on the other hand, it may be very important. Language qualifications for each position should be assessed separately.

Even when the language is the same as your native language, you must be careful. For example, people of Great Britain and Canada both speak English. However, some Canadians follow British spellings. In certain parts of Canada and the United States, people say the accents are nearly indistinguishable. Examples of pronunciation differences include "uh-GAIN" for "again," and "bean" for "been." One-fifth of Canadians speak French as their primary language. (Bosrock, 1995b)

Other problems caused by language diversity include foreigners who speak their native language on the job, a practice that is not viewed favorably by the nationals. Although the main reason foreigners may use their native language is to express their ideas easily, this behavior is interpreted as an attempt to exclude nationals from the conversation and is considered extremely rude.

THE LANGUAGE OF NUMBERS

Number usage can pose special problems with written communication when communicating globally. One such problem is that decimal points are not used in the same way the world over. A number written as 34.5 in the United States is written as 34,5 in Europe. The decimal point is also used for separating thousands in Europe; for example, 8.642 in Europe is equal to 8,642 in the United States. In some countries, the decimal may be located half the distance between the top and bottom of the adjoining numbers (34·5). Another area of confusion is the difference between what constitutes a billion and a trillion. In the United States, Russia, France, Italy, Turkey, Brazil, and Greece, a billion has nine zeros (1,000,000,000) but is called a milliard in Russia, Italy, and Turkey. In Germany, Austria, the Netherlands, Hungary, Sweden, Denmark, Norway, Finland, Spain, Portugal, Serbia, Croatia, and some South American countries, a billion has 12 zeros (1,000,000,000,000), which is equal to the U.S. trillion. Although the British government announced in 1974 that all government reports and statistics would use the U.S. system for billion, you should check figures carefully in Britain (*Names of big numbers,* 2004). Some other interesting variations from what is considered the standard way of writing numbers in the United States include the following: a one (1) may be written so that it looks like a V, seven may be written with a slash across the middle that can be mistaken for a Y or a 4, eight may be started at the bottom loop rather than the top loop, and zero may be crossed (Bermont, 2004).

INFORMAL AND ALTERNATIVE LANGUAGES

Informal language in the United States generally takes the form of slang, colloquialisms, acronyms, euphemisms, and jargon. Alternative languages of a coculture may take the form of cant and argot and may serve various functions. Those engaged in illegal activities may use their specialized language for concealment and to avoid arrest. Alternative languages also give certain groups a sense of identity and cohesiveness (Samovar et al., 2009).

Informal language comes from numerous areas, including the military, sports, computers, law, and engineering. Informal language should be used with caution in intercultural encounters because of potential miscommunication.

Slang includes idioms and other informal language. "Bottom line" and "back to square one" are examples of business slang. Sometimes American slang is misunderstood by people from other cultures; in one situation, the results were tragic.

A Japanese exchange student was looking for a party one evening in 1992 in Baton Rouge, Louisiana. He approached the wrong house by mistake. The owner came out of the house with a shotgun and yelled: "Freeze!" The Japanese student did not understand and continued moving toward the house. The owner shot and killed the student. Subsequently, a Japanese magazine in an article reporting the incident used this headline: "Learn These English Words—or Die!" In addition to the word "Freeze!" ("Do not move or you're dead"), other words international visitors should learn according to this article were "Duck!" ("Something is flying toward you!") and "Spread them!" ("Raise your hands and spread your legs"). (Axtell, 2009, p. 12)

Colloquialisms are informal words or phrases often associated with certain regions of the country. Examples of colloquialisms include "y'all" (you all), "pop" (soda), and "ain't" (is/are not). **Acronyms** are words formed from the initial letters or groups of letters of words in a phrase and pronounced as one word. Examples of acronyms are RAM (random access memory), BASIC (beginner's all-purpose symbolic instruction code), Fortran (formula translation), and OSHA (Occupational Safety and Health Administration). All-cap initialisms are pronounced as separate initials, such as CEO (corporate executive officer), CAR (computer-assisted retrieval), and OJT (on-job-training). **Euphemisms** are inoffensive expressions that are used in place of offensive words or words with negative connotations. Taboo words are dealt with through euphemisms. Examples of euphemisms include "to pass or pass away" (to die), "senior citizens" (old people), "customer service department" (complaint department), and "human relations" (personnel). **Jargon** is technical terminology used within specialized groups, such as engineers, teenagers, and doctors. Examples of jargon include "on the ball" (on top of things), "oiled" (become suddenly wealthy), and "byte" (a string of binary digits) (Ferraro, 2010).

Additional business expressions include the following (DeVries, 1994):

- asleep at the switch: inattentive
- back off: moderate your stand or speed if driving
- blockbuster: great success
- cold turkey: abruptly, without warning
- cutthroat: harsh
- eat one's words: retract

- garbage: nonsense
- get off the ground: start successfully
- have someone's number: know the truth about someone
- kiss-off: dismissal
- miss the boat: lost opportunity
- piece of cake: something easy
- ring a bell: sound familiar
- two-bit: cheap, tacky
- red tape: many steps to completion
- bottom line: profits or loss
- ballpark figure: an estimate or amount that is close

Alternative language is generally begun by people in a subgroup of a community to differentiate themselves from the masses and determine who is a member of the "in group." Argot and cant are examples of alternative languages.

Argot is a vocabulary used by nonprofessional, noncriminal groups. Truck drivers, for example, may use the term "smoky" to refer to the highway patrol. Circus workers use the term "dip" to mean a pickpocket (Klopf & McCroskey, 2007).

Cant is the vocabulary of the undesirable cocultures, such as drug dealers, gangs, prostitutes, or murderers. Expressions used by people who are incarcerated include "doing a stretch" (serving a prison sentence) and "lifeboat" (a pardon). Prostitutes use the term "gorilla" to refer to a person who beats them and "outlaws" to mean prostitutes who do not have a pimp. Gangs use the term "homegirl" to refer to a girl who hangs around the gang and "claim" to mean the area gang members consider their territory (Klopf & McCroskey, 2007).

Some African Americans use a nonstandard form of American English sometimes referred to as **Ebonics**; for example, the word "bad" is used to mean the best. Although some people view Ebonics as a language, others see it as a dialect.

FORMS OF VERBAL INTERACTION

Forms of verbal interaction include verbal dueling, repartee conversation, rituals, and self-disclosure. **Verbal dueling** is like gamesmanship; the object is to see who can gain dominance in a friendly debate rather than who can impart needed information. The competitive conversations are generally meant in jest but are used in nonaggressive societies to release hostility. Often people who are also not familiar with verbal dueling may misunderstand the subtleties of the communication that is taking place. In the United States, urban black adolescent males have a form of insult contest called playing the dozens. The verbal dueling begins when one male insults a member of the opponent's family. The opponent can choose not to play; however, he will normally counter with an insult of his own. The verbal dueling continues until the males become bored or one is "victorious" (Ferraro, 2010). In Germany, France, and England, politics is an appropriate topic for verbal dueling. Verbal dueling may also take place when discussing sporting events, such as which team is better or which team is going to win. In the business environment, verbal dueling may occur when a group is trying to decide on a new ad campaign and members of the group are polarized as to which campaign is best. Many times when companies are interviewing candidates for positions, verbal dueling takes place over who is the best candidate for the job.

Repartee conversation is a conversation in which the parties frequently take turns speaking, usually after the first few sentences. The speakers talk only for short periods and then listen while the other person speaks briefly. Repartee is a favorite form of interaction for people of the United States; they become very irritated when someone speaks for too long. In contrast, Africans and Arabs tend to speak for extended periods.

Excellent speech is important to the French, and repartee is admired. The speaking skill is so important that for a foreigner to function effectively in France, he or she must speak French fluently (Hall & Hall, 1990).

Ritual conversation is culturally based and involves standard replies and comments for a given situation. In the United States, the interchanges are superficial; little meaning is attached to what is said. U.S. people are not actually interested in learning about others or in revealing their own emotions or personal information during such rituals as greeting others upon arriving at work. Latin Americans, on the other hand, discuss health and other personal information for extended periods during ritual conversation. Arabs in ritual conversation invoke Allah's goodwill; however, they avoid discussions of personal situations.

Self-disclosure is another form of interaction that involves telling other people about yourself so they may get to know you better. The amount of self-disclosure a person is willing to give another person is culturally determined. Foreigners who need to know a person to do business with that person become very frustrated with the lack of personal information provided by people in the United States. If people in a culture feel the need to develop friendships prior to conducting business, doing business with U.S. persons can be very disconcerting because U.S. Americans are not viewed as committed to making friendships.

LINEAR AND NONLINEAR LANGUAGE

Linear and nonlinear aspects of language involve cultural thought patterns; they indicate how people in a specific culture think and communicate (Tsunda, 1986).

Linear language is object oriented and logical with a beginning and an end. Linear languages, such as English, look at time on a continuum of present, past, and future. This view has affected communication patterns and business practices in the United States; an example of such business practices is short-range planning.

Nonlinear language is circular, tradition oriented, and subjective. Nonlinear languages, such as Chinese, look at time as cyclical and the seasons as an ever-repeating pattern. The nonlinear concepts are apparent in the long-range planning of the Chinese and Japanese and in the seasonal messages at the beginning of Japanese letters. The short term is unimportant in Asia. In the United States, for example, stockholders tend to sell their ownership in firms that are having short-term problems; Asians, on the other hand, look at the long-term position of the firm and hold on to the stock.

In intercultural business situations, people respond in a dialogue based on their linear or nonlinear orientation. In the United States, linear explanations are given as answers to *why* questions. The Japanese, however, give more details that do not need linear links. The Japanese tell *what* happened and assume the *why*, whereas U.S. people answer *why* and assume the *what*. For example, a U.S. manager might ask a Japanese worker why the production was stopped. The manager would expect a direct answer, such as, "The parts are defective." The Japanese worker would answer nonlinearly with a long, detailed explanation, including what the defects were and other related details. Miscommunication occurred because the Japanese answered with *what* was wrong instead of the *why* response expected by the U.S. manager (Tsunda, 1986).

VOCABULARY EQUIVALENCE

Because language is influenced by various aspects of a culture, exact translations for all words in one language to a second language are not possible. For example, in one language, the word "love" is used to mean love of another person, love of a pet, or love of an object, while in a second language, different words are provided to distinguish between different types of love (see Figure 1).

FIGURE 1 Vocabulary Equivalence

Many vocabulary inequivalences exist, including problems due to idiomatic equivalence, grammatical–syntactical equivalence, experiential equivalence, and conceptual equivalence (Jandt, 2010).

The English language is built on extremes, such as far and near, heavy and light, high and low, good and bad, wide and narrow, old and young, and long and short. These conceptual inequivalences can cause misunderstanding. Words may or may not exist to describe the middle area between the extremes, forcing a person speaking English to use one of the polar ends. The Portuguese language has many words in between the extremes; however, when the Portuguese is translated into English, only the extremes are available. Therefore, when the translation is read in English, it may not have vocabulary equivalence and so will not ask or say what was said in Portuguese. The Portuguese question, "*Qual é a distancia a* New York?" becomes "How far is it to New York?" However, the Portuguese are actually asking for the location in space of New York as opposed to the far or near dichotomy of the English language (Stewart & Bennett, 1991).

The following story is an example of grammatical–syntactical equivalence. A devout Catholic, David drove south from Minnesota to celebrate the papal visit to Mexico. Overcome with emotion, David ran through the streets of Mexico City shouting "¡*Viva la papa! ¡Viva la papa*!" David's newfound Mexican friend, while sharing in his excitement, thought it prudent to correct David's Spanish. "The Spanish word for 'pope' is *el papa*," the Mexican explained. "You're shouting 'Long Live the Potato.'" (Bosrock, 1995b, p. 40)

Language misunderstandings related to vocabulary usage are numerous even between people who speak the same language.

World War II and the use of the atomic bomb may well have been the result of such a translation error. The Japanese government, in response to the ultimatum in the Potsdam Declaration, responded, "The government does not see much value in it. All we have to do is *mokusatsu* it." The Japanese had carefully chosen the word *mokusatsu* and intended it to mean "no comment." The Western translators chose one of the other meanings of the word, which is "to ignore or to treat with silent contempt" (Jandt, 2010, p. 135).

Homonyms, words that sound alike but have different meanings, can be troublesome when learning a new language. The Chinese language is particularly difficult in this regard because even though the word is pronounced the same, the voice tone and pitch can change the entire meaning of a word. Within a family of languages (such as the Romance languages), words with similar spellings and sometimes very similar pronunciations may have very different or very similar meanings. Assuming a similarity could be both costly and embarrassing during intercultural communication encounters (Ferraro, 2010).

Sound alike? Chuck Blethen of Scottsdale, Arizona, recounts his experience when ordering in Spanish at a Madrid restaurant. "I ordered *caballo*. The waiter looked at me indignantly and said, 'Sir, we don't serve horse here.' I thought I was saying *cebolla* which means onion." (Schmit, Richards, & Swingle, 1993, p. 5E)

Experiential equivalence happens when there is no word in one language because the idea or object does not exist. Ideas such as department store, mall shopping, or wind surfing are words that do not always translate well.

PARABLES AND PROVERBS

A **parable** is a story told to convey a truth or moral lesson, and a **proverb** is a saying that expresses a common truth. Parables and proverbs deal with truths simply and concretely and teach the listener a lesson.

Parables and proverbs can help you understand a culture and can help you determine whether it is a group- or individual-oriented culture. Parables and proverbs may also help you understand what is desired and undesired as well as what is considered correct or incorrect in the culture (Ferraro, 2010).

The U.S. proverb, "The squeaking wheel gets the grease," implies that the person who stands out and is the most vocal will be rewarded. The Japanese proverb, "The nail that sticks up gets knocked down," is an expression of their belief that the group is more important than the individual—the idea is that no one should stand out or be more important than anyone else.

Parables and proverbs can provide important information concerning the nature of the culture, such as whether or not it is basically an empathetic culture or an uncaring one.

Here are some other proverbs of selected cultures:

U.S. Proverbs

"The early bird gets the worm."

"Waste not, want not."

"He who holds the gold makes the rules."

"An ounce of prevention is worth a pound of cure."

Chinese Proverbs

"Man who waits for roast duck to fly into mouth must wait very, very long time."

"He who sows hemp will reap hemp; he who sows beans will reap beans."

"Man who says it cannot be done should not interrupt man doing it."

"Give a man a fish, and he will live for a day; give him a net, and he will live for a lifetime."

German Proverbs

"No one is either rich or poor who has not helped himself to be so."

"He who is afraid of doing too much always does too little."

"What's the use of running if you're not on the right road?"

Japanese Proverbs

"Silence is golden."

"Still water runs deep."

"A wise man hears one and understands ten."

"A wise hawk hides his talons."

Other Proverbs

"Words do not make flour." (Italian)

"He that wishes to eat the nut does not mind cracking the shell." (Polish)

"Why kill time when one can employ it?" (French)

"Wealth which comes in at the door unjustly, goes out at the windows." (Egyptian)

CONVERSATION TABOOS

Conversation taboos are topics considered inappropriate for conversation with people in certain cultures or groups. Baldrige (1993), Braganti and Devine (1992), and Devine and Braganti (1991, 1995, 1998, 2000) discuss the culturally preferred topics of conversation as well as those that are considered taboo. Meeting another person usually involves a certain amount of "small talk" before getting down to business, so knowing what topics are considered appropriate and inappropriate is important.

In the United States, the most popular topic of small talk seems to be the weather or comments on some aspect of the physical surroundings, such as the arrangement of the meeting room or some aspect of the building, such as the landscaping or the building location. Topics that are included later in the encounter include favorite restaurants, television programs, cities or countries visited, one's job, recreational interests or hobbies, and news items. Topics people in the United States have been taught to avoid discussing include religion and politics, even in family situations because they are too controversial. In the United States, family members often belong to different religions and political parties. The avoidance of such topics has caused people in other cultures to erroneously conclude that people in the United States are not intellectually capable of carrying on a conversation about anything more complex than weather and sports.

Some topics are considered too personal to discuss, such as the state of one's health or the health of family members, how much things cost, a person's salary, and personal misfortunes. People in the United States have been taught never to ask another person questions related to sensitive areas such as age, weight, height, hair color, or sexual orientation or behavior.

Topics considered inappropriate in the United States are, however, considered appropriate in other cultures. People in Germany and Iran, for example, consider discussing and arguing about politics to be completely acceptable. The state of someone's health and well-being and that of family members is an appropriate topic when people from Spanish-speaking countries meet for the first time. People from Saudi Arabia, on the other hand, would consider questions about the family inappropriate on an initial meeting.

General guidelines to follow when conversing with someone from another culture include the following (Baldrige, 1993):

- Avoid discussing politics or religion unless the other person initiates the discussion.
- Avoid highly personal questions, including "What do you do?"
- Keep the conversation positive. Avoid asking questions that would imply criticism; phrase questions so they can be answered in a positive manner.
- Avoid telling ethnic jokes because of the possibility of offending someone.

A good rule to follow is to take your cue from the other person. Let the other person initiate the discussion, particularly with culture-sensitive topics. Be a good listener and stay informed on a wide variety of topics to expand your conversational repertoire.

Table 1 contains some appropriate and inappropriate topics of conversation in selected countries (Braganti & Devine, 1992; Devine & Braganti, 1991, 1995, 1998, 2000).

TABLE 1 Appropriate and Inappropriate Conversation Topics by Country

Country	Appropriate Topics	Topics to Avoid
Austria	Professions, cars, skiing, music	Money, religion, divorce/separation
France	Music, books, sports, theater	Prices of items, person's work, income, age
Germany	Travel abroad, international politics, hobbies, soccer	World War II, personal life
Great Britain	History, architecture, gardening	Politics, money/prices, Falklands War
Japan	History, culture, art	World War II
Mexico	Family, social concerns	Politics, debt/inflation problems, border violations
Saudi Arabia	Soccer, travel abroad	Personal family matters, politics
South Africa	Weather, beauty of the country, occupation	Personal questions, political situation, ethnic differences

NATURE OF LANGUAGE

Language, according to Klopf and McCroskey (2007), is "a series of sounds, and when these sounds are combined as symbols, they acquire meaning" (p. 178). To most people, language is the means we use to communicate with each other. However, the nature of language depends upon people involved with various aspects of language. For example, **linguists** study the phonetic aspects of language and define language by the sounds speakers produce and listeners receive. **Semanticists** study the meanings of words and where and how the words developed. **Grammarians** study how a language is governed and its grammatical forms, roots, and endings. **Novelists** believe that language is a series of words arranged to produce harmonious sounds or to have a logical effect (Klopf & McCroskey, 2007).

Syntactic Rules

Syntactic rules govern how words are arranged in a sentence. Different languages choose variations. English, French, and Spanish mainly follow a subject/verb/object order. Japanese and Korean use subject/object/verb. Hebrew and Welsh follow verb/subject/object. The object does not come first in any language (Klopf & McCroskey, 2007).

Perceptual Meanings and Verbal Styles

Different perceptual meanings are conveyed depending upon word choice. **Denotative meanings** are definition meanings, such as the name of a type of crab, the Japanese spider crab. **Connotative meanings** are the emotional meanings, such as Alaskan king crab. (The term Alaskan king crab, although it is a type of Japanese spider crab, has a more positive and appealing name.) **Figurative meanings** are descriptive meanings, such as kicking the bucket (Klopf & McCroskey, 2007).

Verbal styles vary across cultures as shown in Table 2 (Klopf & McCroskey, 2007).

TABLE 2 Verbal Styles by Country	
Ethnic Group	**Verbal Style**
Japanese	• They converse without responding to what the other person says. Emphasis is on nonverbal communication, so they do not listen.
	• They prefer less talkative persons and value silence.
	• They make excuses at the beginning of a conversation for what they are about to say. They do not want apologies for what was already said.
	• They have many different meanings for the word "yes."
Mexican	• They seem overly dramatic and emotional to U.S. persons.
	• They rise above and embellish facts; eloquence is admired.
	• They like to use diminutives, making the world smaller and more intimate. They add suffixes to words to minimize importance.
	• They appear to be less than truthful. Their rationale involves two types of reality: objective and interpersonal. Mexicans want to keep people happy for the moment. When asked directions, if they don't know the answer they will create directions to appear to be helpful.

(continued)

Ethnic Group	Verbal Style
Chinese	• They understate or convey meanings indirectly. They use vague terms and double negatives; even criticism is indirect.
	• Harmony is very important. During negotiations, the Chinese state their position in such a way that seems repetitious. They do not change their point of view without discussing it with the group.
	• They speak humbly and speak negatively of their supposedly meager skills and those of their subordinates and their family.
Arabian	• They encourage eloquence and "flowery" prose. They are verbose, repetitious, and shout when excited.
	• For dramatic effect, they punctuate remarks by pounding the table and making threatening gestures.
	• They view swearing, cursing, and the use of obscenities as offensive.
	• They like to talk about religion and politics but avoid talking about death, illness, and disasters. Emotional issues are avoided.
	• The first name is used immediately upon meeting but may be preceded by the title "Mr." or "Miss."
German	• In the German language, the verb often comes at the end of the sentence. In oral communication, Germans do not immediately get to the point.
	• Germans are honest and direct; they stick to the facts. They are low-context people; everything is spelled out.
	• Germans usually do not use first names unless they are close friends (of which they have few).
	• They do not engage in small talk; their conversations are serious on a wide variety of topics. Avoid conversations related to their private life.
U.S. American	• Some words are specific to an age group.
	• Men speak more and more often than women; women are more emotional and use such terms as "sweet," "darling," and "dreadful."
	• Racial and cocultural differences in verbal styles exist.

TRANSLATION PROBLEMS

When languages are translated, the intended meaning may be lost. Although these errors may seem hilarious, they are also costly. Translation is written and does not have the advantage of nonverbal cues. You are also more likely to receive a literal translation than a literal interpretation.

Axtell (1994) identifies a number of U.S. translation problems: (1) General Motors automobile "Nova" in Spanish means "doesn't go"; (2) Pepsi-Cola's "Come Alive with Pepsi" when translated in Taiwanese is "Pepsi brings your ancestors back from the grave"; (3) Electrolux, a Swedish manufacturer, used "Nothing sucks like an Electrolux," which failed because of the negative slang meaning of "suck" in the United States; and (4) Bic pens were originally named Bich by their French manufacturer.

The word or concept may not have an exact duplicate in the other language. All languages do not have the same verb tenses, and many verbs have multiple meanings. In English, for example, the verb "get" can mean to buy, borrow, steal, rent, or retrieve. When a language is the person's second language, slang, euphemisms, and cultural thinking patterns can cause problems.

In preparation for the 2008 Summer Olympics, Beijing city officials decided to replace signs containing bad translations that had delighted foreign visitors to China for many years. The Chinese were tired of being laughed at for their use of "Chingish"; however, people from other countries found the unique translations a source of amusement and lamented their demise. Among the 6,300 road signs that were replaced included "To take notice of safe: The slippery are very crafty." (The intended meaning was "Be careful, slippery.") Some translations were, in fact, offensive. The sign outside restrooms with provisions for handicapped persons read "Deformed Person" along with the usual drawing of a person in a wheelchair. Another sign identifying a men's restroom read "Genitl Emen." A hospital sign that was inoffensive but quite humorous read: "Dongda Hospital for Anus and Intestine Disease Beijing." The sign was replaced with "Hospital of Proctology." (Fong, 2007)

Back translation is the concept of written work being translated to a second language and then being translated back to the first language by another person to determine if the translations are equivalent.

One type of translation assistance is **Group Decision Support System** (GDSS), a software package that allows people to communicate by computer in a meeting by using language translation software that permits participants to comment on a topic at the same time, rank order the comments, and vote on the comments in their own languages. People participate in their own language, which is translated into the other languages just as the others' communication is translated into their own languages. Words that do not translate directly are put in quotation marks to alert the reader to a possible translation problem. Pocket translators are also available to aid in learning and understanding another language.

Those who need oral interpretations or written translations in the United States can contact local universities for names of competent translators or consult the Translation Directory (published by the American Translators Association, http://www.translation-directory.com) or The American Association of Language Specialists in Washington, DC. Rates for on-the-spot verbal translations are charged by the hour or by the day, while written translations are charged by the word and the nature of the material being translated; they sometimes charge flat rates. They usually provide free estimates. AT&T has a Language Line Service (800-225-5254) or http://www.atanet.org to reach language professionals who interpret more than 150 languages 24 hours a day, 7 days a week.

INTERPRETER USE

An interpreter uses the oral or spoken word versus the written word. To be useful in a negotiation situation, an interpreter must be bilingual, bicultural, thoroughly familiar with the business culture of both sides, and able to use the correct meaning in all situations. They should possess a knowledge of the terminology used in your particular field and should have ethnic compatibility with members of the group for whom they will be translating (Samovar et al., 2009). Often, however, the interpreters supplied by the host culture are bilingual but not bicultural and understand at least some business in their own culture and perhaps a little of the other side's business culture. Their loyalty is, of course, with their employer. When an interpreter is not bicultural, his or her thoughts, feelings, and translations are formulated according to the interpreter's native language rather than the second language. When using an interpreter in international negotiations, a missed negative can turn an agreement into a disagreement. A poor translator can be the difference between the success and failure of the negotiation.

Many U.S. business travelers expect everyone to speak English and, therefore, do not feel compelled to get an interpreter. Although people may speak English as a second language, they do not think the same as U.S. businesspeople unless they are bicultural. Because of this, an interpreter can easily misinterpret the English being used by the U.S. businessperson and misstate facts when translating back to English. Unless the traveler is aware of the possibility of misinterpretation and asks additional questions, the traveler could leave with the wrong answer or conception.

Occasionally an interpreter may wisely change the message to diffuse a potentially volatile situation as the following incident illustrates.

U.S. baseball players in Japan often have difficulty communicating. After a U.S. player in Japan was knocked down by the pitcher of the opposing team, the player from the United States visited the opposing catcher during pregame batting practice. He had to communicate through an interpreter since the catcher was Japanese. What the irate U.S. player actually said was: "Listen, you no good SOB, if you have a pitcher throw at my head again, I'll bleeping kill you!" The interpreter's translation: "He is asking you to please not throw at his head anymore; it makes his wife and children worry." (Moran, Harris, & Moran, 2011)

When using interpreters, review with them your notes, slides, presentation, or anything else you have brought with you before the meeting. The advantage of using bicultural interpreters is that you can ask questions if you are not sure what to do next. A bicultural interpreter can also alert you to problems he or she may foresee. Interpreters should be allowed to use notes or a dictionary and be allowed sufficient time to clarify points. Try not to interrupt interpreters while they are translating. Use visuals to support presentations but allow the bicultural interpreter to check them for anything that may be offensive to the other people. Remember to avoid sarcasm or innuendoes because they are very difficult to translate. Try to state concepts in more than one way to be sure the point you are making is understood.

The following tips will help you work with interpreters (Axtell, 1994; Bosrock, 1997; Samovar et al., 2009):

- Get to know the interpreter in advance. Your phrasing, accent, pace, and idioms are all important to a good interpreter.
- Ask about cultural differences in nonverbal behaviors, such as eye contact, and about local customs that may affect the effectiveness of your presentation.
- Review technical terms in advance.
- Speak slowly and clearly.
- Watch the eyes; they are the key to comprehension.
- Insist that the interpreter translate in brief bursts and not wait until the end of a long statement.
- Be careful of humor and jokes; it is difficult to export U.S. humor.
- Use visual aids where possible. By combining the translator's words with visual messages, chances of effective communication are increased.
- Be especially careful with numbers; write out important numbers to ensure accurate communication.

- Confirm all important discussions in writing to avoid confusion and misunderstanding.
- Allow the interpreter to apologize for your inability to speak your counterpart's language.
- Ask your interpreter about meeting styles, small talk, and discussing major issues.
- Locate your interpreter correctly, remembering international protocol.
- Speak to your counterpart, not to the interpreter.
- Keep comments simple and direct.
- Get feedback through questions to be certain that ideas are interpreted and understood correctly.
- Do not make statements you do not want your counterparts to hear, even if these points are not interpreted. Many counterparts can understand your language even if they are not speaking it.
- If the message is complex, meet with the interpreter prior to the meeting so the interpreter will have a clear understanding of what you are saying.
- Have a concluding session with the interpreters to see if they picked up all messages that will not translate.
- Be prepared to give your closing comments in the host country's language.

HOST LANGUAGE

If you choose to use the language of the country you are visiting, the **host language**, be especially cautious. Be sure to speak clearly and slowly and eliminate jargon, idioms, and slang. When in doubt, ask questions. Avoid using expressions or gestures that could be misinterpreted. Find out if the meaning in the host language is modified by cadence, tone, or gestures.

Learning a business partner's language can help you learn how the person thinks. Learning a foreign language and living in another cultural community will affect your view of life. You will begin to think from the other person's perspective and will reevaluate your own cultural heritage. To live in another country, you must develop personal relations and function effectively. To function effectively, some fluency in the language is important. Becoming competent in a foreign language is time consuming, but the process is helped by the language families. The Romance languages (Spanish, French, Portuguese, and Italian) share Latin as their source and therefore have many **cognates** or words that sound the same and have the same meaning. Be careful, however, because not all words that appear to be cognates actually are.

As mentioned earlier, significant differences exist when both people speak the same language in the same country. Those living in the Eastern United States are considered by many people in other parts of the country to be direct, rude, and to the point; Southerners are considered by many to be indirect, friendly, and more likely to skirt issues. When people speak the same language but are from different countries, additional problems are encountered. For example, the English spoken in the United States is different from the English spoken in Australia and Great Britain. The British use a very indirect style of verbalizing, while people of the United States use a more direct style.

The best advice when using the host language is to maintain a pleasant disposition and a positive attitude toward the host language; avoid making comments that could be interpreted as criticism of their language.

The language people speak, the names of the countries, and what the citizens are called can be very confusing. The following list in Table 3 should make references easier (Bosrock, 1995a, p. 53).

TABLE 3 Languages and Citizen References by Country

Country	People	Language
• Austria	• Austrians	• German
• Belgium	• Belgians	
–Wallonia	–Walloons	–French
–Flanders	–Flemings	–Flemish/Dutch
• Canada	• Canadians	• English/French
• Denmark	• Danes	• Danish
• Finland	• Finns	• Finnish
• France	• French	• French
• Germany	• Germans	• German
• Greece	• Greeks	• Greek
• Ireland	• Irish	• English/Irish
• Italy	• Italians	• Italian
• Japan	• Japanese	• Japanese
• Luxembourg	• Luxembourgers	• Luxembourgish/French/German
• Mexico	• Mexicans	• Spanish
• The Netherlands	• Dutch/Netherlanders	• Dutch
• Norway	• Norwegians	• Norwegian
• Portugal	• Portuguese	• Portuguese
• Spain	• Spanish/Spaniards	• Spanish
• Sweden	• Swedes	• Swedish
• Switzerland	• Swiss	• French/German/Italian/Romansch
• Turkey	• Turks	• Turkish
• United Kingdom	• British	• English
–England	–British/English	–English
–Scotland	–Scots	–English/Gaelic
–Wales	–Welsh	–English/Welsh
–Northern Ireland	–Northern Irish	–English

English is spoken as a native language, a semiofficial language, or is studied in the countries listed in Table 4 (U.S. News & World Report, 1995).

THOUGHT

Thinking is universal; however, methods of classifying, categorizing, sorting, and storing information are very different.

Subjective interpretation is an interpretation placed on a message that is affected by the thought processes; it is influenced by personal judgment, state of mind, or temperament. Subjective interpretation is learned through cultural contact. We perceive what is relevant to

TABLE 4 Use of English by Country

Native English	Semiofficial English	English Studied
• North America	• Africa	• North America
–Canada, except Quebec	–Botswana	–Mexico
–United States	–Cameroon	• Central America
• South America	–Ethiopia	• Caribbean
–Guyana	–Gambia	–Costa Rica
• Caribbean	–Ghana	–Cuba
–Bahamas	–Kenya	–Dominican Republic
–Barbados	–Lesotho	–Honduras
–Grenada	–Liberia	• South America
–Jamaica	–Malawi	–Brazil
–Trinidad and Tobago	–Mauritius	–Colombia
• Europe	–Namibia	–Venezuela
–Ireland	–Sierra Leone	• Europe
–United Kingdom	–South Africa	–Austria
• Pacific	–Sudan	–Belgium
–Australia	–Swaziland	–Denmark
–New Zealand	–Tanzania	–Finland
	–Uganda	–France
	–Zambia	–Germany
	–Zimbabwe	–Greece
	• Asia, Pacific	–Iceland
	–Bangladesh	–Italy
	–Fiji	–Luxembourg
	–India	–Netherlands
	–Malaysia	–Norway
	–Myanmar (Burma)	–Portugal
	–Pakistan	–Romania
	–Philippines	–Russian Federation
	–Singapore	–Sweden
	–Sri Lanka	–Switzerland
	–Tonga	• Africa
	–Western Samoa	–Algeria
	• Mideast	–Angola
	–Israel	–Burkina Faso
	–Malta	–Central African Republic
	–Burundi–Central	–Côte d'Ivoire (Ivory Coast)
		–Gabon
		–Guinea
		–Libya
		–Madagascar
		–Morocco
		–Niger
		–Senegal
		–Togo
		–Democratic Republic of Congo
		• Middle East
		–Egypt
		–Jordan
		–Saudi Arabia
		–Syria
		–Turkey
		–Yemen
		• Asia
		–Afghanistan
		–China
		–Hong Kong–Indonesia
		–Japan
		–Nepal
		–S. Korea
		–Thailand

our physical and social survival and classify, categorize, sort, and store it for future use. What is important in one culture may not be important in another.

In the United States, people tend to think in a very functional, pragmatic way; they like procedural knowledge (how to get from point A to point B). Europeans, however, are more abstract; they like declarative knowledge, which is descriptive. The Japanese have a different way of thinking; they like to work with precedents and rules rather than abstract probability (Borden, 1991).

Thoughts and views toward nature, for example, are culturally diverse. U.S. people view nature as something to conquer; however, Native Americans and many Asians view nature as something with which to coexist. Other cultures such as the Colombian *mestizo* consider nature to be dangerous and have a fatalistic attitude toward it and its ability to control their destiny. A culture's perception of nature can be seen in their parables and proverbs, work ethic, and religion (Condon & Yousef, 1975).

A culture's way of thinking adversely affects the culture's capability to make progress. People who worked with the Peace Corps, for example, found that introducing technology to a Third World country could not be accomplished without a change in cultural attitudes toward technology (Condon & Yousef, 1975). Initial plans for people of the Russian Federation following the fall of communism in 1991 were to give them stock in businesses and housing. After generations of being told what to do, however, the people had a difficult time changing their way of thinking to include taking responsibility for themselves.

In our thought processes, we make associations between color and messages. For example, in the United States, red is associated with stop; and green is associated with go. U.S. Americans associate white with purity, but in China, white is associated with death.

LANGUAGE AND CULTURE INTERACTION

Language can be both unifying and divisive. A common native language ties people together, yet the presence of many different native languages in a small geographic area can cause problems. Both culture and language affect each other. We have the chicken and egg dilemma—which came first, the language or the culture? The use of language/culture in creating political, social, economic, and educational processes is a consequence of favoring certain ideals over others. Understanding the culture without understanding the language is difficult.

Colonialism caused many areas of the world to lose or replace their native languages with the colonial language. Because the colonies spoke the colonizers' language, the colonizers treated them from an ethnocentric view. Many areas of the world that once were colonized are now trying to gain back their native language in an effort to regain their ethnic identity (Ferraro, 2010).

Because most U.S. Americans are immigrants and have learned English, they no longer use their native languages. Although many U.S. citizens may not speak the languages of their ancestors, a number of the thought patterns have been passed from generation to generation, such as how a person shows affection for male and female friends, male and female family members, spouse and children, and acquaintances. A person with a strong German background is less likely to hug any of those group members in public; however, someone of Spanish or African descent is much more likely to hug and show affection in public. Often, people want to continue speaking their native language because they are able to express their thoughts clearly and maintain what is culturally comfortable.

English also changes from one region of the nation to another. All these differences cause unequal power relationships to develop between people from different social and power backgrounds. Because language determines your cognition and perception, if you are removed from your linguistic environment, you no longer have the conceptual framework to explain ideas and opinions. The Sapir–Whorf hypothesis and the Bernstein hypothesis offer additional insight into language and culture interaction (Samovar et al., 2009; Weaver, 1998).

Sapir–Whorf Hypothesis

The main idea of the **Sapir–Whorf hypothesis**, named for Edward Sapir and Benjamin Lee Whorf, is that language functions as a way of shaping a person's experience and not just a device for reporting that experience. People adhere to the connections of their language to communicate effectively. Both structural and semantic aspects of a language are involved. The structural aspect includes phonetics and syntax. Although the syntax aspect of language is both influenced by and influences perception and categorization, the semantic aspect of language deals with meaning.

The concept of linguistic determinism is often referred to as the Sapir–Whorf hypothesis because the two men figured predominately in its development. **Linguistic determinism** is the assumption that a person's view of reality stems mainly from his or her language. Even though two languages may be similar, they cannot represent the same social reality; the worlds of the people who speak the two languages are different. So although languages often do have equivalencies in other languages, the social reality cannot be fully conveyed to a person who does not speak the language.

An example of the concept of linguistic determinism is the absence of a word for "snow" in Inuit, the language of the Inuit people. The language does, however, have numerous words for types of snow, while other languages do not have the equivalent of flaky snow or crusty snow, for example. Because snow is important to the Inuit people, they need to be able to describe it precisely (Borden, 1991; Condon & Yousef, 1975; Dodd, 1997; Ferraro, 2010; Samovar et al., 2009).

Bernstein Hypothesis

The **Bernstein hypothesis** explains how social structure affects language and is an extension of the Sapir–Whorf hypothesis. Bernstein considers culture, subculture, social context, and social system to be part of social structure.

According to the Bernstein hypothesis, speech emerges in one of two codes—restricted or elaborated. Communication transmission channels used in the restricted code are oral, nonverbal, and paralinguistic. **Restricted codes** include highly predictable messages; they are for those who know you and what you are talking about well. These codes are similar to argot in that the communication assumes a common interest or shared experience. Because of this shared experience and identity, elaborating on the verbal message is unnecessary. You may, for example, find that your best friend sometimes finishes your sentences or knows what you are going to say before you finish speaking because of shared experiences. **Elaborated codes** are used with strangers; they involve messages that are low in predictability. You need to give explicit information to ensure that the message is understood. The verbal channel is important in elaborated codes, while restricted codes use nonverbal and paralinguistic cues (Dodd, 1997).

Terms

Acronyms
Argot
Back translation
Bernstein hypothesis
Cant
Cognates
Colloquialism
Connotative meanings
Conversation taboos
Denotative meanings
Ebonics
Elaborated codes
Euphemisms
Figurative
  meanings

Grammarians
Group Decision
  Support System
High-context
  language
Homonyms
Host language
Jargon
Linear language
Linguistic
  determinism
Linguists
Low-context
  language
Nonlinear language

Novelists
Parable
Proverb
Repartee conversation
Restricted codes
Ritual conversation
Sapir–Whorf
  hypothesis
Self-disclosure
Semanticists
Slang
Sociolinguistics
Subjective interpretation
Syntactic rules
Verbal dueling

Exercise 1

Instructions: Circle T for true or F for false.

1. T F Nonverbal aspects are very important in low-context cultures.
2. T F The Japanese language and culture are examples of high-context communication.
3. T F The terms "sanitation engineer" and "garbage collector" are examples of colloquialisms.
4. T F Politics is an appropriate topic for verbal dueling in Germany.
5. T F Repartee involves taking turns speaking.
6. T F People of the United States provide very little self-disclosure.
7. T F Chinese is an example of a linear language.
8. T F Conversation taboos in Mexico include politics and border violations.
9. T F The concept of linguistic determinism is related to the Sapir–Whorf hypothesis.
10. T F The Bernstein hypothesis involves restricted and elaborated codes.

Questions and Cases for Discussion

1. Explain how language differentiates us as groups.
2. Teenagers and other groups develop jargon and slang. Give examples of slang or jargon used by people with whom you associate.
3. The United States is a low-context country, and Japan is a high-context country. How would the Japanese react to a flamboyant U.S. salesperson?
4. Give examples of conversation taboos in your home or group of friends.
5. Why is a bicultural/bilingual interpreter better than a monocultural/bilingual interpreter?
6. In what employee positions is knowledge of a foreign language more crucial for a company? Why?
7. Explain how ethnic groups in the United States participate in verbal dueling.
8. What does it mean to say two languages do not have vocabulary equivalence? What does it mean to say the same language does not have vocabulary equivalence?
9. Explain what is meant by argot. Give examples from a culture with which you are familiar.
10. Explain the difference between restricted and elaborated codes in the Bernstein hypothesis.
11. If thinking is universal, how does culture and language affect the way different groups of humans think?

CASES

The following procedure is recommended for analyzing the cases: (a) read the case carefully paying attention to details; (b) read the questions at the end of the case; (c) reread the case, taking notes on or highlighting the details needed for answering the questions; (d) identify relevant facts, underlying assumptions, and critical issues of the case; (e) list possible answers to the questions; and (f) select the most logical response to the question. Your professor may ask that you submit answers to the case questions in writing.

Case 1

In parts of the United States, particularly in Florida where there is a large Latin American population, the suggestion has been made that Spanish should be considered the first language and English the second language and that people whose native language is Spanish should be taught in Spanish with English taught as a second language. Based on the discussion of language in this chapter, what are the advantages and disadvantages of implementing such a system? How would your argument for or against this proposed change apply to similar situations in India, Canada, or the European Union?

Case 2

A U.S. production manager, Joe Sorrells, is sent to manage a manufacturing facility in Mexico. On his arrival, his assistant production manager, Juan Lopez, suggests they go to the factory to meet the workers who have been awaiting his arrival. Joe declines Juan's offer and chooses instead to get right to work on determining why the quality and production rate of the Mexican plant are not equal to the U.S. plant. Juan stresses the importance of getting to know the workers first, but Joe lets Juan know he was sent to Mexico to straighten things out, not to form friendships with the local workers. Without further comment, Juan gets Joe the figures and records he requests. Joe made a number of changes and felt sure the plan he had prepared would improve quality and increase production. After a couple of months, no improvement has been made; Joe cannot understand why the workers seem to resist his plans. What went wrong?

Case 3

You are responsible for hiring a sales manager whose territory will include all of South America. You have narrowed your search to two people. One is a citizen of Brazil who speaks Spanish and Portuguese but very little English. The second is a U.S. citizen who speaks English and a little Spanish. Your product line necessitates that the sales manager hire two additional people in South America, run a sales office with a receptionist/secretary, live in South America, and personally call on customers in the different countries. Which of the two people would you choose? Give reasons for your choice.

Case 4

You are in a meeting in a subsidiary of a German company in the United States. The meeting has two German citizens who are living in the United States and three U.S. citizens all of whom are employees. You have been discussing the packaging of a new product, and suddenly the two Germans begin speaking in German rather than English. You wait for a couple of minutes, become irritated, and leave. Explain what is happening in this situation concerning the use of language.

Case 5

Barbara, a U.S. female manager, was faced with deciding how best to approach an upcoming evaluation session with Carlos, a new employee from Venezuela. Carlos often arrived late and sometimes did not come to work at all; he would later explain that he had a family emergency. In addition, Carlos often spoke Spanish to another Spanish-speaking employee during work hours.

The other employees thought he was probably speaking negatively about them. Female employees were upset because he was overly familiar with them; his terms of endearment and hugs were not appreciated. What factors should Barbara consider when offering constructive criticism to Carlos? Explain how gender may be a factor in this evaluation session.

Activities

1. Prepare a list of countries you have visited or countries in which you have worked. List one U.S. slang expression that has a negative meaning in each country listed.
2. Quote a parable or proverb from one of the countries listed in Activity 1 and indicate how the parable or proverb characterizes some aspect of the culture.
3. List three conversation taboos in the United States and three taboos in one of the countries identified in Activity 1.
4. Write a paragraph about language problems you have encountered when communicating with students from other cultures. Include problems with tone, enunciation, pronunciation, slang, and so on.
5. Review a journal article or a chapter in a book related to the use of interpreters. Prepare a one-page summary for submission to the instructor.
6. Because many books are translations from other languages, the Sapir–Whorf hypothesis states that these translations may not preserve the exact meaning as it was intended. This phrase paraphrased from the Bible, for example, has been translated numerous times: "It is easier for a camel to go through the eye of a needle than for a rich man to enter the kingdom of God" (Mark 10:25). (One other translation is: "The eye of the needle is a narrow doorway in an ancient wall.") Give other examples of exact translations that may make understanding a book difficult.

References

Axtell, R. E. (1994). *The do's and taboos of international trade.* New York: John Wiley & Sons, Inc.

Axtell, R. E. (2009). *Do's and taboos of using English around the world.* New York: Castle Books.

Baldrige, L. (1993). *Letitia Baldrige's new complete guide to executive manners.* New York: Rawson Associates.

Bermont, J. (2004). *How to Europe: The complete traveler's handbook.* Midland, MI: Murphy & Broad Publishing Company.

Borden, G. A. (1991). *Cultural orientation: An approach to understanding intercultural communication.* Upper Saddle River, NJ: Prentice Hall.

Bosrock, M. M. (1995a). *Put your best foot forward—Europe.* St. Paul, MN: International Educational Systems.

Bosrock, M. M. (1995b). *Put your best foot forward—Mexico/Canada.* St. Paul, MN: International Educational Systems.

Bosrock, M. M. (1997). *Put your best foot forward—Asia.* St. Paul, MN: International Educational Systems.

Braganti, N. L., & Devine, E. (1992). *European customs and manners.* New York: Meadowbrook.

Condon, J. C., & Yousef, F. S. (1975). *Introduction to intercultural communication.* New York: Macmillan Publishing Company.

Devine, E., & Braganti, N. L. (1991). *The traveler's guide to Middle Eastern and North African customs and manners.* New York: St. Martin's Press.

Devine, E., & Braganti, N. L. (1995). *The traveler's guide to African customs and manners.* New York: St. Martin's Press.

Devine, E., & Braganti, N.L. (1998). *The traveler's guide to Asian customs and manners.* New York: St. Martin's Griffin.

Devine, E., & Braganti, N. L. (2000). *The traveler's guide to Latin American customs and manners.* New York: St. Martin's Griffin.

DeVries, M. A. (1994). *Internationally yours.* Boston, MA: Houghton Mifflin.

Dodd, C. H. (1997). *Dynamics of intercultural communication* (5th ed.). New York: McGraw Hill.

Ferraro, G. P. (2010). *The cultural dimension of international business* (6th ed.). Upper Saddle River, NJ: Prentice Hall.

Fong, M. (2007, February 5). Tired of laughter, Beijing gets rid of bad translations. *The Wall Street Journal,* pp. A1, A13.

Funakawa, A. (1997). *Transcultural management: A new approach for global organization.* San Francisco, CA: Jossey-Bass.

Fussell, P. (1983). *Class.* New York: Ballantine.

Gilsdorf, J. (2002, July). Standard Englishes and world Englishes: Living with a polymorph business language. *The Journal of Business Communication, 39*(3), 365–378.

Hall, E. T., & Hall, M. R. (1990). *Understanding cultural differences.* Yarmouth, ME: Intercultural Press.

Hodge, S. (2000). *Global smarts: The art of communicating and deal making anywhere in the world.* New York: John Wiley & Sons.

James, M. L., & Peltier, J. (1998). Bridging the gender gap in business communications. *Academy of Managerial Communications Journal, 2*(1), 1–11.

Jandt, F. E. (2010). *An introduction to intercultural communication* (6th ed.). Thousand Oaks, CA: Sage.

Klopf, D. W., & McCroskey, J. C. (2007). *Intercultural communication encounters.* Boston, MA: Pearson Education.

Languages. (2008). *Languages spoken in the U.S.* Retrieved August 18, 2008, from http://www.nvtc.gov/lotw/months/november/USlanguages.html

Moran, R. T., Harris, P. R., & Moran, S. V. (2011). Managing cultural differences (8th ed.). Burlington, MA: Butterworth-Heinemann.

Names of big numbers. (2004). Retrieved July 25, 2004, from http://www.sizes.com/numbers/big_numName.htm

Samovar, L. A., Porter, R. E., & McDaniel, E. R. (2009). *Communication between cultures* (7th ed.). Belmont, CA: Thomson Learning.

Schmit, J., Richards, R., & Swingle, C. (1993, September 14). Travelers' bouts of foot-in-mouth disease. *USA Today,* p. 5E.

Stewart, E. C., & Bennett, M. J. (1991). *American cultural patterns.* Yarmouth, ME: Intercultural Press.

Tannen, D. (2001). *You just don't understand: Women and men in conversation.* New York: Quill.

Tsunda, Y. (1986). *Language inequality and distortion.* Philadelphia, PA: John Benjamin.

U.S. News & World Report. (1995, February 18). In F. E. Jandt, *An introduction to intercultural communication* (4th ed.). Thousand Oaks, CA: Sage.

Weaver, G. R. (1998). American identity movements. Cross cultural confrontations. In G. R. Weaver (Ed.), *Culture, communications, and conflict* (pp. 72–77). Needham Heights, MA: Simon & Schuster.

Glossary

Acronyms are words formed from the initial letters or groups of letters and pronounced as one word.

Argot is a vocabulary of a particular group; it is often regional.

Back translation is the concept of written translation from a first language into a second language, followed by another person's translating it back into the first language to determine if the translations are equivalent.

Bernstein hypothesis explains how social structure affects language; speech emerges in restricted or elaborated codes.

Cant is the vocabulary of the undesirable cocultures, such as drug dealers, gangs, prostitutes, and murderers.

Cognates are words that sound the same and have the same meaning.

Colloquialism refers to informal words or phrases often associated with regions of the country.

Connotative meanings are the emotional meanings of words.

Conversation taboos are topics considered inappropriate for conversation with people in certain cultures or groups.

Denotative meanings are the explicit or direct meanings of words.

Ebonics is a nonstandard form of English used by the U.S. African American subculture.

Elaborated codes are messages that are low in predictability; verbal transmission is important.

Euphemisms are inoffensive expressions used in place of offensive words or words with negative connotations.

Figurative meanings are the descriptive meanings of words.

Grammarians are people who study how a language is governed and its grammatical forms, roots, and endings.

Group Decision Support Systems (GDSS) is a business conference software package.

High-context language is communication that transmits little in the explicit message; nonverbal aspects are important.

Homonyms are words that sound alike and have different meanings.

Host language is the native language of the country.

Jargon refers to technical terminology used within specialized groups.

Linear language has a beginning and an end; logical and object oriented.

Linguistic determinism is the assumption that a person's view of reality stems mainly from his or her language.

Linguists are people who study the phonetic aspects of language and define language by the sounds speakers produce and listeners receive.

Low-context language is communication explicitly coded and given in more than one way to be sure the receiver understands it.

Nonlinear language is circular, subjective, and traditionally oriented.

Novelists are people who believe that language is a series of words arranged to produce harmonious sounds or to have a logical effect.

Parable is a story used to convey a truth or moral lesson.

Proverb is a saying that expresses a commonplace truth.

Repartee conversation is a conversation in which the parties take turns speaking and talk only for short time periods.

Restricted codes include highly predictable messages; use oral, nonverbal, and paralinguistic transmission channels.

Ritual conversation involves standard replies and comments for a given situation, with little meaning attached to what is said.

Sapir–Whorf hypothesis is the belief that language functions as a way of shaping one's experiences; includes structural and semantic aspects of a language.

Self-disclosure is a form of interaction that involves telling other people about yourself so they may get to know you better.

Semanticists are people who study the meaning of words and where and how the words developed.

Slang refers to idioms and other informal language vocabulary.

Sociolinguistics refers to the effects of social and cultural differences upon a language.

Subjective interpretation is interpretation placed on a message that is affected by thought processes; influenced by personal judgment or temperament of a person.

Syntactic rules govern how words are arranged in a sentence.

Verbal dueling is a friendly type of argument or debate.

Answers to Exercises

True/False

1. F
2. T
3. F
4. T
5. T
6. T
7. F
8. T
9. T
10. T

Oral and Nonverbal
Communication Patterns

From Chapter 6 of *Intercultural Business Communication*, Sixth Edition. Lillian H. Chaney, Jeanette S. Martin.

Oral and Nonverbal Communication Patterns

Objectives

Upon completion of this chapter, you will

- be able to evaluate thought patterns and their relationship to intercultural business communication.
- understand how paralanguage affects successful intercultural communication.
- appreciate how attitudes toward time and use of space convey nonverbal messages in intercultural encounters.
- understand the role that eye contact, smell, color, touch, and body language play in communicating nonverbally in cultural situations.
- learn how silence is used to send nonverbal messages in various cultures.
- recognize that nonverbal leakage often occurs in intercultural nonverbal communication.

Successful multicultural business encounters depend to a large extent on effective oral and nonverbal communication. Although much communication in the global arena is oral, the nonverbal aspects can contribute significantly to understanding and interpreting oral communication. **Nonverbal communication** refers to nonword messages such as gestures, facial expressions, interpersonal distance, touch, eye contact, smell, and silence.

Costly business blunders are often the result of a lack of knowledge of another culture's oral and nonverbal communication patterns. Knowledge of these aspects of intercultural communication is essential for conducting business in the international marketplace.

THOUGHT PATTERNS

Patterns of thought or processes of reasoning and problem solving are not the same in all cultures, but they all have an impact on oral communication.

Most people in the United States use the deductive method of reasoning to solve problems. The **deductive method** goes from broad categories or observations to specific examples to determine the facts and then the solution to the problem. The line of reasoning used by people in many other cultures, such as Asians, is typically the **inductive method**. People who use this approach start with facts or observations and go to generalizations. Thought patterns also include the pace or speed with which problems are solved or decisions made. Making quick decisions is a characteristic of an effective manager in the United States, although this behavior is viewed as impulsive by the Japanese. The slower method of problem solving is often a source of frustration for U.S. managers when conducting business with the Japanese. Recognizing that people from other cultures may have different thought patterns is important to communicating and negotiating successfully in the global business environment.

PARALANGUAGE

Paralanguage is related to oral communication; it refers to the rate, pitch, and volume qualities of the voice that interrupt or temporarily take the place of speech and affect the meaning of a message. Paralanguage includes such vocal qualifiers as intensity (whether loud or soft); pitch (either high or low); extent (drawls and accents); vocal characterizers, such as crying and laughing; and vocal segregates, such as saying "uh" and "uh-huh." Paralanguage conveys emotions. Negative emotions of impatience, fear, and anger are easier to convey than the more positive emotions of satisfaction and admiration. An increased rate of speech could indicate anger or impatience; a decrease in rate could suggest lack of interest or a reflective attitude. An increased volume could also indicate anger; a lower volume is nonthreatening and sympathetic (Samovar, Porter, & McDaniel, 2009).

In the United States, people usually have no difficulty distinguishing the speech of persons from specific regions of the country. Although the rate of speech and dialect may vary from region to region, they rarely cause major problems in the communication process.

Learning the nuances in speech that affect verbal messages will help when communicating with people of other cultures. Differences in volume of speech, for example, are culture specific as well as gender specific. Arabs, for example, speak loudly, feeling that this shows strength and sincerity. People from the Philippines, however, speak softly, as they believe that this is an indication of good breeding and education. Thais also speak softly, speaking loudly only when they are angry. When they first hear U.S. Americans speak, the Thais think the U.S. Americans are angry because of the loudness of their speech. Males usually speak louder and in a lower pitch than females. Differences also exist in the rate at which people speak. U.S. Americans living in the northern states usually speak faster than those in the south; Italians and Arabs speak faster than do people of the United States. People who speak slowly sometimes have difficulty understanding the speech of those who speak rapidly. Accent is also an aspect of paralanguage. Some British are able to discern a person's educational background by his or her accent. In the United States, accent has been related to hiring decisions. In one U.S. research study, standard language speakers were given more supervisory positions while persons with accents were given more semiskilled positions (Jandt, 2010; Samovar et al., 2009).

CHRONEMICS

Chronemics (attitudes toward time) vary from culture to culture. Two kinds of time are involved in chronemics. One is objective time, which involves clocks and calendars; the other is subjective time, which relates to how an individual perceives time. For example, to the young, time passes slowly; as people age, however, time seems to pass quickly. In addition, time flies when we are having fun but seems to drag when we are bored. In Western cultures, objective time is far more prevalent than subjective time (Klopf & McCroskey, 2007).

Two of the most important time systems that relate to international business are monochronic and polychronic time. Countries that follow **monochronic time (M-time)** perform only one major activity at a time; countries that follow **polychronic time (P-time)** work on several activities simultaneously.

The United States is a monochronic culture; other monochronic countries are England, Switzerland, and Germany. In monochronic cultures, time is regarded as something tangible; people use such terms as "wasting time" or "losing time." Time is seen as lineal and manageable. In monochronic cultures, it is considered rude to do two things at once, such as reading a journal in a meeting or answering the telephone while someone is in your office. Schedules and keeping appointments are consistent with values of people in monochronic cultures (Klopf & McCroskey, 2007).

Polychronic cultures include people of Latin America, Southern Europe, and the Middle East. These people are well adapted to doing several things at once and do not mind interruptions. People are more important than schedules to members of polychronic cultures. The result is a lifestyle that is more unstructured than that of monochronic people (Samovar et al., 2009).

People from low-context cultures are usually monochronic, while people from high-context cultures tend to be polychronic. The two time systems do not mix. People from monochronic cultures take deadlines and meeting commitments seriously; they are punctual. People in polychronic cultures, however, are often late and do not take schedules and deadlines seriously (Klopf & McCroskey, 2007).

Table 1 contains a summary of generalizations related to monochronic and polychronic time systems (Hall & Hall, 1990).

Being on time for work, business appointments and meetings, and social engagements is very important in the United States. Punctuality is considered a positive attribute that conveys the nonverbal message of being respectful of other persons. Tardiness is interpreted as rudeness, a lack of consideration for others, or a lack of interest in the job or meeting. Being

TABLE 1 Monochronic and Polychronic Time Systems

Monochronic People	Polychronic People
Do one thing at a time	Do many things at once
Concentrate on the task	Are highly distractible and subject to interruptions
Take time commitments seriously and value promptness	Consider time commitments more casually; promptness based on the relationship
Are committed to the task	Are committed to people
Show respect for private property; rarely borrow or lend	Borrow and lend things often
Are accustomed to short-term relationships	Tend to build lifetime relationships

late also sends the nonverbal message that you are not well organized. Being on time for business meetings is also important in Germany; Germans view punctuality as a sign of respect and good manners. Being punctual is also important for business events in China, India, Taiwan, and Singapore, as well as to people in many other countries of the world (Klopf & McCroskey, 2007).

The length of time someone has to wait to see another person also sends a message. In the United States, the length of the wait is associated with the person's status and importance. The person perceived as high status is seen immediately; the implied message is, "You are important; your time is just as valuable as mine." Generally in the United States, keeping a person with a business appointment waiting for five minutes is acceptable. Keeping a person waiting 15 minutes clearly implies that you consider yourself more important than your visitor. With a 20- to 30-minute wait, the message becomes stronger and implies contempt and/or annoyance; it also sends the message that the other person's time is not important (Fast, 1991). In time-conscious cultures, being aware of the subtextual implications associated with different lengths of waiting can be extremely important to avoid unintentionally demeaning or insulting a person with whom you want to have a business relationship.

People of Germany and Switzerland are even more time conscious than are people from the United States. In fact, northern Europeans regard tardiness as a characteristic of an undisciplined person. Scandinavians are also time conscious, with the exception of Iceland, where people are a bit more flexible regarding punctuality. A telephone call is appropriate when you are delayed (Turkington, 1999). Being on time is important to the people of Singapore and Hong Kong (except at banquets in Hong Kong—nobody arrives at the time stated on the invitation). Being punctual is also important in Malaysia and Indonesia, particularly when meeting with a person of superior status. Unlike the people in their neighboring countries, Iraqis value punctuality, so it is important to be on time for appointments in that country (Devine & Braganti, 1991). Likewise, people of India appreciate punctuality but may not be punctual themselves. Also, in Australia and New Zealand, punctuality is important for both business appointments and social events. Arriving late for meetings and appointments signifies a careless attitude toward business (Morrison & Conaway, 2006).

In Algeria, however, punctuality is not widely regarded. In Latin American countries, the *mañana* attitude (putting off until tomorrow what does not get done today) has been a source of frustration for time-sensitive U.S. executives when conducting business with people of that culture. Because their first obligations are to family and friends, Latin Americans consider a request from a family member or friend to take precedence over a business meeting (Bosrock, 1997). People in the Arabic cultures also have a more casual attitude toward time; this attitude is related to their religious belief that God decides when things get accomplished (Engholm, 1991).

The manager of a German bank offered to host a cocktail party for the South American delegation to a bankers' conference in Hamburg. The invitation stated that cocktails were at 7 P.M., so the banker and his wife were ready to greet guests at 6:30 P.M. When no guests had arrived by 8:45 P.M., he asked his staff, "What kind of people have we invited?" The response: South Americans. (Bosrock, 1997)

In southern Europe, people are also more casual about punctuality, but position and relationship to the other party are considerations. In Spain, for example, specific but unwritten rules exist concerning who can be late and by how long in both social and business situations. The waiting also depends on whether you want something from the other person or whether they want something from you. Arriving early is not recommended as this implies being too eager (Engholm & Rowland, 1996).

To work harmoniously with persons from other cultures, you should consider these different attitudes toward time. When conducting business with persons from cultures whose attitude toward time differs from your own, you should verify whether the meeting time is, for example, Latin American time or U.S. time.

PROXEMICS

Communicating through the use of space is known as **proxemics**. The physical distance between people when they are interacting, as well as territorial space, is strongly influenced by culture.

You should consider interpersonal space when conversing with others. Hall and Hall (1990) report that psychologists have identified four zones from which U.S. people interact: the intimate zone, the personal zone, the social zone, and the public zone. The **intimate zone**, less than 18 inches, is reserved for very close friends; it is entered by business colleagues briefly, such as when shaking hands. The **personal zone**, from 18 inches to 4 feet, is used for giving instructions to others or working closely with another person. The **social zone**, from 4 to 12 feet, is used for most business situations in which people interact more formally and impersonally, such as during a business meeting. The **public distance**, over 12 feet, is the most formal zone; therefore, fewer interactions occur because of distance.

A psychology professor at a southern university gave his students an assignment to test elevator proxemics, the use of space in such crowded places as an elevator. They reported the usual U.S. behaviors of facing the front and watching the illuminated floor indicator, assuming the Fig Leaf Position (hands/purses/briefcases hanging down in front of the body), and positioning themselves in the corners or against the elevator walls. The professor then added another assignment: students were to break the rules and get on the elevator, stand at the front facing the other occupants, and jump backward off the elevator just before the door closed. One of the elevator occupants was heard to whisper, "Call 911; we've got a real weirdo here." (Axtell, 1998)

People of the United States tend to need more space than do persons of certain cultures, such as Greeks, Latin Americans, or Arabs. When interacting with persons of these cultures, U.S. Americans back away because the person is standing too close. On the other hand, the Japanese stand farther away than do U.S. people when conversing. Negative nonverbal messages often conveyed by standing too close to a person who requires more space include being pushy or overbearing; standing too close may also be interpreted as an unwelcome sexual advance.

People also communicate through space by the arrangement of desks and chairs. When U.S. people are conversing, they generally prefer the face-to-face arrangement of chairs placed at right angles to one another. People of other cultures, such as the Chinese, prefer the side-by-side arrangement; this preference may be related to the custom of avoiding direct eye contact in that culture.

In the United States, nonverbal messages are sent by other aspects of the office environment. Private offices and offices with windows have more status than inside offices, and large offices have more status than small ones. In addition to office size, higher-ranking executives have their territory better protected than do lower-status employees; doors and secretaries are often used as barriers to access. Messages related to authority and position are also conveyed by the selection and arrangement of furniture. A large wooden desk and desk chairs with arms convey power and authority. Placing the desk and chair in front of a window or an arrangement of pictures on the wall creates a throne-like effect that adds to the sense of power (Chaney & Lyden, 1996). Office location also conveys the presence or absence of power and status. Offices on the fourth floor have more status than offices on the first floor. The top floors of office buildings are generally occupied by the top-level executives not only in the United States but in Germany as well. However, French top-level executives occupy a position in the middle of an office area with subordinates located around them. The purpose of this arrangement is to help upper management stay informed of activities and to maintain control over the work area. The Japanese also do not consider private offices appropriate. In traditional Japanese firms, only executives of the highest rank have private offices, and they may also have desks in large work areas (Gudykunst & Ting-Toomey, 1988).

OCULESICS

Some cultures place more emphasis on **oculesics** or oculemics (gaze and eye contact) than others. People of the United States, as well as people in Canada, Great Britain, and Eastern Europe, favor direct eye contact. The eye contact, however, is not steady; it is maintained for a second or two and then broken. Eye contact is considered a sign of respect and attentiveness in these countries. People who avoid eye contact may be considered insecure, untrustworthy, unfriendly, disrespectful, or inattentive.

Students in a business communication class at a Mid-South university were asked to test the concept of gaze and eye contact in the United States by maintaining steady eye contact with a person in the car next to them when they stopped at a traffic light. Responses varied from obscene gestures to making faces to returning the gaze. Students concluded that U.S. persons are very uncomfortable with prolonged eye contact.

In other cultures, there is little direct eye contact. The Japanese direct their gaze below the chin; they are uncomfortable with maintaining direct eye contact throughout the conversation. People in China and Indonesia also lower the eyes as a sign of respect, feeling that prolonged eye contact shows bad manners. Likewise, Latin Americans and Caribbeans, as well as people in parts of Africa, show respect by avoiding direct eye contact. In some countries, such as India and Egypt, eye contact is related to position and gender. In India, eye contact is avoided between people who are on different socioeconomic levels, while in Egypt there is no eye contact between men and women who do not know each other. Germans value direct eye contact; however, their eye contact is more intense than U.S. persons are accustomed to (Samovar et al., 2009). In addition, in the Middle East, the eye contact is so intense that it exceeds the comfort zone for most people in the United States. Prolonged eye contact with women, however, is considered inappropriate.

Cultural variations in eye contact vary from prolonged eye contact to little eye contact as shown here.

Very direct eye contact:	Middle Easterners
	Some Latin American groups
	The French
Moderate eye contact:	Mainstream Americans
	Northern Europeans
	The British
Minimal eye contact:	East Asians
	Southeast Asians
	East Indians
	Native Americans

Very direct eye contact can be misinterpreted as hostility, aggressiveness, or intrusiveness when the intended meaning was just to appear interested. Minimal eye contact may be misinterpreted as lack of interest or understanding, dishonesty, fear, or shyness when the intended meaning was to show respect or to avoid appearing intrusive.

Barbara Walters, a television newscaster, was interviewing Mu'ammar Gadhafi and could not understand why he would not look into her eyes. She learned later that he was showing her respect by not having direct eye contact. Arabic men do not have direct eye contact with women unless they are members of their family.

The eyes can be very revealing during negotiations. The pupils of the eyes constrict or dilate in response to emotions. Well-trained negotiators watch the pupils for signs that the person is willing to make concessions (Borden, 1991).

A prolonged gaze or stare in the United States, Japan, Korea, and Thailand is considered rude. In most cultures, men do not stare at women. In France and Italy, however, men can stare at women in public. In the United States, staring at a person is considered a sign of interest and may even be interpreted as sexually suggestive.

OLFACTICS

Olfactics, or smell, as a means of nonverbal communication is important. A person's smell can have a positive or negative effect on the oral message. The way someone smells remains in our memory after the person has gone.

Most people of the United States respond negatively to what they consider bad odors, such as body odor, breath odor, or clothes that emit unpleasant aromas such as perspiration. They place great importance on personal hygiene and consider it normal for people to remove body odors by bathing or showering daily and by brushing teeth to remove mouth odors. Advertisements on U.S. American television and in newspapers and magazines for underarm deodorants, perfumes, colognes, and mouthwash emphasize the importance U.S. Americans place on personal hygiene. In a television commercial that epitomizes the fixation that U.S. Americans have concerning body odor, a young woman states, "If a guy smells, it's such a turnoff." People in the United States are not comfortable discussing the topic, however, and generally will not tell another that his or her body odor is offensive; instead, they simply avoid being close to the person and end the discourse as quickly as possible.

Other cultures have different concepts of natural odors; they consider them as normal and think attitudes of people in the United States are unnatural. Arabs, for example, are comfortable with natural odors. Other cultures in which smell plays an important role include the Japanese and Samoans. Cultures that include little meat in the diet, such as the Chinese, say that people who consume a lot of meat, such as U.S. Americans, emit an offensive odor (Samovar et al., 2009).

A medical doctor from Saudi Arabia was completing an internship in a hospital in the southern United States. Problems arose when patients refused to have the Saudi doctor examine them. Interviews with patients revealed two problems: He "smelled bad," and he breathed on the patients. The doctor's orientation had apparently failed to include the incongruence between Arabic and U.S. American olfactory perceptions and practices.

To maintain harmonious intercultural business relationships, remember these diverse attitudes toward smell and, if possible, adopt the hygiene practices of the country in which you are conducting business.

HAPTICS

Haptics, or touch, refers to communicating through the use of bodily contact. When used properly, touch can create feelings of warmth and trust; when used improperly, touch can betray trust and cause annoyance (Fast, 1991). Some cultures are very comfortable with bodily contact, and others avoid it. People in the United States are taught that appropriate touch includes shaking hands but that in business situations giving hugs or other expressions of affection to supervisors and coworkers encourages familiarity that is generally considered inappropriate. Because touching may be interpreted as a form of sexual harassment, it is necessary to refrain from touching in business situations to avoid the appearance of impropriety.

Another consideration when using touch in the United States is knowledge of the hierarchy involved. People of higher rank (the president of the company) may touch those of lower rank (office employees), but secretaries may not touch the president. Doctors may place a comforting arm around a patient, but patients may not touch doctors. Adults may touch children, but children should not touch adults unless they know them. Equals may touch each other. The general rule is that people who are older or of higher status may touch those who are younger or of lower status (Fast, 1991).

Several years ago, when President Carter was mediating peace talks between Egypt and Israel, Anwar Sadat frequently placed his hand on President Carter's knee. Although this subtextual message was intended as a gesture of warm friendship, the subtler message Sadat was conveying to the world was that he was President Carter's equal. (Fast, 1991)

Axtell (1998) and others classified the following cultures as "touch" and "don't touch" (see Table 2).

In touch-oriented cultures, such as those of Italy, Greece, Spain, and Portugal, both males and females may be seen walking along the street holding hands or arm in arm. Cultural

TABLE 2 Touch and Don't Touch Cultures

Don't Touch	Middle Ground	Touch
Japan	Australia	Latin American countries
United States	France	Italy
Canada	China	Greece
England	Ireland	Spain and Portugal
Scandinavia	India	Some Asian countries
Other Northern European countries	Middle East countries	Russian Federation

Source: Based on a chart in *Gestures* (p. 40), by R. E. Axtell, 1998. Hoboken, NJ: John Wiley & Sons, Inc.

variations also exist in the extent of touching between persons of the same gender. In Mexico, Eastern Europe, and the Arab world, embracing and kissing are common, especially between friends. In Finland, however, hugs or kisses on the cheek are not appropriate in public (Samovar et al., 2009). In other cultures, such as in the Latin America, touching between men is considered acceptable (Figure 1).

A Mexican male will stand close to a male colleague and even hold him by the lapel or shoulder. Behavior between men in the Middle East is similar, but you should avoid touching the person with the left hand because the left hand is considered unclean and is reserved for personal hygiene. In other countries, such as in the United States, touching between men may be construed as an indication of homosexuality.

An additional aspect of tactile communication concerns the location of the touch. In Thailand and India, it is offensive to touch the head, as this part of the body is considered sacred. In fact, avoid touching all Asians on the head, including small children. Even placing a hand on the back of an Asian worker's chair is considered inappropriate. Although Muslims hug another person around the shoulders, in Korea young people do not touch the shoulders of their elders (Axtell, 1998). In Hong Kong, avoid initiating any type of physical contact. Tactile behavior is highly cultural; knowing when and how to touch in various cultures is important to conducting business globally.

FIGURE 1 Touch-Oriented Culture

KINESICS

Kinesics is the term used for communicating through various types of body movements, including facial expressions, gestures, posture and stance, and other mannerisms that may accompany or replace oral messages.

Facial Expressions

The face and eyes convey the most expressive types of body language. People of all cultures learn how to control facial expressions to mask emotions that are inappropriate in a specific setting, such as crying when being reprimanded or yawning when listening to a boring presentation. In some countries, such as China, people rarely show emotion. Koreans seldom smile; they perceive people who smile a great deal as shallow. The following proverb from the Korean culture illustrates the Asian attitude concerning the meaning of a smile: "The man who smiles a lot is not a real man." People of Thailand, on the other hand, smile a great deal, which may be why Thailand has been called "The Land of Smiles." The Japanese may smile to cover a range of emotions, including anger, happiness, or sadness, although the smile to people in the United States means happiness. Asians smile or laugh softly when they are embarrassed or to conceal any discomfort (Samovar et al., 2009). To interpret facial expressions correctly, you should take the communication context and the culture into account.

During the weightlifting event of the 2008 Summer Olympics in Beijing, an Asian athlete was attempting his third try in the clean and jerk competition. Although the athlete leaned down as if he were about to make his final attempt, he did not even try to lift the weight but simply stood up and walked away. The announcer said: "He's laughing! I don't believe I would be laughing after that performance." The announcer apparently did not understand that Asians often laugh when they are embarrassed.

Gestures

Gestures are another important aspect of body language. Gestures can be emblems or symbols ("V" for victory), illustrators (police officer's hand held up to stop traffic), regulators (glancing at your watch to signal that you are in a hurry), or affect displays (a person's face turns red with embarrassment).

Gestures are used to add emphasis or clarity to an oral message. Although the meaning of gestures depends on the context, following are some general guides to interpreting the meaning of gestures in the United States (Axtell, 1998):

- Interest is expressed by maintaining eye contact with the speaker, smiling, and nodding the head.
- Open-mindedness is expressed by open hands and palms turned upward.
- Nervousness is sometimes shown by fidgeting, failing to give the speaker eye contact, or jingling keys or money in your pocket.
- Suspiciousness is indicated by glancing away or touching your nose, eyes, or ears.
- Defensiveness is indicated by crossing your arms over your chest, making fisted gestures, or crossing your legs.
- Lack of interest or boredom is indicated by glancing repeatedly at your watch or staring at the ceiling or floor or out the window when the person is speaking.

Although regional differences exist, people in the United States typically use moderate gesturing. They rarely use gestures in which the elbows go above the shoulder level as this is interpreted as being too emotional or even angry; one exception is waving hello or good-bye. Italians, Greeks, and some Latin Americans use vigorous gestures when speaking, although Chinese and Japanese people tend to keep their hands and arms close to their bodies when speaking. Most cultures have standard gestures for such daily situations as greeting someone and saying good-bye; learn and respect such gestures when conversing with persons of another culture.

Following are some additional guidelines for gesturing in various cultures (Axtell, 1998):

- The "V"-for-victory gesture (Figure 2), holding two fingers upright with palm and fingers faced outward, is widely used in the United States and many other countries. In England and in New Zealand, however, it has a crude connotation when used with the palm in.
- The vertical horns gesture (raised fist, index finger and little finger extended [Figure 3]) has a positive connotation associated with the University of Texas Longhorn football team. This gesture has an insulting connotation in Italy, but in Brazil and Venezuela it is a sign for good luck. This symbol has various meanings in U.S. subcultures, including serving as a satanic cult recognition sign signifying the devil's horns. This symbol should be used only when you are sure the other person understands its intended meaning.

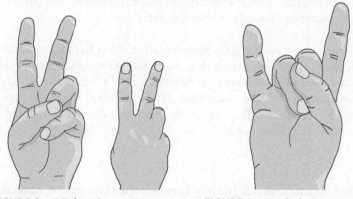

FIGURE 2 "V"-for-Victory Gesture   **FIGURE 3** Vertical Horns Gesture

- The "thumbs-up" gesture (Figure 4) has been widely recognized as a positive signal meaning "everything is OK" or "good going." Although well known in North America and most of Europe, in Australia and West Africa, it is seen as a rude gesture.
- The "OK" sign (Figure 5), with the thumb and forefinger joined to form a circle, is a positive gesture in the United States, although in Brazil it is considered obscene. The gesture has yet another meaning in Japan—it is a symbol for money; in Belgium, it means zero. The "OK" sign should be used with great care in Tunisia; you would be saying, "I will kill you."

An American engineer, sent to Germany by his U.S. firm that had purchased a German company, was working side by side with a German engineer on a piece of equipment. When the American engineer made a suggestion for improving the new machine, the German engineer followed the suggestion and asked his American counterpart whether or not he had done it correctly. The American replied by giving the U.S. American "OK" gesture, making a circle with the thumb and forefinger. The German engineer put down his tools and walked away, refusing further communication with the American engineer. The U.S. American later learned from one of the supervisors the significance of this gesture to a German: "You asshole." (Axtell, 1998)

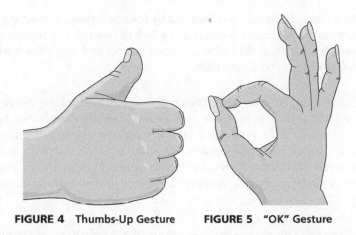

FIGURE 4 Thumbs-Up Gesture   **FIGURE 5** "OK" Gesture

- The beckoning gesture (Figure 6), fingers upturned, palm facing body, is offensive to Filipinos as it is used to beckon animals and prostitutes. Vietnamese and Mexicans also find it offensive.

FIGURE 6 Beckoning Gesture

- The head nod in most countries means "yes," but in Bulgaria it means "no."

Because one culture's gestures may be misinterpreted by people in another culture, avoid using gestures when communicating in international business settings until you become knowledgeable about the meaning of such gestures.

Posture and Stance

Posture, the way someone stands, sits, or walks, can send positive or negative nonverbal messages. Posture can signal agreement or disagreement. For example, when people in a business meeting share a point of view, they are likely to mirror each other's posture. When a person disagrees with others in the group, his or her posture also disagrees with that of other group members. Posture can convey self-confidence, status, and interest. Confident people generally have a relaxed posture yet stand erect and walk with assurance. Walking with stooped shoulders and a slow, hesitating gait projects such negative messages as lack of assurance and lack of confidence. Walking rapidly and swinging the arms indicates that the person is goal oriented. A preoccupied walk, with hands clasped behind and head lowered, is thoughtful. Men who walk with hands on hips convey the message of wanting to get to their destination as quickly as possible (Fast, 1991). The posture of persons of higher status is usually more relaxed than that of their subordinates. Interest is demonstrated by leaning forward toward the person you are conversing with, while sitting back communicates a lack of interest. The posture of people in the United States tends to be casual; they sit in a relaxed manner and may slouch when they stand. This behavior in Germany is considered rude.

President Ronald Reagan was well known for using posture to convey subtextual messages. In a 1985 article in the *New York Times*, a reporter described how President Reagan's posture revealed his emotions during an interview. He said that much of the time President Reagan settled back comfortably. When the issue of Star Wars was brought up, his posture changed; he leaned forward in his chair and became totally engaged. When the talk shifted to Soviet violations, however, he placed his back straight against the chair. (Fast, 1991)

Posture when seated also varies with the culture. When seated, people in the United States often cross their legs; women cross at the ankle, and men cross with their ankle on the knee (Figure 7). Crossing the leg with ankle on the knee would be considered inappropriate by most people in the Middle East. In the Arab world, correct posture while seated is important; avoid showing the sole of your shoe or pointing your foot at someone, as the lowest part of the body is considered unclean. People from a number of countries—Turkey, India, Egypt, Saudi Arabia, Singapore, and Thailand—feel that showing the bottom of your feet is insulting, so it is important to avoid sitting such that the soles of the shoes are visible.

When communicating with persons of another culture, follow their lead; assume the posture they assume. Remember that in most cultures, standing when an older person or one of higher rank enters or leaves the room is considered a sign of respect.

An awareness of cultural differences in facial expressions, gestures, and posture is important to successful intercultural encounters. Body language can enhance the spoken message or detract from it. Even though we usually believe that actions speak louder than words, in intercultural interactions what the person says may give a clearer picture of the intended message than the accompanying body language. However, if a gesture is used in the wrong context, it may be difficult for a foreigner to understand the intended message. The best advice is probably to keep

FIGURE 7 Sitting Postures

gestures to a minimum when communicating with persons in other cultures; learn the words for "good" or "yes" in the local language rather than relying on gestures.

CHROMATICS

Chromatics, or color, can affect your mood, your emotions, and your impression of others. Certain colors have both negative and positive connotations. In the United States, for example, black is considered a sophisticated color, but it may also represent sadness. White is pure and peaceful, but in some cultures it is associated with mourning. Blue may represent peace and tranquility or sadness and depression, as in "I feel blue."

Color may be used to symbolize such things as patriotism. People in the United States associate red, white, and blue (the colors in the flag) with patriotism. Cultural differences associated with colors include the following (Axtell, 1998; Ricks, 2006; Scott, 2002):

- Black is the color of mourning to many Europeans and U.S. Americans, but white is worn to funerals in Japan and many other nations. Red has funereal connotations in African countries.
- In the United States, brides typically wear white; however, in India, brides wear red or yellow. White is associated with mourning in parts of Asia.
- Purple is sometimes associated with royalty, but it is the color of death in many Latin American countries.
- Red (especially red roses) is associated with romance in some cultures, including the United States. Red is not an appropriate color for wrapping gifts in Japan.
- Green is not used for wrapping packages in Egypt because green is the nationalist color (as red, white, and blue are the nationalist colors in the United States).
- In many countries of the world, blue is considered a masculine color, but to people of France and the United Kingdom, red is more masculine. Blue, in Iran, is an undesirable color.
- Although people of the United States consider pink to be the most feminine color, persons in most other countries think of yellow as the most feminine color.

United Airlines unknowingly got off on the wrong foot during its initial flights from Hong Kong. To commemorate the occasion, they handed out white carnations to the passengers. When they learned that to many Asians white flowers represent bad luck and even death, they changed to red carnations. (Ricks, 2006)

Color also has an influence on foreign sales. In a study of consumers' color preferences for various countries reported by Madden, Hewett, and Roth (2000), blue was ranked as the most preferred color by people of Austria, China, and the United States (and ranked second in Brazil); other colors ranked in the top five by these four countries were white, green, black, and red. Firms who sell their products in other countries should be aware that the color used in packaging a product may influence the purchasing decisions of potential customers. For example, packaging a product in red would be appealing to customers in China but less appealing to potential buyers in South Korea because of the possible association of red with communism (Scott, 2002).

Determining cultural meanings of various colors is advised to ensure that nonverbal messages associated with color are positive ones.

SILENCE

Silence is a form of nonverbal communication that may be interpreted in various ways, depending on the situation, the duration of the silence, and the culture. Interpretations of silence include agreement or disagreement, lack of interest, or contempt. Silence can also mean that the person is giving the topic some thought. Silence can be used to indicate displeasure in the United States and in other cultures (Samovar et al., 2009).

Other aspects of silence should also be considered: the duration, appropriateness, and relationship between people who are conversing. A prolonged silence following a question could be interpreted to mean that the person does not know the answer. Silence following an inappropriate statement, such as the telling of a tasteless joke, is usually interpreted as disapproval. Silence following a conversation with someone you know well could be interpreted as dissent or disapproval (Samovar et al., 2009).

People of the United States are rather uncomfortable with periods of silence except with people they know well. They use fillers, such as comments on the weather, to avoid silence. Talking is considered an important means of communication and as an enjoyable pastime in the United States. Perhaps one reason U.S. Americans are considered "masters of the art of chitchat" is that they enjoy talking—often on nonsubstantive topics. In addition to people of the United States, Germans, Arabs, the French, and Southern Europeans are uncomfortable with silence.

In some cultures, periods of silence are appropriate when communicating. People in East Asia consider silence an integral part of business and social discourse, not a failure to communicate. Silence in East Asia and Finland is associated with listening and learning; silence protects your privacy and individualism and shows respect for the privacy and individualism of others. Silence in these cultures is viewed as restful and as appropriate lulls in conversation (Lewis, 2006). The Japanese are comfortable with silence and use it as a bargaining tool when negotiating with persons from the United States. They know that U.S. Americans are not comfortable with long periods of silence and that a U.S. businessperson will offer a price concession just to get the discussion going again. Learn to remain silent when negotiating with the Japanese; they like periods of silence and do not like to be hurried. People who converse with no pauses are viewed as having given little thought to what they are saying and as having unfocused thinking (Axtell, 1998). Breaking the silence may also give the impression that your proposal is flawed. Japanese proverbs such as "Those who know do not speak—those who speak do not know" emphasize the value of silence over words in that culture.

An appropriate caution is to watch the behavior of the persons you are talking with and match their style. For example, allow pauses when speaking with Asians and avoid pauses when dealing with those from the Middle East. Knowing cultural variations in the use of silence and other forms of nonverbal communication is helpful when conversing with persons of another culture.

NONVERBAL LEAKAGE

Nonverbal leakage occurs when people are unsuccessful in their attempt to control the messages sent by their behavior, gestures, facial expressions, and other forms of nonverbal communication. The person's actual feelings or attitudes, which may be incongruent with what has been said, are inadvertently revealed. People are often successful in controlling facial expressions; however, nonverbal leakage occurs in the arms and hands, as well as the feet and legs, since these areas are more difficult to control. For example, people who are being deceptive will often lick their lips, grip an arm rest, or tap their fingers on a table. In addition, those who are trying to deceive someone will shuffle their feet or cross and uncross their legs. People who are untruthful often gulp, perspire, or play with a pen. They also avoid getting close to another person. When body language contradicts what a person says, body language is more indicative of the actual meaning than the verbal message. In intercultural encounters, observing nonverbal leakage may provide useful clues to a person's intended message. Observing physiological changes, such as changes in pupil size and skin color, are outside someone's conscious control and may be reliable indicators of the truth. You have to learn the meaning of the leakage in other cultures because nonverbals do not always mean the same thing in different cultures (Martin & Chaney, 2012).

Visitors to certain areas in many international cities should be aware of the messages they may be sending by their body language. In one research study, convicted muggers, who were interviewed separately, viewed videotapes of pedestrians in public places and were asked to identify the ones they would target as potential victims. The muggers, who become experts at nonverbal leakage, identified the same pedestrians as being most vulnerable. (Fatt, 1998)

OBJECTS, SIGNS, AND SYMBOLS

Objects, signs, and symbols are useful nonverbal communicators, especially in the presence of linguistic barriers in intercultural situations.

Objects that can provide useful nonverbal information include articles of clothing. In addition to the type of clothing, messages can be conveyed through accessories, such as sunglasses.

U.S. Marines, during the occupation of Iraq, were given important information about the symbolic meaning of their desert camouflage clothing: In some countries (Latin America, Africa, and the Middle East), the wearer might be perceived as being a member of an unpopular faction; thus, the attire can be unsafe. Marines were advised to wear dark-green uniforms instead. In addition, they were cautioned against wearing sunglasses because Iraqis prefer direct eye contact. Marines would be more successful in establishing rapport with the local people without their sunglasses. (Dresser, 2005)

Clothing can send positive or negative nonverbal messages. For example, casual attire may suggest to international visitors that they are not sufficiently important to warrant your wearing professional attire. In some cultures, dressing casually during business encounters with international visitors may convey a lack of respect. Clothing is also associated with credibility; people who are dressed professionally have higher credibility than those who do not dress in a professional manner. In some cultures clothing reflects cultural values. In England, for example, dressing conservatively is associated with social status. Likewise, clothing is important to Arabs; to upper-class Arabs, dress is associated with social standing, self-respect, and wealth (Klopf & McCroskey, 2007; Martin & Chaney, 2012). An article of clothing that sends negative nonverbal messages in some cultures is a green hat, a fact a U.S. couple learned too late.

A U.S. couple who entertained some English-speaking Taiwanese business associates decided to make the social event a St. Patrick's Day celebration since the party was in March. In addition to serving green beer and corned beef and cabbage, the hosts had shamrock decorations and wore green hats; they gave their guests green hats to wear as well. The guests were able to hide their discomfort over wearing green hats, and the hosts did not learn until a year later—after the Taiwanese associates became better acquainted with their hosts—that green hats are associated with infidelity for many Chinese people. (Dresser, 2005)

In addition to clothing, nonverbal messages are sent by such impersonal objects as office furnishings. To imply that a business has international interests or contacts, a firm may display in the lobby framed pictures of the world or several clocks, each labeled with the name of a different city of the world, such as London, Delhi, and Tokyo. Other objects that may have a positive impact on wealthy international clients are displays of antiques, works of art, and wall hangings of substantial monetary value (Chaney, 2004; Martin & Chaney, 2012).

Signs and symbols are especially helpful to travelers who do not know the country's language. Signs, which are typically simpler than symbols, may include arrows to point direction, running figures to indicate exits, and circles containing diagonal lines across pictures/figures to convey negation. Symbols may be based on likeness, such as a picture of a cup and saucer for a coffee shop. Symbols may also be arbitrary, such as the color red to symbolize Christian charity (Jandt, 2010). Signs containing symbols help those who travel by automobile. Signs with a symbol of a knife and fork, for example, inform travelers where to exit for a restaurant; other signs containing a company's advertising logo, such as McDonald's golden arches and Shell's yellow silhouette sea shell with a heavy red border, are easily recognized and provide information about services that are available at upcoming exits. Examples of other road signs that alert drivers to information they need to know without words include a yellow sign with a picture of an alligator in the center, which warns Florida travelers about the possibility of their encountering an alligator on the road. Other countries use similar signs. In Europe, a red triangle with the picture of a turtle inside warns drivers that they may encounter turtles crossing the road. Signs made up of symbols are also found in airports around the world to assist travelers in locating various services, such as the baggage claim area (suitcase), toilets (man/woman), and ground transportation (bus/taxi). Additional signs that are universally recognized include a circle with a diagonal line through a picture of a burning cigarette, which means "No smoking," and a sign containing a picture of a person walking with a diagonal line through it, which means "Do not walk."

Some symbols are easily recognized and interpreted, while others are recognized primarily by a subgroup within the macroculture, as the following incident illustrates.

A high school teacher who observed a student's necklace featuring a comedy/tragedy dual mask commented: "Oh, I see you are a thespian." The student became very upset and even threatened the teacher. The teacher did not know that the theater symbol was also a gang symbol that means, "First you laugh, and then you cry." Another reason the student—who did not know the meaning of *thespian*—was irate was that she thought the teacher was making a comment about her sexual orientation. (Dresser, 2005)

A well-known symbol that is recognized not only by U.S. citizens but by visitors from other countries as well is the Statue of Liberty, located on Liberty Island in New York Harbor. This gift from France to celebrate the country's first 100 years as a nation is widely recognized as a symbol of freedom. Symbols of peace are also recognized around the world; however, the peace symbol may vary according to the country. For example, the traditional peace symbol to the Greek people is the olive branch; while in the Far East, the red crowned crane is a symbol of peace. The Italian symbol of peace is the peace flag, which features seven rainbow stripes with the word *Pace* ("Peace" in Italian) printed in the center. The peace sign, which is a broken upside-down cross, is now recognized as the symbol for peace around the world (Martin & Chaney, 2012).

Some symbols are not universally understood. In many countries, for example, a red cross on a white background symbolizes emergency medical assistance; this symbolic meaning can be traced back to 1863 when a red cross identified ambulances and medics in war zones. In some countries, however, the cross is considered a Christian symbol; thus, other symbols, including the red crescent, were used instead of a cross. Eventually, in 2006 the International Committee of the Red Cross officially recognized a third symbol, the red crystal (a red square resting on one corner), as a humanitarian symbol. Now, when medical personnel enter war zones, they must use one of these three symbols: red cross, red crescent, or red crystal (Jandt, 2010).

A symbol that has been devised in recent years is the widely recognized red AIDS ribbon to raise public awareness of the Acquired Immune Deficiency Syndrome (AIDS) epidemic. Other symbolic ribbons that are perhaps less widely recognized are the pink ribbon for breast cancer research and the lavender ribbon to raise awareness of abused women (Jandt, 2010).

Some symbols evoke an emotional response. The swastika symbol, for example, is associated with the Nazis in some countries, including the United States and Europe, and evokes a negative emotional response. Hindus, on the other hand, view the symbol in a positive manner; they have used it to signify peace for many years (Jandt, 2010; Ricks, 2006). Another symbol that often evokes an emotional response is a country's flag. The red, white, and blue U.S. flag, often called the Stars and Strips or Old Glory, is a symbol of patriotism. The historic significance of the flag's design is familiar to U.S. citizens: The 50 stars symbolize the country's 50 states; the 13 stripes represent the original 13 colonies. The flag is expected to be treated with great respect; special rules govern its use, handling, and disposal. Britain's widely recognized red, white, and blue flag, the Union Flag (popularly known as the Union Jack), is actually made up of three flags: St. George's Cross (England); St. Andrew's Cross (Scotland); and St. Patrick's Cross (Northern Ireland). More recently, the English flag (a red cross on a white background) has been displayed at numerous important events, perhaps to symbolize English nationalism now that Scotland and Wales have their own parliaments.

During groundbreaking ceremonies for a Japanese company's U.S. subsidiary, Kentucky's governor presented the visiting Japanese dignitaries with a flag of the Commonwealth of Kentucky. After opening the flag, the Japanese executives, who were unaware of U.S. customs concerning flags, dragged it on the ground. Many U.S. audience members were offended at such disrespect for the state flag. What they did not know is that the Japanese do not treat flags with the respect they are shown in the United States and that they meant no disrespect. (Ricks, 2006)

Burning a country's flag is widely recognized as a symbol of protest against the country and its citizens. However, one U.S. patriot had this to say about burning her country's flag: "Some people say you should never burn the flag. But you won't destroy my ideas about America by setting the flag on fire. The American flag is not a weapon; the American flag is a promise" (Schultz, 2011, p. 15).

In intercultural situations, objects, signs, and symbols are important sources of nonverbal communication that cross language barriers and make international travels easier. Travelers depend upon these nonverbal communicators to navigate their way through international airports, along highways in other countries, and during visits to destination locations.

A summary of guidelines related to various aspects of nonverbal communication for the 10 countries with which the United States conducts much of its international business follows.

Brazil

While punctuality is typically important in the workplace, starting meetings a little late is not uncommon in larger cities because of heavy traffic. In social situations, hosts expect their guests to arrive about 15 minutes later than the time indicated on the invitation. Standing close during conversations is the norm; Brazilians also touch each other while conversing. Touch is inappropriate, however, between strangers or between those of unequal status or ages. Brazilians maintain eye contact during conversations; however, they will lower their gaze when interacting with someone they perceive to be their superiors to show respect. Silence is uncommon when Brazilians converse; they often interrupt and are enthusiastic conversationalists. They use their hands during conversations. Gesturing is common. Some gestures, however, are rude and/or vulgar and should be avoided; these include the "OK" sign, holding up the middle finger, and hitting a clenched fist with an open palm.

Canada

Punctuality is equally important to Canadians and to people of the United States. Being on time for business functions is expected; being 15 minutes late for evening social occasions is permitted. People stand farther apart in Canada than do persons of Latin America or the Far East. The standard space between people who are conversing is about 4 feet or 1.2 meters; however, French Canadians often stand closer. Little touching is seen except between relatives and good friends. However, French Canadians commonly touch while conversing. Eye contact is important when conversing with someone and during greetings. Eye contact conveys sincerity and helps establish credibility. Gestures are similar to those used in the United States. Because some gestures may offend people of a certain cultural group, gesturing should be kept to a minimum. Pointing with the index finger is considered rude; the entire hand should be used to motion to someone. Beckoning is done with the fingers pointing up and motioning toward one's body with the palm inward. The U.S. "thumbs-down" gesture used to indicate "no" or that something is bad is offensive in Quebec, as is slapping an open hand over a closed fist. Appropriate seated posture for men includes legs crossed at the ankles or at the knees or one ankle crossed on the other knee; appropriate seated posture for women is crossing legs at the ankle. Avoid sitting with legs apart; do not place your feet on furniture (Axtell, 1998; Martin & Chaney, 2012, 2009).

China

Punctuality is important to the Chinese. When invited to dinner or when attending a business meeting, arriving early is recommended to show respect. Touching is not common among the Chinese. They do not usually hug or kiss each other when greeting. Smiling when being introduced is not customary. Touch is generally limited to shaking hands. Public displays of affection, even between people who are married, are not acceptable. Silence is valued; it is associated with politeness. Avoid interrupting others during conversations. The Chinese tend to stand closer together than do U.S. Americans. Direct eye contact is limited, and staring is uncommon. Gesturing is somewhat limited in China. Using the open hand rather than one finger to point is important. Although many U.S. gestures are familiar to the Chinese, the "OK" sign is not widely understood. Using good posture is important to the Chinese; feet should remain on the floor and should not be placed on chairs or desks (Axtell, 1998; Martin & Chaney, 2009; Turkington, 1999).

Germany

Being on time for all business and social engagements is perhaps more important in Germany than in any other country in the world. Being only two to three minutes late is insulting to German managers; an explanatory call is expected if you are delayed. Eye contact is expected during conversations; it shows sincerity. Avoiding eye contact suggests that you are not trustworthy. Respect the space needs of Germans; the German sense of territoriality is evidenced by their keeping their office doors closed. Gestures/behaviors considered inappropriate in Germany include talking with your hands in your pockets and chewing gum in public. Pointing the index finger to the temple and making a twisting motion is an insult to another person; the meaning is "you are crazy." Rather than crossing the fingers to wish a person good luck, Germans make a fist, folding the thumb in and pounding lightly on a surface. The gesture for waving good-bye is extending the hand upward, palm out, and waving the fingers up and down rather than side to side, which means "no." When trying to get someone's attention, such as a waiter, raise the hand, palm out, with only the index finger extended; do not wave. People of Germany avoid public displays of affection and do not typically touch each other. In addition, Germans do not want anyone to touch their cars. Posture is important; people should cross their legs with one knee over the other; feet should not be placed on furniture (Axtell, 1998; Martin & Chaney, 2009).

Japan

Punctuality is valued. Being late to a business meeting is considered rude, but being late for social occasions is acceptable. Because the Japanese are a "do not touch" culture, avoid standing close, patting a person on the back, or any prolonged physical contact. Prolonged eye contact should also be avoided; indirect eye contact is used to show respect. The U.S. "OK" gesture may signify "money" in Japan. The gesture for beckoning someone is placing an arm out, palm down, and making a scratching motion with the fingers. Chewing gum or yawning in public is impolite; standing with your hands in your pockets is inappropriate. Also avoid shouting or raising your voice in anger; the Japanese are a polite, gracious people and show great restraint. The correct seated posture includes having both feet on the floor and arms placed on chair armrests or in the lap. Slouching, leaning back in a tilted chair, or placing your feet on a table are inappropriate. Crossing the legs at the knees or ankles is acceptable; placing an ankle over a knee, however, is improper (Axtell, 1998; Martin & Chaney, 2009; Sabath, 2002).

Mexico

Punctuality is not highly regarded in Mexico; 30 minutes past the scheduled meeting time is considered punctual by Mexican standards. Foreigners, however, are expected to be on time for business meetings. For social engagements, being 30 minutes to an hour later than the time stated on the invitation is expected. Time may be stated as *la hora Americana*, meaning that punctuality is expected; *la hora Mexicana* implies a more relaxed time frame. People of

Mexico usually stand close together while conversing and sometimes touch the other person's clothing, shoulders, or arm. Avoid the temptation to step back; this indicates that you are unfriendly. Increased touching should be viewed positively as it usually indicates the development of a good relationship. Hand and arm gestures are often used during a conversation. Most people of Mexico are familiar with U.S. gestures; however, the "V"-for-victory sign, when made with the nose in the wedge of the "V" and mouth covered with the palm, is a very rude gesture. The U.S. gesture for "thumbs down" is vulgar in Mexico; the "thumbs-up" gesture means approval. Waving the hand from side to side with the index finger pointed up and palm facing forward means "no." Avoid standing with your hands on your hips as this implies that you are angry. Standing with your hands in your pockets is considered rude and often suggests anger (Axtell, 1998).

The Netherlands

Punctuality is very important to the Dutch; they expect punctuality at meetings and appointments. You are expected to call ahead with an explanation if you must be late. The Dutch are somewhat reserved and do not use nonverbal communication to the extent that many other European countries use it. They prefer direct eye contact and a distance of about an arm's length during conversations. They do not pat each other on the back or hug or touch each other in public, unless they are relatives or close friends. Chewing gum in public and standing with hands in pockets is considered rude. Interpreting gestures used by the Dutch should be done cautiously because some of their gestures may have a different meaning to people in other countries. For example, using the index finger to make a circular motion near the ear is a signal that the person is crazy in many countries; however, the Dutch use it to signal that a person has a telephone call. Their gesture to signal that someone is crazy is tapping the middle of the forehead (Axtell, 1998; Martin & Chaney, 2009; Sabath, 1999).

Singapore

Punctuality is expected for both business and social events in Singapore; being kept waiting is viewed as an insult. Touching or patting another person is to be avoided as it is demeaning. Constant eye contact is inappropriate; breaking eye contact during introductions and conversations is recommended. A smile does not always convey happiness; it may mean embarrassment or unhappiness. Gestures to avoid include touching a person's head, standing with hands on hips, and hitting the palm of the hand with the fist. Pointing should be done with the hand open, not with the index finger. Avoid sitting so that the bottom of the foot points at another person. Avoid the "okay" sign as it is viewed as rude. One gesture may be confusing to Westerners: the side-to-side head toss; it signals agreement rather than disagreement.

South Korea

Although punctuality is important in South Korea, top-level executives may occasionally be a little late for meetings or appointments. Western businesspersons, however, are expected to be on time. Direct eye contact is appreciated, but touching on the arm or back is not. In public, people may stand close together while shopping or while riding on buses because of space limitations. Using correct posture when seated is important. Although it is preferable to sit with legs uncrossed, it is acceptable to cross the legs at the knees. Putting your feet on a chair or table is considered rude. Visitors should remember that South Koreans may laugh when embarrassed or when they are frustrated as well as when something is funny; they also cover the mouth when laughing. Avoid speaking or laughing loudly. Using the index finger to beckon someone is impolite. Passing objects with the right hand or with both hands is customary (Axtell, 1998; Martin & Chaney, 2012; Sabath, 2002).

United Kingdom (England, Scotland, Wales, and Northern Ireland)

Being punctual is very important to the people of the United Kingdom. Because the British are polite and reserved, they respect another's personal space and do not like someone to get too close when conversing. The British do not always look at the person with whom they are conversing. Touching is avoided; do not put your arm around a colleague's shoulder or slap him or her on the back. Avoid excessive enthusiasm; the British do not typically display emotions. Many of the gestures used in the United States and Canada are recognized and used in the United Kingdom; however, the "V"-for-victory sign (usually with the palm out) is rude and offensive when used with the palm inward. The accepted seated posture for men is crossing the legs at the knees rather than placing one ankle across the other knee; for women, crossing the legs at the ankle is the accepted seated posture (Axtell, 1998; Martin & Chaney, 2012, 2009).

United States

Punctuality is very important to people of the United States. Being late for business or social appointments is extremely rude; the messages conveyed for arriving late range from lack of respect for the person or occasion to poor organizational skills. Space is an important consideration in the United States; people prefer a distance of about an arm's length when interacting. Little touching is considered the norm. In business situations, acceptable touching is usually limited to the handshake. In social situations, people may be seen hugging during greetings; however, this type of touching is not typical of people of the U.S. macroculture. Direct eye contact is important in the United States during both business and social encounters. Avoiding eye contact sends negative messages, including lack of respect, inattentiveness, or disinterest. Smiling while making eye contact is common, including smiling at complete strangers. Moderate gesturing is the norm for people of the United States. Some typical gestures include the thumbs-up sign or "OK" signal to indicate that everything is great, the "V" sign to mean victory, and the thumbs-down gesture to indicate disapproval. Gestures to avoid because of their negative connotations include using a single finger to point at someone, holding up the middle finger by itself, and using the forearm jerk. The posture of people of the United States is rather casual; their seated posture is relaxed. They typically cross their legs; women cross at the ankle, while men cross their legs with the ankle on the knee.

Terms

Chromatics	Monochronic time	Paralanguage
Chronemics	(M-time)	Personal zone
Deductive method	Nonverbal	Polychronic time
Haptics	communication	(P-time)
Inductive method	Nonverbal leakage	Proxemics
Intimate zone	Oculesics	Public distance
Kinesics	Olfactics	Social zone

Exercise 1

Instructions: Circle T if the statement is true or F if false.

1. T F Asians typically use the deductive method of reasoning to solve problems.
2. T F People in the United States speak faster than Italians and Arabs.
3. T F Latin Americans need more space than people of the United States.
4. T F Punctuality is not widely regarded in Algeria.
5. T F Private offices are generally reserved for top-level executives in all cultures.
6. T F When conversing with the Japanese, it is best to keep steady eye contact throughout the dialogue.
7. T F People of all cultures respond negatively to body and breath odor.
8. T F More bodily contact occurs between Western men than between Arab men.
9. T F Touching the head of a Thai is forbidden.
10. T F Smiling is interpreted as happiness in all cultures.

Exercise 2

Instructions: Match the following terms with their definition.

_____ 1. Space
_____ 2. Body language
_____ 3. Smell
_____ 4. Gaze/eye contact
_____ 5. Symbols, illustrators, regulators, or affect displays
_____ 6. Goes from facts to generalizations
_____ 7. Time
_____ 8. Color
_____ 9. Volume, pitch, and rate that affects message meaning
_____ 10. Touch

A. Chromatics
B. Chronemics
C. Deductive approach
D. Gestures
E. Haptics
F. Inductive approach
G. Kinesics
H. Oculesics
I. Olfactics
J. Paralanguage
K. Proxemics

Questions and Cases for Discussion

1. Explain how thought patterns and problem solving differ in the United States and other cultures.
2. Discuss differences in paralanguage of people in various cultures.
3. Explain how attitudes toward time vary from culture to culture.
4. Discuss differences in space needs of persons in the United States, Japan, Greece, and Latin America.
5. Identify cultures that favor direct eye contact and those that avoid eye contact.
6. Give examples to show how olfactics is an important aspect of intercultural nonverbal communication.
7. Identify cultures that are comfortable with bodily contact and those that avoid bodily contact. Give examples of appropriate and inappropriate bodily contact in the United States.
8. Discuss cultural differences in body language of people in the United States, Japan, China, Italy, Greece, and Latin America.
9. Explain how the use of color communicates nonverbal messages.
10. Identify cultures that are comfortable with silence and those that are not. Discuss possible meanings of silence in various situations.

CASES

The following procedure is recommended for analyzing the cases: (a) read the case carefully paying attention to details; (b) read the questions at the end of the case; (c) reread the case, taking notes on or highlighting the details needed for answering the questions; (d) identify relevant facts, underlying assumptions, and critical issues of the case; (e) list possible answers to the questions; and (f) select the most logical response to the question. Your professor may ask that you submit answers to the case questions in writing.

Case 1

Barbara works for a subsidiary of a German corporation in the United States. Her job involves ordering products from Germany and following-up on the status of deliveries. Barbara does not speak, read, or write German; however, this is not a problem, as Barbara's contact Anna speaks, reads, and writes English. Normally all of Barbara's e-mails, letters, and faxes from Anna are written in English. Lately, the German factory has been having difficulty, and Barbara has been sending e-mails to Anna with inquiries about the product delays. In her last e-mail, Barbara asks why the Germans cannot get their materials shipped on time. The answer to Barbara's question comes back in German. Discuss what nonverbal communication was being conveyed in the situation and how you would change the behavior to be more positive.

Case 2

A U.S. company has sent a representative to negotiate a contract with a Japanese firm. The U.S. representative arrives at the appointed time for his meeting and is shown to the meeting room, where six representatives from the Japanese firm meet with him. During his presentation, the Japanese move their heads in an up-and-down motion; however, they say very little. The presentation was given in English, as the representative had been

told the Japanese understood English. When the representative asked if there were any questions, everyone nodded politely; however, no one said a word. After a few minutes, the representative asked if they were ready to sign the contracts. One of the Japanese said, "It is very difficult for us to sign." At this point the representative said, "Should I leave the contract with you?" The Japanese said, "Yes." The U.S. representative returned to the United States expecting the Japanese to return the contract, which did not happen. Explain what the Japanese were really saying by nodding their heads and using the word "difficult."

Case 3

On his first trip to Mexico, Harry, a U.S. manager interested in negotiating a contract for his firm with a Mexican firm, was invited to a dinner party by his Mexican counterpart. The invitation indicated that cocktails would begin at 7 P.M., so Harry arrived promptly at that time. His host seemed surprised, and no one else had arrived. People began arriving about 8 P.M.; Harry knew he had read the invitation correctly but felt he had gotten off to a bad start. What advice would you have given Harry?

Case 4

Fred, the manager of a large U.S. bookstore, hired Ching Wu, a newcomer from China, as one of his clerks. In an attempt to get to know Ching Wu better, Fred invited her to join him for coffee. Throughout their conversation, he noticed that Ching Wu always looked down at the floor and never gave him eye contact. He interpreted this as a lack of respect. Discuss the nonverbal communication differences in this situation.

Case 5

A Canadian professor accepted a two-year teaching assignment at a South American university. Despite the professor's guidelines for appropriate classroom conduct that had been conveyed at the first class meeting, students continued to come to class 20–30 minutes late. In addition, instead of quietly taking a seat, they came to the front of the class and apologized to the professor and to the other students for the tardiness. Often the reasons they gave for arriving late were related to family problems. Explain the cultural differences involved in this situation.

Activities

1. Write a paragraph describing an incident from your own experience involving oral and/or nonverbal miscommunication with someone from another culture. Suggest a plausible explanation for the miscommunication.

2. Prepare a short skit to illustrate nonverbal communication blunders that a person from the United States might make in a country of your choice.

3. Demonstrate a gesture (such as the "thumbs-up" or the U.S. "OK" sign) and ask class members to explain its meaning in a specific country.

4. Demonstrate the amount of space considered acceptable when interacting with persons in Latin America, the United States, and Egypt.

5. Demonstrate the amount of eye contact considered appropriate in the United States, Japan, and the Middle East.

6. Access online (www.aiga.org/symbol-signs/) the 50 copyright-free international symbols developed by AIGA (the Professional Association for Design) to guide travelers through worldwide transportation facilities. Suggest possible changes/improvements to these symbols or additions to this list based on your own travel experiences.

References

Axtell, R. E. (1998). *Gestures*. New York: John Wiley & Sons, Inc.

Borden, G. A. (1991). *Cultural orientation: An approach to understanding intercultural communication*. Upper Saddle River, NJ: Prentice Hall.

Bosrock, M. M. (1997). *Put your best foot forward: South America*. St. Paul, MN: International Educational Systems.

Chaney, L. H. (2004, August/September). Curb appeal. *OfficePRO, 66*(6), 28–29.

Chaney, L. H., & Lyden, J. A. (1996, April). Impression management: The office environment. *Supervision, 57*(4), 3–5.

Devine, E., & Braganti, N. L. (1991). *The traveler's guide to Middle Eastern and North African customs and manners*. New York: St. Martin's Press.

Dresser, N. (2005). *Multicultural manners: Essential rules of etiquette for the 21st century*. Hoboken, NJ: John Wiley & Sons.

Engholm, C. (1991). *When business east meets business west*. New York: John Wiley & Sons, Inc.

Engholm, C., & Rowland, D. (1996). *International excellence*. New York: Kodansha International.

Fast, J. (1991). *Body language in the workplace*. New York: Penguin.

Fatt, J. P. T. (1998). Nonverbal communication and business success. *Management Research News, 21*(1), 4–5.

Gudykunst, W. B., & Ting-Toomey, S. (1988). *Culture and interpersonal communication*. Newbury Park, CA: Sage.

Hall, E. T., & Hall, M. R. (1990). *Understanding cultural differences: Germans, French, and Americans*. Yarmouth, ME: Intercultural Press.

Jandt, F. E. (2010). *An introduction to intercultural communication: Identities in a global community* (6th ed.). Thousand Oaks, CA: Sage Publications.

Klopf, D. W., & McCroskey, J. C. (2007). *Intercultural communication encounters*. Boston, MA: Pearson Education.

Lewis, R. D. (2006). *When cultures collide: Leading across cultures* (3rd ed.). Boston, MA: Nicholas Brealey International.

Madden, T. J., Hewett, K., & Roth, M. S. (2000). Managing images in different cultures: A cross-national study of color meanings and preferences. *Journal of International Marketing, 8*(4), 90–107.

Martin, J. S., & Chaney, L. H. (2009). *Passport to success: The essential guide to business culture and customs in America's largest trading partners.* Westport, CT: Praeger.

Martin, J. S., & Chaney, L. H. (2012). *Global business etiquette: A guide to international communication and customs* (2nd ed.). Westport, CT: Praeger.

Morrison, T., & Conaway, W. A. (2006). *Kiss, bow, or shake hands* (2nd ed.). Holbrook, MA: Bob Adams.

Ricks, D. A. (2006). *Blunders in international business* (4th ed.). Malden, MA: Blackwell.

Sabath, A. M. (1999). *International business etiquette: Europe.* Franklin Lakes, NJ: Career Press.

Sabath, A. M. (2002). *International business etiquette: Asia and the Pacific Rim.* New York: ASJA Press.

Samovar, L. A., Porter, R. E., & McDaniel, E. R. (2009). *Communication between cultures* (7th ed.). Belmont, CA: Thomson Learning.

Schultz, D. (2011, July 3). A grand old flag. *Parade*, pp. 14–15.

Scott, J. C. (2002, October). The colorful world of international business. *Business Education Forum, 57*(1), 40–43.

Turkington, C. (1999). *The complete idiot's guide to cultural etiquette.* Indianapolis, IN: Alpha Books.

Glossary

Chromatics is the use of color to communicate nonverbally.

Chronemics is the use of time to communicate nonverbally.

Deductive method refers to problem solving that goes from broad categories or observations to specific examples to determine the facts and then the solution to the problem.

Haptics is the use of touch to communicate nonverbally.

Inductive method is problem solving that starts with facts or observations and goes to generalizations.

Intimate zone is the physical distance between people in the United States, less than 18 inches; reserved for close friends.

Kinesics refers to various types of body language, including facial expressions, gestures, posture and stance, and other mannerisms used to communicate or that accompany verbal messages.

Monochronic time (M-time) is a system of time that allows for performing only one major activity at a time.

Nonverbal communication includes nonword messages, such as gestures, facial expressions, interpersonal distance, touch, eye contact, smell, and silence.

Nonverbal leakage occurs when people try unsuccessfully to control messages sent through various forms of nonverbal communication.

Oculesics refers to the use of eye contact as a way of communicating nonverbally.

Olfactics refers to the use of smell to communicate nonverbally.

Paralanguage refers to the linguistic elements of speech, such as pitch, loudness, quality, rate, or dialect, that interrupt or temporarily take the place of speech and affect the meaning of a message.

Personal zone refers to the physical distance between people; in the United States, from 18 inches to 4 feet; used for giving instructions to others or working closely with another person.

Polychronic time (P-time) is a system of time that allows for performing several activities simultaneously.

Proxemics refers to communicating through the use of space.

Public distance in the United States is the physical distance between people of about 12–25 feet.

Social zone in the United States refers to physical distance of 4–12 feet between people; used for business situations in which people interact in a more formal, impersonal way.

Answers to Exercises

Matching

1. K
2. G
3. I
4. H
5. D
6. F
7. B
8. A
9. J
10. E

True/False

1. F
2. F
3. F
4. T
5. F
6. F
7. F
8. F
9. T
10. F

Written Communication Patterns

From Chapter 7 of *Intercultural Business Communication*, Sixth Edition. Lillian H. Chaney, Jeanette S. Martin.

Written Communication
Patterns

Objectives

Upon completion of this chapter, you will

- know the guidelines for writing international messages in English.
- be familiar with letter formats commonly used by U.S. business firms and how they differ from formats used in other countries.
- understand how facsimiles are commonly used for communicating between U.S. firms and those in other countries.
- understand how writing tone and style vary from culture to culture.
- understand cultural differences in other types of written communication such as the résumé and related job-search documents.

Many U.S. companies correspond with foreign corporations; it is important, therefore, to be aware of differences in the format, tone, and style of written communication. Research results show that 97% of outgoing international correspondence is sent in English, with about 1% each in Spanish, French, and German. Percentages for incoming international messages are similar: 96% are in English with the remaining 4% divided between French, German, and Spanish (Green & Scott, 1992). Because English is used for most international written messages, making these messages as clear as possible is important. Understanding the business communication practices of the culture you are writing to will help you to communicate effectively.

INTERNATIONAL ENGLISH

International English is English for businesspeople who deal with cultures whose native language is not English or for whom English may be a second language; it is limited to the 3,000–4,000 most common English words. An excellent reference is Collin, Lowi, and Weiland's

Beginner's Dictionary of American English Usage (2002). In order to use international English, three cultural factors are important: an understanding of business communication in the other culture, an idea of how business communication is taught in the other culture, and a knowledge that content errors are more difficult than language errors for people in another culture to discern.

Content errors are **lexical errors** and refer to errors in meaning. **Syntactic errors** are errors in the order of the words in a sentence. A native speaker of a language will discover the syntactic errors in a sentence much easier than the lexical errors.

EXAMPLES OF LEXICAL ERRORS

We baste (based) this opinion on our many years of experience.

Thank you for your patients (patience).

The device omits (emits) a high-pitched signal when it is receiving.

We realize that your office will be closed on this wholey (holy) day.

It is there (their) material.

We except (accept) your invitation to dinner.

Business communication is not necessarily taught in other countries as it is in the United States. The course may not contain any information on the theory of communication and what happens between the sender and receiver. Many of the business communication courses being taught in a country that desires to do more business with the United States are simply translation courses.

Guidelines for "internationalizing" the English language have been developed to enable both native and nonnative speakers of the language to write messages clearly to decrease the possibility of misunderstanding between people of different cultures. The following guidelines were adapted from those developed by Weiss (2005) and Riddle and Lanham (1984–1985); they are important for situations in which both cultures speak English as well as for situations in which English may be a second language for one or both of the communicators:

- Use the 3,000–4,000 most common English words. Uncommon words such as "onus" for "burden" and "flux" for "continual change" should be avoided.
- Choose words that have only one meaning. The word "high" has 20 meanings; the word "expensive" has 1. When it is necessary to use words with multiple meanings, use only the most common meaning.
- Select action-specific verbs and words with few or similar alternate meanings. Use "cook breakfast" rather than "make breakfast"; use "take a taxi" rather than "get a taxi."
- Avoid redundancies (interoffice memorandum), sports terms (ballpark figure), and words that draw mental pictures (red tape); also avoid what Winston Churchill called "adverbial dressing gowns" (thoroughly understand or utterly reject—just use "understand" and "reject").
- Avoid using verbs containing two or more words (take offense at); also avoid making verbs out of nouns (impacting the economy and faxing a message) and nominalizations or "smothered verbs" (have knowledge of).
- Avoid wordy expressions for time, such as interval of time (interval) and three weeks' duration (three weeks).

- Be aware of words with a unique meaning in some cultures; the word "check" outside the United States generally means a financial instrument and is often spelled *chéque*.
- Be aware of alternate spellings in countries that use the same language, such as theatre/theater, organisation/organization, colour/color, and judgement/judgment.
- Avoid creating or using new words; avoid slang.
- Use the formal tone and correct punctuation to ensure clarity; avoid the use of first names in letter salutations. If you know the other country's salutation and closing, use them. End with a closing sentence that is thoughtful.
- Conform to rules of grammar; be particularly careful of misplaced modifiers, dangling participles, and incomplete sentences.
- Use more short, simple sentences than you would ordinarily use; avoid compound and compound-complex sentences.
- Clarify the meaning of words that have more than one meaning.
- Adapt the tone of the letter to the reader if the cultural background of the reader is known, for example, use unconditional apologies if that is expected in the reader's culture.
- Try to capture the flavor of the language when writing to someone whose cultural background you know. Letters to people whose native language is Spanish, for example, would contain more flowery language (full of highly ornate language) and would be longer than U.S. letters.
- Avoid acronyms (ASAP, RSVP), **emoticons** (:-o), and shorthand (U for "you" and 4 representing "for") in writing letters, faxes, or e-mail messages.
- If photocopies to other members of the organization are appropriate, be sure to send them a copy or ask who should receive copies.
- Remember that numbers are written differently in some countries; for example, 7,000 may be written 7.000 or 7000. In addition, money designations are also often written differently.

THE IMPORTANCE OF GRAMMAR

The Associated Press, London, June 19, 1999—A comma in the wrong place of a sales contract cost Lockheed Martin $70 million, the *Financial Times* reported Friday. An international contract for the U.S.-based aerospace group's C-130J Hercules had the comma misplaced by one decimal point in the equation that adjusted the sales price for changes to the inflation rate, the London-based newspaper said. In Europe, commas are used instead of periods to mark decimal points. "It was a mistake," the newspaper quoted James A. "Micky" Blackwell, president of Lockheed's aeronautics division. But the customer, who Lockheed refused to name, held them to the price. "That comma cost Lockheed $70 million," said Blackwell.

WRITING TONE AND STYLE

The tone and writing style of correspondents from foreign countries are usually more formal and traditional than that typically used by U.S. companies. When the tone and style differ greatly from that used by the recipient, the intended positive message may be negatively received.

Authors of business communication textbooks in the United States recommend using the direct approach for beginning good news, direct request/inquiries, and neutral messages.

You should use the indirect approach for bad-news messages. The direct approach means that you begin with the good news or other pleasant ideas in the good-news message, begin with the request or inquiry in request/inquiry messages, and begin with the most important idea in neutral messages. When using the indirect approach, beginning with a buffer is recommended. A **buffer** is a paragraph that tells what the letter is about with a pleasant tone but says neither yes nor no.

Park, Dillon, and Mitchell (1998), in their research comparing U.S. and Korean business letters, concluded that both U.S. and Korean letters used direct and indirect request strategies. In both countries, the structure used for direct requests was "Please" plus the imperative (*Please let us know the shipment date*). The structure for indirect requests, however, differed. Korean letters seemed to prefer "wishful" requests (*We hope you will replace the damaged shipment*). U.S. letters avoid "wishful" requests; they call for a specific action (*Your replacing the damaged shipment will be appreciated*).

In the United States, we also teach using a "you approach" or "reader orientation"; however, in a collectivistic country, you should use an inclusive approach such as "we" or "our" to avoid making the reader lose face or be singled out. In a collectivistic culture, it is improper for one person to be addressed because the whole team is responsible for the outcome.

Women writing to men internationally must be very careful about the tone and word choice. Women have to make an exceptionally good impression if they are to be taken seriously. Flattering statements when written to a man must be carefully worded so they cannot be interpreted as flirtatious. Compliments should be given from the company or the department rather than from the woman directly. Many countries do not consider women as serious businesspeople and would regard a woman as too assertive if she used firm and direct words. Direct words such as "expect" or "require" should be softened to "would appreciate" (DeVries, 1994).

Although Germans use the buffer occasionally, they are usually more direct with negative news. Latin Americans do not use buffers; they avoid the negative news completely, feeling it is discourteous to bring bad news. This practice of omitting buffers was confirmed in research of communication in Latin America conducted by Conaway and Wardrope (2004). Thus, U.S. Americans must be able to read between the lines of letters from Latin American businesspeople. The Japanese begin letters on a warm, personal note, which is an inappropriate way of beginning a U.S. letter. The Japanese try to present negative news in a positive manner, a quality that has sometimes caused a U.S. counterpart to feel that the person was deceitful. In research conducted by Azuma (1998) to determine Japanese strategies for writing negative messages compared to U.S. strategies, findings revealed that the three areas present in Japanese letters but absent in U.S. letters were comments about the weather or seasons, congratulations to the recipient on his or her prosperity or success, and requests for forgiveness or understanding.

> The Japanese begin a letter, regardless of the type of news, with a statement about the season: "It is spring, and the cherry blossoms smile to the blue sky."
>
> Islamic people use the phrase, "God willing" (*Inshallah* in Arabic).

A way to show respect is to include common phrases of the country that help make the recipient feel comfortable. Most nations consider politeness to be a very important quality in business encounters. A compliment showing knowledge of the cultural heritage of the country is also appreciated.

U.S. businesspeople tend to be very direct in discussing business and do not want to waste anyone's time. However, showing politeness and a little small talk is considered the proper way of doing business in most countries in the world.

Also, what U.S. persons view as a request can appear to be boasting, obnoxious, or arrogant in another culture because of the way the request is phrased.

In the United States, ending negative messages on a positive note is important, although the French do not consider this important. Beginnings and endings of French business letters are very formal, but endings tend to be somewhat flowery: "Sir, please accept the expression of my best feelings." The French organize some types of business letters differently. They recommend apologizing for mistakes and expressing regret for any inconvenience caused. U.S. business letter writers, on the other hand, avoid apologies and simply state objectively the reason for the action taken. Endings of German letters tend to be formal (Kilpatrick, 1984; Varner, 1987, 1988).

An awareness of the differences between the format, tone, and style of written communication can go far in building goodwill between cultures. If you receive a letter in which you are addressed "Dear Prof. Dr. Judith C. Simon," you need to be able to read past the unimportant style or tone differences and look for the meaning in the letter. The overuse of politeness is very common for many cultures and should not distract U.S. readers. However, as a writer, keep these cultural differences in mind to avoid sounding harsh and insensitive to the reader.

British writers assume less shared knowledge than Finnish writers (Lampi, 1992). Politeness strategies differ when a group of Dutch businesspeople use their native language or use English. The type and frequency of the use of politeness change when a second language is used. (Geluyckens & van Rillaer, 1996)

U.S. letters tend to be shorter than letters written in other cultures. As a sign of friendship, U.S. businesspeople should change the tone of their letters when writing to businesspeople in another culture. The **parochialism** or ethnocentrism that so many U.S. people display in their writing to other cultures can easily be tempered with knowledge of the person to whom they are writing.

LETTER FORMATS

Letter formats used by other countries often differ from styles used by U.S. businesses. Some countries, such as France, still use the indented letter style with closed punctuation. Latin American countries prefer the modified block format, which features the date and closing lines beginning at the center and paragraphs beginning at the left margin (Conaway & Wardrope, 2004). The preferred styles in the United States are the block (all lines beginning at the left margin) and modified block (date and closing beginning at the center and paragraphs blocked). Writing styles use either standard punctuation (colon after the salutation and comma after the closing) or open punctuation (no punctuation after either the salutation or the closing).

The French tend to use the indented style for business letters. The French place the name of the originating city before the date (*Norvége, le* 15 *décembre* 2——). (Use the overstrike function, symbol function, or multinational insert function of your word processing software to type special marks used in other languages.)

The format of the inside address may vary. In the United States, the title and full name are placed on the first line; street number and name on the second line; and city, state, and ZIP code on the last line. The format used in Germany puts the title (*Herr, Frau, or Fräulein*) on the first line, full name on the second line, street name followed by the street number on the third line, and ZIP code, city, and state on the last line. Spanish-language writers also place the recipient's title (*señor, señora, señorita*) on the first line above the person's name (Conaway & Wardrope, 2004). The street number also follows the name of the street in Mexico and South America.

Although U.S. letters always place the date before the inside address, the French sometimes place the date after the inside address. In their letters, the inside address is typed on the right side with the ZIP code preceding the name of the city (74010 PARIS); in U.S. letters, the inside address is on the left. The punctuation style used in French letters differs from that used in U.S. correspondence; the salutation is followed by a comma rather than a colon or no punctuation, which is used in standard and open punctuation styles of U.S. letters. The complimentary close is rather formal in French business letters; the writer's title precedes the writer's name. Care should be taken to format the inside address and the envelope address exactly as it is shown on the incoming correspondence.

Guidelines for addressing the envelope if you do not have an address to copy are as follows:

Mr./Mrs./Ms./or appropriate title plus first, then last name
Street number followed by street name
ZIP code information placed sometimes before and sometimes after the city

The country name typed in full capital letters (whether the country and city are at the beginning or at the end of the address determined by the collectivistic or individualistic nature of the society)

Examples:

Herr Hans-Dieter Duden	JAPAN, Tokyo	Mr. John R. Smith
Bosch Gmbh	Hachioji-shi	2350 Walnut Grove
1600 Bretton Due	47–25 Nanyodai	Memphis, TN 38152
GERMANY	Nakamura Yoko	USA

Dates are written differently also. Although people in the United States would use "January 5, 2——," in many other countries, the date would be written as "5th of January 2——" or "5 January 2——." Numerals should not be used for both the month and the day as it is difficult to know which numeral is the day and which number is the month.

U.S. business letters are single spaced, but in many other countries, they may be either single spaced or double spaced. In U.S. letters, the name of the writer is typed four lines below the complimentary close with the title placed on the next line. In German letters, the company name is placed below the complimentary close; the writer signs the letter, but the writer's name and position are not typed in the signature block. In Japan and China, the surname is always placed before the given name (such as Smith Jack rather than Jack Smith).

> Depending on how international the Japanese, Chinese, or Far Eastern businessperson is, he or she may switch the names to make you comfortable.
>   Example: Wu Chei will change his name to Chei Wu (surname last) to please you.

Salutations and closings are more formal in many other countries. Salutations for German letters are the English equivalent of Very Honored Mrs. Jones and in Latin American countries, My Esteemed Dr. Green. Complimentary closings are often the English equivalent of Very respectfully yours (Kilpatrick, 1984; Varner, 1987, 1988).

DIPLOMATIC TITLES

Written Forms of Address and Salutations

Title and Address Form	Salutation
AMBASSADOR	
His/Her Excellency (name)	Excellency: (or)
The Ambassador of (country)	Dear Mr./Madame Ambassador:
CHARGÉ D'AFFAIRES	
The Honorable (name)	Dear Sir/Madame:
Chargé d'Affaires of (country)	Minister:
The Honorable (name)	Dear Sir/Madame:
The Minister of (country)	Dear Mr./Madame Minister:
CONSUL GENERAL	
The Honorable (name)	Dear Mr./Ms. (name):
Consul General of (country)	
CONSUL	
The Honorable (name)	Dear Mr./Ms. (name):
Consul of (country)	

Source: Put your best foot forward: Europe (p. 54) by M. M. Bosrock, 1995, St. Paul, MN: International Education Systems.

Samples of Japanese, French, Spanish, and Chinese letters that have been translated into English from the native language are shown, respectively, in Figures 1 through 4. Samples of a British and a U.S. letter are shown, respectively, in Figures 5 and 6.

AZ409
April 7, 2 ---

Showa Machine Works Ltd.
Attention of Sales Department

5-1 Moriyama Maguro
Moriyamaku, Nagoya 463
Asumi Trading Co., Ltd.

President: Nobuaki Iwai

Allow us to open
with all reverence to you:

The season for cherry blossoms is here with us and everybody is beginning to feel refreshed. We sincerely congratulate you on becoming more prosperous in your business.

We have an inquiry from a foreign customer and shall be very happy to have your best price and technical literature for the item mentioned below:

Wire Drawing Machine
6 units for Taiwan

Specifications:

1. Finished sizes:	0.04 mm to 0.10 mm
2. Spooler:	Single
3. Speed:	Min. 1500 meters/min.
4. Type of spooler:	Expanding arbor
5. Capstan:	Must be covered with ceramic
6. Dimension of spool:	Flange diam. 215 mm
	Barrel diam. 163 mm
	Bore diam. 97 mm
	Traverse 200 mm

The above are all the information available for this inquiry. We ask you to recommend a machine that can meet these specifications.

We shall be very pleased if you will study the inquiry and let us have your reply as soon as possible. We solicit your favor.

Let us close with
great respect to you.

FIGURE 1 **Japanese Letter**

Marie Portafaix
7, Avenue Felix
75541 Paris

Mr. Pierre DESBORDE
Professor d'économie politique
IUT BB Commericial Techniques
Doyen Gosse Place
38000 GRENOBLE

MTP/GM/05.22

Paris, 25 September 2–––

Sir,

We are in receipt of your letter and have given our best attention to your request.

We are unhappy to inform you, we are not able to give your proposition a favorable report.

As a matter of fact we are grateful for the interest and your support, but we must consider essential publications hereafter for the media.

We want to renew our regrets and thank you for your belief. Sir, be assured our sentiments are the best.

Public Relations Director
Marie Thérése PORTAFAIX

FIGURE 2 French Letter

8 June 2–––

Zapatería Elegánte, S.A.
May 5 Avenue
Caracas, Venezuela

Esteemed clients and friends:

Permit us to communicate to you that the fabric of the shoes of Miss Modalo that were ordered has been discontinued. Therefore much to our regret we will not be able to serve you in this situation.

We always want to fill your catalog requests, and if you find another model from the enclosed catalog that you like we would be very glad to send them.

We regret your loss and hope to be able to serve you on another occasion as you deserve.

Very cordially yours,

CIA. LATINOAMERICANA, S.A.

José Mendoza Lopez General Manager

FAL/age

Enclosure: 1 catalog

FIGURE 3 Spanish Letter

The Japanese have a traditional format beginning with the salutation followed by a comment about the season or weather.

A kind remark about a gift, kindness, or patronage will follow. Then they include the main message and close with best wishes for the receiver's health or prosperity (Haneda & Shima, 1982). Japanese who are doing business internationally are adjusting and changing the way they write. They are using a shorter seasonal greeting and writing the business message sooner. Studies show that Japanese businesspeople are using both deductive and inductive writing patterns (Kubota, 1997).

In the letter from France, notice the "we" attitude and manner of indirect apology; note also the way of explaining the situation and the format: typing the surname in all capital letters. The date, salutation, and closing also differ from the U.S. letter.

EXAMPLES OF SEASONAL GREETINGS

January—I feel my body frozen as severe cold days continue.

Full scale "Winter Shogun" has arrived. (An analogy between Shogun and nature is used.)

February—Hope you are coping with the last phase of the cold season.

Cold winter still remains strong.

March—Spring has just begun on the calendar, but the cold wind reminds us winter is not over yet.

Glad to smell the soil covered by snow for a long winter.

April—Buds of cherry tree are getting large.

Spring has arrived and every field is covered by hundreds of flowers.

May—Wind blowing over the field feels like a beginning of the summer.

Flapping wind kite in the sky looks great.

June—Rice paddy fields are ready to be planted.

Continuous rain ended, and it is a beautiful day.

July—It was the hottest day of the year.

It is a season of summer festivals and people having fun.

August—Indian summer is still around this week.

Keeping a lot of summer memories in my heart.

September—Hope you are in good health with the cool weather.

The sun is still strong and casting shadow reminds me the summer season is not over.

October—It is autumn, when the sky is blue and people have an appetite.

The smell of Matsutake reminds me of fall.

November—The tree on the boulevard is bare of leaves.

All mountains are burning with crimson foliage.

December—Frost is on the ground and breath is white.

The year is almost over.

Source: M. Tsuji, personal interview, October 27, 1998.

Similarities and differences between the Spanish letter and the U.S. letter include the date, salutation, and closing.

The letter from China in Figure 4 is shown as it was received; notice how the syntactic errors develop when people are not writing in their native language. Also notice that the writer has used the U.S. format in deference to another culture.

April 5, 2---

Prof. L. S. St. Clair
71 South Perkins Extd.
Memphis, TN 38117-3211

Dear Prof. St. Clair:

I've received your letter of Jan. 30 and your report passed on to me by Dr. Jones of CSU, Long Beach. Thank you deeply for your kindness to let me have it. I have perused it and found it very creative and enlightening, I especially admire your servant and ingenious analysis. I fully support your suggestion to establish course in intercultural business communication. Never has it been so important to globalize business communication education as it is today. It is time now to join our effort in this important area.

I made a report on the development of BC in the U.S. at a convention in Chicago last month.

You are welcome to visit China and help us with the development of business communication in China.

Sincerely,

Feng Xiang Chun
Vice President

FIGURE 4 Letter Written in English by Chinese Writer

As shown in Figure 5, the British do not use a period after Mr, Mrs, Ms, or Dr. The British are very conscious of forms of titles and addresses and expect others to use them appropriately (Janner, 1977). The British class system is becoming less rigid; how you address someone is less

23 October 2----

Mr Stevens J. Martin, Jr.
AOC Incorporated
1627 Byhalia Road
Collierville, TN 38067

Dear Mr Martin:

I have pleasure in submitting our quotation as follows:

A.   Cost incurred to date.
     1.   Design. All designs presented to date and working drawings to entire booth to enable USA contractor to build.
          1,500.00
     2.   Model. Production, packing and shipment.
          1,100.00
B.   Refurbishment of existing display.
          9,425.00

I hope the above meets with your approval and should you have any queries, please do not hesitate to contact Alan Roast at Walker Roast.

It is essential that our contractors are instructed to proceed today to meet the shipping deadline. I apologise for putting pressure on this decision but time is now of the essence.

Yours sincerely,

Edward Bales

FIGURE 5   **British Letter**

formal than a few years ago. However, if you do not know someone well, you need to use his or her title and surname. When writing about someone in a letter, you should include after the name, the abbreviations for military and civil orders and decorations, highest degree or diploma, professional memberships, and professions. In the typed signature line, include in parentheses the title you prefer to use, such as Ms. (Scott, 1998).

In the example of a U.S. letter that conveys bad news (Figure 6), notice the use of a buffer in the first paragraph, which does not suggest a negative message. In the second paragraph, the bad news is placed in a dependent clause to deemphasize it. The letter ends with an action close, avoiding any reference to the bad news. The letter style is blocked with standard punctuation.

September 15, 2----

Mr. Larry Green
2871 Goodlett Street
Memphis, TN 38817

Dear Mr. Green:

A beautiful driveway not only enhances the beauty of a home, but it also increases a home's value.

Although the driveway we installed at your home six years ago is no longer under warranty, we will be glad to send one of our service representatives to inspect your driveway and give you a free estimate on repairing or replacing it.

Please call 767-6334 to arrange a time for one of our representatives to evaluate the condition of your driveway.

Sincerely,

Thomas L. Johnson

pl

FIGURE 6   U.S. Letter

FACSIMILES (FAX)

Multinational businesses in the United States have found that the facsimile (fax) machine is more dependable than the mail service in many countries. However, in some countries the telephone system is also poorly managed; this poor management often suggests that using the fax machine may not be better than using the mail. Poor service of both mail and telephone systems occurs during the stormy seasons that a number of countries experience. In addition, many countries lack regular mail and telephone service in their remote areas. However, through telecommunication satellites and cell towers, telephone service is becoming more dependable than the mail in many locations around the globe.

The fax should be written as you would write a letter. If you are sending production schedules, budgets, or other types of written information, then a cover letter or transmittal sheet should be used so that the operator knows to whom the fax is directed, from whom the material originates, and how many total pages are included. Figure 7 is an example of a fax.

ELECTRONIC MAIL (E-MAIL)

A question that often arises is whether electronic mail (e-mail) is suitable for international correspondence. In some countries it may be preferable to send a traditional letter as an e-mail attachment. The e-mail message would simply consist of one sentence that transmits the letter. In such

To: Jim Cain, President
Cainable Vegetables

From: Wu H. Chu

I received your fax message delightly. How is your business doing? I really think that our election was better for all business in Korea. If you can make a video-tape of Ray Manner' farm, that would be great. Videotape, Blueprints together you can send me by airmail *not by ship,* regardlessly special or regular with the bill I would appreciate it very much. In designing of my vegetable farm I am take your experienced advice in good consideration. Thank you. I will look for your advices more.

FIGURE 7 Korean Fax

countries as France, for example, recipients may get a negative impression when important information is transmitted in the typical casual e-mail style. Even when the choice is made to send a traditional letter as an attachment, there are other considerations, such as whether or not the recipient welcomes attachments and whether the recipient's system is capable of downloading large attachments. Since attitudes toward use of e-mail vary not only by industry and country but also by age of correspondents, it is probably advisable to consider whether e-mail is the most appropriate communication channel for corresponding with international business colleagues (Weiss, 2005).

The vice president of a company in Canada, who was born in South Africa and lived in England before moving to Canada, emphasized that styles of e-mail vary depending upon the country. She said, "The North American way of e-mail communication is very direct and abrupt and in no way kind on relationships." She added that in countries where people focus more on the relationship than on the task, it is wise to spend time building the relationship rather than simply introducing the task. She further suggests that in their initial e-mail to Chinese counterparts, U.S. persons should introduce themselves and inquire about the Chinese colleague's family. "If you build the relationship, it is much easier to get the task done," she says. (Gohring, 2004, p. 45)

When using e-mail internationally, you should use the same writing techniques you use for a letter. However, because the format is a memorandum with TO, FROM, DATE, and SUBJECT already stated, you do not use an inside address.

Proper e-mail courtesy includes addressing the receiver by name in the opening sentence (i.e., Mr. Slovinsky, thank you for sending me the figures I requested). Avoid addressing the person by his or her first name unless permission has been granted to use the first name. You should check your e-mail inbox at least once a day and respond promptly, preferably within 24 hours. Keep messages concise and brief; most messages should be kept to a maximum of two screens. You should also devise an electronic "signature" because, unlike a letter, e-mail is not on company letterhead (Sabath, 2002).

Lash (2007) offers these suggestions for writing e-mail messages to international colleagues:

- In your introductory e-mail, include some phrases, such as "hello" and "good-bye," in the customer's language. Mention places you enjoyed visiting if you have traveled in the customer's country.

- Use a collaborative tone; ask for feedback at the conclusion of your e-mail messages. State that you are enjoying working with the person and use such phrases/sentences as "I appreciate" and "Thank you for your feedback." Avoid humor because humor does not cross cultures easily. Be positive and cheerful; be honest but do not emphasize any negatives in your message.
- Avoid dwelling on cultural differences; concentrate on similarities in experiences and attitudes. Admit your own biases.
- Use short, simple sentences; show humility; and be deferential. Avoid abbreviations, contractions, possessives, parenthetical phrases, and slang, jargon, or idioms. Use only present and past tense; avoid progressive tenses.
- Be explicit; emphasize your desire for feedback on your ideas. Always include your relation to Greenwich Mean Time (GMT) when referring to time in the message (GMT minus seven hours, for example).
- Do not use all capital letters and avoid exclamation marks. In addition, do not ask questions starting with the word "why" because such questions seem to require that readers defend their positions.
- Be generous with compliments. Include such statements as "I like your suggestion" and "I am happy you thought about that."
- Maintain a consistent pattern in the way you organize your e-mail messages. Boilerplate paragraphs are useful for messages used for recurring situations, such as delivery instructions.
- Learn how to handle problem situations. When you do not understand, always ask for clarification. When you are angry, avoid expressing your feelings in the e-mail message. Simply ask questions and say that you wish to clear up any misunderstandings. If you do make a mistake, apologize—even though you may feel that you are not at fault. Do not attempt to assign blame.

Major cities around the world are connected by the Internet and have e-mail available. E-mail is a very convenient way to send documents, and many times the printout is clearer than when using a fax machine. Telephone lines are a problem in some countries, and the cost may be much higher than in the United States.

RÉSUMÉ AND JOB SEARCH INFORMATION

Globalization has definitely expanded the information people need to get a position in a country other than their own. Variations exist in the styles and contents of résumés as well as the style, content, and format of the letter of application.

Mohammed Al-Ali (2004) found that different rhetorical strategies were used based on whether or not the writer was English speaking or Arabic speaking. English cover letters used supportive discussions in support of the writer's candidacy and explicit requests for a job interview; Arabic letters did not. Arabic letters of application glorified the company being contacted and asked for compassion; English letters did not.

Job-search information needed to find a position in Brazil, Canada, China, Germany, Japan, Mexico, The Netherlands, Singapore, South Korea, United Kingdom, and the United States follows.

Brazil

Brazil has many trade, professional, and social networking organizations that can help with finding a position. Sites such as http://www.goingglobal and http://www.jobline.net list by country where to find positions and discuss the requirements for working in the country. Receiving a visa to work in Brazil can be a lengthy process so starting the job hunting early is recommended. Résumés or CVs (curriculum vitae), as they are usually called, are similar to résumés in the United States in information requirements except that they may also include some personal information such as marital status, number of children, and organizations of which you are a member as many European countries also require.

Since Brazil is a more contact-oriented culture, one should be prepared for more physical contact such as hugs and touching of the arms and such during conversations. Because Brazilians are a relationship-oriented country, applicants should plan on long interviews to give the Brazilians time to get to know them.

Because Brazil graduates more individuals from college than there are positions available, it is very difficult for someone outside of the country to get a position. In Brazil bureaucracy runs everything, so it is important to learn how to get things done in this country. Speaking Portuguese fluently is highly recommended, as well as being able to understand the language when it is spoken very fast. Executive search firms tend to help applicants find a position only if they have the exact position for which the person is seeking.

Canada

Canadian hiring officials prefer résumés that include information similar to that included on U.S. résumés: educational background, work experience, skills, achievements, and references. No personal information is included in Canadian résumés. Canadian employers stress the importance of selecting keywords carefully, including use of industry jargon in describing skills and qualifications, as larger companies use résumé scanning software. Like U.S. employers, Canadians recommend using the combination résumé, rather than the functional or chronological résumé, for job seekers who have gaps in their work history. They also emphasize the importance of writing a cover letter that is tailored to the specific company and that is free of mistakes in spelling and grammar. Additional job-search information for Canada is available at http://www.goinglobal.com.

Workopolis.com, which is offered in English and French, is Canada's largest online job site; it offers more than 30,000 jobs each day in Montreal and Toronto, as well as some other Canadian cities. Job seekers may search by location, keyword, job category, and so on. The *Toronto Star* is Canada's largest daily newspaper and has numerous job listings.

It is difficult to get a long-term work visa in Canada; however, short visits for academic study or employment are possible.

China

Résumés or CVs as they are called in China contain personal information. In addition to the name, address, phone number, and e-mail address, applicants include date and place of birth, gender, marital status, and information about their children. After the personal information, the job objective is listed, followed by education or employment history, depending on which is most relevant. Schools attended are listed including dates of attendance, location, and degree(s) received. A section on Specialized Training typically follows Education. This section includes computer skills and language competencies (which should include Mandarin). Employment history, including company name and location, dates of employment, and job titles, are listed as Work Experience. Duties and responsibilities are described using action verbs. Both education and Work Experience are listed in reverse chronological order with the most recent school attended or job experience given first. References are usually omitted—the statement "References furnished on request" is usually placed at the end of the résumé. Information about careers in China is available at http://www.goinglobal.com.

The visa system takes a long time to complete. It is highly regimented. It is not easy to get a position in China unless you want to teach English, have a doctorate and can teach at the university level, or have a skill that they need. It is important to learn as much about the employer as possible. Many business organizations and trade councils in China assist people looking for positions in China.

Germany

The German résumé is a complete dossier of the candidate. A length of 20–30 pages is not unusual. The résumé should include positions the candidate has held, photocopies of diplomas and degrees the candidate has earned, letters of recommendation, verification of previous employment, a recent photograph, and a statement of computer and language skills. It is preferred that workers speak German. Other information includes the names and professions of the candidate's parents; names of brothers, sisters, spouse, and children; religious affiliation; and financial obligations. In addition to the diplomas and degrees, transcripts are provided to certify all course work completed. Professional activities, including publications and personal references, are also given. A typed letter of application that is one to two pages in length accompanies the résumé. The style should be very conservative and formal.

In Germany, students often enter into a contract with a company while in college. College internships are very important. The two largest newspapers where employment ads are placed are the *Frankfurter Allgemeine Zeitung* and *Suddeutsche Zeitung*. Additional information on positions may be found at http://goinglobal.com.

Japan

Finding a position in Japan generally requires having the skills directly related to the position and having a personal introduction. Work permits or visas must be processed in the jobseekers country of residence through the local embassy or consulate of Japan. Without the correct introduction you probably will not receive an interview.

A simple résumé should be handwritten in Japanese. It should list the dates and locations of your education and work experience. Networking is very important in Japan and with the right introductions an interview may be a formality. If you are interviewed, they will be looking not only for qualifications but to see if there is a fit between you and the organization. More information is available at http://goinglobal.com.

Mexico

Finding a position in Mexico is done through contacts and networking. A visa is needed for a stay of more than 180 days, a return air ticket, and a passport that is good for six months beyond the departure date. Many international firms in Mexico seek foreign workers or transfer foreign workers to Mexico.

Mexican résumés are lengthy. The résumé includes a cover page with the applicant's name and the word curriculum vitae. Beyond the standard education, work experience, and job objective, you would find personal information such as age, marital status, gender, place and date of birth, and a photograph. Since education is very important in Mexico, include awards, courses, and training you have received. Likewise titles are very important so when choosing references be sure to list their titles and positions. Since punctuation and grammar are very important in Spanish be sure to have someone proofread your résumé carefully. More information is available at http://goinglobal.com.

The Netherlands

A resident permit and social security card are required after three months. Many people are turned down due to the number of people who apply. In The Netherlands a small amount of information is better than a lot of information. The résumé follows the format of a U.S. résumé. Name, date and place of birth, address, e-mail address, driver's license number, education, work experience, and leisure and volunteer activities are included on the one to two page resume. It is correct to write the résumé in Dutch. If you are being seriously considered for a position, school grades and letters of recommendation will be requested later. During the interview (of which there will be several), applicants may be asked personal questions, such as marital status; applicants feel free to ask questions about salary and company benefits.

Many newspapers such as *NRC Handelsblad, Volkskrant, De Telegraaf,* and *Algemeen Dagblad* have job openings listed. Plus websites such as the EURES website, Monsterboard.nl, and Werk.nl list job openings and interview advice. Additional information is available at http://www.goinglobal.com.

Singapore

Résumés in Singapore begin with personal information (name, address, telephone number, e-mail address, nationality, date of birth, and gender). The sections that follow include education and qualifications, work experience, activities and hobbies, and special skills and training (computer skills and languages written and spoken). Military service should also be listed. The length of the résumé is usually one page but should not exceed three pages. The cover letter should be addressed to a specific person; applicants should remember that a Chinese surname will be written first.

Job sites include Monster, Contact Singapore, JobStreet, and JobsCentral.

South Korea

Permission to enter South Korea is granted or denied at the point of entry even for people who have a visa. A visa should be obtained before arrival but does not guarantee entry. Personal contacts are important in order to obtain a position in South Korea; however, recruiters and governmental employment agencies are also helpful.

A cover letter and résumé are required by South Korean companies. Job applicants in Korea are advised to use reverse chronological order when listing information related to work experience and education on the résumé. Name and address of employers, job title, and details of achievements and duties are included. Job seekers are expected to complete a standard application form typically used by Korean companies.

Job fairs are held in the COEX Convention Center several times each year; they provide job seekers an opportunity to meet with numerous representatives of South Korea's midsized companies. Additional information is available at http://www.goinglobal.com.

United Kingdom (England, Scotland, Wales, and Northern Ireland)

The curriculum vitae or CV as the résumé is called in the United Kingdom (UK) is one to two pages in length, typed, and does not include a photograph. The CV is accompanied by a cover letter. The CV contains a professional objective, name, address, phone number, e-mail address, professional experience, education, hobbies and other activities, and references. Include "References are available on request" at the end of the CV. Military service is not listed, and there is no personal information.

A visa is required to work in the United Kingdom and involves extensive documentation. Positions may be found in newspapers such as *The Guardian, The Daily Telegraph, The Sunday Times,* and *The Financial Times.* Additional information may be found at http:/goinglobal.com.

United States

U.S. hiring officials have indicated a preference for résumés that are one to two pages long. Important résumé items include personal information (name, address, telephone number, and e-mail address), job objective (to give the reader an idea of the type of work desired and plans for advancement), work experience (current position, company name and location, job title, dates employed, responsibilities, and accomplishments), and educational background (universities attended and degrees received). Most hiring officials prefer three or four references (names of people who can verify your work experience, educational achievements, and character). Information about your family, age, religion, ethnicity, or gender should not be included, nor should a photograph be included. The résumé is accompanied by an application (cover) letter.

In the United States, good sources of job opportunities are the Sunday edition of major newspapers in cities where you are interested in working. *The Wall Street Journal* on Tuesdays has a special employment section and also produces a newspaper, *Employment Weekly,* which is a collection of all employment advertising for the previous week in all U.S. regions of *The Wall Street Journal.* In larger cities, public and private employment agencies are also adept at helping people find positions.

Many companies now post position openings on their websites; therefore, applicants can go to the company's website to apply. Networking is one of the best ways to obtain a position in the United States. U.S. recruiters expect candidates to know the employer, its competitors, and its customers before interviewing.

In the United States there are a number of visas that are divided into immigrant (permanent resident) and nonimmigrant (temporary resident) visas. All workers need a Social Security Card.

A number of sources of books, websites, and government documents are available to help prevent a faux pas (a social blunder or error in etiquette). The Department of State's *Background Notes* by country, the *CultureGram* series, the Department of Commerce's *Overseas Business Reports,* the *World Factbook,* the *Statesman's Yearbook*, and http:/goinglobal.com are good sources for specific information on various cultures and finding positions in different countries.

Terms

Buffer	International English	Parochialism
Emoticons	Lexical errors	Syntactic errors

Exercise 1

Instructions: Circle T for true or F for false.

1. T   F   Native speakers of a language will discover lexical errors easier than the syntactic errors.
2. T   F   The writing style of U.S. letters is more formal than most foreign correspondents.
3. T   F   The use of a buffer in bad-news messages is typical of the writing style of Latin Americans.
4. T   F   The Japanese try to present negative news in a positive manner.
5. T   F   Ending messages on a positive note is important in both French and U.S. letters.

6. T F   The indented letter style for business letters is used by the French.
7. T F   Salutations of German letters are more formal than in the United States.
8. T F   The Japanese traditionally begin letters with comments about the season or weather.
9. T F   Résumés submitted to a German firm are typically longer than those submitted to a U.S. firm.
10. T F   Spanish résumés are typically in letter form.

Questions and Cases for Discussion

1. Explain how the format of business letters differs in U.S. correspondence and in Latin American countries.
2. How does the tone and writing style of Japanese letters differ from those of the United States?
3. To use international English, what cultural factors do you have to understand?
4. Explain the difference between lexical and syntactic errors.
5. Explain why people from two cultures who speak the same language may have difficulty in communicating.

6. Define a buffer and how it is used.
7. Which countries expect the reader "to read between the lines" for meaning?
8. What are some guidelines for writing e-mail messages to international colleagues?
9. What items are currently included in résumés in the United States?
10. Explain the major differences between résumés of the United States and of other cultures.

CASES

The following procedure is recommended for analyzing the cases: (a) read the case carefully paying attention to details; (b) read the questions at the end of the case; (c) reread the case, taking notes on or highlighting the details needed for answering the questions; (d) identify relevant facts, underlying assumptions, and critical issues of the case; (e) list possible answers to the questions; and (f) select the most logical response to the question. Your professor may ask that you submit answers to the case questions in writing.

Case 1

You work in the personnel division of a multinational organization. You have been asked to provide a list of potential candidates for a management position in the corporation's German office. Because of their laws, you want a German national for the position. How would you go about obtaining résumés to review?

Case 2

If you are dealing with a foreign corporation in which no one speaks English as a native or second language, what may be necessary for your corporation and the foreign corporation to work together? How does a U.S. corporation react when the other corporation does not speak its language? If the corporation has the flexibility to deal with another company in which someone speaks its language versus one in which no one does, which company would receive the order?

Case 3

A U.S. executive was working with a convention booth builder in England. The English were not working on the booth and would not give a date of completion for the booth or a shipping date to the United States. For six consecutive weeks, the U.S. executive called to inquire about the state of the booth. One day, the executive was called and was given the usual litany of excuses, so he gave the English an ultimatum. The next week, the English had not acted on the ultimatum, so the U.S. executive informed the company he would have a trucking company pick up and ship the booth to the United States. Twice the trucking company went to pick up the booth and was told by the English company that they were not authorized to pick up the booth. The U.S. executive finally had to hire the advertising firm in England that had originally hired the booth manufacturer to intervene and get the booth shipped. When the booth arrived in the United States, it had not been packed properly and required additional work. What cultural differences were involved in this situation? How could the executive have handled the situation differently?

Case 4

A British national was sent to the United States to work in a subsidiary. He was an engineer in a management position in charge of building a new factory for the corporation. He was initially offered intercultural training; however, he felt comfortable because both countries spoke the same language and declined the training. The British engineer later complained to the home office that he was not getting the cooperation he needed. The home office hired an intercultural trainer to go to his office to review his correspondence and sit in on some of his meetings. The intercultural trainer discovered that the U.S. employees did not understand his communications. The engineer was interjecting British humor and sarcasm in both his oral communication and his e-mail messages. The U.S. subordinates did not know when he was serious about a problem and when they were to ignore his statements. What are some examples of humor used by people of the United States with foreigners that U.S. persons expect foreigners to understand?

Case 5

Virtual teams, comprising people who work together through the use of e-mail and other communication technologies to complete a task while in separate locations, are becoming more commonplace for working with international colleagues. Virtual teams have a number of advantages, including elimination of travel time and elimination of such negative behaviors as team members who are late, interrupt, and talk incessantly. An added advantage is that members from different cultures are often more comfortable expressing themselves in writing than in speaking. However, there are a number of disadvantages, especially when people from different cultures are involved. What are some of the concerns, issues, or disadvantages of a virtual team that communicates primarily via e-mail and that is composed of members from China, France, Mexico, and the United States?

Activities

1. Examine the Latin or Germanic roots of simple and difficult words in the English language.
2. Take a passage from a journal or textbook in another language and compare it, in terms of sentence and paragraph length, to a passage from a journal or textbook written in English.
3. Modify a bad-news letter so that it is effective for a reader who is Japanese, French, Spanish, or German.
4. Search the want ads of the local newspaper; bring to class a job announcement of a position with a multinational corporation, a position involving overseas travel, or a position located in a foreign country.
5. Prepare a résumé to be sent to a multinational company applying for an overseas assignment in a country of your choice.
6. Write a letter of application to accompany the résumé prepared in Activity 5.
7. Write a letter in English to someone who speaks English as a second language following the international English guidelines.
8. Find the errors in Figure 4 and explain why these particular errors may have happened.
9. Read the following two faxes and determine the reader's probable reaction. What choice of words could have been improved on? The first fax is from the U.S. corporate office to Taiwan; the second is from Taiwan to the U.S. corporate office.
10. Have an international student write a letter for you in English but with their native language style, tone, and format. Compare the letter to the style, tone, and format of U.S. letters.

References

Al-Ali, M. N. (2004). How to get yourself in the door of a job: A cross-cultural contrastive study of Arabic and English job application letters. *Journal of Multilingual and Multicultural Development, 25*(1), 1–23.

Azuma, S. (1998). How do Japanese say "no" in the written mode? *Academy of Managerial Communications Journal, 2*(2), 18–29.

Bosrock, M. M. (1995). *Put your best foot forward: Europe.* St. Paul, MN: International Education Systems.

Collin, P. H., Lowi, M., & Weiland, C. (2002). *Beginner's dictionary of American English usage.* Lincolnwood, IL: National Textbook Company.

Conaway, R. N., & Wardrope, W. J. (2004, December). Communication in Latin America.

DeVries, M. A. (1994). *Internationally yours: Writing and communicating successfully in today's global marketplace.* Boston, MA: Houghton Mifflin.

Geluyckens, R., & van Rillaer, G. (1996, March 26–31). *Face-threatening acts in international business communication: A quantitative investigation into business writing.* Paper presented at the 22nd and 23rd LAUD Symposium, Duisburg.

Green, D. J., & Scott, J. C. (1992). International business correspondence: Practices and perspectives of major U.S. companies with related implications for business education. *NABTE Review, 19,* 39–43.

Gohring, N. (2004, November). Face time. *PM Network,* pp. 41–45.

Haneda, S., & Shima, H. (1982). Japanese communication behavior as reflected in letter writing. *Journal of Business Communication, 19*(1), 21–32.

Janner, G. (1977). *The businessman's guide to letter writing and to the law on letters* (2nd ed.). London: Business Books.

Kilpatrick, R. H. (1984). International business communication practices. *Journal of Business Communications, 21*(4), 40–42.

Kubota, R. (1997). A reevaluation of the uniqueness of Japanese written discourse. *Written Communication, 14*(4), 460–481.

Lampi, M. (1992). Rhetorical strategies in "Chairman's Statement" sections in the annual reports of Finnish and British companies: Report on a pilot study. In P. Nuolijarvi & L. Tiittula (Eds.), *Talous ja Kieli* 1 [Language and Economics 1] (pp. 127–143). Helsinki: Helsinki School of Economics and Business Administration. Helsingin kauppak-orkcakoulun julkaisuja D-169.

Lash, B. (2007, May). Communicating across cultures by e-mail: Advice for consultants. *Intercom, 54*(5), 23–25, 42.

Park, M. Y., Dillon, W. T., & Mitchell, K. L. (1998, July). Korean business letters: Strategies for effective complaints in cross-cultural communication. *The Journal of Business Communication, 35*(3), 328–345.

Riddle, D. I., & Lanham, Z. D. (1984–1985, Winter). Internationalizing written business English: 20 propositions for native English speakers. *Journal of Language for International Business, 1,* 1–11.

Sabath, A. M. (2002). *Business etiquette: 101 ways to conduct business with charm and savvy.* Franklin Lakes, NJ: Career Press.

Scott, J. C. (1998). Dear ???: Understanding British forms of address. *Business Communication Quarterly, 61*(3), 50–61.

Varner, I. I. (1987). Internationalizing business communication courses. *Bulletin of the Association for Business Communication, 1*(4), 7–11.

Varner, I. I. (1988). A comparison of American and French business correspondence. *Journal of Business Communication, 25*(4), 55–65.

Weiss, E. H. (2005). *The elements of international English style.* Armonk, NY: M. E. Sharpe.

Glossary

Buffer is a paragraph used to begin a bad news letter; tells what the letter is about, is pleasant, but says neither yes nor no.

Emoticons are symbols used to convey emotions within e-mail messages.

International English is a limited vocabulary for international businesses using the 3,000–4,000 most common English words.

Lexical errors are language content errors.

Parochialism is the same as ethnocentrism.

Syntactic errors are errors in the order of the words in a sentence.

Answers to Exercises

True/False

1. F
2. F
3. F
4. T
5. F

6. T
7. T
8. T
9. T
10. T

Global Etiquette

From Chapter 8 of *Intercultural Business Communication*, Sixth Edition. Lillian H. Chaney, Jeanette S. Martin.

Global Etiquette

Objectives

Upon completion of this chapter, you will

- understand cultural differences in making introductions, greetings, and handshakes as well as customs related to business card exchange.
- understand how position and status affect cultural interaction.
- be familiar with rules of etiquette that apply to communicating by telephone and electronically with persons of other cultures.
- understand how cultural differences in dining practices may affect intercultural communication.
- be familiar with the cultural nuances of tipping.
- understand how practices of giving gifts vary from culture to culture and the role of gift giving in establishing favorable intercultural relations.
- learn the importance of travel etiquette in conveying a positive image of a person's firm and country.

When you conduct business abroad or in the United States with someone of another culture, knowledge of certain rules of business and social etiquette is important. **Etiquette** refers to manners and behavior considered acceptable in social and business situations. **Protocol** refers to customs and regulations dealing with diplomatic etiquette and courtesies expected in official dealings (such as negotiations) with persons in various cultures.

President Clinton, during his first state dinner abroad on a visit to Korea, confused his translator and embarrassed South Korean officials when he stepped to the microphone to give his dinner speech and invited a translator to stand between him and President Kim Young Sam. Because in South Korea it is an insult for anyone to stand between two heads of state, President Clinton had committed a serious *faux pas*. (Kim, 1993, p. A5)

Proper social behavior includes learning cultural variations in making introductions, exchanging business cards, recognizing position and status, communicating interculturally, dining practices, tipping etiquette, giving gifts, and traveling.

INTRODUCTIONS, GREETINGS, AND HANDSHAKES

Being sensitive to cultural variations when making introductions will ensure that your first encounter with a person from another country leaves a positive impression. First impressions are made only once but are remembered for a long time.

The procedure for making introductions varies from culture to culture. People from the United States and England use first names almost immediately; however, introductions are more formal in some other cultures. Titles are used when introducing people in Germany and Italy; titles often indicate the person's profession or educational level. Germans always address each other as "Herr Guenther" or "Frau Kurr" in and out of the office, reserving first names for close friends and family.

Remember that in some cultures, such as the Chinese, the surname comes first and the given name last. Ching Lo Chang would be addressed as Mr. Ching.

President Clinton, in a meeting in Korea, addressed South Korean President Kim Young Sam's wife, Mrs. Sohn Myong-suk, as Mrs. Kim. He should have addressed her as Mrs. Sohn because in Korea, it is the custom for women to maintain their maiden name when they marry. (Kim, 1993, p. A5)

Men and women from the Latin American countries often add their mother's maiden name to their surname, so you should use the next-to-last name when addressing them. Thus, Evelyn Rodrigues Castillo would be addressed as Señorita Rodrigues. When women marry, they drop their mother's surname and add their husband's father's surname. When in doubt, ask what name is to be used (Martin & Chaney, 2012). Egyptians use the title plus the first name when making introductions. In some cases, the French form of address is used for women, for example, Madame Susan. In Iraq and in India, titles such as Professor and Doctor, used with the last name, are used as part of the introduction. In African countries, such as Nigeria and Kenya, titles are used with last names until you get to know the Nigerians and Kenyans well and they ask you to call them by their first name (Devine & Braganti, 1991, 1995, 2000). Because of such widely diverse customs in the use of titles, it is wise to research the customs of the particular culture involved.

A handshake, an embrace, or a bow, depending on the culture, accompanies introductions. Handshakes may vary from the soft handshake of the British to the firm handshake of U.S. people. Hugging or embracing when being introduced is considered inappropriate in business situations in the United States but is common in many South American countries. The bow, common in China and Japan, is uncommon in many other cultures.

Customary greetings vary from culture to culture. Persons from other cultures are struck by the informality of U.S. Americans who often say "Hi!" to complete strangers. In most countries of the world, this practice is uncommon. People of the United States are often perceived as insincere when they use the standard greeting of "Hi, how are you?" which does not mean that they are actually inquiring on the state of someone's health. This outward show of friendliness is often misleading because people from the United States are actually private and slow to form friendships. The use of "Hello, I'm pleased to meet you" is preferable, as it conveys a more sincere message.

British-born journalist Henry Fairlie, in writing "Why I Love America," recalled this encounter with a four-year-old boy riding his tricycle in the suburbs shortly after his arrival in the United States:

"As I passed him, he said Hi!—just like that. No four-year-old boy had ever addressed me without an introduction before. Recovering from the culture shock, I found myself saying in return: Well—hi! He pedaled off, apparently satisfied."

Fairlie, who comes from a country where you can tell another person's class from their greeting, observed that the greeting "Hi!" is a democracy. In America, anyone can say "Hi!" to anyone else. (Fairlie, 1983)

In addition to the informal "Hi!" often used when meeting someone, persons of the United States engage in other ritualistic greeting behavior. When greeting an office colleague, one person will say, "Good morning, how are you?" The appropriate response is, "Fine, thank you. And how are you?" Some people make the mistake of forgetting that this is only a ritual and proceed to describe in detail the state of their health. Remember, the appropriate response is, "Fine, thanks."

Gunter Lensges, an exchange student from Germany, recalled his experience with ritualistic greetings when he returned to the campus apartment he shared with three U.S. students following his first day of classes.

When one of his roommates said, "Hey, man, what's going on?" he was impressed that they seemed interested in how his day had gone and proceeded to recount his experiences in his classes. Noticing the strange expressions on his roommates' faces, he asked, "Did I say something wrong?" They then explained to him, "When we say, 'Hey, man, what's going on?' we don't really want to know. You're supposed to say, 'Not much, man, and what's going on with you?' Then we'll say, 'Not much.'"

When greeting people, the handshake is customary in many countries. Egyptians, both men and women, shake hands when being introduced. Men of India shake hands with other men but not with women. In African countries, such as Nigeria and Kenya, shaking hands is customary. In Saudi Arabia, handshakes are numerous and elaborate. In Finland, handshakes are firm and are typical greeting behavior for men and women—women are customarily greeted first. Although a firm handshake is considered the norm in the United States, it may be considered impolite in some cultures. Handshakes in other cultures vary from the soft grasp of the British to the brusque grasp of Germans. A summary of how various cultures differ in their ideas of a proper handshake follows in Table 1.

Although a kiss or hug is considered inappropriate as a form of greeting in the United States, in other countries it is customary. For example, in Saudi Arabia, the handshake is accompanied with a light kiss; even males in Saudi Arabia kiss both cheeks after a handshake. In the Russian Federation, the "bear hug" may follow a strong, firm handshake between good male friends; neighboring Finns, on the other hand, do not hug, kiss, or have body contact with strangers. People in Latin American countries also embrace, often accompanied by a couple of slaps on the back (Samovar, Porter, & McDaniel, 2009) (see Figure 1). Egyptian women who are close friends, as well as women in some African countries, often hug or kiss each other as part of the greeting.

Asians, Northern Europeans, and most North Americans are uncomfortable with touching and hugging. People of Greece have no firm customs for greeting others; they may shake hands, embrace, and/or kiss a person at the first meeting or at every meeting. Bowing is the customary form of greeting in Japan. In China, bowing is also customary, but a handshake is

TABLE 1 Handshakes by Culture

Culture	Type of Handshake
U.S. American	Firm
Asian	Gentle (shaking hands is unfamiliar and uncomfortable for some; the exception is the Korean, who usually has a firm handshake)
British	Soft
French	Light and quick (not offered to superiors); repeated on arrival and departure
German	Brusque and firm; repeated on arrival and departure
Latin American	Moderate grasp; repeated frequently
Middle Eastern	Gentle; repeated frequently

Source: Adapted from these books: *International Business Etiquette: Asia and the Pacific Rim* (2002); *International Business Etiquette: Europe* (1999); and *International Business Etiquette: Latin America* (2000) by Ann Marie Sabath, Franklin Lakes, NJ: Career Press.

also acceptable. When conducting business with people of Japan or China, the handshake is often combined with a bow so that each culture shows the other proper respect (Baldrige, 1993; Samovar et al., 2009) (see Figure 2). In India, the traditional greeting is the *Namaste*, which a person says while pressing palms together with fingers up and placing the hands below the chin; a slight bow accompanies this gesture when greeting supervisors or others to whom you want to show respect (*CultureGrams*, 2010).

FIGURE 1 Greetings in Latin American Countries

FIGURE 2 Greetings in Japan Involve Bowing at the Waist

BUSINESS CARD EXCHANGE

An important aspect of business protocol is the proper procedure for exchanging business cards. Because all business contacts require a business card, the admonition of a well-known credit card company, "Don't leave home without it," applies.

Although most U.S. businesspeople carry business cards, they do not always exchange them when meeting unless there is a reason to contact the person later. Rank, title, and profession are taken seriously in some cultures, so it is important to include your position and titles or degrees in addition to your company name on your card. Include foreign head-quarters where appropriate, as well as your fax number and perhaps e-mail address. Avoid colored type and paper. Be conservative by choosing white paper with black ink (Martin & Chaney, 2012).

Cultural variations exist in the presentation of the card. The practice in the United States of glancing at the business card and promptly putting it in the pocket is considered rude in countries like Japan. The Japanese examine the business card carefully and make some comment while accepting it. During meetings, place the business cards of others attending in front of you on the conference table to refer properly to names, ranks, and titles. Use both hands when presenting your card in Japan or South Korea; position the card so that the person can read it (Axtell, 1993; Baldrige, 1993; Chaney & Martin, 2007) (see Figure 3).

FIGURE 3 **Business Card Presentation in Japan**

An exchange of business cards is an expected part of all business introductions and most personal ones in Europe, including the Scandinavian countries. Because Scandinavians are respectful of age, include your company's date of establishment on your business card when the company's history is a long one (Turkington, 1999). Other parts of the world in which an exchange of business cards is the norm include the Middle East, the Pacific, Asia, and the Caribbean. Australian businesspersons do not usually carry business cards; thus, when you offer them your card, you may not receive one in return. In Latin American countries, business titles are important, so be sure to include them on your business cards (Moran, Harris, & Moran, 2011). In most countries of Southeast Asia, Africa, and the Middle East (with the exception of Israel), avoid presenting the card with your left hand as the left hand is reserved for taking care of bodily functions. In non-English speaking countries, have the information on your card printed in English on one side and in the local language on the other.

POSITION AND STATUS

Position and status may have an impact on the success of intercultural communication encounters. No standard definition of social class exists that applies to all countries because people in different cultures have their own way of identifying the classes. Some cultures believe that people should occupy their proper places and that some are entitled to more respect than others.

Most people of the United States show limited respect for rank and authority, although many other cultures are very conscious of position and power.

Although the United States is not considered a nation of classes, distinctions in position and status do exist. Because class distinctions in the United States are subtle, visitors from other cultures may not be able to spot the existence of a class structure and may believe the official propaganda of social equality. Visitors to New York, Washington, DC, and other cities, however, may see both the homeless and more affluent persons in public places. Although a system of inherited titles and ranks does not exist in the United States, certain factors distinguish between the top class, the upper-middle class, the mid-middle class, and the lower-middle class. Money is one factor associated with class. Further distinctions are made between those who have inherited money but are not currently employed and those who have inherited money and are employed. Style, taste, and awareness are equally important. Social class is also associated with educational opportunities and a person's occupation or profession (Fussell, 1983).

Status is associated with education in a number of cultures. Educational titles are used in introductions as a sign of respect and acknowledgment of the person's educational achievement. In Germany and Italy, executives and other professionals are proud of titles preceding their names, as they often reflect their education or profession. People with a college degree are entitled to be called Doctor (*Dottore* in Italian); the same rule applies to architects and lawyers. In Germany, the U.S. equivalent of president or managing director of a company is called *Herr Direktor*; a female doctor is addressed as *Frau Doktor*; and a female engineer is addressed as *Frau Ingenieur*. In Mexico, a lawyer is addressed as *Licenciado,* a title that is considered very important. In England, special protocol exists for addressing royalty, peers, clergy, and others. The managing director in a British firm is usually the top official and equivalent to a U.S. corporate president (U.S. corporate vice presidents do not carry much clout abroad) (Axtell, 1990).

In some cultures, such as India, a very rigid class system exists, with a society divided into castes. The particular caste a person belongs to is determined at birth; each **caste system** has its status, rights, and duties. Although discrimination based on caste has been outlawed, in many areas, particularly rural ones, it is still a major influence on life in India. In India's rigid caste system, interaction between members of different castes is often limited, as in the case of India's untouchables (Samovar & Porter, 2003).

Cultural differences also exist concerning the status of women in a society. Women in some cultures play a less prominent role in business than do men. In South Korea, women are considered inferior to men and thus have lower social status. Women, even those with college degrees, are rarely employed as executives; they usually hold jobs as teachers or secretaries. Social and economic inequality between men and women is also apparent in China, Malaysia, and Singapore; men are clearly the ones in positions of authority (Chaney & Martin, 2007; Turkington, 1999).

The Arabs are becoming more accustomed to women executives, and they are beginning to accept women executives from other countries. U.S. women doing business with the Arabs should understand this difference in cultural attitude and should make a special effort to conduct themselves appropriately, including dressing very modestly. In some Middle Eastern countries, men may refuse to work with women; women executives in Latin America may not receive the same respect given to men executives.

Women in the United States are being given increased opportunities for business travel, management positions in overseas operations, and transfers to overseas assignments. The progress U.S. women have made in the workplace is viewed by many as setting a precedent for other countries because the United States is often perceived as a catalyst for international change.

In some cultures, such as the Chinese, people are very aware of age and hierarchy. Age is viewed as an indication of seniority. In addition to the Asian culture, the Arabian world has a great respect for age. Advanced years represent wisdom and respect. Age takes precedence over rank, but rank is still important. In the Japanese society, knowing the rank of the people with whom you come in contact is important. The middle-level manager in a large company outranks a department head from a smaller company. The higher the rank of the person you are introduced to, the lower you bow. The person of lower rank bows first and lowest. Status is also shown by who goes first when entering a room or an elevator. Those of lower rank wait for those of higher rank to precede them. If you are the foreign guest, you may be expected to enter a room ahead of others, so if you are motioned to enter the room, do so quickly. When the Chinese or Japanese enter a room, they generally enter in protocol order, with the highest-ranking person entering first. They will also assume that the first member of your negotiating team to enter the room is the head of your group and has the higher rank. Sitting in rank order from highest to lowest during a meeting is helpful (Axtell, 1998; Turkington, 1999).

A consulting firm trying to establish a partnership between a Mexican and U.S. client arranged a party at a local hotel to celebrate the new business. Invitations were sent to all those involved. Only Mexican administrative assistants attended; none of the executives attended. The party organizers later learned that Mexican companies are very hierarchical and do not mix socially with people of other ranks. Mexican executives chose not to attend upon learning that administrative workers were also invited. (Wilen, 2000, pp. 71–72)

ELECTRONIC COMMUNICATION ETIQUETTE

Aspects of protocol related to successful intercultural communication include telephone manners and cyberspace etiquette, sometimes referred to as **netiquette** (network etiquette).

Many intercultural encounters are via the telephone. When talking on the telephone, the initial impression is formed mainly by vocal quality (70%) rather than on the words spoken (30%). Thus, opinions are formed more on how something is said and the voice tone rather than on what the person actually says (Mitchell, 2000).

Good telephone manners include answering the phone promptly (first or second ring), identifying yourself properly by giving your department and your name, and being courteous at all times, including the frequent use of "please" and "thank you." Successful telephone communication involves recognizing and avoiding behaviors that typically irritate others. Avoid putting people on hold as this has been identified as the single most irritating behavior. Other negative behaviors that should be avoided include making mouth noises, not paying attention, and having a negative or rude attitude. A positive behavior appreciated by callers is "the voice with a smile." Callers also appreciate a cheerful attitude.

When voice mail is used, be brief but complete when leaving a message. Include your name, company, the date, and the time of the message. Give your phone number slowly and include a brief summary of what the call concerns.

Because more companies are communicating by e-mail, certain rules of etiquette should be observed. E-mail is more informal than a letter or memorandum and is inappropriate for conveying certain types of messages. Negative information, such as a person's failure to get a promotion, and personal information, such as announcing the birth of a baby, is not an appropriate use of e-mail. Proper "netiquette" avoids the following:

- **shouting**—typing the message in all capital letters.
- **dissing**—speaking ill of someone.
- **flaming**—sending vicious, insulting messages.
- **spamming**—mass mailings of commercial advertisements or material cross posted to numerous news groups (Segaloff, 1998).

In addition to these suggestions, avoid the use of humor and sarcasm. Remember that cultural variations exist in what is perceived as humorous. Also avoid a tone that is even slightly critical (Miller, 2001).

Because a firm may be liable for information leaked into cyberspace, employees should be very careful about the messages they send. A good rule to follow: If you would not want your message posted on the company bulletin board, do not send it via e-mail. Pressing the Delete key after sending a message does not mean that it cannot be tracked back to you (Miller, 2001).

Care should be taken in deciding how a message should be sent. The advantages of using e-mail include low preparation, fast delivery time, personal, and convenient for the receiver. The disadvantages are lack of confidentiality and the lack of nonverbal interaction (Kenton & Valentine, 1997). Certainly, not all countries use e-mail with equal frequency. According to Internet World Stats, June 30, 2011, the two countries with the highest number of Internet users are China, comprising 23.0% of world users, and the United States, with 11.6% of world users. In China, the number of Internet users is 485 million, representing 36.3% of the population; in the United States the number of Internet users is 245 million, comprising 78.2% of the population. Other countries in the top 10 Internet users (from highest to lowest) are India, Japan, Brazil, Germany, Russia, United Kingdom, France, and Nigeria.

When corresponding with international persons via e-mail, avoid addressing people by their first names. Be sure to write out the name of the month when specifying a date, include country codes for telephone numbers, and indicate which time zone is being referred to when making such statements as "I will telephone you at 2 P.M. Friday."

The use of fax messages is increasing as a quick method of communication between countries. Points of etiquette regarding the transmission of fax messages are as follows:

- Call ahead to confirm the fax number and to alert the person that you are sending a message (in case the fax machine shares a line with a person's telephone). The message should follow within 15 minutes.
- Certain documents should not be faxed—documents of more than 10–15 pages, personal or confidential information, and negative news.
- Avoid using the fax when impressions are important. Résumés and proposals submitted on fax paper will not get the same attention as those submitted on good-quality, linen finish paper (Ford, 2003; Glassman, 1998).

DINING PRACTICES

Cultural dining practices vary widely. In many parts of the world, the main meal is at noon, although in the United States, the main meal is in the evening. In Mexico, lunchtime is from 2 P.M. to 4 P.M. and is the main meal of the day. However, in places near the U.S.–Mexican border, local businesses conform more to the U.S. lunchtime of noon to 2 P.M. The dinner hour also varies. In the United States, the dinner hour varies from 5 P.M. to 7 P.M., but in such countries as Spain, it may be as late as 10 P.M. In some cultures, business meals are eaten in private homes, although in other cultures, they are usually eaten at restaurants. When entertaining visitors from other countries, be considerate and ask them whether they prefer the main meal at noon or in the evening and take them to restaurants where they have a choice of a light or heavy meal (Devine & Braganti, 2000; Martin & Chaney, 2012).

Cultural variations exist in the number of courses typically served. A formal luncheon usually consists of two to three courses, and a formal dinner consists of three to seven courses. In some countries, including those in Latin America, even informal meals typically have numerous courses. In Italy and France, salads are often served after the main course rather than before.

Dining practices are viewed differently in various cultures. A U.S. dining practice that seems unusual to people of other cultures is the serving of a glass of iced water at most restaurants. Other countries that serve water do so without ice or serve bottled mineral water. Another dining practice that is viewed with astonishment is the habit of offering coffee at the beginning of a meal; serving coffee at the end of the meal is common in most cultures. The popularity of decaffeinated coffee in the United States has not yet spread to other countries, so visitors are often surprised by a waiter's question of, "Will you have regular coffee or decaf?" Another U.S. custom that sometimes amazes people from other cultures is designating certain sections in restaurants as smoking and nonsmoking. A practice that makes little sense in other cultures is the U.S. custom of conducting business at breakfast. The French especially do not like breakfast meetings; they prefer a leisurely breakfast with time to read the paper in the morning. The French do conduct business over lunch; however, the meal may last two hours or more. Another U.S. business custom questioned by people in other cultures is the lengthy cocktail "hour" before dinner. Italians have commented that the endless rounds of cocktails before ordering a meal are exhausting and may result in discussions that make little sense (Baldrige, 1993; Martin & Chaney, 2012).

The manner of eating is also diverse. The **U.S. eating style** uses the "zigzag" technique: cutting the meat with the knife held in the right hand and the fork in the left, then placing the knife on the plate, shifting the fork to the right hand, and eating. Diners using the **Continental eating style** place the fork in the left hand and knife in the right; they use the knife to push food onto the back of the fork, and then move the food into the mouth with the tines of the fork down. Asians typically use chopsticks especially for eating rice but may or may not use a spoon for soup. They appreciate foreigners' attempting to use chopsticks and are often willing to demonstrate correct usage. Chopsticks are placed on the chopstick rest at the conclusion of the meal (or when pausing during the meal); they should not be placed in an upright position in the rice bowl (Martin & Chaney, 2012; Sabath, 2002).

Other cultural variations in dining also exist. Tahitian food is eaten with the fingers. In the Middle East, be prepared to eat with your fingers if your host does so but use the right hand only. In Bolivia, you are expected to clean your plate; Egyptians and Filipinos, however, consider it impolite to eat everything on your plate (Axtell, 1993; Turkington, 1999). In China, avoid taking the last item of food from the serving platter unless you want to convey to the host that you are still hungry (Turkington, 1999).

When dining in other countries, be aware that animals considered delicacies in some countries are viewed as pets in others. For example, dogs may be on the menu in such Asian countries as South Korea, while they are considered pets in the United States.

When a man from Tonga went to a U.S. neighbor's home to purchase a pony that had been advertised in the local newspaper, the neighbor, who asked why the Tongan wanted the pony, was told that he was buying it for his son's birthday. While the neighbor watched in shocked disbelief, the Tongan struck the pony in the head, put the dead pony in his truck, and drove home. The police were called; when they arrived, they found a birthday party in progress. They also observed that the pony was being cooked for a typical Tongan birthday feast. (Ricks, 2006, p. 5)

Dining in Japan, especially in Japanese homes, requires sitting in a kneeling position on a *tatami* mat. Men keep their knees three or four inches apart; women keep their knees together. Being able to lower yourself to this position and rise from it gracefully requires practice. If you have frequent contact with the Japanese, practicing this art is warranted (Axtell, 1993).

TIPPING

People communicate nonverbally by their tipping practices; those who are basically miserly and those who are generous reveal these traits by their tipping behavior. Although it is difficult to establish definite rules for tipping, generally when service has been good or when service people go out of their way to do a favor, a tip is merited. If the service is very bad, you are not expected to leave a tip but should report the situation to the manager. "Insult tipping" (leaving a few coins) shows a lack of respect and is inappropriate regardless of how poor the service.

Trends in tipping appear to have changed in the past few years. Although a tip of 15% of the bill was considered to be a generous tip in fine restaurants, 20% is now closer to the norm when the service is excellent.

Traveling in the United States involves numerous situations in which tipping is expected. When traveling, have a supply of $1 and $5 bills in your pocket for tipping the cab driver, the bellhop, and other service personnel who may carry your luggage, summon a cab, or perform other services, such as delivering food or small appliances to your hotel room. Travel tipping needs to be included in anticipated travel expenses; tipping service personnel at a resort or luxury hotel may add an additional 25% to your bill (Chaney & Martin, 2007; Martin & Chaney, 2012).

Tipping in a nontipping culture can offend or insult the people of that culture. However, letters of thanks to people who have been especially helpful, including hotel managers, are very much appreciated. Tipping in Japan is frowned on. People in this culture consider helping you with your luggage a gesture of hospitality and would be offended if you tipped them. If a hotel employee has performed an extra service that you want to reward, place the yen in an envelope because the Japanese would consider openly receiving money as embarrassing or as "losing face." Likewise in Singapore and South Korea, tipping is not expected, although this practice seems to be changing in hotels where international businesspersons stay (Martin & Chancy, 2012).

A U.S. professor with little travel experience, while attending a business conference in Puerto Vallarta, visited a nice restaurant recommended by the concierge at the conference hotel. When she received the bill, she noticed that 15% had been added, assumed that this was the tip, and left no extra amount. As she was leaving the restaurant, the server ran after her, pointed to the bill, and said, "*La propina!*" The professor tried to explain that the tip was included in the bill, but the server was clearly unhappy at receiving no tip. (What the professor did not know was that the amount added was a tax and that she was expected to leave a tip of 15–20%.) (Martin & Chaney, 2012, p. 121)

In many places, such as Europe, a service charge is added to the restaurant and hotel bill. Although no additional tip is expected, the trend is to leave an extra amount, especially if the service was good. In the absence of a service charge, leaving the usual 15–20% that is customary in the United States is recommended. Observing cultural differences in tipping can communicate nonverbally that you have researched the country and that you consider local customs to be important (Axtell, 1993; Sabath, 1999, 2000, 2002).

GIFT GIVING

Each country has its seasons and occasions for giving gifts. Gift giving in some cultures is an art and is considered an integral part of building intercultural professional and social relationships. The careful selection and wrapping of a gift and presenting it at the proper time with panache (style) conveys to others your social sensitivity and good manners.

Business gifts in the United States are very modest in price; the rule to follow (because of tax regulations) is to limit the price to $25 or less. Business gifts are sometimes given to members of your staff on such occasions as birthdays and Christmas. In addition, secretaries are generally treated to flowers and/or lunch on Secretaries' Day. Remember that business gifts to staff members should be personal; an electric pencil sharpener is inappropriate. However, they should not be too personal—cologne or lingerie to a member of the opposite gender could be misinterpreted. A gift certificate to the person's favorite restaurant or specialty shop is in good taste. Subordinates wait for their supervisors to set the tone on gift giving. If you are new in an office, ask what tradition is usually followed in exchanging gifts. Several years ago when the office Christmas party was popular, colleagues often exchanged gifts as part of the occasion. The practice of exchanging gifts among colleagues, even token gifts (the office grab bag), seems to have been discontinued in many firms in favor of contributing the amount of money you would spend on such gifts to a local food bank or pooling the amount to give gifts of food or money to members of the custodial staff (Martin & Chaney, 2012).

In the United States, gifts are opened in front of the giver. The gift is admired, and appreciation is expressed verbally. The oral expression of thanks is followed by a written note of appreciation unless the gift is small and is used as an advertisement (e.g., a paperweight with the company logo). Business gifts to the office or department, such as a basket of fruit or box of candy, are opened immediately and shared by all. (The manager's taking the gift home to share with his or her family is considered to be in poor taste.) The manager writes a note of thanks to the company that sent the gift and conveys expressions of appreciation from staff members (Samovar & Porter, 2004). Gifts are also opened in the presence of the giver in Brazil and Belgium. In the Arabian countries, you must present a gift when others are present so it will not be interpreted as a bribe. In some countries, however, gifts are not opened in the presence of the giver. In Taiwan, Hong Kong, and Korea, you should not open a gift in front of the giver, and you should accept the gift with both hands (Bosrock, 1995, 1997a, 1997b).

Although flowers make appropriate gifts, learn cultural taboos related to color, variety, and number. Red roses are associated with romance in some cultures. In some countries, such as China, white is the color of mourning, and gladioli are often used in funeral sprays; thus, a gift of white gladioli is inappropriate in China. Although a gift of flowers in any color is considered appropriate by most Brazilians, purple flowers should probably be avoided as they are associated with death by some segments of the population. In most European countries, avoid a gift of carnations, which are for cemeteries only. Chrysanthemums are inappropriate in Belgium, Japan, and Italy; they are associated with funerals and mourning. Although flowers are not expected by a Mexican host, they are appreciated; however, avoid sending yellow, red, or white flowers as these colors have negative connotations for some Mexican people. In some cultures, the number of flowers given has a special significance (Barnum & Wolniansky, 1989). Armenians give an odd number of flowers on happy occasions; even numbers of flowers are associated with death. For the Chinese, four is the most negative number (it sounds like their word for death), so gifts of four flowers—or four of anything else—should be avoided (Dresser, 2005). Because in Thailand and Hong Kong three is a lucky number, give gifts in threes in these countries (Bosrock, 1997a). A flower shop in the host country is the best place to get information concerning local customs about giving flowers (Sabath, 2002).

Exhibitors at a trade show could not understand why Chinese visitors were not stopping by their booth. Workers were wearing green hats and were using them as giveaways as well. They later learned that for many Chinese, green hats are associated with infidelity; the Chinese expression "He wears a green hat" indicates that a man's wife has been cheating on him. When they discarded the green hats and gave out T-shirts and coffee mugs instead, they had a number of Chinese visitors. (Dresser, 2005)

Gift giving is very much a part of conducting business in such countries as Japan. Japan's major gift-giving times are *Ochugen* (July 15) and *Oseibo* (December). Companies give gifts to their customers as an expression of appreciation for past and future business. They also reward their employees at these times with large bonuses. U.S. companies that have ongoing business relationships with the Japanese should remember their associates with a gift at both of these times. Because Japan is one of the United States' largest trading partners, knowing the nuances associated with Japanese gift giving is considered an important aspect of protocol with people in that culture (Samovar et al., 2009).

The Japanese are a gracious people for whom gift giving seems to be an art. The wrapping of the gift and the manner of presenting it are just as important as the gift itself. Gifts are beautifully wrapped but without the ornate bows and other decorations typically used on gifts in the United States. The color of the wrapping should be consistent with the occasion: red, gold, and white for happy events; black and purple or black and white for other occasions. The Japanese do not open a gift in front of the giver, so you should avoid opening your gift in their presence. Also avoid giving a gift when someone else is present. Do not surprise your Japanese host with a gift, as it might cause the person to lose face. Let your host know ahead of time by mentioning, for example, that you have found a special commemorative coin to add to his collection. Favorite gifts with the Japanese are imported liquor, consumables of high quality, and designer-made products with such names as Gucci, Tiffany & Co., or Mark Cross. Musical tapes and CDs are also good choices. Avoid giving gifts manufactured elsewhere in Asia, as this is an insult (Baldrige, 1993; Sabath, 2002).

A Japanese American whose firm conducted business in Japan told how he once averted a near disaster in U.S.–Japanese relations. His company selected and addressed 500 Christmas cards to its Japanese joint-venture partner. The cards were red (in Japan, funeral notices are red). The Japanese American manager stopped the mail just in time. He said, "We almost sent 500 funeral cards to our Japanese partner!" (Engholm, 1991, p. 228).

These additional guidelines for gift giving in Asian countries should be observed because of the importance placed on this aspect of developing and maintaining harmonious business relationships:

- Take time to research the perfect gift; it could be related to the Asian counterpart's profession or hobby. Adding an item to a person's collection is much appreciated.
- Always wrap gifts (no bows) and include an appropriate card. Although wrapping the gift in red paper (the color of luck) is appropriate, using red ink when addressing the card or writing the accompanying note is not; in China, using red ink indicates a desire to sever a relationship forever.
- Be aware of superstitions and taboos related to gifts. Avoid any gift depicting white wolves because the wolf is symbolic of cruelty and greed. Also avoid a gift of straw sandals in China.
- Recognize the significance of numbers in gift giving: Three is a lucky number in Thailand; eight and nine are lucky in Hong Kong (the word for "eight" sounds like "prosperity"; the word for "nine" is a homonym for "eternity").
- Expect a gift to be declined out of politeness at least once in some Asian countries; they will then accept. You are expected to decline once and then accept with thanks (Engholm, 1991). Because gift giving is very important in the Japanese culture, asking advice from a Japanese colleague or from someone who has lived in Japan is recommended (Axtell, 1993; Yager, 2001).

Knowing when to present the business gift is also important. In Korea, business gifts are usually given at the beginning of formal negotiations. In Germany, however, business gifts are seldom exchanged at the beginning of negotiations but may be given at their conclusion. In Latin American countries, present gifts only at the conclusion of negotiations.

Other gift-giving practices and guidelines in various cultures include the following:

- When dining in a person's home in Western Europe, present your gift when you arrive so that it does not appear to be intended as payment for the meal.
- Avoid giving gifts to the French until a personal relationship has been developed. Avoid gifts of perfume or wine; those are their specialties.
- Gifts to Germans should not be wrapped in black, brown, or white.
- Avoid gifts of a clock in the People's Republic of China, as the clock is considered a symbol of bad luck. (In Korea, however, the clock is considered good luck and is an appropriate gift.)
- A striped tie is not an appropriate gift to a British man; it may represent a British regiment other than his own.
- Avoid gifts of a knife or handkerchief to persons in Latin America. The knife is interpreted as a desire to cut off the relationship; the handkerchief is associated with tears.
- Avoid gifts of liquor or wine for an Arab. Because alcohol is illegal in Islamic cultures, the gift would be confiscated by customs.
- Because the cow is sacred in India, do not give any gifts made of cowhide.
- In Islamic countries, exercise restraint in admiring personal possessions; you will probably find yourself the recipient of the object you have admired (Axtell, 1993; Stewart, 1997).

When people of the United States select business gifts for people in other countries, they should remember that the gifts should be made in the United States, be utilitarian, and have conversational value. Good choices include things that are representative of the United States, such as Native American art or jewelry, DVDs of U.S. movies, U.S.-made sports equipment, or food that is unique to the United States, such as candy, nuts, and California wines. Avoid gag gifts; people of some other cultures do not appreciate them (Stewart, 1997).

TRAVEL ETIQUETTE

Travel etiquette begins with a pleasant, positive attitude and a sense of adventure, especially in international travel. People who approach international travel with eager anticipation—who look forward to meeting new people, seeing new places, and experiencing a new culture—seem to have more favorable experiences than those who approach travel with a sense of foreboding. In other words, people seem to get what they expect.

Because most international travel is by airplane, etiquette in this section concentrates on air travel and covers such topics as dressing and packing for the trip, behaving properly on the plane, and handling problem situations.

Travel dress is important because the people you meet, including ticket agents, will be strangers who will judge you first by your appearance. Being well dressed makes a favorable impression on others and in many cultures is associated with competency and respect. You are a representative of your company and your country; dressing professionally sends the message that you care about the impression you make on your compatriots and on persons of other cultures. Another benefit of being well dressed (wearing a suit or executive casual) when traveling is that you get better service from airline personnel and from hotel employees on your arrival. Women may want to wear their business blouse and jacket with coordinating slacks and then carry a skirt in the carry-on luggage and change in the plane lavatory just before landing. This is especially important when a presentation is scheduled for the same day or when you are being met at the airport by a business colleague from the host country (Chaney & Martin, 2007).

When packing for a trip, keep in mind that conservative business attire is usually preferred in other countries. This means dark suits for men and women, classic leather shoes, and good-quality accessories. Your luggage should also be of good quality to create a positive impression. All belongings should be packed in the luggage; carrying personal belongings in shopping bags does not convey a professional image. Checking large suitcases and limiting carry-on luggage to the size and number specified by the airline is important. Women should remember that they are responsible for their own luggage, including lifting a suitcase to the overhead bin of the airplane. Luggage with wheels is a good investment. With multiple bags, a porter or a cart may be used.

Travel etiquette also involves courteous treatment of airline personnel. When flights are late or canceled, travelers should remain calm and be polite to travel clerks who are anxious to get them to their destinations. Passengers who are courteous when they are inconvenienced often receive better treatment, including free food and lodging, than those who are rude and insensitive. Flight attendants should also be treated with respect. Although they are not tipped, flight attendants, as well as the captain/cocaptain, should be thanked when they are standing near the exit (Chaney & Martin, 2007).

A passenger standing in line at an airline ticket counter listened to a person yelling and screaming at the ticket agent. After the mad, rude customer left, the passenger complimented the ticket agent on his patience, attitude, and calm demeanor. The clerk replied, "Thank you for your kind words, but don't worry; it's all right." The passenger asked, "How can it be all right?" The clerk answered, "It's all right because, you see, that man is going to Cleveland, but his luggage is going to Singapore." (Dosick, 2000, p. 50)

Proper behavior during the flight is especially important because of the close quarters. Complete strangers are forced into another person's intimate space. Therefore, airline passengers should be especially considerate of those around them and careful that their behavior does not offend anyone. Because of the limited space, passengers should refrain from wearing strong fragrances. They should respect the preferences for conversation of those seated next to them. Those who do not want to talk can take out a book or papers to work on to discourage a conversation. Do not put the seat back in a reclining position when traveling in the main cabin without first asking permission of the person seated behind you. Because of the limited space, it is difficult for the person seated behind you to exit, to eat or drink, or to work with the seat in front of him or her in a reclining position. Passengers should also remember to stay out of the aisles as much as possible and limit their time on the telephone and in the bathroom. If they are traveling with their family, passengers should make sure that their children do not engage in such activities as kicking the seat back of the person in front of them or standing up in the seat and staring at the person behind them (Chaney & Martin, 2007).

Sometimes problem situations arise because other passengers do not know or practice proper etiquette. When confronted with an incessant talker, you might say, "I would like to talk more, but I must finish this report." To the person in coach who reclines his seat, you might respond, "Would you please pull your seat forward while I am eating?" (Asking the flight attendant to make this request is also appropriate.) If you are seated next to a crying baby or a loud, obnoxious person, ask the flight attendant for another seat assignment.

International businesswomen typically travel as part of their jobs; they will benefit from knowing and following certain guidelines to make their travel experiences safe and enjoyable. Safety suggestions include taking a taxi rather than public transportation at your destination, selecting a nice hotel and eating there, and avoiding driving in other countries. (Hiring local drivers or taking taxis for special side trips is recommended.) Practice hotel safety; make sure other people do not know your room number; check escape routes in case of an emergency evacuation; put valuables in the room safe-deposit box; hang a "Do Not Disturb" sign outside your door whenever you are in your room; and do not open the door when someone knocks. If you plan to shop or explore the city, ask the concierge about sections of the city considered unsafe for women (Axtell, Briggs, Corcoran, & Lamb, 1997; Martin & Chaney, 2012). Women travelers should also practice street safety; wear your handbag next to your body using a long strap placed around your neck (or wear the handbag underneath a top coat) and keep matches from your destination hotel with you in case you wish to take a taxi back to your hotel and encounter a taxi driver who does not speak your language. (Matches usually contain the hotel's name, address, and phone number.) Taking with you a personal safety device, such as an alarm, may provide a sense of security. Rather than taking your usual early morning jog, pack a jump rope and exercise in your room (Martin & Chaney, 2012).

A summary of rules for business and social etiquette for the 10 countries with which the United States conducts most of its international trade follows.

Brazil

Use titles when making introductions. To show respect, the title *Doutor* or *Doutoro* (Doctor) is used, especially with older people, even though they may have neither an MD nor a PhD degree. Brazilians shake hands when greeting each other. During personal greetings, women include one to four air kisses to each cheek when shaking hands. The number of kisses has significance; married women usually kiss twice, while single women kiss three times. Although men do not kiss each other during personal greetings, they do pat each other on the back. Business cards should be printed in English on one side and in Portuguese on the reverse side. Brazilians use the Continental style of eating. Visitors should remember to avoid eating with the hands and to keep both hands above the table while dining. In addition, one should drink from a cup or glass, not from a bottle or can. A tip of 10–15% is appropriate in a restaurant when a tip has not been added to the bill. Business gifts are appreciated but are not usually given at the first meeting. Mementos of the visitor's country are appropriate; inappropriate gifts include knives or anything sharp (suggests a desire to sever the relationship) and handkerchiefs (associated with funerals). Gifts are opened in the presence of the giver.

Canada

Social and business etiquette in Canada is similar to that of the United States, but Canadians are more conservative than people of the United States. As in the United States, a firm handshake accompanied by eye contact is the customary greeting when meeting someone; the handshake is repeated on departure. Greeting behavior among French speakers will usually include cheek kissing. Both the American and Continental styles of eating are common. Do not eat food while walking on the street; always sit down or stand while consuming food. You may refuse food offered without causing offense. Most business entertaining is done in restaurants, and tipping is about the same as in the United States. Visitors to Canada should remember that in addition to the Goods and Services Tax that is included on the bill, they are expected to tip an additional 15–20%. Because of the strong French influence in certain parts of Canada, French cuisine is offered in many restaurants. If invited to someone's home, take flowers (but not white lilies, as they are associated with funerals) to the hostess; chocolates are also appropriate. Gifts are opened immediately in the presence of the giver (Axtell, 1993; Martin & Chaney, 2009, 2012; Powell, 2005).

China

Because greeting someone is a solemn occasion, the Chinese bow or nod without smiling. When greeting Westerners, however, they usually offer a handshake. Remember that rank is important in China, so the senior person should be acknowledged first. In establishing business relationships, dining plays an important role. Business entertaining is typically conducted in restaurants at lunch or dinner. Because seating etiquette is important, waiting for your Chinese host to indicate where you are to sit is recommended. Leaving a small amount on your plate is a good idea to indicate your satisfaction with the food. Although the Chinese do not tip, foreigners are expected to tip. A common practice when tipping restaurant servers or taxicab drivers is to give them a handful of change. Giving gifts is a common practice except at a first meeting. Expect the Chinese to decline a gift three times before they eventually accept it. The Chinese do not open gifts in the presence of the giver (neither should you when you are given a gift). Recommended gifts (wrapped in red) are pens of high quality or a paperweight. Gifts to avoid are clocks, white flowers, and handkerchiefs because of their association with death. In addition, knives and other cutlery should be avoided as they suggest a wish to sever ties (Martin & Chaney, 2009, 2012; Powell, 2005; Sabath, 2002).

Germany

When you greet people in Germany, remember to use last names and a firm handshake. Maintain eye contact during introductions. Status is recognized; men allow people of higher status or older women to precede them when entering a door or elevator. When dining in a restaurant, a service charge of 10–15% is generally added to the check. Although you do not need to leave an extra tip, it is customary to round up to the next large number. Tipping too much should be avoided as it is viewed as showing off. Try some German specialties: beers, sausages, and potato pancakes. Eating everything on your plate is considered polite. When invited to a German home, bring the hostess a gift of flowers (an odd number except 13 and no red roses). Gifts to your German host should be simple and rather inexpensive as Germans consider expensive gifts to be in bad taste. A gift of a good wine is also appreciated; however, do not give a gift of beer since the Germans are considered the world's beermeisters (Braganti & Devine, 1992; Powell, 2005; Sabath, 1999).

Japan

In Japan, the usual form of greeting is a bow rather than a handshake; however, many Japanese who regularly associate with persons of other cultures may use both a bow and a handshake. Follow the lead of your Japanese host. The exchange of business cards is common, so be sure you have a good supply. These should be printed on one side in English and the other side in Japanese. Remember to address your Japanese host by his last name; only family members and close friends use the first name. Most business entertaining is done in Japanese restaurants. Some Japanese specialties include *sake* (rice wine) and *sashimi* (sliced raw fish). Do not tip in restaurants; the waiter will return the money if you do. Although being invited to a Japanese home is not the norm, if invited, remember to remove your shoes at the entrance of the home. A box of candy, rather than flowers, is an appropriate gift for the hostess. Because social and business etiquette are very different in Japan, do a thorough study of the culture and its customs before you go (Axtell, 1993; Devine & Braganti, 1998; Martin & Chaney, 2009, 2012; Sabath, 2002).

A world traveler from Switzerland describes how he temporarily lost his fondness for eating fish while dining at a lavish Tokyo restaurant. After he had sampled numerous delicacies, the *piéce de résistance* was served: A live fish still flopping on the platter was brought to the table; the *maitre d'* then delicately sliced the live fish and served it to the guests. (Axtell, 1993)

Mexico

Shaking hands is the usual greeting in Mexico, and people also shake hands when saying good-bye. People who are friends will greet each other with an embrace or touch on the elbow. Kissing on the cheek is also common. When introduced to a woman, a man will bow slightly and will shake hands if the woman initiates it. Address the person by his or her last name, as first names are not used during initial meetings. Business cards are exchanged at a first meeting but remember to include the Spanish translation on your cards. Be sure to indicate your position with your company and your university degrees. Deference is shown to someone whose age, social status, or position warrants it. The altitude of Mexico City may affect your digestion, so eat lightly and carefully. Always order bottled water as tap water is not considered safe. Although Mexicans expect you to sample the fare, they will understand if you decline dishes such as *tripe* (stomach of sheep). Unlike many European cultures, Mexicans do not expect you to eat everything on your plate. You might want to sample such national dishes as *mole poblano de guajolote* (turkey in a sauce of spices, herbs, and chocolate), *quesadillas* (folded tortillas filled with cheese), and *frijoles refritos* (mashed and fried cooked beans). If invited to a Mexican home, send flowers ahead of time; avoid marigolds (used to decorate cemeteries) and red flowers (used for casting spells). Appropriate gifts include U.S. cigarettes, a gold cigarette lighter, a gold pen, art books, or a bottle of scotch (Devine & Braganti, 2000; Martin & Chaney, 2009; Powell, 2005; Sabath, 2000).

The Netherlands

In the Netherlands, both men and women shake hands when greeting each other. The handshake is firm and accompanied by eye contact. Waving when greeting another person from a distance is acceptable, but shouting is considered impolite. Although men do not kiss each other as part of the greeting, women who are good friends may kiss on both cheeks. Business cards are typically exchanged at initial meetings. Because English is spoken by most Dutch businesspeople, business cards may be in English only. The Dutch expect you to clean your plate and to rest both wrists on the table while dining. Visitors will want to try some Dutch specialties, such as *erwtensoep* (a thick pea soup) and *lamstongen met rozijnensaus* (lamb's tongue with a white wine sauce). Dining in restaurants is expensive, so you might want to try the numerous alternatives that are available: snack bars, cafes, street stalls, and restaurants that sell only pancakes. Since restaurants include a 10% service charge on the bill, you do not need to add an extra amount. However, adding 10% when the service is good is appreciated. When invited to your Dutch host's home, it is appropriate to bring flowers or to send them the following day. Business gifts should be given only after a relationship has been developed with your Dutch associate. Appropriate gifts include desk accessories or books (Braganti & Devine, 1992; *CultureGrams*, 2010; Martin & Chaney, 2012; Powell, 2005; Sabath, 1999).

Singapore

Greeting behavior in Singapore varies according to the culture, but most residents are now comfortable with shaking hands. Since Singaporean men are unsure about whether businesswomen shake hands, women should be prepared to initiate the handshake or to simply nod the head in response to being introduced. Following the lead of your Singaporean host is recommended when it comes to greeting behavior because of cultural differences in bowing, touching, and shaking hands. After introductions, business cards, which may be printed in English only, are commonly exchanged using both hands. Tipping in restaurants is usually 10–15%, which may be included in the bill. Taxi drivers and hotel personnel are not generally tipped unless some extra service is provided. Eating customs depend upon the culture, for example, Malays and Indians often sit on the floor while dining rather than eating at a table. Gift giving is as important in Singapore as it is in other countries of Asia. Appropriate gifts include brand-name items and gifts that are typical of your city or area of the country. Avoid gifts of scissors or knives (convey a desire to sever the relationship), clocks (bring bad luck), or flowers and handkerchiefs (have funereal connotations). Since numbers have significance to your Chinese and Indian business colleagues, give gifts in even numbers to those of Chinese descent and uneven numbers to Indians (signify good luck).

South Korea

In South Korea, the usual greeting between men is a bow, accompanied by a handshake. To show respect, the left hand is placed below the right forearm while shaking hands. Women do not shake hands as frequently as men. Following the handshake, business cards are exchanged between professionals during initial encounters; the cards are presented and received with both hands. Both age and social standing are taken into consideration when greeting someone. Because Koreans are proud of their cuisine, you will want to sample some of their spicy foods and such delicacies as *pulkogi* (strips of beef that are marinated and barbecued) as well as the alcoholic drink *soju,* which is frequently served with meals. Those who conduct business in South Korea should remember that meals are served and eaten, usually with periods of silence, before socializing begins. When invited to a Korean home, it is appropriate to bring a small gift, such as fruit, flowers, or candy. Business gifts, although not a necessity, are appreciated and should be made in the giver's country. Gifts should be of good quality, yet inexpensive; they are opened in private rather than in the presence of the giver (Bosrock, 1997a; *CultureGrams,* 2010; Martin & Chaney, 2012; Sabath, 2002).

United Kingdom (England, Scotland, Wales, and Northern Ireland)

A soft handshake accompanied by "How do you do?" is the common greeting in the United Kingdom. Although the typical U.S. greeting of "Hi" is acceptable in casual situations, it is too informal for business occasions. In addition, avoid saying "Have a nice day" when departing (the British interpret it as a command). As in the United States, first names are often used after knowing the person only a short time. When dining in various parts of the United Kingdom, you might want to try some of their specialties: crumpets, steak and kidney pie, or Scotch eggs, which are deep-fried hardboiled eggs with a coating of sausage and breadcrumbs. Pubs and restaurants, rather than private homes, are used for most business entertaining. Although restaurants typically add a service charge, you are expected to add an additional 10% when the service is good. When invited to dine in a British home, a flower bouquet (except for white lilies) is an appropriate gift for the hostess. A bottle of good wine is also appreciated (Axtell, 1993; Martin & Chaney, 2009, 2012; Powell, 2005; Sabath, 1999).

United States

Introductions are important to making a favorable initial impression in the United States. During introductions, it is important to mention first the name of the person having the highest rank; age and gender are no longer considerations in whose name should be mentioned first. Both men and women are expected to rise, smile, and shake hands when being introduced in business situations. (Women may choose to remain seated and refrain from shaking hands on social occasions.) The typical U.S. handshake is firm and brief; it lasts only a couple of seconds. Eye contact is expected when shaking hands. Business cards are exchanged on business occasions only when the parties plan to contact each other at a later time. There is no set ritual for the exchange of business cards. People of the United States use the American zigzag style of eating. Using good table manners is important. Refusing food offered is impolite; taking at least a small amount of food is expected. People usually leave some food on the plate to indicate they have had enough to eat. Tipping is expected; the amount to tip in restaurants ranges from 15 to 20%, depending upon the service and the restaurant. Gifts in the United States must be quite modest due to the legal limit of $25 that can be spent on a business gift. Gifts to people of other countries should be U.S.-made; local crafts, Native American art, wines or liquors, and food items are appropriate choices.

A helpful rule to remember in most cultures is to follow the lead of the people in the other culture. If they shake hands, so do you. Eat what they eat and when they eat. If the other person gives you a gift, be prepared to reciprocate. Researching the country before you travel is always good advice.

Terms

Caste system	Etiquette	Shouting
Continental eating style	Flaming	Spamming
	Netiquette	U.S. eating style
Dissing	Protocol	

Exercise 1

Instructions: Encircle T for true or F for false.

1. T F In Japan, a business card should be presented with both hands.
2. T F Throughout Latin America, the main meal of the day is in the evening.
3. T F Flaming and dissing are terms associated with "netiquette."
4. T F Introductions are more formal in Germany than in the United States.
5. T F Bolivians expect visitors to eat everything on their plate.
6. T F Tipping is more common in the United States than in China and Japan.
7. T F The practice of serving a glass of water with meals is universal.
8. T F In China, the gift of a clock is considered a symbol of good luck.
9. T F In Germany, business gifts are usually exchanged at the beginning of formal negotiations.
10. T F When selecting travel attire, the main consideration is comfort.

Questions and Cases for Discussion

1. How do introductions vary between the United States and other cultures?
2. Describe cultural variations in business card exchange.
3. Explain class distinctions in the United States and India.
4. How are gender and age related to position and status in the United States?
5. Identify some guidelines for proper telephone etiquette.
6. Explain the difference between the terms "flaming" and "shouting" in relation to netiquette.
7. What are some advantages and disadvantages of using e-mail?
8. Identify some cultural differences in dining practices.
9. Explain the difference between the U.S. and Continental eating styles.
10. What are some guidelines for tipping appropriately? How do tipping customs vary?
11. What are some guidelines for effective business gift giving in the United States?
12. What are some cultural differences in gift-giving practices? What gifts are considered appropriate for a person from the United States to give to someone in another culture?
13. Identify some cultural taboos concerning giving flowers as gifts.
14. Give some guidelines for airline travel attire and suggestions for proper behavior during the flight.
15. What are some travel guidelines for international businesswomen?

CASES

The following procedure is recommended for analyzing the cases: (a) read the case carefully paying attention to details, (b) read the questions at the end of the case, (c) reread the case, taking notes on or highlighting the details needed for answering the questions, (d) identify relevant facts, underlying assumptions, and critical issues of the case, (e) list possible answers to the questions, and (f) select the most logical response to the question. Your professor may ask that you submit answers to the case questions in writing.

Case 1

Mark was in charge of a negotiating team sent to Japan. On learning the importance of gift giving to a successful business relationship in this culture, prior to departure he asked his secretary to wrap these gifts: a clock with the company logo, a leather briefcase, a country ham, and a pen and pencil set marked "Made in Japan." His secretary wrapped the gifts attractively in bright red paper and with matching bows and mailed them to his Japanese hosts. What rules for appropriate gift giving in this culture have been followed? Which have been violated?

Case 2

A U.S. executive was invited to dine in the home of a Latin American businessman. The dinner invitation was for 9 P.M. The U.S. executive arrived promptly at 9 P.M. bearing a gift of an unwrapped bottle of Scotch for his host and a dozen yellow and white chrysanthemums for the businessman's wife. Discuss the appropriateness of the U.S. executive's behavior.

Case 3

Joe Anthony, a U.S. graduate student, was beginning a semester-long internship in Mexico City with an international health care products firm. After he had been there about a week, some male employees invited him out to a bar to sample the local specialty, bull's testicles. Joe had heard about this practice considered a sign of young Mexican machismo (male power). The idea did not appeal to him because something he had eaten recently had made him queasy. What are Joe's options? What are the possible implications or consequences of each option? What would you do in such a situation?

Case 4

When Sara Canton boarded her flight to Barcelona in New York City, she was seated in the middle with an unkempt person who apparently had not bathed recently on one side and a crying baby on the other. The person in front of her immediately reclined his seat. Sara knew she would not be pleased making a seven-hour trip under these circumstances. What can Sara do to make the trip more bearable?

Case 5

A businessman from Singapore, upon visiting the United States for the first time, was unfamiliar with U.S. tipping customs. He could not understand the cool reception he received when he did not tip the taxi driver who took him to his Dallas hotel, the bellman who helped him with his luggage, the concierge who provided special services, or the server in the hotel restaurant. Explain what the visitor from Singapore should have known about U.S. tipping customs, including specific amounts and/or percentages, in each of these situations. Be prepared to cite specific books on etiquette that include U.S. tipping information.

Activities

1. Practice introducing your U.S. manager to each of the following:
   a. An Italian manager, John Giovanni, with a college degree
   b. Chung Lo Wang, a manager from China
   c. Marco Comerlato Velasquez, a business associate from Brazil
   d. Thomas Edward Peacock, a British associate who has been knighted

2. Role-play to show how a business card is presented to someone from Japan.
3. Review back issues of the *Wall Street Journal* or a news magazine such as *Time* and make a copy of an article related to a cultural faux pas committed by either a person from the United States when traveling abroad or someone from another culture when visiting the United States. Share your information with the class.

4. Research the dining practices of such countries as Zimbabwe, Samoa, and Tanzania; write a one-page summary identifying major differences between dining practices in the United States and these countries.
5. Research the tipping practices of a European and an Asian country of your choice and make a comparison with tipping practices in the United States. Report your findings to the class.

6. Research the gift-giving practices of one of the following countries and make a brief report to the class: Japan, Taiwan, Egypt, Argentina, or Germany. Include appropriate and inappropriate gifts and other related information, such as gift presentation and reciprocation.

References

Axtell, R. E. (1990). *Do's and taboos of hosting international visitors.* New York: John Wiley & Sons, Inc.

Axtell, R. E. (1993). *Do's and taboos around the world.* New York: John Wiley & Sons, Inc.

Axtell, R. E. (1998). *Gestures: The do's and taboos of body language around the world.* New York: John Wiley & Sons, Inc.

Axtell. R. E., Briggs, T., Corcoran, M., & Lamb, M.E. (1997). *Do's and taboos around the world for women in business.* New York: John Wiley & Sons, Inc.

Baldrige, L. (1993). *Letitia Baldrige's new complete guide to executive manners.* New York: Rawson Associates.

Barnum, C., & Wolniansky, N. (1989, April). Glitches in global gift giving. *Management Review, 78,* 61–63.

Bosrock, M. M. (1995). *Put your best foot forward: Europe.* St. Paul, MN: International Education Systems.

Bosrock, M. M. (1997a). *Put your best foot forward: Asia.* St. Paul, MN: International Education Systems.

Bosrock, M. M. (1997b). *Put your best foot forward: South America.* St. Paul, MN: International Education Systems.

Braganti, N. L., & Devine, E. (1992). *European customs and manners.* New York: Meadowbrook.

Chaney, L. H., & Martin, J. S. (2007). *The essential guide to business etiquette.* Westport, CT: Praeger.

CultureGrams. (2010). Ann Arbor, MI: ProQuest CSA.

Devine, E., & Braganti, N. L. (1991). *The travelers' guide to Middle Eastern and North African customs and manners.* New York: St. Martin's Press.

Devine, E., & Braganti, N. L. (1995). *The travelers' guide to African customs and manners.* New York: St. Martin's Griffin.

Devine, E., & Braganti, N. L. (1998). *The travelers' guide to Asian customs and manners.* New York: St. Martin's Griffin.

Devine, E., & Braganti, N. L. (2000). *The travelers' guide to Latin American customs and manners.* New York: St. Martin's Griffin.

Dosick, W. (2000). *The business bible.* Woodstock, UT: Jewish Lights Publishing.

Dresser, N. (2005). *Multicultural manners.* Hoboken, NJ: John Wiley & Sons, Inc.

Engholm, C. (1991). *When business east meets business west: The guide to practice and protocol in the Pacific Rim.* New York: John Wiley & Sons, Inc.

Fairlie, H. (1983, July 4). Why I love America. *The New Republic,* p. 12.

Ford, C. (2003). *21st-century etiquette.* Guilford, CT: Penguin Putnam Publishing.

Fussell, P. (1983). *Class.* New York: Ballantine.

Glassman, A. (1998). *Can I FAX a thank-you note?* New York: Berkley.

Internet World Stats Usage and Population Statistics. (2011, June 30). Retrieved February 5, 2012, from http://www.internetworldstats.com/top20.htm

Kenton, S. B., & Valentine, D. (1997). *Crosstalk: Communicating in a multicultural workplace.* Upper Saddle River, NJ: Prentice Hall.

Kim, J. Y. (1993, July 11). Clinton couldn't get protocol right to save his Seoul. *The Commercial Appeal,* p. A5.

Martin, J. S., & Chaney, L. H. (2009). *Passport to success: The essential guide to business culture and customs in America's largest trading partners.* Westport, CT: Praeger.

Martin, J. S., & Chaney, L. H. (2012). *Global business etiquette: A guide to international communication and customs* (2nd ed.). Westport, CT: Praeger.

Miller, S. (2001). *E-mail etiquette.* New York: Warner Books.

Mitchell, M. (2000). *The complete idiot's guide to etiquette.* New York: Alpha Books.

Moran, R. T., Harris, P. R., & Moran, S. V. (2011). *Managing cultural differences* (8th ed.). Burlington, MA: Butterworth-Heinemann.

Powell, M. (2005). *Behave yourself! The essential guide to international etiquette.* Guilford, CT: The Globe Pequot Press.

Ricks, D. A. (2006). *Blunders in international business.* Malden, MA: Blackwell.

Sabath, A. M. (1999). *International business etiquette: Europe.* Franklin Lakes, NJ: Career Press.

Sabath, A. M. (2000). *International business etiquette: Latin America.* Franklin Lakes, NJ: Career Press.

Sabath, A. M. (2002). *International business etiquette: Asia and the Pacific Rim.* New York: ASJA Press.

Samovar, L. A., & Porter, R. E. (2003). *Intercultural communication: A reader* (10th ed.). Belmont, CA: Wadsworth.

Samovar, L. A., & Porter, R. E. (2004). *Communication between cultures* (5th ed.). Belmont, CA: Wadsworth.

Samovar, L. A., Porter, R. E., & McDaniel, E. R. (2009). *Communication between cultures* (7th ed.). Belmont, CA: Thomson Learning.

Segaloff, N. (1998). *The everything etiquette book.* Holbrook, MA: Adams Media Corporation.

Stewart, M. Y. (1997). *The new etiquette.* New York: St. Martin's.

Turkington, C. (1999). *The complete idiot's guide to cultural etiquette.* Indianapolis, IN: Alpha Books.

Wilen, T. (2000). *International business: A basic guide for women.* n.p.: Xlibris Corporation.

Yager, J. (2001). *Business protocol: How to survive & succeed in business.* New York: John Wiley & Sons, Inc.

Glossary

Caste system is the rigid system of class in India. The society is divided into castes where a person is determined to belong at birth. Each caste has its status, rights, and duties.

Continental eating style is a manner of eating in which the eater places the fork in the left hand and knife in the right, uses the knife to push food onto the back of the fork and then moves the food into the mouth with the tines of the fork down.

Dissing is a term meaning to speak ill of someone.

Etiquette refers to the manners and behavior considered acceptable in social and business situations.

Flaming refers to sending vicious, insulting messages via e-mail.

Netiquette refers to cyberspace or network etiquette.

Protocol refers to customs and regulations having to do with diplomatic etiquette and courtesies expected in official dealings with persons in various cultures.

Shouting is typing a message (via e-mail) in all capital letters.

Spamming refers to the cyberspace term for mass mailings of commercial advertisements or material cross-posted to numerous newsgroups.

U.S. eating style is a zigzag style of eating used by people in the United States: cutting the meat with the knife held in the right hand and the fork in the left, then placing the knife on the plate, shifting the fork to the right hand, and eating.

Answers to Exercises

True/False

1. T
2. F
3. T
4. T
5. T
6. T
7. F
8. F
9. F
10. F

Business and Social Customs

Objectives

Upon completion of this chapter, you will

- learn customary verbal expressions of persons of various countries.
- understand the importance of a knowledge of male/female relationships and workplace equality to successful intercultural communication.
- learn the roles that humor, superstition, and taboos play in understanding persons of other cultures.
- understand the role that dress and appearance play in interacting with persons from other countries.
- learn the importance of knowing about the customs associated with holidays and holy days of the country in which you are traveling or conducting business.
- understand that office customs vary from culture to culture.
- understand the importance of appropriate demeanor/behavior in intercultural encounters.
- recognize that bribery is culturally relative and plays an unofficial role in doing business in many cultures.
- recognize special food and meal customs considered typical of various cultures and how to show respect for consumption taboos of other countries.

Customs are behaviors generally expected in specific situations and are established, socially acceptable ways of behaving in given circumstances. Customs vary not only by country but also by regions or locations within a country. For example, in the United States, customs differ along north–south lines and urban–rural lines. In addition, religious backgrounds and ethnic identities account for differences in customs.

People of the United States have customary behaviors associated with certain holidays, such as eating turkey on Thanksgiving, giving gifts at Christmas, and staying up until midnight on New Year's Eve. Other customary behaviors are associated with greetings and verbal expressions, male/female relationships, dress and appearance, use of humor, belief in superstitions, and special foods and consumption taboos. Although it is impossible to identify all customs of a particular culture, certain customs are important to conducting business interculturally.

> Learning the customs of the country with whom you plan to do business shows respect and conveys a sincere commitment to developing a successful business relationship. (Stoller, 2007)

VERBAL EXPRESSIONS

Although you are not expected to learn the language of every country with whom you may conduct business, if you plan an extended relationship with a particular culture, learning to speak the language (especially commonly used expressions) is important because you may have to communicate with persons who do not speak your language.

Make an effort to learn to say such basic expressions as "please" and "thank you," greetings, and other terms commonly used by people in the culture. Examples of such terms in French, German, and Spanish are listed in Table 1.

In addition to learning these expressions, knowing other verbal expressions customarily used in a culture is useful. In the United States, people often respond to someone with a one-word reply: "sure," "okay," and "nope." Although such brevity seems blunt and abrupt by foreign standards, it is simply an indication of the informality typical of U.S. persons. Some expressions are used only in certain regions of the United States. For example, people in the southern United States often say "Y'all come to see us" when bidding someone good-bye. The expected reply is "Thanks! Y'all come to see us, too." This verbal exchange should not be taken as an invitation to visit but is rather only a friendly ritual. In many other cultures and certain regions in the United States, however, such an expression is meant to be an actual invitation to visit (Martin & Chaney, 2012).

TABLE 1 Basic Expressions by Culture

English	French	German	Spanish
Good day	*Bonjour* (bawn-JHOOR)	*Guten Tag* (GOO-tun TAHK)	*Buenos días* (BWAY-nos DEE-ahs)
Good-bye	*Au revoir* (o reh-VWAHR)	*Auf Wiedersehen* (owf VEE-der-zeyn)	*Adiós* (ah-DYOS)
Please	*S'il vous plait* (seel-voo-PLEH)	*Bitte* (BIT-teh)	*Por favor* (POR fah-vor)
Thank you	*Merci* (mehr-SEE)	*Danke* (DUNK-uh)	*Gracias* (GRAH-see-ahs)
Good evening	*Bonsoir* (bawn-SWAHR)	*Guten Abend* (GOO-tun AH-bent)	*Buenas noches* (BWAY-nahs NO-chase)
Excuse me	*Excusez-moi* (ex-kyou-zay MWAH)	*Verzeihung* (fare-TSY-oong)	*Perdóneme* (per-DOH-nay-may)

Other expressions, such as "Don't mention it" and "Think nothing of it" in response to a courtesy or favor, are considered rude by persons of other cultures. These expressions, however, are consistent with the U.S. custom that people should be modest and should not brag on themselves. Some persons feel awkward when people compliment or thank them and simply do not know how to respond. When being thanked for a courtesy, a response of "You are welcome" is preferable. Other confusing verbal expressions used in the United States are "What's up?" and "How's it going?" Persons for whom English is a second language have no idea what the phrases mean. Avoid using idioms and slang when conversing with new speakers of English because they rely on the literal translation of words. For example, a newcomer to the United States did not accept a job on the "graveyard shift" because he thought he would be working in a cemetery (Dresser, 2005).

On meeting someone for the first time, U.S. persons engage in **chitchat** (small talk or light conversation). Small talk is important in getting to know another person before concentrating on business. In most cultures, starting business without light conversation is rude and insensitive. Chitchat often includes comments about the weather, the physical surroundings, the day's news, or almost anything of a nonsubstantive nature (Baldrige, 1993). People of the United States excel at small talk, as do Canadians and Australians. The British and the French are likewise masters of small talk. In the United States, small talk does not include topics related to politics, religion, personal income, or personal life. Likewise in Saudi Arabia, conversations about family members are usually inappropriate. In Latin America and Mexico, on the other hand, it is not only appropriate to inquire about the health of family members but also to have lengthy discussions about their well-being. Any inquiries in the United States about one's family are brief; for example, "How is your wife?" is answered with "Fine, thanks." Small talk seems to pose problems for people of some cultures. Germans, for example, simply do not believe in it. Swedes, usually fluent in English, have little to say in addition to talking about their jobs, which lasts 10–15 minutes. People of Finland actually buy books on the art of small talk (Lewis, 2006).

South Americans can talk incessantly for hours, despite their relatively deficient foreign language skills. Author Richard Lewis reported attending an all-Latin American cocktail party in Caracas that lasted from 7 P.M. to 1 A.M. He said, "There were 300 people present, very little to eat, nobody stopped talking, except to draw breath, for six hours flat; I do not remember a single word that was said." (Lewis, 2006, p. 89)

In Asian and Pacific Rim countries, variations exist not only in the use of chitchat but also in the topics that are considered appropriate. The Japanese are uncomfortable with small talk. The Chinese consider small talk useful during initial meetings; appropriate topics include travel experiences and such personal topics as salary and marital status. South Koreans also consider asking personal questions to be appropriate. People of Australia and New Zealand enjoy chitchat and often initiate conversations with strangers in pubs and other public places; they enjoy discussing sports, the weather, and international politics (Martin & Chaney, 2012).

When engaging in chitchat with someone of another culture, the best advice is probably to follow the other person's lead. When a person from another culture talks about his or her family, then talk about yours. If he or she initiates discussions of a political nature, continue the discourse with your own perceptions.

MALE/FEMALE RELATIONSHIPS AND WORKPLACE EQUALITY

In high-context societies such as the Arab culture, people have definite ideas on what constitutes proper behavior between males and females. In low-context cultures such as the United States, little agreement exists. Both people of the United States and visitors from other cultures have difficulty knowing how to proceed in male/female relationships in the United States because a wide range of behaviors may be observed.

A problem with understanding acceptable male/female relationships in any culture is the stereotypes that exist. For example, a stereotype of U.S. women originating primarily from U.S. television shows and movies is that they are aggressive, glamorous, and promiscuous (Axtell, Briggs, Corcoran, & Lamb, 1997). Correspondingly, U.S. men are viewed as weak men who permit women to dominate them.

The equality of men and women in the workplace has been a sensitive issue in the United States. Although 60% of U.S. women of employment age work, they still do not receive equal pay and responsibility. Some U.S. men feel threatened by the more assertive roles many women are assuming. However, most people accept that men and women can work side by side in the workplace and that they can have a friendship that does not have a sexual component. U.S. men and women often have business colleagues of the opposite gender. These work relationships may involve business travel, and no assumption is made about any sexual involvement.

In other countries, however, treatment of men and women in the workplace differs substantially from that of the United States. In Mexico, for example, male supervisors customarily kiss their female secretaries on the cheek each morning or embrace them. Despite this custom (seen as undue familiarity by U.S. managers), problems with sexual harassment and gender discrimination are uncommon according to Mexican managers. U.S. managers interviewed, however, reported that Mexican managers do have such problems (Stephens & Greer, 1995).

In the Scandinavian countries, women and men are treated equally. Many Swedish women hold middle-management positions in business. In addition, Swedish women are found in political positions, including parliament. In Iceland, the first country to have a woman's party, women are very evident in the workplace. In fact, 70% of women in Iceland have jobs. In Finland, women hold about 38% of positions in parliament. However, women in Finland, like U.S. women, do not earn as much as men (Turkington, 1999).

In India, women do not enjoy the same privileges as men; in addition, in Saudi Arabia, women are not considered equal to men. In Egypt, only one-tenth of workers are women. Although they hold positions as doctors and secretaries, few women hold executive jobs.

Korean women have traditionally not held prominent positions in government and business. Although some progress in this area has been made, women still hold low-ranking jobs. China, too, is a male-dominated country; however, women do hold important managerial positions in business (Bosrock, 1997a).

Women in the Netherlands comprise less than one-third of the workforce. In the Netherlands 75% of the 71.5% of women who are employed work part time. Women who work outside the home usually have low-paying jobs; few hold managerial positions. A wage gap of 11.3% exists between women and men. Likewise, in Belgium and Germany, women are more likely to be in support staff jobs rather than in managerial positions. In both countries, women seem to be making progress in assuming leadership positions as the younger generation is more accepting of women in higher-level positions (Bosrock, 1995). Brazilian women are not only accepted but are also well respected in business, medicine, and education (Bosrock, 1997b).

HUMOR IN BUSINESS

As more and more companies conduct business internationally, frequent opportunities exist for businesspersons to interact in an attempt to develop a good relationship. Using humorous anecdotes is a way of breaking the ice and establishing a relaxed atmosphere prior to the start of business in international meetings.

Although humor is a universal human characteristic, what is perceived as humorous varies from culture to culture. In the United States, presentations are often started with a joke or cartoon related to the topic to be covered. In addition to the United States, most European countries use humor during business meetings. The British, especially, intertwine humor in business discussions. When humor is used in business situations with Asian audiences, on the other hand, few are amused (except for Koreans, who seem to appreciate everybody's jokes). British humor is often self-deprecating. Egyptians, too, have a good sense of humor that is self-deprecating. Visitors, however, should not join in. Although it is fine for Egyptians to laugh at themselves, others may not do so (Turkington, 1999). Asian humor finds little merit in jokes about sex, religion, or minorities; however, Asians will laugh out of politeness when a joke is told. They take what is said literally and do not understand U.S. humor. Germans, too, find humor out of place during business meetings. They take business seriously and do not appreciate joking remarks during negotiations. When a presentation in Germany was begun with a cartoon deriding European cultural differences, no one laughed. As the week progressed, people started laughing both in and out of the sessions. Later the presenters learned that cartoons were not appropriate in a professional setting of strangers. At the conclusion of negotiations, however, Germans enjoy relaxing and telling jokes in local bars or restaurants (Axtell, 1999; Trompenaars & Hampden-Turner, 1998).

Members of cross-cultural teams may have difficulty interpreting teasing and other forms of humor from their colleagues. A U.S. team member working with Australians asked about the meaning of the constant sarcastic remarks and put-downs of other team members. The Australian's response was that the teasing and put-downs show that "we accept you and like you, mate." (Schmidt, Conaway, Easton, & Wardrope, 2007, pp. 132–133)

Is there such a thing as international humor? Yes—some humor is acceptable internationally, such as slapstick, restaurant jokes, and humorous stories about golfers. Even in international jokes, however, people have their own nuances to make the jokes/anecdotes amusing to members of their own culture. In the United States, for example, sarcasm and kidding accompany humor; in Australia, humor is barbed and provocative (Lewis, 2006). In some countries, the people enjoy making citizens of a neighboring country the object of their jokes. Belgians, for example, like to direct humor at their neighbors, the Dutch, and likewise the Dutch direct humor at the Belgians. The same is true of the British and the Irish (Axtell, 1999).

Some businesspersons with global experience recommend that jokes be avoided with people of diverse cultures; they maintain that American humor is hard to export and appreciate. Even though the intention of humor is to put your international colleagues at ease and create a more relaxed environment, there is great risk of offending someone of another culture or of telling a story that no one understands. In short, we do not all laugh at the same things (Axtell, 1999).

A New York businessman who frequently traveled to Japan on business often used a translator for his speeches. After one such speech, he learned that the Japanese interpreter's version of his opening remarks went like this:

"American businessman is beginning speech with thing called joke. I am not sure why, but all American businessmen believe it necessary to start speech with joke. (Pause) He is telling joke now, but frankly you would not understand joke so I won't translate it. He thinks I am telling you joke now. Polite thing to do when he finishes is to laugh. (Pause) He is getting close. (Pause) Now!"

The audience not only laughed appreciatively, but stood and applauded as well. Later the U.S. businessman commented to the translator, "I've been giving speeches in this country for several years, and you are the first translator who knows how to tell a good joke." (Axtell, 1990)

SUPERSTITIONS AND TABOOS

Superstitions are beliefs that are inconsistent with the known laws of science or what a society considers to be true and rational. Examples of superstitions include a belief that special charms, omens, or rituals have supernatural powers. Superstitions that are treated rather casually in Europe and North America are taken seriously in other cultures. Although few U.S. persons consult astrologers or fortune-tellers for advice on business matters, in other cultures, spiritualists are highly regarded and may be consulted in making business decisions. When doing business with persons who take business advice from seers, it is best to respect these beliefs. In parts of Asia, for example, fortune-telling and palmistry are considered influential in the lives and business dealings of the people.

In many cultures, bad luck and even death are associated with certain numbers. People of the United States, for example, think that 13 is an unlucky number. Most U.S. hotels do not have a 13th floor, and even a hotel number ending in 13 may be refused. Friday the 13th is perceived as an unlucky day. Many U.S. persons will not schedule important events, such as weddings or major surgery, on this day. The Chinese, who also believe that good or bad luck is associated with certain numbers, feel that four is the most negative number because it sounds like the word for death. Hotels in China, Hong Kong, and Taiwan often have no fourth floor, and some Asian airports have no Gate 4. Conversely, some numbers have positive meanings. In China, for example, the number six represents happiness, and nine represents long life. The number of people in a photograph also has significance. Many Chinese believe that having an uneven number of people in a photograph will bring bad luck and that having three people in a photograph will result in dire consequences—the middle person will die (Dresser, 2005). Those who take pictures as mementos for their Chinese business friends should keep this in mind.

Other superstitions held by persons in some cultures include the following:

- Events on New Year's Day predict what will happen for the entire year.
- Sweeping the floor on New Year's Day may sweep away your good luck for the coming year; likewise, bathing on this day washes away your good luck.
- Performing certain rituals protects a newborn child from evil spirits.
- Attaching old shoes to the car of newlyweds ensures fertility.
- Walking under a ladder or breaking a mirror brings bad luck.
- Giving too much attention to a newborn places the child in jeopardy; the evil spirits will harm the baby if it receives a lot of attention (Dresser, 2005).

Many South Americans respect these superstitions:

- Bringing coral or shells into your home brings bad luck.
- Putting your purse on the floor results in your money running away.
- Passing salt hand to hand brings bad luck.
- Scheduling important events on Tuesday the 13th should be avoided as this is an unlucky day (Bosrock, 1997b).

Taboos are practices or verbal expressions considered by a society or culture as improper or unacceptable. Taboos often are rooted in the beliefs of the people of a specific region or culture and are passed down from generation to generation. In Arab countries, for example, it is considered taboo to ask about the health of a man's wife. In Taiwan, messages should not be written in red ink as this has death connotations. Writing a person's name in red also has negative associations in Korea, parts of Mexico, and among some Chinese (Lewis, 2006).

An American English teacher made comments and constructive criticisms in red ink on her students' papers. Although U.S. students were accustomed to this practice, her Korean students were not. These red-inked notes sent shock waves through the families of Korean students, who associated red ink with death. When the families told the principal of this taboo, he asked all teachers to refrain from using red ink on any student's paper. (Dresser, 2005)

In Malaysia, pointing with your index finger is taboo, but you may point with the thumb. Indonesia has certain taboos related to the head. Because the head is considered a sacred part of the body, it should not be touched by someone else. The practice in the United States of patting young children on the head would be cause for great concern in Indonesia. Another taboo is placing your head in a higher position than the head of a senior person. People of the Russian Federation have numerous taboos, including no whistling in the street and no lunches on park lawns. Taboos of the people of Madagascar are perhaps the most unusual: Pregnant women are forbidden from eating brains or sitting in doorways, women may not wash their brothers' clothes, and children are not permitted to say their father's name or make reference to any part of his body (Lewis, 2006).

DRESS AND APPEARANCE

What you wear sends a nonverbal message about you and your company. Because clothes can enhance or destroy your credibility, you should determine what attire is customary in the countries you visit. According to Axtell (1993), the general rule for business everywhere is to be "buttoned up": conservative suit and tie for men and dress or skirted suit for women.

An American television program investigated the impact of an attractive, well-groomed appearance in both social and business situations. "Well-groomed men and women were placed in identical situations with less polished participants who had neglected their appearance. Every single time, the more highly groomed individual got not only the date or the help with a flat tire but also the job offer and the higher salary." (Bixler, 1997, p. 16)

According to U.S. researchers and image consultants, people who wear suits, whether male or female, are perceived as more professional than those who wear any other type of attire.

Wearing professional attire is recommended when a person wants to be taken seriously. For men, professional attire includes very dark suits in charcoal gray or navy with a white, pastel, or pinstripe long-sleeved cotton shirt; for women, a medium-range or navy blue suit with a white blouse. A second choice for women is a beige suit with a light blue blouse (Baldrige, 1993; Molloy, 1996). Fabric is also important in projecting credibility, status, and power. Fabrics of pure fibers (silk, wool, and cotton) or fabrics that have the look of pure fibers convey higher credibility and status than synthetic fibers such as polyester. The recommended suit for both men and women is 100% wool (Martin & Chaney, 2012; Molloy, 1996).

Business dress in Canada, England, France, Germany, Japan, and Mexico is similar to that worn in the United States with slight variances. In Canada, people dress more conservatively and formally than people in the United States. The French are very fashion conscious as France is considered a leader in fashion. When conducting business in Europe, remember that dress is very formal; coats and ties are required for business. Jackets stay on in the office and restaurants even when the weather is hot (Braganti & Devine, 1992). Dress in Japan is also formal. Japanese women dress very conservatively and usually wear muted colors to the office. (This custom seems to be changing somewhat in larger cities, especially in companies that conduct business globally.) Care should be exercised in wearing very casual attire in public in these countries as this practice is considered inappropriate (Devine & Braganti, 1998).

Dress standards in the U.S. workplace became increasingly casual in the 1990s as did dress standards in many European companies. However, this trend toward casual office attire in the United States appears to be over (Fenton, 2002). Companies became concerned with their corporate image, as many employees seemed to be unable to distinguish between casual and slovenly. As a result, numerous companies revoked their casual dress policies a decade after the trend started; casual attire was wreaking havoc on the workplace, and some firms felt that dressing too casually was costing their company business (Hudson, 2002). Because people, particularly those from other cultures, tend to make assumptions about another person's educational level, status, and income based on dress alone, those interested in career advancement and in careers in international business should probably dress conservatively in traditional business attire—suits for men and suits or dresses for women (Martin & Chaney, 2012).

> At a Washington firm, a group of Japanese businessmen who came for a meeting on a Friday found a room full of casually dressed people. They made a hasty retreat, believing they had the wrong office. (Alvarez-Correa, 1996, p. 134)

Casual attire that is even more informal than is the norm in the United States is appropriate in certain cultures. In the Philippines, men wear the *barong*—a loose, white- or cream-colored shirt with tails out and no jacket or tie. In Indonesia, *batiks* (brightly patterned shirts worn without tie or jacket) are worn (Axtell, 1993).

Although Western business dress has been widely adopted among other cultures, you might want to learn cultural distinctions in appropriate business attire. In Saudi Arabia, for example, the Saudi might wear the traditional Arabic white, flowing robe and head cloth. You would not, however, attempt to dress in a similar manner. You would dress in the same manner as you would for an important meeting in your U.S. office.

Color of clothing is also a consideration because in some cultures color has strong associations. Do not wear black or solid white in Thailand because these colors have funereal connotations. Avoid wearing all white in the People's Republic of China as white is the symbol of mourning. Avoid wearing yellow when visiting Malaysia as certain shades are reserved for the royal families in that country. When visiting Germany, women should not wear flowered prints; such attire suggests frumpiness (Binkley, 2007). In the United States, black is typically worn at funerals but has no special significance in business situations (Martin & Chaney, 2012).

Shoes are considered inappropriate in certain situations in various cultures. They should not be worn in Muslim mosques and Buddhist temples. Shoes should also be removed when entering most Asian homes or restaurants. Place them neatly together facing the door you entered. Following the host's lead is good advice; if the host goes without shoes, so do you. Remember that in the Arab culture, the soles of the feet should not be shown, so keep both feet on the floor or the bottoms of your feet covered.

Women who conduct business abroad should be especially careful to conform to local customs concerning appropriate attire. Women conducting business in the Arabian countries, for example, should avoid wearing slacks and should wear clothes that give good coverage, such as long-sleeved dresses and dress/skirt lengths below the knees. In Europe, women do not wear slacks to the office or to nice restaurants. Ask before you go; consult a colleague who is familiar with the culture (Axtell, 1993; Devine & Braganti, 1998, 2000; Turkington, 1999).

A female sales executive from the United States, while attending a meeting in Scandinavia, was informed that the afternoon business session would be held in the sauna. The U.S. executive was not prepared for the regional custom of conducting business in a sauna in the nude. Fortunately, she had packed a bathing suit that was considered acceptable attire. Later, as she recounted the embarrassing situation to her U.S. colleagues, she said, "I just didn't know where to look." (Binkley, 2007)

CUSTOMS ASSOCIATED WITH HOLIDAYS AND HOLY DAYS

An awareness of the holidays and holy days of other cultures is important in scheduling telephone calls and business trips.

Holidays may celebrate a prominent person's birthday (Washington's Birthday) or a historic event (Independence Day) or pay homage to a group (Veterans' Day and Memorial Day). Holy days are associated with religious observances (Ramadan, Christmas, Easter, and Yom Kippur). Because business may not be conducted on some of these special days, consider this information when planning a trip abroad.

People who travel to the United States, for example, should understand that it is not customary to conduct business on Christmas Day or Thanksgiving. Business is rarely conducted on the Fourth of July when Independence Day is celebrated with fireworks, picnics, parades, and parties. Many businesses, with the exception of retail establishments, are closed on Sunday, which is the Sabbath for many religions. The Sabbath in Israel, on the other hand, is observed on Saturday, while the Arabs observe the Sabbath on Friday.

In some countries, holidays are similar to those celebrated in the United States. Some Catholic countries have a carnival season (similar to New Orleans' Mardi Gras), which is not a good time for conducting business. Many countries celebrate the New Year; the nature, duration, and time of the year of the celebration may vary. In Mexico, for example, the two-week period including Christmas and New Year's Day is not a good time for business, nor is the two-week period prior to Easter. Businesspeople are usually traveling with their families during this time.

The holidays observed in the United States and those observed by the 10 countries with which the United States conducts most of its international business are listed here (*CultureGrams,* 2010; Sabath, 1999, 2002).

Brazil	Carnival (five-day festival preceding Ash Wednesday)
	Tiradentes Day (April 21)
	Easter
	Labor Day (May 1)
	Independence Day (September 7)
	Memorial Day (November 2)
	Republic Day (November 15)
	Christmas Eve and Christmas
Canada	New Year's Day (January 1)
	Easter Sunday and Monday*
	Labor Day (May 1)
	Victoria Day (third Monday in May)
	Canada Day (July 1)
	Thanksgiving Day (second Monday in October)
	Christmas (December 25)
	Boxing Day (December 26)
	Quebec has two additional holidays: The Carnival de Quebec (February) and St. Jean Baptiste Day (June 24)
China	New Year's Day (January 1)
	Chinese Lunar New Year and Spring Festival*
	International Working Woman's Day (March 8)
	Labor Day (May 1)
	Youth Day (May 4)
	Children's Day (June 1)
	People's Liberation Army Day (August 1)
	National Day (October 1)
Germany	New Year's Day (January 1)
	Good Friday*
	Easter Sunday and Monday*
	Labor Day (May 1)
	Ascension Day*
	Whit Monday*
	Day of German Unity (October 3)
	All Saints' Day (November 1)
	Day of Prayer and Repentance*
	Christmas (December 25)
Japan	New Year's Day (January 1)
	Coming of Age Day (January 15)

(continued)

	National Foundation Day (February 11)
	Vernal Equinox (March 21)
	Greenery Day (April 29)
	Constitution Day (May 3)
	Children's Day (May 5)
	Bon Festival (August 15)
	Respect for the Aged Day (September 15)
	Autumnal Equinox (September 23)
	Sports Day (October 10)
	Culture Day (November 3)
	Labor Thanksgiving Day (November 23)
	Emperor Akihito's Birthday (December 23)
Mexico	New Year's Day (January 1)
	St. Anthony's Day (January 17)
	Constitution Day (February 5)
	Carnival Week*
	Birthday of Benito Juarez (March 21)
	Easter*
	Labor Day (May 1)
	Cinco de Mayo (May 5)
	Corpus Christi*
	Assumption of the Virgin Mary (August 15)
	President's Annual Message (September 1)
	Independence Day (September 16)
	Columbus Day (October 12)
	All Saints' Day (November 1)
	All Souls' Day (November 2)
	Revolution Day (November 20)
	Day of the Virgin Guadalupe (December 12)
	Christmas (December 25)
The Netherlands	New Year's Day (January 1)
	Queen Beatrix's Birthday (April 30)
	Liberation Day (May 5)
	Christmas (December 25–26)
Singapore	The New Year (January 1)
	Chinese New Year*
	Easter*

(continued)

Business and Social Customs

(*continued*)

	Vesak Day (celebrates Buddha)*
	Labor Day (May 1)
	National Day (August 9)
	Christmas (December 25)
South Korea	The New Year (January 1–3)
	The Lunar New Year (January or February*)
	Independence Day (March 1)
	Buddha's Birthday (April or May*)
	Memorial Day (June 6)
	Constitution Day (July 17)
	Liberation Day (August 15)
	Ch'us̆ok, Harvest Moon Festival (September or October*)
	National Foundation Day (October 3)
	Christmas (December 25)
United Kingdom (UK)	New Year's Day (January 1)
	Good Friday*
	May Day*
	Easter Sunday and Monday*
	Spring Bank Holiday*
	Late Summer Holiday*
	Christmas (December 25)
	Boxing Day (December 26)
	(Northern Ireland also observes St. Patrick's Day on March 17 and Battle of the Boyne on July 12)
	(Wales also celebrates Patron Saints Day or St. David's Day on March 1)
	(Scotland also celebrates Robert Burns' Birthday on January 25 and Remembrance Day, the Sunday closest to November 11)
United States	New Year's Day (January 1)
	Birthday of Martin Luther King Jr. (third Monday in January)
	Presidents' Day (third Monday in February)
	Memorial Day (last Monday in May)
	Independence Day (July 4)
	Labor Day (first Monday in September)
	Columbus Day (second Monday in October)
	Thanksgiving (fourth Thursday in November)
	Christmas (December 25)

*Dates vary.

212

In addition to their holidays, some countries have other times during which business is curtailed. Do not expect to conduct business in Europe during August as this is considered the vacation month, and many people close their businesses during this time. In addition to the Sabbath, little business is conducted with the Arabs during Ramadan, the month long Islamic fast. In Japan, many companies close from April 29 to May 5 to celebrate various holidays and birthdays.

OFFICE CUSTOMS AND PRACTICES

Office customs and practices include typical hours of work, lunch and break times, degree of formality, and hiring/firing.

Customarily, hours of work in U.S. offices are 9 A.M.–5 P.M. Employees are expected to start work promptly and to stay busy even during slow periods. In other words, employees are expected to find work to do and never be idle. In many countries, on the other hand, employees feel free to read the newspaper or visit with colleagues when there is nothing pressing, especially when the supervisor is out of the office.

Office hours in other countries vary. In Iran, for example, business hours are from 9:30 A.M. to 1 P.M. and from 2 P.M. to 5 P.M., Monday through Friday. In some South American countries, such as Brazil and Colombia, the workweek is 8 A.M.–6 P.M., Monday through Friday. Some offices and stores close from noon to 2 P.M. for lunch. Peru has one of the longest workweeks in the world: 48 hours with businesses open at least six days a week (Bosrock, 1997b).

The lunch period in U.S. firms may vary from 30 minutes to an hour, and break times are usually one 15-minute period in the morning with a second 15-minute period in the afternoon. These should be kept to the time specified; extended periods result in a reprimand because in the United States "time is money." U.S. persons, who are time and productivity conscious, seriously question the workday customs that are commonplace throughout Europe. For example, Europeans have a 1–1 1/2-hour lunch break, 20-minute morning and afternoon breaks (often including beer or wine), and 15 minutes at the end of the workday for cleanup time. Thus, their nine-hour workday is, in reality, a seven-hour workday (Utroska, 1992).

Hiring and firing practices vary according to the culture. In the United States, people are hired with the understanding that retention and promotions depend on performing the job satisfactorily and on getting along with their colleagues. In other words, hiring and retention are based on job effectiveness and job performance. Although workers cannot legally be fired without cause, it is understood that no job is permanent. In Europe, on the other hand, everyone in the firm has a contract that virtually guarantees permanent employment regardless of the financial condition of the company. Likewise, in such countries as Japan, employers consider an employee's job to be permanent unless the person breaks the law or is guilty of a moral turpitude. In such socialist countries as France and England, the only grounds for job termination are criminal behavior. Employees who are dismissed receive generous severance pay by U.S. standards. Employees receive a three-month notice at full salary and benefits while they look for a new job. Executives receive an even more generous severance package: a full year's salary plus one month's pay for each year of company service plus accumulated vacation pay (Utroska, 1992). In many Asian cultures, the company is considered an extension of the family. In the United States, workers are simply employees, and the company does not serve as an extended family. Problems sometimes arise when Japanese companies take over U.S. firms. Because Japanese managers assume their employees will be with them their entire careers, they think they are entitled to ask personal questions related to the prospective employee's home life and even make recommendations regarding the improvement of their personal appearance. They then discover that such questions and comments are illegal in the United States (Dresser, 2005).

The degree of formality found in U.S. offices varies; in major corporations, especially financial institutions and those in large cities, more formality often exists than in small companies in rural areas. Characteristics of an informal atmosphere include the use of first names at all levels, frequent small talk and joking, and, in recent years, more casual attire. This informal atmosphere does not indicate a lack of respect as would be the case in many European countries.

Another important aspect of office relationships is the appropriateness of showing emotions at work. Cultures that are primarily affective feel it acceptable to show emotions; those who are emotionally neutral control or mask their feelings. In an exercise reported by Trompenaars and Hampden-Turner (1998), participants from various cultures were asked whether they would express their feelings openly if they became upset about something at work. The highest percentage of persons who would not show their emotions openly were from Ethiopia, Japan, and Poland, although the lowest percentages of persons who would not express emotions were from Kuwait, Egypt, Spain, and Cuba. No pattern was apparent by continent; the United States was in the middle range, with 43% of persons indicating they would not show emotions at work.

CUSTOMARY DEMEANOR/BEHAVIOR

What is considered customary behavior in one culture may be unacceptable in another. **Demeanor** involves a person's conduct or deportment and is influenced by culture. Behavior in public places is culture specific. U.S. Americans speak louder in public than people of Germany, and people from Brazil or Nigeria speak louder than people of the United States. The type of public place also affects the voice volume that is considered acceptable. At sports events, it is acceptable to make more noise than inside a shopping mall or health club. Good advice to follow when in a foreign country is to observe the behavior of the nationals and avoid calling attention to yourself by speaking louder than those around you speak.

The following rules apply to appropriate behavior in public places in the United States:

- Keep to the right when walking in malls or on the street.
- Wait your turn when standing in line at the post office, bank, or theater.
- Give priority to the first person who arrives (rather than to people who are older or wealthier as is done in Asian cultures).
- Do not block traffic.
- Do not block someone's view at a ball game or other public event.
- Be considerate of nonsmokers.
- Treat clerks, taxi drivers, and other service personnel with courtesy and respect because in the United States the principle of equality prevails.

Courtesy is, in fact, important in most areas of the United States. The use of "please" when you are making a request is expected; "thank you" is considered appropriate when someone has granted a request or performed a service. People of all social and educational levels are accorded equal courtesy.

Another behavior that varies with the culture is the extent of touching in public places. People in the United States usually avoid situations in which they would be touching strangers in public. They avoid getting on a crowded elevator because they are uncomfortable with physical contact. If they must get on a crowded elevator, they observe "elevator etiquette," refraining from speaking, facing the front, and watching the floor indicator. One exception seems to be subway trains, where people are often too crowded to move. People in South America, on the other hand, think nothing of squeezing onto a crowded bus or elevator and pushing through a crowd.

A behavior of U.S. Americans that seems unusual to those of many other countries is doing "menial" jobs. In fact, the United States is often referred to as a "do-it-yourself" society. Regardless of wealth, position, or social standing, people of the United States are often found mowing their lawn, washing their car, or building a patio. Reasons for this custom vary; some U.S. persons point out that hiring household help or a gardener represents a loss of privacy. Others reason that they prefer to do the work themselves and use the money they would spend on service personnel for vacations, sports, and labor-saving appliances. When both adults work, home cleaning services or domestic help may be used for a limited number of hours each week. In many European and South American countries, on the other hand, numerous service people are often employed by businesspersons, government officials, and professionals. Households commonly have a cook, maid, and gardener.

BRIBERY

A custom that has undergone close scrutiny in the past few years is bribery. **Bribery** is giving or promising something, often money, to influence another person's actions. In Mexico, bribes are known as *mordida*; in Southeast Asia, *kumshaw*; and in the Middle East, *baksheesh*. Although bribery is not officially sanctioned or condoned in any country, it is unofficially a part of business in many cultures. The practice is often referred to as "greasing the palm" and is considered neither unethical nor immoral in a number of countries. In Nigeria, for example, a person must pay the customs agent in order to leave the airport; in Thailand and Indonesia, getting a driver's license involves giving a tip to an agent (Engholm & Rowland, 1996).

> According to Indonesians, bribery saves time and effort when dealing with top officials who make final decisions. In this country businesspeople have found that bribing a top government official to get a big contract is far less time consuming than preparing a good proposal for bidding. (Hodge, 2000, p. 222)

The United States has the most restrictive laws against bribery in the world. Companies found guilty of paying bribes to foreign officials can be fined up to $1 million, and guilty employees may be fined up to $10,000 (Engholm, 1991). Many U.S. competitors, including Italian, German, and Japanese firms, not only use bribery in international transactions but also may deduct the amount of the bribe on their taxes as a necessary business expense.

> Mike Lorelli of Pizza Hut shared this experience related to bribery in other cultures:
> In the Middle East or Brazil, they would think you are crazy for not offering a bribe because to them there is absolutely nothing wrong with bribery. You're an oddball, but there is not a thing you can do about it. (Engholm & Rowland, 1996, p. 133)

Managers in the United States are faced with situations that are considered illegal in their country and that are not only lawful but also an accepted part of doing business in other countries. They must, therefore, be aware that as business becomes globalized, different perceptions exist regarding the appropriateness of certain incentives. What is perceived as bribery is culturally relative just as a person's conscience can become "culturally conditioned." What is considered a tip (to ensure promptness) in one culture is considered illegal in another (Moran, Harris, & Moran, 2011). Although people of the United States are not legally permitted to accept bribes, many U.S. businesspersons provide favorite clients with box seats at sporting events or entertain them lavishly (Dresser, 2005). Some consider this practice a form of bribery.

SPECIAL FOODS AND CONSUMPTION TABOOS

Most cultures have unusual foods that are viewed with surprise or even disdain by persons in other cultures. Foods that are common in the United States that people in other cultures find unusual include corn on the cob (in some countries considered a food for animals), grits, popcorn, marshmallows, and crawfish (Axtell, 1993) (see Figure 1).

Foods in other cultures that concern some U.S. Americans include Japanese sushi (raw fish), shark fin soup in Hong Kong, dog meat in South Korea, and sheep's eyeballs in Saudi Arabia. In parts of Mexico, chicken soup may contain the chicken's feet; in China, you may be served duck's feet (see Figure 2).

A college professor from the United States who had just arrived in La Paz, Bolivia, for a two-year teaching assignment at the local university was invited to dine with U.S. colleagues at a well-known local restaurant. She was assured that the best dinner choice was the eatery's specialty, mixed grill—a variety of meats grilled at the table. After consuming one chewy morsel, she made the mistake of asking what it was. The reply: stuffed cow's teats! (Martin & Chaney, 2012, p. 113)

FIGURE 1 Popcorn (a), Crawfish (b), and Corn on the Cob (c)

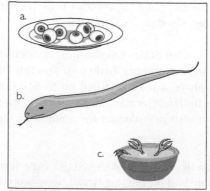

FIGURE 2 Sheep's Eyeballs (a), Snake (b), and Chicken Soup Containing the Feet (c)

A U.S. businesswoman visiting Spain was served a food that appeared to be noodles but was actually baby eels. She noticed that no one else at the table had been served them; she later learned that baby eels are quite expensive. Though a bit apprehensive, she knew that failure to eat this delicacy would be very rude; she reported that she actually enjoyed them. On another trip to Mexico City, the same businesswoman was served fried grubs seasoned with garlic. This businesswoman recommended that when you are served something that looks strange, tell yourself that others have survived eating this dish and that you can probably survive also. (Whitmore, 2005)

Because you are expected to eat what you are served in other countries, you may find it advisable to swallow quickly, avoid asking what it is, or pretend to eat by moving the food around so that it changes form. People who are experienced travelers also advise cutting the food into very thin slices and imagining that the unusual food, such as snake or dog meat, looks or tastes like something palatable (e.g., chicken).

Master of five languages, Patrick Larbuisson eats sheep intestines to help grease business deals in Saudi Arabia. He swallows with a smile but is "sick like hell the next day." (Jones, 1993)

Knowing consumption taboos of the host culture is important. People in the United States, for example, do not knowingly eat horse meat, although no religious taboo is associated with this practice. South Koreans, on the other hand, consider dog meat a delicacy. Strict Muslims do not consume pork (or any animal that is a scavenger) or alcohol. Orthodox Jews eat neither pork nor shellfish. They also observe such rules as not serving meat and dairy products together and requiring that cattle or fowl be ritually slaughtered (i.e., kosher). Strict Muslims also observe ritual slaughtering. Hindus do not eat any beef because the cow is considered sacred. People from such countries as India are often vegetarians because of personal or religious beliefs (Axtell, 1993).

Because business encounters are often conducted in social settings, you should become familiar with special foods associated with the host culture as well as consumption taboos so that your lack of knowledge of cultural eating habits will not negatively affect the communication process. The following section identifies special foods and consumption practices/taboos associated with the United States and with the 10 countries with which the United States conducts most of its international business: Brazil, Canada, China, Germany, Japan, Mexico, the Netherlands, Singapore, South Korea, and the United Kingdom. To secure information about countries not specifically identified, consult such sources as *CultureGrams* published by ProQuest CSA (the 2010 edition contains briefings on more than 200 countries), Martin and Chaney's *Global Business Etiquette* (2012), and Martin and Chaney's *Passport to Success* (2009) published by Praeger, the sources used for much of the following country-specific information on food customs.

Brazil

Breakfast in Brazil is typically *café com leite* (coffee with milk), fruit, and buttered bread. Food specialties in Rio de Janeiro include *feijoada* (black beans with pork, sausage, beef, and tongue), *moqueca* (seafood stew), and *carurur* (a pepper, onion, shrimp, and okra mixture). *Bife à cavalo com fritas* (meat with egg and French fries) is a favorite food in many parts of Brazil. In addition to coffee, milk, fruit juices, and soft drinks, an herbal tea called *mate* is a favorite beverage in the southern states.

Canada

Although the majority of Canadian people eat many of the same foods as people in the United States, the French influence is apparent in restaurants in many parts of Canada. Canadians along the Atlantic seaboard maintain a diet of seafood, including lobster and seaweed. Canadians along the Pacific Ocean are partial to smoked salmon. Canadians in the interior eat more grain products and red meats. As in the United States, ethnic and international cuisine is readily available in the metropolitan areas.

China

Food specialties in China vary from region to region. Roast Peking duck served with thin pancakes is a famous specialty in northern China. In Canton, a specialty is *dim sum*, which is a light meal consisting of small portions of food such as steamed meat and shrimp dumplings or steamed rolls with chicken served in bamboo baskets. Stuffed bean curd is also a Cantonese specialty. In Shanghai, a typical dish is sweet-and-sour spareribs. In other parts of China, *man tou* (steamed bread) is a favorite food. Noodles, rice, potatoes, and tofu are staples in the Chinese diet. Although dairy products are not readily available, fresh fruits and vegetables are enjoyed when they are in season. Dessert usually consists of fruit; seeds and nuts are typical snack foods.

Germany

Germany, like England, tends to have a cuisine that is meat and potatoes oriented. Because many cuts of meat are tough in texture, most foods are cooked for a lengthy time or cut up and served with sauces. Foods considered unusual by U.S. standards include *eisbein* (pig's knuckle), *schavelfleish* (raw hamburger), and *hasenpfeffer* (rabbit stew). The serving of warm beer, wine, and soft drinks is common in Germany.

Japan

An example of a food a U.S. person would consider unusual is dried squid, a food that is symbolic of happiness and served at New Year's in Japan. Another unusual food is *fugu* (blowfish or glowfish), which requires special preparation as the liver and ovaries contain a dangerous poison. The Japanese diet consists of very little meat and large quantities of rice and vegetables. Coffee has surpassed tea as the preferred drink. Food presentation is a very important part of the meal.

Mexico

Typical Mexican cuisine includes tortillas, beans, and various soups, such as *sopa de lima* (chicken and lime soup). An *hors d'oeuvre* that people of the United States find unusual is *chicharrón* (pork crackling served with a piquant sauce). In some parts of Mexico, a favorite dish is *pollo borracho* (chicken flavored with a tequila sauce). Other foods include *ceviche* (raw fish with onions, tomatoes, lime juice, and chiles) and *huevos motuleños* (corn tortillas with black beans, ham, fried eggs, and tomato sauce). Many foods are highly spiced; bland foods, such as breads and rice, are used to temper the hot seasonings.

The Netherlands

The Dutch are famous for their pastries. For breakfast or lunch, most Dutch people like something sweet, such as a chocolate spread on their bread or raisin rolls. Seafood is part of their diet, including eel and herring. The Dutch like French fries, but they are eaten with mayonnaise, rather than ketchup. Dutch people are well known for their breaks at 10 A.M. and 4 P.M. at which time they have coffee, usually with cream and sugar, and pastries or cookies.

Singapore

Food preferences of the people of Singapore vary according to the ethnic culture: Chinese, Indian (many of whom are Hindu), and Malay (usually Muslim). Food consumed by Hindus and Buddhists does not include beef, and the food of Muslims does not include pork. In addition, a large number of residents are vegetarians. Singaporean delicacies include *Satay* (or *Sate*), marinated, skewered and grilled meat, which may be beef, chicken, fish, goat, mutton, or tofu. Other favorite foods include *Roti prata*, an Indian bread, and *Kway tiao*, fried black noodles. Various soups and noodle dishes are popular, as well as *Dim sum* (Chinese dumplings). Desserts include Ice *Kachang* (flavored ice), grass jelly (black jelly), and *Chendol* (a coconut-flavored dessert); fruits commonly available are bananas, mangoes, and papaya.

South Korea

The diet of Koreans includes spicy foods, such as their pickled cabbage. They consume various types of soups and dishes that combine rice with such foods as red beans and with meats, especially chicken and beef. Fish and seafood, including squid, sea cucumbers, and octopus, are also part of the Korean diet. Barley tea is a favorite beverage. Visitors may want to avoid dog soup and live octopus. Although alcoholic beverages are an important part of business entertaining, women should consume only nonalcoholic drinks, such as juices or sodas.

United Kingdom (England, Scotland, Wales, and Northern Ireland)

Consumption practices of the people of the United Kingdom are somewhat similar to those in the United States; for example, the British now eat more fast foods. In fact, hamburger restaurants are currently almost as popular as fish-and-chips restaurants. Pizza places are also becoming popular. Poultry and pasta dishes are often preferred to traditional beef-and-potato meals. Some food preferences are different from those enjoyed by people of the United States. For example, Yorkshire pudding and steak and kidney pie are traditional fare in the United Kingdom. In addition, *Cawl* (a soup) and *bara brith* (current cake) are foods that are native to Wales. In Scotland, *haggis* (ground sheep entrails cooked with spices and oats) is the national dish. Irish stew, tarts, and *pasties* (small meat pies) are traditional dishes in Northern Ireland. Dessert, typically a sweet or pudding, is served at the end of the meal.

United States

The majority of U.S. people eat the meat of selected animals except for certain parts of the animal, such as the feet and eyes. Most U.S. people do not feel comfortable eating something they cannot easily identify. Meats that are consumed are beef, pork, and fowl as well as fish and shellfish. U.S. people do not knowingly eat horse meat (a cowboy's best friend); however, horse meat may be on restaurant menus in Belgium, France, and Japan. Dog meat is not eaten as dogs are considered pets; however, dogs are considered a delicacy in several Eastern countries and in

Korea. In addition, U.S. people do not eat grasshoppers (considered pets in China and eaten as an appetizer in Northern Thailand) (Chaney & Martin, 2007).

U.S. Americans are great supporters of the fast-food industry, frequenting such restaurants as McDonald's, Pizza Hut, Kentucky Fried Chicken (KFC), and Taco Bell. In metropolitan areas, ethnic and international cuisine is readily available.

Terms

Bribery	Customs	Superstitions
Chitchat	Demeanor	Taboos

Exercise 1

Instructions: Circle T for true or F for false.

1. T   F   Customs may vary by regions within a country in addition to by country.
2. T   F   In India women enjoy the same privileges as men.
3. T   F   The cost of items is an appropriate topic for small talk in most cultures.
4. T   F   People in Mexico do not waste time with small talk but get right down to business.
5. T   F   A stereotype of U.S. women is that they are aggressive.
6. T   F   What is perceived as humorous in the United States may not be humorous in Japan.
7. T   F   When conducting business in another country, wear what the people in that country typically wear.
8. T   F   In some cultures, bad luck is associated with certain numbers.
9. T   F   In the United States, employees consider their jobs to be permanent.
10. T   F   What is perceived as bribery is culturally relative.

Questions and Cases for Discussion

1. Explain how high-context societies differ from low-context societies in male/female relationships.
2. Identify some verbal expressions used in the United States that when translated literally have little meaning and are confusing to persons for whom English is a second language.
3. Give examples of how variations in the English language exist within regions of the United States.
4. How do you say "Good day" in French, German, and Spanish?
5. Explain differences in the use of humor in business in the United States and Germany.
6. Explain how women in business are treated differently in the United States and Mexico.
7. What superstitions related to numbers are held by people of the United States and China?

8. In what countries is business dress similar to that worn in the United States?
9. Identify cultures in which business dress may be different from that worn in the United States.
10. What guidelines for business dress should women observe in cultures other than their own?
11. Describe how hiring/firing practices of the United States and Japan differ.
12. Identify some rules for appropriate behavior in public places in the United States.
13. How is knowledge of holidays and holy days helpful when conducting business with another culture?
14. What U.S. foods do people of other cultures find unusual? What foods of other cultures do people of the United States consider unusual?
15. List some consumption taboos of people in various cultures.

CASES

The following procedure is recommended for analyzing the cases: (a) read the case carefully paying attention to details; (b) read the questions at the end of the case; (c) reread the case, taking notes on or highlighting the details needed for answering the questions; (d) identify relevant facts, underlying assumptions, and critical issues of the case; (e) list possible answers to the questions; and (f) select the most logical response to the question. Your professor may ask that you submit answers to the case questions in writing.

Case 1

Your organization is having a large party for its worldwide distributors in the United States. Because there will be people from all over the world, what would you serve for meals to avoid offending anyone?

Case 2

You have unknowingly arrived in Mexico during Carnival Week. Because people are busy partying and celebrating, they are not interested in meeting with you to discuss business. However, because you are here, they have invited you to join in their activities. Should you accept or reject their invitation?

Case 3

A Japanese businessman on his first visit to the United States was pleased to be invited to a U.S. executive's home for cocktails. He arrived promptly at 7 P.M. The host introduced him to a small group of people, and then returned to the front door to greet others who were arriving. The Japanese businessman seemed to have nothing to contribute on the seemingly mindless topics that were discussed. After a few minutes, the others in the group wandered off to join other groups, and he was left alone. Because the host did not return to introduce him to others at the party, he left and returned to his hotel. What, if any, rules of proper etiquette were breached?

Case 4

At his first meeting with Mina Van Buren, a U.S. manager, Juan Velasquez, an Argentine businessman, complimented her on her appearance and invited her out for drinks and dinner that evening. Ms. Van Buren refused, saying that she preferred to keep their relationship on a professional level. Discuss the appropriateness of Mr. Velasquez's invitation and Ms. Van Buren's response and the implications for building a solid business relationship.

Case 5

In China business attire is very formal. For example, women generally wear blouses that are buttoned to the top, dark, skirted suits, and plain shoes with low heels. Women with long hair wear it up in a bun or braided close to the head. What opinions would the Chinese have of women in the United States who give business presentations in form-fitting, bright-colored clothes with short hemlines and with their long hair trailing down their backs?

Activities

1. Research appropriate business and social dress in one of the following countries: India, Israel, Thailand, or Saudi Arabia.

2. List some religious taboos associated with food consumption in a coculture of the United States or a culture of your choice.

3. Write a paragraph summarizing your experience in trying a food for the first time.
4. Practice saying the following in French, German, and Spanish: "please," "thank you," "good-bye," and "excuse me."
5. Research superstitions of a country of your choice and make an oral report to the class.
6. Search online for holidays celebrated by a country of your choice (other than those listed in the text). Choose one or two holidays celebrated by the people of the country selected. Prepare a one-page abstract summarizing how the holiday(s) is celebrated, including such activities as parades, dancing, and parties. Also include special foods associated with the celebration.

References

Alvarez-Correa, W. (1996, October). Relax, it's Friday. *The Washingtonian*, pp. 134–137.

Axtell, R. E. (1990). *Do's and taboos of hosting international visitors*. New York: John Wiley & Sons, Inc.

Axtell, R. E. (1993). *Do's and taboos around the world*. New York: John Wiley & Sons, Inc.

Axtell, R. E. (1999). *Do's and taboos of humor around the world*. New York: John Wiley & Sons, Inc.

Axtell, R. E., Briggs, T., Corcoran, M., & Lamb, M. E. (1997). *Do's and taboos around the world for women in business*. New York: John Wiley & Sons, Inc.

Baldrige, L. (1993). *Letitia Baldrige's new complete guide to executive manners*. New York: Rawson Associates.

Binkley, C. (2007, December 6). Where yellow's a faux pas and white is death. *The Wall Street Journal*, pp. D1, D8.

Bixler, S. (1997). *The new professional image*. Holbrook, MA: Adams Media Corporation.

Bosrock, M. M. (1995). *Put your best foot forward: Europe*. St. Paul, MN: International Education Systems.

Bosrock, M. M. (1997a). *Put your best foot forward: Asia*. St. Paul, MN: International Education Systems.

Bosrock, M. M. (1997b). *Put your best foot forward: South America*. St. Paul, MN: International Education Systems.

Braganti, N. L., & Devine, E. (1992). *European customs and manners*. New York: Meadowbrook.

Chaney, L. H., & Martin, J. S. (2007). *The essential guide to business etiquette*. Westport, CT: Praeger.

CultureGrams. (2010). Ann Arbor, MI: ProQuest CSA.

Devine, E., & Braganti, N. L. (1998). *The travelers' guide to Asian customs and manners*. New York: St. Martin's Griffin.

Devine, E., & Braganti, N. L. (2000). *The travelers' guide to Latin American customs and manners*. New York: St. Martin's Griffin.

Dresser, N. (2005). *Multicultural manners*. Hoboken, NJ: John Wiley & Sons, Inc.

Engholm, C. (1991). *When business east meets business west*. New York: John Wiley & Sons, Inc.

Engholm, C., & Rowland, D. (1996). *International excellence*. New York: Kodansha International.

Fenton, L. (2002, March 24). Casual-dress craze in the workplace is over. *The Commercial Appeal*, p. E8.

Hodge, S. (2000). *Global smarts: The art of communicating and deal making anywhere in the world*. New York: John Wiley & Sons.

Hudson, R. (2002, April 15). "Business casual" on the wane. *Seattle Post-Intelligencer*, p. E4.

Jones, D. (1993, September 14). More business travelers going global. *USA Today*, p. E1.

Lewis, R. D. (2006). *When cultures collide: Leading across cultures* (3rd ed.). Boston, MA: Nicholas Brealey International.

Martin, J. S., & Chaney, L. H. (2009). *Passport to success: The essential guide to business culture and customs in America's largest trading partners*. Westport, CT: Praeger.

Martin, J. S., & Chaney, L. H. (2012). *Global business etiquette: A guide to international communication and customs* (2nd ed.). Westport, CT: Praeger.

Molloy, J. T. (1996). *New women's dress for success*. New York: Warner.

Moran, R. T., Harris, P. R., & Moran, S. V. (2011). *Managing cultural differences* (8th ed.). Burlington, MA: Butterworth-Heinemann.

Sabath, A. M. (1999). *International business etiquette: Europe.* Franklin Lakes, NJ: Career Press.

Sabath, A. M. (2002). *International business etiquette: Asia and the Pacific Rim.* Franklin Lakes, NJ: Career Press.

Schmidt, W. V., Conaway, R. N., Easton, S. S., & Wardrope, W. J. (2007). *Communicating globally.* Thousand Oaks, CA: Sage.

Stephens, G. K., & Greer, C. R. (1995, Summer). Doing business in Mexico: Understanding cultural differences. *Organizational Dynamics, 24*(1), 39–56.

Stoller, G. (2007, August 24). Doing business abroad? Simple faux pas can sink you. *USA Today,* p. B2.

Trompenaars, F., & Hampden-Turner, C. (1998). *Riding the waves of culture* (2nd ed.). New York: McGraw-Hill.

Turkington, C. (1999). *The complete idiot's guide to cultural etiquette.* Indianapolis, IN: Alpha Books.

Utroska, D. R. (1992, November). Management in Europe: More than just etiquette. *Management Review, 81,* 21–24.

Whitmore, J. (2005). *Business class: Etiquette essentials for success at work.* New York: St. Martin's Press.

Glossary

Bribery refers to giving or promising to give something, often money, to influence someone's actions.

Chitchat is small talk or light conversation.

Customs are socially acceptable ways of behaving; also refers to enforcement of export and import laws of a country.

Demeanor refers to a person's conduct, behavior, deportment, and facial appearance.

Superstitions are beliefs that are inconsistent with the known laws of science or what a society considers true and rational.

Taboos are practices or verbal expressions considered by a society or culture as improper or unacceptable.

Answers to Exercises

True/False

1. T
2. F
3. F
4. F
5. T
6. T
7. F
8. T
9. F
10. T

Intercultural Negotiation Process

From Chapter 10 of *Intercultural Business Communication*, Sixth Edition. Lillian H. Chaney, Jeanette S. Martin.

Intercultural Negotiation Process

Objectives

Upon completion of this chapter, you will

- be able to define the intercultural negotiation process.
- understand the steps in the negotiation process.
- know how to avoid mistakes commonly made in intercultural negotiations.
- be knowledgeable about intercultural negotiation models.
- understand negotiation strategies, including conflict resolution, in intercultural negotiations.
- understand various trade agreements that affect intercultural negotiation.

The increasing globalization of industries has necessitated an increase in strategic alliances and hence intercultural negotiations. **Intercultural negotiation** involves discussions of common and conflicting interests between persons of different cultural backgrounds who work to reach an agreement of mutual benefit. How competent and competitive firms are both domestically and internationally and how they handle customers and vendors from other cultures will determine how successful a firm is internationally. Some of the reasons global joint ventures and strategic alliances are on the increase include economic deregulation, rapid technological changes, large capital requirements, government-supported industries, economic maturation, and improved communications.

One of the most important differences in negotiating internationally rather than domestically is culture. Negotiators find out the negotiation model that their counterparts will use and then compare and contrast it with their own. A major mistake is to stereotype a national culture. Although you can learn a lot about how people in another culture negotiate, all negotiators from a country will not be the same. The less homogeneous a country is, the larger the range of negotiator styles you will find. This chapter includes steps in the negotiation process, intercultural negotiation models, and negotiation strategies.

STEPS IN THE NEGOTIATION PROCESS

Because negotiating with people from other cultures can be challenging, it is important to first get an overview of the negotiation process by examining the steps typically followed. These steps include site and team selection, relationship building, opening talks, discussions, and agreement. The negotiation process sets the stage for successful cross-border deals.

Preparation and Site Selection

When preparing to negotiate with a person of another culture, such variables as customs, etiquette, languages, and beliefs, in addition to product issues of price and terms, must be considered. Consulting someone who has lived in the target country or who has worked there is advisable. In addition, written materials and videos on negotiating in different countries are valuable resources.

The negotiation site is relatively unimportant to U.S. negotiators; they are comfortable negotiating in their office, over the telephone, or in another country. In some countries, however, the negotiation location is an important consideration. You may be expected to go to their country. Latin Americans and Asians, for example, expect you to go to them initially as they are more comfortable in their own territory (Leaptrott, 1996).

Other preparation includes locating an appropriate room that is large enough to accommodate seating, bearing in mind that seating is very important in cultures in which hierarchy must be acknowledged. In addition, remember that in Hong Kong, Taiwan, and Singapore, round conference tables are preferred, while in South Korea and Japan, rectangular tables are used. No one is seated at the ends of the table; the guests are seated on the "wall of honor," which is the side of the table near the wall that is farthest from the door (Wilen, 2000).

Team Selection

To have a successful negotiation experience, it is important to select the team members carefully. The number of people on the team; the age, gender, rank, and expertise of team members; and the personalities of potential team members are all important considerations. Whenever possible, include someone on the team who either is from the target culture or has spent time there. Expertise in the language is also a consideration; unless a team member can speak the language, the services of an interpreter may be necessary. The number of members on the team could range from two to three typically found on U.S. and Mexican teams to four to seven on Japanese teams. Inquiring ahead of time as to the size of the opponent's team is recommended so that team sizes are balanced. Age, gender, and rank are important considerations in most Asian countries as well as in Africa and the Middle East. Keeping the same team throughout negotiations is important for building a solid business relationship.

Negotiator selection is an important aspect of conflict resolution. Negotiators should be selected for their background (technical or social), emotional makeup, values, and viewpoints. It is important to find a negotiator whose qualifications most closely fit the requirements for the negotiations that will take place. Some important areas to be considered are gender, age, political affiliation, social class, cooperativeness, authoritarianism, and risk-taking propensity. Evaluating the negotiators from the other perspective is helpful in selecting or adapting your strategy (Cohen, 1998).

Evaluating yourself as an intercultural negotiator within the constraints of the situation is important. Be sure you clearly perceive your objectives, know the facts, and choose your strategies and tactics carefully. Negotiation is essentially communication with an encoder and a decoder. To the extent that the encoder and decoder share the same perceptions is the degree to which their communications will be sent and received as intended. Communicating successfully with someone in your own society is often difficult; when you add different cultural concepts, different experiences, and different languages and word meanings, the possibility for miscommunication increases (Cohen, 1998).

Relationship Building

Although relationship building is relatively unimportant in the United States, in some countries sufficient time must be spent getting acquainted with the person with whom you want to conduct business. In Argentina, as in other Latin American countries, personal relationships are very important. To conduct business with governmental representatives, you need an intermediary to even get an appointment. In fact, all Hispanic countries have agents who specialize in making contacts between local firms and foreign companies (Leaptrott, 1996). In India, small talk and tea are important aspects of the negotiation process. The sweet milky tea that is offered should be accepted after an initial refusal; refusing the refreshments offered entirely is considered an insult (Morrison & Conaway, 2006). In Central and Eastern Europe, building relationships prior to conducting business is also important. Introductions are a necessary part of building the relationship. Establishing a relationship is also important in the Arab countries. Because Arabs conduct business only with friends, taking time to build a friendship is a necessity. However, with the friendship comes the implicit agreement to give assistance and support when needed. Although personal relationships are necessary to conducting business in Asian countries, establishing a friendship with potential business associates is not necessary. Locating an agent to serve as an intermediary with the targeted firm is recommended (Leaptrott, 1996).

Opening Talks

In the United States, as in many cultures, opening talks begin promptly, often with a short time spent in small talk. When negotiating with Australians, expect to engage in small talk for a short time to establish rapport before getting down to business (Morrison & Conaway, 2006). In Scandinavian countries, differences exist in what is considered customary during opening talks. People from Sweden arrive promptly, have a meeting agenda, and engage in small talk. Opening the presentation with a joke, however, is a mistake because the Swedes do not use humor during negotiations. In Finland, on the other hand, there is no small talk; they prefer to get down to business promptly (Turkington, 1999). Agendas, although viewed in a positive manner in the United States, may not be viewed as positive in some countries, such as in Latin America and the Middle East. In these countries more open interaction is preferred; agendas are viewed as a hindrance to effective negotiations. Likewise, in Japan agendas may not be used because Japanese negotiators prefer to discuss several topics at the same time. When negotiating with Asians, it is important to remember that during opening talks, they will expect your top-level executives to be present (Leaptrott, 1996).

In Arabic-speaking Islamic cultures, time is viewed in two ways: first, the earthly existence from birth until death and second, the heavenly existence that does not have a beginning and an end. While the two domains share the unit of time, the ratio is one earth day is equal to 50,000 heaven days. Also the heaven domain dominates the earth domain. Earth time is event oriented rather than clock oriented. Event time and clock time exist in the Arab world. Event time happens when something is ready, such as a meal has been prepared. In the past appointment times were unknown. Time is measured by how long it takes to complete a task. Western time is clock time, and time controls everything in Western life (Alon & Brett, 2007).

Discussions

During discussions, it is important to keep in mind that a variety of behaviors may be seen as the norm in certain countries. In Argentina, for example, negotiators may become quite emotional, although in France you may expect a lively discourse because they enjoy debating. Concessions during the discussions should be thought out ahead of time and handled skillfully. Your plan for concessions should take into account that in some countries, such as Mexico and the Middle East, compromise is viewed negatively. In addition, the timing and amount of the concession should vary with the country. In Australia, concessions tend to increase during negotiations, although in India they tend to decrease. During discussions with Asians, it is wise to keep in mind that they may smile, which usually indicates lack of understanding, or they may say, "Yes," which may actually mean, "Yes, I understand." In negotiations with Asians, it is sometimes advisable to move discussions to a more informal location, such as a restaurant or a golf course (Leaptrott, 1996).

Agreement

Closing the negotiations properly is very important. Delays are to be expected in such countries as India, so it is advisable to allow sufficient time for completing the deal. Likewise, when completing negotiations in India, it is wise to get both tax and legal advice prior to the final agreement (Morrison & Conaway, 2006). Delays are also common in Asian and Latin American countries; after reaching agreement, there is typically a long wait before final approval. The final written contract is vague by U.S. standards and is viewed as a guide for future negotiations rather than as a binding agreement as is true of U.S. contracts. You may, therefore, be continuing negotiations for some time even after both sides have signed the agreement (Leaptrott, 1996). Documenting the agreement is a stage where cultural differences need to be addressed (King & Segain, 2007).

To be successful in distributor agreements, Axtell (1994) suggests the following points that should be covered and agreed upon to assure success:

1. Effective dates of the agreement
2. Options at the end of the agreement
3. Place of jurisdiction
4. Terms of termination before agreement ends
5. Arbitration
6. Geographic boundaries of agreement
7. Degree of exclusivity
8. Description of products being distributed
9. Agreed-on sales quotas
10. Responsibility for import duty, freight, and insurance
11. Responsibility for warehousing, inventory control, and accounting
12. Information that must be reported to the sourcing company
13. Currency to be used for payment
14. Terms of payment
15. Provisions for secrecy
16. Competitive products that can or cannot be carried
17. Responsibility for warranty and repairs
18. Responsibility for advertising, merchandising, and public relations
19. Protection of patents and trademarks

20. Responsibility associated with drop shipments and payment
21. Payment provisions of commissions and bonuses
22. Responsibility for taxes
23. Responsibility for indemnification
24. Responsibility for translation
25. Consideration of legal assignment, waivers, *force majeure*, notices, severability, and Foreign Corrupt Practices Act
26. Responsibility for setting prices

Many of these points can be handled ahead of negotiations and are controlled by lawyers during negotiations between U.S. firms. However, when you are dealing interculturally and multinationally, these points need to be addressed so that everyone understands both the letter and the intent of the contract.

When barriers develop during the negotiations, the negotiators need to be creative if the negotiations are important to their company. The negotiators must sift through the information to look for the conflict, look at the goals that underlie the demands, seek ways to reconcile the two sides, and, if agreement is not reached, decide whether to pursue the negotiations by changing the goals (Pruitt, 2000).

MISTAKES COMMONLY MADE DURING NEGOTIATIONS

Although effective negotiators are generally successful in their negotiation attempts, mistakes are sometimes made during the negotiation process that may have a negative impact on the outcome. Cellich (1997) identified the following mistakes sometimes made by negotiators:

1. Making a negative initial impression
2. Failing to listen and talking too much
3. Assuming understanding by the other culture
4. Failing to ask important questions
5. Showing discomfort with silence
6. Using unfamiliar and slang words
7. Interrupting the speaker
8. Failing to read the nonverbal cues
9. Failing to note key points
10. Making statements that are irritating or contradictory
11. Failing to prepare a list of questions for discussion
12. Being easily distracted
13. Failing to start with conditional offers
14. Failing to summarize and restate to ensure understanding
15. Hearing only what they want to hear
16. Failing to use first-class supporting materials

Skilled negotiators should avoid the preceding list of common mistakes, emphasize areas of agreement, and consider the long-term consequences of their agreements. A mistake sometimes made by U.S. negotiators because of their self-imposed time constraints is making concessions prematurely. Many times, the size of the concession is larger than necessary had more time been taken. If a concession is made too soon or if a large concession is made, the opponent is not as likely to see the concession as much of a gain. The Russians and the Chinese are very good at making concessions work for them. People of the United States also look at negotiations from a legal point of view. Most cultures are not as concerned with the legal view but are concerned with having a good agreement, a shared perception, and a trust of the other side (Berger, 2006).

INTERCULTURAL NEGOTIATION MODELS

The model you choose to use when negotiating interculturally will depend on the people with whom you are negotiating as well as on your own personal biases. Research has shown that social, cultural, political, and legal issues; timing of delivery; payment; terms of payment; role of consultants; and authority to make binding decisions take up most of the negotiation time, so researching a particular company and culture could greatly reduce the time spent in negotiation (Ghauri, 1983).

People tend to negotiate interculturally as they do intraculturally unless they realize they need to adapt to another culture. The effect of culture in intercultural negotiation is one of relative, not absolute, values. The negotiations will proceed as smoothly as the abilities of all participants to be empathetic and to adapt to each other's cultural constraints. For example, the Russian negotiating tactics include a need for authority, a need to avoid risk, and a need to control. Negotiating style is not neutral; it is culturally based and somewhat subconscious. A clash of negotiating styles can lead to a breakdown in the negotiation (Cohen, 1998).

Protocol helps maintain the cultural values of a country. Therefore, businesspeople who are going to negotiate outside their own culture need to learn as much about the other culture as possible. When you understand the opposition, you can formulate a course of action more accurately and obtain your goals (Leaptrott, 1996).

Game theory holds that protocol ensures that the rules of behavior are the same for both parties; however, if one party does not understand the rules, that party will not win in the negotiations.

For example, the Japanese protocol is to never say "no." A negotiator must know and understand the many meanings of "yes" to know whether a contract is forthcoming or not. (Leaptrott, 1996)

Two main negotiating styles used currently are the problem-solving approach and the competitive approach. Interculturally, the **problem-solving approach** has been identified with the need to consider national cultural characteristic differences and/or organizational cultural differences that lead to differences in communication. The **competitive approach** is more individualistic and persuasion oriented. The competitive approach also looks at a solution that is best for the negotiator's own side versus a win–win style of negotiation. The problem-solving approach to negotiation leads to adaptation by the negotiator to the negotiator's counterpart through information exchange of needs. This is accomplished by gaining information on the opposition's people. Each of the variables are affected by the cultural protocol from which both sides come, and the more difference there is between their cultures on the protocols, it follows that more problems could exist when they are working through the negotiation variables. The more the negotiators are problem-solving oriented, the more they will use the problem-solving approach to negotiation. The competency of businesspersons' intercultural communication will determine how effective they are in using the problem-solving approach (Chaisrakeo & Speece, 2004).

Three other negotiation approaches have been promulgated: compromising, forcing, and legalism. **Compromising** seeks a middle ground between the two parties. Although compromising distributes the outcomes equally between the parties, it does not maximize the joint gain. **Forcing** is used to make the other party comply and is closer to the competitive approach. **Legalism** uses legal documentation to force the other partner to comply and is again closer to the competitive approach (Lin & Miller, 2003).

A Thai working in a Swiss multinational says: "National culture always influences the style of negotiation either directly or indirectly....This culture comes into our life from everywhere in our country. So there is no doubt…it must affect our bargaining style."

In contrast, a United Kingdom worker says: "I don't see that culture will affect my bargaining style. I got bargaining skills from my working experience. I also learned it from my supervisor and my friends. Individual personality should be another factor that has an effect on negotiating style but not national culture." (Chaisrakeo & Speece, 2004, p. 274)

A person's negotiating strategy may achieve a compromise agreement (distributive deal) or an integrative agreement (integrative deal). The **compromise agreement** is reached when two parties find a common ground between their individual goals; the result is a lower joint benefit. For example, if one side offers to sell a product for $35 per unit and the other side offers to buy it for $25, a compromise of $30 can be reached that yields a lower joint benefit. With an **integrative agreement**, the two parties reconcile their interests to yield a high joint benefit. Negotiators should seek integrative agreements rather than compromise agreements because integrative agreements tend to be more stable and more mutually rewarding and usually benefit the broader community represented by the two parties. Research does not support one culture's using either an integrative or a distributive strategy primarily. Negotiators tend to learn to use both during negotiations (Brett, 2007).

The five methods of reaching integrative agreements described by Pruitt (2000) are expanding the pie, nonspecific compensation, logrolling, cost cutting, and bridging. Expanding the pie involves receiving additional resources. Nonspecific compensation involves repaying the party who does not receive what he or she requests in some unrelated way. Logrolling, which may be viewed as a variant of nonspecific compensation, involves both parties, rather than only one, being compensated for making concessions requested by the other party. Each party makes concessions on low-priority issues in exchange for concessions on high-priority issues. The cost-cutting solution involves the reduction of one person's costs while the other person gets what he or she wants. Bridging involves devising a new option for situations in which neither person gets his or her initial demands (Brett, 2007; Pruitt, 2000).

A cease-fire in the Yom Kippur War found the Egyptian Third Army surrounded by Israeli forces. A dispute arose about the control of the only road available for bringing food and medicine to this army, and the two parties appeared to be at loggerheads. After a careful analysis, the mediator, Henry Kissinger, concluded that Israel wanted actual control of the road while Egypt wanted only the appearance that Israel did not control it for the sake of public relations. A bridging solution was found that involved continued Israeli control but the stationing of United Nations soldiers at checkpoints on the road so that the Egyptians seemed to control it. (Pruitt, 2000, p. 503)

The high or low national cultural context of a negotiator, the organizational culture, the negotiator's own cultural context, and the cultural contexts of their counterparts determine the negotiators' abilities to adapt to each other during the negotiation process. This ability of the people in an organization to integrate other cultures' views into their own cultural intelligence is paramount to an organization's being successful in negotiating in other cultures.

For a negotiation to be effective, the people must work toward an agreement. This involves the people's working to build a relationship rather than a transaction. They need to exchange information honestly and openly. The negotiators must be careful in their use of persuasion tactics. Although Western societies favor rational argument, which can be aggressive and competitive, their Eastern counterparts tend to be more polite and restrained (Thomas & Inkson, 2004).

Kozicki (1998) presents a four-stage negotiation model—investigative, presentation, bargaining, and agreement. The investigative stage includes preparation or knowledge gathering about the other side and their goals. The presentation stage is a challenge because of cultural, perceptual, environmental, and power differences. The bargaining stage depends on cultural differences and the ability to stay disciplined and controlled. The agreement stage is the point at which the negotiators finalize the deal and set the stage for a continued relationship. Often people associate negotiation with only the bargaining stage, but negotiations are much more than bargaining.

Although these four stages work well in the United States, when negotiating internationally, it may be advisable to change your strategy. According to Brett (2007), those negotiators who negotiate the high-net-value integrative and distributive deals across cultures can be described as pragmatic individualists, cooperative pragmatists, and indirect strategists. The pragmatic individualist sets high targets, searches for information, makes trade-offs, and avoids distraction concerning power. The downside of the pragmatic individualist is time because their partner may feel a long-term relationship is not being established. The cooperative pragmatist is concerned with the outcome for all parties. Many questions will be asked and answered, and power will be dealt with indirectly. Cooperative pragmatists negotiate integrative deals and realize distributive outcomes. As long as the trust is genuine between the two sides in a negotiation, there should be few problems. However, a pragmatic individual may take advantage of a cooperative pragmatist because of the cooperative's need to trust. Indirect strategists are not sure about the power situation and choose to search for information indirectly. This tends to be successful within a culture that uses the indirect strategy but a problem when negotiating with a culture that is not using the indirect strategy. The indirect strategy uses cues that may be too subtle for many cultures. It is also difficult for negotiators from indirect strategy cultures to negotiate with members from a direct strategy culture. When you have direct and indirect negotiators, the conflict will not make integrative agreements possible but will make distributive agreements possible. Because these three models are used in different cultures, successful negotiators need to learn about all three and be able to use the method that will work best with the particular culture with whom they are negotiating. U.S. Americans, in particular, need to be aware of their shortcomings, which are well known to many of their opponents. To people of many cultures, people in the United States always seem to be in a hurry. It is generally known that U.S. negotiators are often in a rush and may not be as completely prepared as the other side.

A young U.S. businessman related a story about negotiating a joint venture with a Japanese company. As they negotiated, it was apparent that the Japanese company knew everything about the U.S. company—who its customers were, production capacity, sales history, financial status—and the U.S. firm had only a little data on the Japanese firm. The Japanese had expected the U.S. firm to be better prepared for their visit and took their business elsewhere.

NEGOTIATION STRATEGIES

Negotiation strategies are plans organized to achieve a desired objective. Because strategies are used to elicit desired responses, negotiations can take many forms. Predicting the opponent's response is essential to strategic planning. Intercultural negotiation strategies differ from intra-cultural styles for most cultures.

> Mark McCormack explained how negotiations can be win–win in his book, *What They Don't Teach You at Harvard Business School*:
>
> "I find it helpful to try to figure out in advance where the other person would like to end up—at what point he will do the deal and still feel like he's coming away with something. This is different from 'how far will he go?' A lot of times you can push someone to the wall, and you still reach an agreement, but his resentment will come back to haunt you in a million ways." (McCormack, 1984, p. 149)

Upon what are negotiation strategies based? Assuming that people act on the basis of their own best interests, the question then becomes how to determine whether this is the deal to accept, or, more broadly, how to determine the truth? Different cultures arrive at truth in negotiations in one of three ways: faith, fact, and feeling. Persons operating on faith care that your religious or political ideology matches theirs. For example, small nations that believe in self-sufficiency may reject a good deal simply because they want their own people to do the work, even though your product is clearly superior and lower priced. Thus, presenting facts to these persons is futile. Persons who believe in facts are often predictable; they give the contract to the lowest bidder. Most of the people in the world are more concerned with feelings and relationships; they believe in building a relationship over time and will not buy from someone else just because they can get a lower price. Both sides have to have an idea of their Best Alternative to a Negotiated Agreement (BATNA). BATNA is a process of determining the terms that are too unfavorable and the terms that are in your interest to accept; you then make sure you do not reject the acceptable terms and that you reject the unfavorable terms. BATNA becomes your lowest denominator—the price at which you will walk away from the negotiations (Berger, 2006).

U.S. Americans tend to make fewer adjustments to their opponent's behavior, and they change their negotiation strategy less than other cultures when dealing interculturally. This tendency is partially due to the fact that U.S. persons lack sufficient motivation to change their behavior in negotiation encounters because, in the past, the world has wanted what the United States produced. The more U.S. negotiators learn about negotiation styles of other cultures, however, the more they are beginning to make adjustments.

Negotiation strategies also include the preparation details; tactics; conflict resolution and mediation; and observations, analysis, and evaluation.

Preparation

Choosing where the meeting will be held is the first consideration in making preparation. When a meeting is held on your turf, you have more power; but you also have more responsibility for seeing to your counterpart's comforts. If the meeting is held on your counterpart's turf, he or she has the power and responsibilities. When it is held at a neutral location, members of each team are responsible for their own comforts.

In addition to selecting the location and determining the cultural protocol of the location, Leaptrott (1996) points out that preparation involves gathering information about the members of the other negotiation team, defining objectives, preparing a strategic plan, gathering ideas on applying your strategies within the protocol, researching the etiquette rules of the other culture, and viewing negotiations as an obstacle course to complete in order to achieve your goal. Although it is important to be prepared for questions, it is also important to safeguard strategic information that you do not want to share.

Tactics

Tactics are maneuvers used for gaining advantage or success. Tactics can take the form of verbal, nonverbal, or situational tactics. The attributes the receiver attaches to the tactic can be so distracting that the receiver has a distorted perception of the point that is communicated. Jokes often used by people of the United States to "break the ice" are examples of such tactics. Although these work well when the negotiations are between U.S. companies, jokes generally do not translate well to other cultures. Jokes are often perceived as derogatory toward a particular person, and in group-oriented cultures, this type of humor may be considered offensive (Berger, 2006).

In addition to jokes, other verbal tactics are promises, threats, recommendations, warnings, rewards, punishments, normative appeals, commitments, self-disclosure, questions, and commands. Nonverbal tactics include tone of voice, facial expressions, body distance, dress, gestures, silence, and symbols. Situational tactics include location, time constraints, and physical arrangements.

Distracting tactics can be detrimental to the negotiation process. Allowing insufficient time for the negotiations is typical of cultures that want to get "right to business." By doing so, the other negotiating team may feel you are uninterested in a long-term relationship; consequently, they are not interested in what your team may have to say.

Whether the climate during negotiations is supportive or defensive depends on how the cultures negotiating view each other. What one culture considers defensive, dominating, retaliatory, and threatening may be considered normal by the other culture. However, if a negotiator is perceived, rightly or wrongly, as defensive or supportive, the other team will respond according to its perceptions and not according to what was intended. Climate is a very important area to research to read your opponents correctly. One way to avoid being defensive is to ask questions and learn what your opponent is thinking. Clarify or restate what you understand to have been said and ask if that is correct. Try to follow the other side as it explores the issues rather than always taking the leadership role. Use role reversal to understand and appreciate the other side's position.

Conflict Resolution and Mediation

Conflict resolution involves a series of questions: How do we know if there is conflict? Is the conflict increasing or decreasing? Is the time to resolve the conflict now? What are the tactics to resolve the conflict? Is the conflict irresolvable? How do you tell if there is conflict or simply a lively debate? What is often an emotional, verbal disagreement for one culture can be a display of sincerity for another culture. In many countries and cultures, courts are third-party intermediaries.

Learning the social system and cultural values of the other negotiators will help you identify the signs of conflict or prevent the conflict from developing. Knowing whether to cultivate a personal relationship, being conscious of rank and position, understanding the thought patterns of other negotiators, and knowing how to establish trust are essential to successful conflict resolution. Because of culture differences, negotiators may focus on different aspects of the negotiations as being more important. A U.S. negotiator, for example, may focus on legal and financial agreements, although the Mexican or Japanese negotiator may emphasize personal relationships (Samovar, Porter, & McDaniel, 2009). Communicating respect, being nonjudgmental, realizing that perceptions are personal, showing empathy, and tolerating ambiguity can help you avoid conflict and negotiate successfully.

> A U.S. software engineer, while working with an Israeli client on a project, observed the Israeli's different ways of approaching and discussing issues. He observed, "There is something pretty common to the Israeli culture; they like to argue. I tend to try to collaborate more, and it got very stressful for me until I figured out how to kind of merge the cultures." (Brett, 2007, p. 33)

If you have done your homework and are still having conflicts that defy resolution, you might want to turn to a third party, a mediator. Mediation is the use of a third party to settle differences between negotiating teams to bring them to common agreement. Mediation may be the fastest road to discovering the negotiation barriers. If you are dealing with members of a culture who do not like confrontation, who are afraid of losing face, or who are causing you to lose face, using a mediator may be the best path to follow (Berger, 2006).

According to Lewicki, Barry, Saunders, and Barry (2011), a mediator can sometimes productively solve disputes. A mediator first stabilizes the setting, including greeting the participants, designating seating, identifying each person, stating the purpose of the mediation, and confirming his or her neutrality. After setting this stage, the mediator gets a commitment from the participants to proceed in a businesslike manner. The second step helps the parties communicate in an orderly fashion. The mediator decides who is to speak first and provides a rationale to the group. As each participant speaks, the mediator takes notes, actively restates the points being made, is a calming influence, and focuses on the issues. The mediator then summarizes, asking the speakers for their agreement. Next, the mediator helps the participants set priorities. The third step is to help the parties solve their disagreements. The negotiator asks everyone to list alternative possibilities for settlement and a workable alternative, increases understanding of the alternatives, and rephrases them if necessary. Finally, the fourth step involves clarifying the agreement, checking to be sure both sides are in agreement and understand the terms, establishing a time for follow-up, emphasizing that the agreement belongs to the parties and not the mediator, and congratulating the negotiators on their resolution.

The best way to avoid conflict is to prepare, plan, and respect the culture with whom you are negotiating before negotiations commence. Be sure you know and respect the customs of the other negotiator's culture and be careful of gestures, nuances in meanings, and taboos of the other culture. Avoid using jargon, idioms, or slang. Realize that even if you are using a bicultural interpreter, often equivalent concepts do not exist between different languages. Many times a picture will help with explanations; therefore, you might want to bring photographs, drawings, overhead transparencies, samples, or anything else that can help the other side understand your presentation.

For the negotiation process to proceed expeditiously, observing, analyzing, and evaluating what happens between negotiators is important.

Observations, Analysis, and Evaluation

As negotiations proceed, you need to be very observant of changes from your initial expectations, analyze the differences, and adapt your negotiation strategy accordingly. Constant evaluation of verbal, nonverbal, and group interaction is necessary to negotiate from the best position possible.

For negotiations to be successful, they must allow both parties to gain something—a win–win situation—although the parties probably will not gain equally.

Analysis involves defining the problem by separating and subjectively assessing probabilities, values, risk attitudes, time preferences, structuring and sequencing of the counterpart's choices, and the unknown. In addition, the people who are involved in the negotiation, their style of negotiating, the national culture, the differences in the two cultures, and the interpreters and translators need to be analyzed and evaluated. The developmental process of observing, analyzing, and evaluating is completed for each step in the negotiation process. Detailed outlines of the items in the negotiation process that need to be constantly observed, analyzed, and evaluated include the following (Casse & Deol, 1991):

1. Physical location of the negotiations
   * managing power
   * time and opportunity management—timely actions based on opportunity analysis provide needed edge in highly competitive situations

2. Agenda or policy issues in the negotiation
   * basic concept of negotiation
   * selection of negotiators
   * role of individual aspirations
   * concern with protocol
   * significance of type of issue

3. Preliminary statement and limitation considerations
   * complexity of language—need a means to communicate clearly
   * nature of persuasive argument
   * value of time
   * appreciation of cultural differences—anticipation of their moves
   * mutual understanding
   * negotiation is more art than science—be natural
   * statement of anticipation for the negotiations

4. Deliberation and solution of some issues and identification of the issues of no agreement
   * bases of trust
   * risk-taking propensity
   * internal decision-making systems
   * persuasion—establish credibility
   * selling—create the need

5. Preliminaries to final negotiations
   * narrow down differences—achieve consensus
   * emphasize commonalities of interest
   * understand limitations of your counterparts—use empathy
   * systematically search for alternatives
   * use conflict management

6. Final negotiations
   * give and take necessary in bargaining process
   * win–win negotiations for generating positive feelings

7. Contract or confirmation of agreement
   - satisfactory agreement
   - including country of dispute resolution
   - importance of written documents in countries involved
8. Implementation of the agreement
   - Both written and unwritten aspects of negotiation are important

Intercultural negotiation assumes that the parties are from different cultures and may not share the same values, beliefs, needs, and thought patterns. During the interaction periods of the negotiation, the values, beliefs, needs, and thought patterns that are not shared by both groups can cause many unanticipated problems. The negotiator must become adept—through continual observation, analysis, and evaluation—at catching the problems and adapting the negotiation strategy accordingly.

TRADE AGREEMENTS

Trade agreements are the laws under which U.S. business must function when exporting. All exports are controlled by the government of the country where they are produced. General and validated are two types of trade agreement licenses. Because the general license is never actually issued, many firms do not realize they are operating under such a license. The validated license is very specific, and the Department of Commerce will assist companies with the regulations that apply. The **validated license** allows a specific exporter to export specific products to specific places. To find out more about validated licenses, obtain a copy of *Export Administration Regulations* from the Department of Commerce. Another book from the Department of Commerce that will prove useful to the overseas negotiator is *Basic Guide to Exporting*, United States Government Subscription, http://bookstore.gpo.gov/index.html.

Free trade zones (FTZ) or **trade blocs** are zones of international commerce where foreign or domestic merchandise may enter without formal customs entry or custom duties. The North American Free Trade Agreement (NAFTA) is an expansion of the FTZ concept, as is the European Union (EU).

The NAFTA, among the United States, Canada, and Mexico, was ratified in 1993 (see Figure 1) and took effect January 1, 1994. In 2008, all import and export taxes on qualified

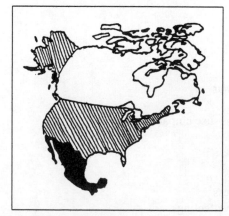 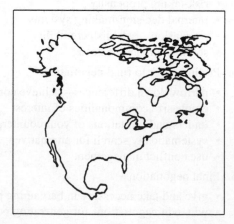

FIGURE 1   Before and After NAFTA

goods between the three countries was revoked, and all qualified materials and services flowed freely among the three countries. NAFTA deals with trade in goods, technical barriers to trade, government procurement, investment, services and related matters, intellectual property, and administrative and institutional provisions. The objectives of NAFTA are the following:

1. To eliminate barriers to trade and facilitate cross-border movement of goods and services
2. To promote fair competition
3. To increase investment opportunities
4. To provide adequate and effective protection for intellectual property
5. To develop effective procedures to handle disputes
6. To expand cooperation and increase benefits to the three countries (North American Free Trade Agreement [NAFTA], 1992)

Many different products are covered by NAFTA; tariff implementation was completed in 2006. Regional economic integration is happening all over the world. A few of the current trade blocs are provided in Table 1 (ALADI, 2012; Asia-Pacific Economic Cooperation [APEC], 2008; Bolivarian, 2012; Community, 2011, European Union, 2008; Free trade agreement, 2012; Foxley, 2010; Trade bloc, 2008).

TABLE 1 Trade Agreements

Acronym	Name	Member Nations
AEC	African Economic Community	(It is expected that the ECOWAS, CEMAC/ECCAS, SACU/SADC, COMESA/IGAD, and EAC will all join the AEC in 2019)
ALADI	Latin American Integration Association	Argentina, Bolivia, Brazil, Chile, Colombia, Ecuador, Mexico, Paraguay, Peru, Uruguay, Venezuela
ALBA	Bolivarian Alternative for the Americas	Antigua and Barbuda, Bolivia, Cuba, Dominica, Ecuador, Nicaragua, St. Vincent and Grenadines, and Venezuela
APEC	Asia-Pacific Economic Cooperation	Australia, Brunei, Canada, Chile, China, Hong Kong, Indonesia, Japan, South Korea, Malaysia, Mexico, New Zealand, Papua New Guinea, Peru, Philippines, Russia, Singapore, Taiwan, Thailand, United States, and Vietnam
ASEAN	Association of Southeast Asian Nations	Brunei, Cambodia, Indonesia, Laos, Malaysia, Myanmar, Philippines, Singapore, Thailand, and Vietnam
CACM	Central American Common Market (block currently stalled because of DR-CAFTA)	Guatemala, Costa Rica, El Salvador, Honduras, and Nicaragua
DR-CAFTA	Dominican Republic-Central America Free Trade Agreement	United States, Costa Rica, El Salvador, Guatemala, Honduras, Nicaragua, and the Dominican Republic

(continued)

TABLE 1 Continued

Acronym	Name	Member Nations
CAN	Andean Community	Bolivia, Colombia, Ecuador, and Peru
CARICOM	Caribbean Community	Antigua, Barbuda, Bahamas, Barbados, Belize, Dominica, Grenada, Guyana, Haiti, Jamaica, Saint Kitts and Nevis, Saint Lucia, Saint Vincent and the Grenadines, Suriname, Trinidad, and Tobago
CEFTA	Central European Free Trade Agreement	Croatia, Albania, Bosnia, Herzegovina, Macedonia, Moldova, Serbia, and Montenegro
CEALC	Latin American and Caribbean Community (New is in the formation stage, meetings suggest 2013 as activation date)	Antigua and Barbuda, Argentina, The Bahamas, Barbados, Belize, Bolivia, Brazil, Chile, Colombia, Costa Rica, Cuba, Dominica, Dominican Republic, Ecuador, El Salvador, Grenada, Guatemala, Guyana, Haiti, Honduras, Jamaica, Mexico, Nicaragua, Panama, Paraguay, Peru, Saint Kitts and Nevis, St. Lucia, St. Vincent and the Grenadines, Suriname, Trinidad and Tobago, Uruguay, and Venezuela
CEMAC	Economic and Monetary Community of Central Africa	Cameroon, Central African Republic, Chad, Republic of the Congo, Equatorial Guinea, and Gabon
COMESA	Common Market for Eastern and Southern Africa	Sudan, Ethiopia, Eritrea, Djibouti, and Comoros
EAC	East African Community	Burundi, Kenya, Rwanda, Tanzania, and Uganda
ECOWAS	Economic Community of West African States	Benin, Burkina Faso, Cape Verde, Côte d'Ivoire, Gambia, Ghana, Guinea, Guinea-Bissau, Liberia, Mali, Niger, Nigeria, Senegal, Sierra Leone, and Togo
EU	European Union	Austria, Belgium, Bulgaria, Cyprus, Czech Republic, Denmark, Estonia, Finland, France, Germany, Greece, Hungary, Ireland, Italy, Latvia, Lithuania, Luxembourg, Malta, Netherlands, Poland, Portugal, Romania, Slovakia, Slovenia, Spain, Sweden, and United Kingdom
EEC	Eurasian Economic Community	Belarus, Kazakhstan, Kyrgyzstan, Russia, Tajikistan, and Uzbekistan
EFTA	European Free Trade Association	Iceland, Norway, Switzerland, and Liechtenstein

(*continued*)

TABLE 1 Continued

Acronym	Name	Member Nations
GAFTA	Greater Arab Free Trade Area	Bahrain, Egypt, Iraq, Jordan, Kuwait, Lebanon, Libya, Morocco, Oman, the State of Palestine, Qatar, Saudi Arabia, Sudan, Syria, Tunisia, the United Arab Emirates, and Yemen
G-3	G-3 Free Trade Agreement	Mexico, Colombia, and Venezuela
GUAM	Organization for Democracy and Economic Development	Azerbaijan, Georgia, Moldova, and Ukraine
MCCA	Central American Common Market	Costa Rica, El Salvador, Guatemala, Honduras, and Nicaragua
MERCOSUR	Southern Common Market	Brazil, Argentina, Paraguay, and Uruguay
NAFTA	North American Free Trade Agreement	Canada, United States, and Mexico
PARTA or PIF	Pacific Regional Trade Agreement	Fiji, Kiribati, Marshall Islands, Micronesia, Nauru, Palau, Papua New Guinea, Samoa, Solomon Islands, Tonga, Tuvalu, and Vanuatu
PICTA	Pacific Island Countries Trade Agreement	Cook Islands, Fiji, Kiribati, Nauru, Niue, Palau, Papua New Guinea, Samoa, Solomon Islands, Tona, Tuvalu, and Vanuatu
SAARC	South Asian Association for Regional Cooperation	Afghanistan, Bangladesh, Bhutan, India, Maldives, Nepal, Pakistan, and Sri Lanka
SACU	Southern African Customs Union	Botswana, Lesotho, Namibia, South Africa, and Swaziland
SAFTA	South Asia Free Trade Agreement	India, Pakistan, Nepal, Sri Lanka, Bangladesh, Bhutan, and the Maldives
UNASUR/ UNASUL	Union of South American Nations (will join MERCOSUR and ANDEAN)	Argentina, Bolivia, Brazil, Chile, Colombia, Ecuador, Guyana, Paraguay, Peru, Suriname, Uruguay, and Venezuela

Free trade zones are not without problems. The Brazilian government delegates said before signing the hemisphere-wide free trade zone that the United States was pushing too hard on Brazil. The Free Trade Area of the Americas (FTAA) talks at points came to a halt. Brazil was not pleased with the U.S. demand that private firms have the right to sue the Brazilian government over international investment issues; Brazil was also less than pleased with the request to tighten patent rights for U.S. pharmaceuticals (Samor, 2004). The FTAA was implemented in 2005.

The World Trade Organization (WTO) is a multinational trade agreement of which the United States is a member. WTO provisions are continually being negotiated or renegotiated. Many stalemates have occurred as countries vie to protect specific industries or commodities. The WTO deals with intellectual property, services, national treatment for services (members must treat other nations' members equal to or better than service suppliers in their own nation), market access for services, foreign investment, antidumping, subsidies, textiles, agriculture, market access, dispute settlement, and telecommunications. Small modifications to a product can change its tariff classification.

The European Union is a FTZ that continues to add countries. The EU is still working out problems due, in part, to the breakdown of the communist bloc countries, but the popularity of the EU is expected to grow in the future. The number of active trade agreements between the United States and other countries for specific products grows every year.

Currently the United States has free trade agreements in force with 17 countries: Australia, Bahrain, Canada, Chile, Costa Rica, Dominican Republic, El Salvador, Guatemala, Honduras, Israel, Jordan, Mexico, Morocco, Nicaragua, Oman, Peru, and Singapore. As of October 21, 2011, President Obama signed free trade agreements with Colombia, Korea, and Panama, but they have not yet been implemented. The United States is also negotiating the Asia-Pacific trade agreement, which will be known as the TPP agreement (Free-trade Agreements, 2012).

NEGOTIATION STYLES

The following sections summarize the negotiating styles of the United States and selected countries, including the countries with which the United States conducts most of its international trade. Because individual differences exist in all cultures, it is wise to research the negotiation styles of countries with which you plan to conduct business.

Brazil

Negotiating with Brazilians can be time consuming as building a relationship before conducting business with someone is important. Brazilians will choose negotiation team members who are well informed and well educated. Keep the same members of your team throughout negotiations. Since Brazilians value personal relationships, changing team members would necessitate building new relationships that would extend negotiations. Team members should expect simultaneous, rather than sequential, discussions of all aspects of the contract. Using a local accountant and lawyer is recommended. Since Brazil is a hierarchical society, understanding how decisions are made is necessary. When compared to other countries in Latin America, Brazilians are more individualistic; team consensus is not a major consideration. Since Brazilians consider themselves Americans, U.S. negotiators should avoid using America to refer to the United States (Moran, Harris, & Moran, 2011; Morrison & Conaway, 2006).

Canada

Canada is a bilingual country, with French as the primary language in the province of Quebec and English in the other provinces. The English spoken is closer to British English in some areas and closer to U.S. English in other areas. Recently, a large group of Hong Kong-based businesspeople immigrated to Canada during the takeover of Hong Kong by the People's Republic of China; this move has introduced another culture into the country (Moran, Harris, & Moran, 2011). Canadians appear to be open and friendly, yet they are reserved, conservative, and very formal. They are also patriotic and lawful and observe strict rules of etiquette. Canadians are not and do not like being considered to be the same as U.S. people, nor do they consider their country part of the United States. Canadians tend to be individualistic. Respect the fact that Canadians are very proud of their heritage and that they were descendants of Loyalists and did not fight for independence from England. Otherwise, negotiation practices are similar to those in the United States.

China

China has been very ethnocentric because of its chosen isolation behind the Great Wall for some 2,300 years. Westerners have had difficulty doing business with the Chinese because they lack an understanding of the Chinese culture and the intrinsic differences between Eastern and Western mind-sets. Protocol to follow during the negotiation process includes giving small, inexpensive presents. The Chinese require a high degree of interpersonal interaction and a high level of character from those with whom they do business. It is necessary to develop a relationship with the Chinese; they believe this takes time and cannot be accomplished in meeting rooms alone (Owen, Javalgi, & Scherer, 2007; Sprong, 2004). The Chinese may not openly state everything during negotiations. They do use silence, postponement of the current discussion, or changing the subject to indicate that they disagree with what is being proposed or said. However, disagreeing with a foreigner is acceptable because of the desire to reach a consensus. The more they are interested in an agreement, the more they entertain. When they are happy with an agreement, they will smile; however, very little negative emotion will be shown when there is disagreement. Disagreements are handled politely, such as proposing an alternative. Chinese negotiators prefer face-to-face meetings over written communication (Ngai, 2000).

The Chinese trust those who are in some way connected to other people they trust. Personal connections are the key to success in China. Finding a common friend to make introductions will help build such relationships quicker. However, the Chinese are some of the toughest negotiators in the world. Technical competence of the negotiators is necessary as well as a noncondescending attitude. The Chinese research their opponents thoroughly to gain competitive advantage during negotiation. Nothing is final until it is signed; they prefer to use an intermediary. The Chinese rarely use lawyers, and interpreters may have inadequate language skills and experience. The Chinese are very high context in their use of language and will not always state exactly what they want. Although Chinese negotiators imply that there is no compromise or third choice, in reality there is ample room for compromise. The Chinese look at a relationship as long term and are very good at stalling during negotiations (DeLozier & Chi, 2000; Moran et al., 2011; Owen et al., 2007).

France

France was the largest country in Western Europe before the reunification of Germany. Needless to say, this change has not enhanced French self-esteem. The French expect everyone to behave as they do when conducting business, including speaking their language. They are individualists and have a sense of pride that is sometimes interpreted as supremacy. The French enjoy conversation for the sake of conversation, but they are also very pragmatic about details of the proposed agreement during negotiations. During conversations away from negotiations, keep in mind that the French consider themselves world leaders in fashion, art, literature, cuisine, and diplomacy. The French follow a type of logic referred to as "Cartesian" logic when negotiating; it is based on principles previously established and proceeds from what is known, in point-by-point fashion, until agreement is reached.

Protocol, manners, status, education, family, and individual accomplishments are keys to success when dealing with the French (Moran et al., 2011). Trust has to be earned; they are impressed by results. The French prefer detailed, firm contracts.

The difference in the U.S.–French cognitive patterns and styles can be seen in reactions by the French to the Richard Nixon and Bill Clinton presidential scandals. The French have a difficult time understanding why people of the United States would want to drive a president from office over a moral or ethical issue. The French view the U.S. need to be morally correct in international situations as unnecessary.

Germany

Germany is now a unified country with the dismantling of the Berlin Wall in late 1989. In business, Germans are typically group oriented; however, as a people, they are rather individualistic. Protocol and regulations are important. Germans prefer explicit contracts and regulations and use power in negotiations (Tinsley, 2001). Dressing conservatively during negotiations, as well as using correct posture and manners, is strongly recommended. Germans tend to use a handshake at the beginning and end of meetings. Remember to use titles when addressing members of the negotiating team and to use "please" and "thank you" freely. Because the Germans believe friendships and personal relationships can complicate negotiations, they prefer to keep a distance between themselves and the other team of negotiators.

Germans tend to be detail oriented, so having technical people as part of the negotiation team is important. Being punctual is expected. Contracts are firm guidelines to be followed exactly. Corporate decisions are made at the top but with a great deal of input from workers. Quality is important, and decisions are pondered and carefully scrutinized to be sure that such quality exists in any projects they undertake. To a U.S. person, Germans may seem pessimistic because of their ability to entertain every conceivable negative point. After they accept a project, however, they give 100% to its successful implementation (Samovar et al., 2009; Tinsley, 2001).

India

In India, business is conducted in a formal yet relaxed manner. Bribery is common, and having connections is important. The left hand is not used in greetings and eating; it is important to request permission before smoking, entering the room, or sitting. Building relationships is important, and an introduction is necessary. Use titles to convey respect. Knowledge of local affairs is important to people of India. Intermediaries are commonly used. Because people of India place importance on building relationships, the negotiation process can be rather long by U.S. standards. Indian management is paternalistic toward subordinates. Because of status differences, Indians generally do not use group orientations; the decisions will be made by senior management. Indians, in an effort to maintain harmony, may tell the other party what it wants to hear. The phrase "no problem" should not be taken literally. People of India do not approve of displays of emotion. Negotiators must use patience and allow the Indians to take the lead in the negotiations. While punctuality is important, patience is required (Moran et al., 2011).

Japan

The negotiating practices of the Japanese companies are based on the keiretsu systems. A **keiretsu system** is a company group formed by the principal company and the partner companies that supply parts, equipment, financial support, or distribution of the final products. In Japan, every company in the keiretsu works to provide the customer the best product for the lowest price while maintaining an acceptable return on investment. A keiretsu group is viewed as a long-term commitment (Yonekura, 1991).

Communication is very complex with the Japanese. To avoid having someone lose face, lose the group harmony, or disappoint another person, the Japanese use very subtle and complex verbal and nonverbal cues. You need to read between the lines to interpret what has been said and to use more silence and less eye contact than is considered normal for U.S. Americans. Because the Japanese do not use "no" and have such subtle verbal and nonverbal cues, ask a number of questions to be certain you understand the intent of what is being communicated (Brett, 2007). Silence is an important aspect of Japanese nonverbal communication and should not be interrupted. Standing at the table, slouching, doodling, crossing the legs, or other informal behavior by sellers is considered disrespectful. The Japanese use status and power in negotiations as well as interest strategies and regulation arguments (Tinsley, 2001).

If a problem is found even after a written agreement is signed, the Japanese will resolve the difference through mutual agreement with the other party as they always consider contracts flexible instruments. Because Japan has very few business lawyers by U.S. standards, the Japanese are very suspicious of a negotiating team that includes lawyers.

Latin America

Latin Americans, which include people from Mexico and Central and South America, are quite different from U.S. persons in their manner of conducting business. Because Latin Americans may have trust issues with U.S. Americans, a negotiator must be careful to maintain the self-esteem of the Latin Americans. When trust is questionable or lost, the opportunity to negotiate is probably lost as well. Relationships are important because of the need to have contacts. Bribery is common, so the local contacts can help you determine who should be approached to get the business moving. The government is very involved in business.

> Latinos emphasize general principles more than problem solving. A story told by a U.S. businessman illustrates the difference in approaches. The U.S. businessman was invited by a Guatemalan to supply equipment for a cereal factory the Guatemalan was planning to open in his country. The U.S. supplier focused on the financing of the purchases, the Guatemalan's credit rating, and how the Guatemalan was going to pay the supplying company. A German contractor, who eventually received the production line order, concentrated on how the production line was going to operate and meet the Guatemalan's needs. The Germans even sent a representative of the company to live on site for the first three months of production. The U.S. interest in the financial aspects of the contract was a turnoff to the Guatemalan. (Axtell, 1994)

Negotiators are chosen on the basis of their family connections, political influence, education, and gender. Latin Americans are very individualistic in business; however, they are very group oriented concerning family and friends. Handshaking and asking about the health and well-being of business contacts and their families are expected.

Because most agreements are consummated over lunch, suitable luncheon accommodations are important. Many meetings are held to allow a personal relationship to develop. Numerous meetings are the norm, and time is not seen as important. Latin Americans are people oriented rather than task oriented. Because body language is important and different from that in the United States, researching nonverbal aspects of communication is recommended (Moran et al., 2011).

The Netherlands

The Dutch have always been internationally oriented due to their trade dependency. They are a very open country and are very proud of their heritage and culture.

> Lawmaker Geert Wilders called for a five-year halt to non-Western immigration after the killing of Dutch filmmaker Theo van Gogh by a Muslim extremist. He stated: "We are a Dutch democratic society. We have our own norms and values. If you choose radical Islam, you can

leave; and if you don't leave voluntarily, then we will send you away. This is the only message possible. The Netherlands has been too tolerant to intolerant people for too long. We should not import a retarded political Islamic society to our country. There is nothing to be ashamed of to say this." (Deutsch, 2004, p. A8)

Dutch negotiators are efficient and straightforward. However, because decisions are based on consensus, the decision-making process can be rather slow. The Dutch are tolerant and willing to listen to divergent points of view. After a decision has been made to proceed with the project, however, those involved will act quickly. Being punctual during negotiations is important; keeping promises is also important. Presentations during negotiations should include facts to back up claims. When negotiating with the Dutch, keep in mind that they admire education, humor, honesty, and modesty (Morrison & Conaway, 2006).

Nigeria

In Nigeria, negotiation in the form of bargaining in the marketplace is practiced from childhood. Therefore, Nigerians are very skillful negotiators. Because Nigerians are individualistic, negotiations are viewed as a competitive process. Age is equated with wisdom and is an important criterion when selecting negotiators. Gender, cultural background, and educational credentials are also important considerations.

Developing a personal relationship is important to the success of the negotiators. Time is not particularly important; therefore, negotiations may be lengthy. An intermediary should make the initial introductions. Being well dressed is important, and conscious demonstration of courtesy and consideration is expected. A successful negotiation is completed when the parties reach a verbal understanding. Contracts are considered flexible and may be oral or written. A person's word is more important than the legal documents. Business relationships follow from personal friendships. Nigerians are very loyal to their tribe and family, and trust is important (Moran et al., 2011).

Russian Federation

The Russian Federation, which is now divided into 21 autonomous republics and 49 regions, has experienced numerous political and economic changes. In 1991, the government and production facilities were decentralized. Despite these changes, some negotiation tactics may remain the same while others will probably change as various management practices are initiated. In the past, negotiation sessions with the Russians have been long with the Russians controlling the agenda. The Russians look at compromise as a weakness and try to wait out their opponents to get more concessions. The Russian negotiators tend to be very animated in their discussions. Russians seem to be concerned with age, rank, and protocol. They are addressed by their full name and tend to be somewhat formal. Like U.S. people, Russians see time as money, and friendships are not crucial to business. Russians are not concerned with equality between business partners but are concerned with maximizing their own profits. Contracts are interpreted rigidly (Elashmawi & Harris, 1998; Samovar et al., 2009).

Singapore

Singapore is unique in the ethnic backgrounds which are Chinese, Malay, and Indian. Cultural differences among the three groups necessitate knowing with whom you are negotiating. The English that is spoken is a blend of English, Cantonese, Hokkien, and Malay. So even though Singaporeans speak English, it may be different from the English to which you are accustomed.

Thus, you will need to be sure details of the negotiations are understood by both sides. Being on time is important; however, due to the number of people in the city, it is not always easy to get to your destination on time.

Negotiations are completed in a very civil manner with plenty of time given between speakers to allow for understanding. Saving face is important, and when someone laughs it may be out of embarrassment. Because Singaporeans will try to get their way does not mean that they are not good negotiators. Relationships are important, so do not change members of your team when negotiating with the Singaporeans (Morrison & Conaway, 2006).

South Korea

When negotiating with South Koreans, remember that getting to know each other is important before beginning business discussions. Because relationships are important, plan to take time to build a solid business relationship. Decision making may be somewhat slow, especially by European or North American standards. Because age and status are respected by South Koreans, it is advisable to include in the negotiating team older, senior executives from your firm. Sometimes silence during negotiations indicates a lack of understanding, so it is wise to ask if additional information is needed or to simply rephrase what was previously said. The initial offer should leave room to negotiate because South Koreans typically begin with an extreme position; they are willing to compromise to assure a win–win situation. Remember that as in other Asian countries, people are not as direct as are people from the United States; they are likely to say what they think the other person wants to hear rather than being totally candid (Morrison & Conaway, 2006).

Taiwan

In Taiwan, trust and respect are very important in business relationships. Because relationship building is important in this country, it is wise to take time to get to know your Taiwanese counterparts. Delays are common, and the decision-making process is somewhat slower than is customary in Europe or the United States. Because both age and seniority are admired in Taiwan, it is a good idea to include on your negotiating team older, senior executives. Women are not typically included on teams, so you should mention ahead of time when you plan to include a woman on your team to allow time for your Taiwanese counterparts to become accustomed to the idea. Suggestions for negotiating with the Taiwanese include being respectful to the elderly, protecting individual dignity, and being honest, modest, and sincere. Avoid criticizing competitors, speaking loudly or with your hands, and displaying emotions (Morrison & Conaway, 2006).

United Kingdom (England, Scotland, Wales, and Northern Ireland)

British negotiators reflect their cultural characteristics; they are very formal and polite and place great importance on proper protocol. They are also concerned with proper etiquette. The British are not as casual or as quick to make friends as are people of the United States; however, this is not considered necessary for conducting any business in the United Kingdom. The British can be tough and ruthless; they excel at intelligence gathering and political blackmail. Because they sometimes appear quaint and eccentric, negotiators from other cultures may underestimate their skill. As U.S. law is based on English law, understanding the meaning of a British contract is relatively easy for U.S. negotiators. Differences exist behaviorally between the Scots, Welsh, British, and the other ethnic groups. Many of the Scottish, Welsh, and Irish do not like to be referred to as Brits although the people in England tend to refer to them as Brits (Cohen, 1998; Moran et al., 2011).

As Ritzer (2007) emphasizes, negotiating on a global scale can present tremendous opportunities. Corporations can expand their markets, increase their profits and productivity, and lower their costs by negotiating globally.

United States

According to Graham and Herberger (1983), the following statements are characteristic of the U.S. style of negotiating:

- "I can handle this by myself" (to express individualism).
- "Please call me Steve" (to make people feel relaxed by being informal).
- "Pardon my French" (to excuse profanity).
- "Let's get to the point" (to speed up decisions).
- "Speak up; what do you think?" (to avoid silence).
- "Let's put our cards on the table" (to convey the expectation of honesty).
- "A deal is a deal" (to indicate an expectation that the agreement will be honored).

The space requirements in the United States have a direct bearing on negotiations. Entering the intimate space (up to 18 inches) of a person from the United States causes great discomfort. Another consideration when negotiating with people of the United States is related to their attitude toward saving face. Because people of the United States are not as concerned with saving face as are people of other cultures, they may be quick with "constructive criticism" that may be a source of discomfort or even humiliation for persons in other cultures.

U.S. negotiators have tended to focus on interest strategies in the past due to the valuing of individualism, egalitarianism, and polychronicity; however, this focus on interest strategies is changing (Tinsley, 2001).

Terms

Competitive approach	Free trade zones	Negotiation strategies
Compromise agreement	Intercultural negotiation	Problem-solving
Compromising negotiation	Integrative agreement	approach
approach	Keiretsu system	Tactics
Forcing negotiation	Legalism negotiation	Trade blocs
approach	approach	Validated license

Exercise 1

Instructions: Circle T for true or F for false.

1. T F In intercultural negotiation, the meeting location is associated with power and responsibilities.
2. T F Social class is unimportant in negotiator selection.
3. T F Failing to listen and talking too much are mistakes made during negotiations.
4. T F Relationship building is important in Arab and Latin American countries.
5. T F Constantly evaluating verbal and nonverbal behaviors of negotiators is unnecessary during negotiations.
6. T F Protocol is important when dealing with the French.
7. T F Bribery is a common part of conducting business in India.

8. T F The Japanese prefer negotiating teams rather than a single negotiator.
9. T F Gender is important when negotiating in the Latin American countries.
10. T F Russian negotiating strategies include a need to control.

Questions and Cases for Discussion

1. Give three reasons why global joint ventures and strategic alliances are increasing.
2. What are the steps in the negotiation process?
3. When analyzing a negotiation situation, what are the models to consider?
4. Explain why following the saying, "When in Rome, do as the Romans do," is appropriate to the negotiation process.
5. Are most negotiation conflicts culturally based?
6. How can you prepare for cultural shock in negotiations?
7. What is the difference between compromise and integrative agreements?

8. Regional free trade zones are becoming popular. What are the negative and positive aspects of such trade zones? How will they help or hinder global organizations?
9. Which factors would you include in developing a negotiation model when negotiating with Canadians?
10. Intercultural negotiations have many implications. Discuss how two of these implications would affect negotiations between a U.S. negotiation team and a Japanese negotiation team. Discuss how two of these implications would affect negotiations between a Japanese negotiation team and a Mexican negotiation team.

CASES

The following procedure is recommended for analyzing the cases: (a) read the case carefully paying attention to details; (b) read the questions at the end of the case; (c) reread the case, taking notes on or highlighting the details needed for answering the questions; (d) identify relevant facts, underlying assumptions, and critical issues of the case; (e) list possible answers to the questions; and (f) select the most logical response to the question. Your professor may ask that you submit answers to the case questions in writing.

Case 1

A U.S. corporation has sent four people to meet with a group from a Russian organization. As the groups have had previous negotiations and contact, the U.S. group is hoping to go home with an agreement. The first meeting lasts 12 hours and ends in a deadlock. After agreeing to meet the next day, one of the U.S. negotiators notices the Russians leaving for an evening on the town. The next morning, the meeting is a repeat of the first, except that it is cut short so that the Russian

negotiators can play golf. All agree to meet the next morning. The U.S. lead negotiator asks his company for time to wait out the Russians. Three weeks later (after many repeat meetings with no concessions), the Russians begin to make concessions. What do you know of the Russian culture that could explain what happened? Did the U.S. negotiator make the right move, or would pressure have made the Russians move faster?

Case 2

A U.S. salesman is in Spain negotiating a contract with a Spanish company. He has expressed to his Spanish colleagues an interest in attending a bullfight, so they invite him to one. As the first bull is released, the salesman jokingly says, "So who's going to win? I'll put my money on the bull." The Spaniards remained silent. The salesman felt very uncomfortable during the rest of the bullfight. Explain the salesman's faux pas and the negative effects it may have on his progress. If the salesman had taken time to research bullfighting, how might he have better handled the situation?

Case 3

International negotiators must diagnose meaning, motive, and intention on the spot if they are to get the contract or sale. How does someone become nonethnocentric and "do as the Romans do" in order to get the contract? How much will previous experience help or hinder the progress of the sale? Why does the visible part of the iceberg overshadow the hidden parts of the iceberg?

Case 4

The comparison chart (Ping, 2000, p. 523) in Table 2 is for a U.S. person who wants to sell a Chinese person a piece of expensive equipment. As you can see, the two gentlemen are not interpreting, perceiving, or expecting the same thing. Using this list, discuss what will probably happen to these negotiations and why if the two sides do not adapt. Now look at the individual factors that must change for there to be a win–win situation for the negotiations.

Case 5

The following case concerns negotiations by KE Electronics (a South Korean company) and JCP (a Japanese company) to license each other their patents. JCP and KE were discussing KE's producing plasma display products (PDP).

KE asserts that JCP has demanded excessive royalties, has asked the South Korean government to restrict imports of JCP products sold in South Korea, is considering referring the patent infringement problem to the WTO, and contends that JCP is using the legal action as a diversionary tactic to curb KE's growth in the PDP industry. JCP has filed a court injunction in Japan to halt the sales of PDPs produced by KE. JCP asserts that KE has violated its patents on dissipation of heat when the panels are operated and has asked Tokyo Customs to suspend imports of KE PDPs.

Describe the important points in the case, including the differences in cross-cultural negotiation components and protocols that these two companies exhibit.

TABLE 2 Expectations and Behaviors of U.S. Americans and Chinese

	Person Expectations	Expected Conversations	Behaviors	Unfulfilled Expectations
U.S. American	Complete job; obtain contract; close deal	Equipment; specification; price; contract terms	Professional; technically oriented	Disappointed and confused
Chinese	Establish long-term relationship; obtain contract; confirm relationship built; begin working on future	Background; introduction to company; training and services	Hospitable; less technically oriented	Hurt and not respected

Activities

1. Invite three or four businesspersons with experience in international negotiation to serve as a panel to discuss "Negotiating with the Japanese" (or another culture of your choice).

2. Prepare a negotiation profile for a person who will be negotiating with representatives of a manufacturing firm in Mexico. Include verbal and nonverbal dos and don'ts.

3. Select a book containing information on international negotiation, such as Jeanne M. Brett's *Negotiating Globally* (2007) or Roger E. Axtell's *The Do's and Taboos of International Trade* (1994), and prepare a one-page summary of nonverbal aspects of negotiating with persons of a culture you choose.

4. Review recent issues of a business journal or newsmagazine for an article related to international negotiation to be used as a basis for class discussion.

5. Prepare a list of possible problems U.S. businesswomen might encounter when negotiating with Arabs.

References

ALADI (2012). Retrieved March, 2012, from http://www.aladi.org/nsfaladi/arquitec.nsf/VSITIOWEB/paises_miembros

Alon, I., & Brett, J. M. (2007). Perceptions of time and their impact on negotiations in the Arabic-speaking Islamic world. *Negotiation Journal, 23*(1), 55–73.

Asia-Pacific Economic Cooperation. (2008). Retrieved July 14, 2008, from http://www.apec.org/apec/member_economies.html

Axtell, R. E. (1994). *The do's and taboos of international trade.* New York: John Wiley & Sons, Inc.

Berger, K. P. (2006). *Private dispute resolution in international business: Negotiation, mediation, arbitration, Volume 11: Handbook.* The Netherlands: Kluwer Law International.

Bolivarian Alternative for the Americas. (2012). Retrieved from http://en.wikipedia.org/wiki/Bolivarian_Alternative_for_the_Americas

Brett, J. M. (2007). *Negotiating globally: How to negotiate deals, resolve disputes, and make decisions across cultural boundaries* (2nd ed.). San Francisco, CA: Jossey-Bass.

Casse, P., & Deol, S. (1991). *Managing intercultural negotiations.* Washington, DC: Sietar.

Cellich, C. (1997, July 1). Communication skills for negotiations. *International Trade Forum, 3*, 22–28.

Chaisrakeo, S., & Speece, M. (2004). Culture, intercultural communication competence, and sales negotiation: A qualitative research approach. *Journal of Business & Industrial Marketing, 19*(4), 267–282. Retrieved September 6, 2004, from the Emerald.

Cohen, R. (1998). *Negotiating across cultures.* Washington, DC: United States Institute of Peace Press.

Community of Latin American and Caribbean States (2011). Retrieved from http://en.wikipedia.org/wiki/Community_of_Latin_American_and_Caribbean_States

DeLozier, M. W., & Chi, Y. (2000). Rules to follow for successful Chinese business relationships. In D. L. Moore & S. Fullerton (Eds.), *International business practices: Contemporary readings* (pp. 179–184). Ypsilanti, MI: Academy of Business Administration.

Deutsch, A. (2004, November 20). Dutch official takes aim at radical Islam. *The Commercial Appeal,* p. A8.

Elashmawi, F., & Harris, P. (1998). *Multicultural management 2000.* Houston, TX: Butterworth-Heinemann.

European Union. (2008, July 14). Retrieved July 14, 2008, from http://europa.eu/abc/european_countries/index_en.htm

Foxley, A. (2010). *Regional trade blocs: The way to the future?* Washington, DC: Carnegie Endowment for International Peace.

Free Trade Agreements. (2012). Retrieved March, 2012, from http://www.ustr.gov/trade-agreements/frec-trade-agreements

Ghauri, P. N. (1983). *Negotiating international package deals.* Doctoral dissertation, Acta Universitatis Upsaliensis Studia Oeconomiae Negotiorum.

Graham, J., & Herberger, R. (1983). Negotiators abroad: Don't shoot from the hip. *Harvard Business Review, 61*(4), 160–169.

King, C., & Segain, H. (2007). Cross border negotiated deals: Why culture matters? *European Company & Financial Law Review, 4*(1), 126–166.

Kozicki, S. (1998). *Creative negotiating.* Holbrook, MA: Adams Media Corporation.

Leaptrott, N. (1996). *Rules of the game: Global business protocol.* Cincinnati, OH: Thomson Executive Press.

Lewicki, R. J., Barry, B., Saunders, D. M., & Barry, B. (2011). *Essentials of negotiation* (5th ed.). New York: McGraw-Hill.

Lin, X., & Miller, S. J. (2003). Negotiation approaches: Direct and indirect effect of national culture. *International Marketing Review, 20*(3), 286–303.

McCormack, M. (1984). *What they don't teach you at Harvard Business School.* New York: Bantam.

Moran, R. T., Harris, P. R., & Moran, S. V. (2011). *Managing cultural differences* (8th ed.). Burlington, MA: Butterworth-Heinemann.

Morrison, T., & Conaway, W. A. (2006). *Kiss, bow, or shake hands* (2nd ed.). Avon, MA: Adams Media.

Ngai, P. B. (2000). Nonverbal communicative behavior in intercultural negotiations: Insights and applications based on findings from Ethiopia, Tanzania, Hong Kong, and the China Mainland. *World Communication, 29*(4), 5–34.

North American Free Trade Agreement between the government of the United States of America, the government of Canada, and the government of the United Mexican States. (1992). Washington, DC: U.S. Government Printing Office.

Owen, C. L., Javalgi, R. G., & Scherer, R. F. (2007). Success strategies for expatriate women managers in China. *Review of Business, 27*(3), 24–31.

Ping, M. D. (2000). Culture and business: Interacting effectively to achieve mutual goals. In G. R. Weaver (Ed.), *Culture, communication, and conflict* (pp. 518–526). Boston, MA: Pearson.

Pruitt, D. G. (2000). Achieving integrative agreements in negotiation. In G. R. Weaver (Ed.), *Culture, communication, and conflict* (pp. 499–507). Boston, MA: Pearson.

Ritzer, G. (2007). *The globalization of nothing 2.* Thousand Oaks, CA: Pine Forge.

Samor, G. (2004, November 16). Gaps between Brazil, U.S. threaten trade talks. *Wall Street Journal,* p. A22. Retrieved November 18, 2004, from ProQuest.

Samovar, L. A., Porter, R. E., & McDaniel, E. R. (2009). *Communication between cultures* (7th ed.). Belmont, CA: Wadsworth/Thomson Learning.

Sprong, J. W. (2004). *The truth about sourcing.* Vital Sourcing, LLC. Retrieved July 13, 2008, from http://vitalsourcing.com.

Thomas, D. C., & Inkson, K. (2004). *Cultural intelligence: People skills for global business.* San Francisco, CA: Berrett-Koehler Publishers, Inc.

Tinsley, C. H. (2001). How negotiators get to yes: Predicting the constellation of strategies used across cultures to negotiate conflict. *Journal of Applied Psychology, 86*(4), 583–593.

Trade bloc. (2008, July 10). Retrieved July 13, 2008, from http://en.wikipedia.org/wiki/Trade_bloc

Turkington, C. (1999). *The complete idiot's guide to cultural etiquette.* Indianapolis, IN: Alpha Books.

Wilen, T. (2000). *International business: A basic guide for women.* n.p.: Xlibris Corporation

Yonekura, S. (1991). *What's the "keiretsu?"* Unpublished paper, Hitotsubashi University, Japan.

Glossary

Competitive approach looks at a solution that is best for the negotiator's own side.

Compromise agreement is a negotiation strategy agreement reached when two parties find a common ground between their individual desires that results in a lower joint benefit.

Compromising is an approach to negotiation that seeks a middle ground between the two parties.

Forcing negotiation approach is used to make the other party comply and is closer to the competitive approach.

Free trade zones (FTZ) are areas of international commerce where foreign or domestic merchandise may enter without formal customs entry or customs duties.

Integrative agreement is a negotiation strategy in which two parties reconcile their interests to yield a high joint benefit.

Intercultural negotiation is discussion between persons of different cultural backgrounds who work toward mutual agreement.

Keiretsu system refers to Japanese negotiating practices in which a company group formed by the principal company and the partner companies supply parts, equipment, financial support, or distribution of the final products.

Legalism uses legal documentation in negotiations to force the other partner to comply.

Negotiation strategies are plans organized to achieve a desired working relationship.

Problem-solving approach is a negotiating style identified with the need to consider national cultural characteristic differences that lead to differences in communication.

Tactics are any maneuvers used for gaining advantages or success.

Trade blocs are zones of international commerce where foreign or domestic merchandise may enter without formal customs entry or custom duties.

Validated license allows a specific exporter to export specific products to specific places.

Answers to Exercises

True/False

1. T
2. F
3. T
4. T
5. F

6. T
7. T
8. T
9. T
10. T

Intercultural Negotiation Components

Objectives

Upon completion of this chapter, you will

- understand the elements of cross-cultural negotiation.
- consider stereotypes that affect intercultural negotiations.
- take into consideration comparative negotiation styles.
- identify characteristics of effective negotiators.
- understand the importance of protocol in intercultural negotiations.
- understand how group and individual orientation, face-to-face strategies, and the media affect negotiations.
- understand how personal constructs affect negotiations.

Intercultural negotiation requires choosing the appropriate communication strategies depending upon the many individual cultural and personal characteristics the negotiators have. The greater the difference between cultures, the greater the likelihood that miscommunication could result in negative outcomes.

CROSS-CULTURAL NEGOTIATION COMPONENTS

Before negotiating with persons from another culture, you should consider the players and the situation, cultural noise, national character, power and authority, perceptions, use of interpreters and translators, gender, environment, and relationships and substantive conflicts.

The Players and the Situation

According to Fisher (1980), you should learn how the negotiators and negotiating teams were selected. Try to determine the background of the players to anticipate the counterpart's behavior.

From Chapter 11 of *Intercultural Business Communication*, Sixth Edition. Lillian H. Chaney, Jeanette S. Martin.

Determine the expectations of the other negotiators, their negotiating style, and the role they have played in past negotiations. Attempt to provide an environment that is free of tension and conducive to an exchange of ideas and problem resolution.

Successful companies choose the players or team members carefully. If possible, have a local person on the team handle introductions, translations, explanations of cultural differences, permits, and navigation of the laws and customs of the country. Many times it is possible to hire such an individual through a local law firm, accountant, bank, or trade organization. If the negotiations are to take place in a hierarchical society, then be sure the people on the negotiating team come from the correct levels of seniority. As Malaysians say, "match eagles with eagles." Also, if you bring management from your home country, they should be part of the negotiation team. Because many cultures consider relationships vital, changing people after negotiating a contract could be viewed very negatively. A company has to consider how the team members' negotiating experience, seniority, political affiliation, gender, ethnic ties, kinship, technical knowledge, and personal attributes will relate to the individuals with whom the team members will be negotiating (Moran, Harris, & Moran, 2011). During negotiation orientations, U.S. Americans need to learn to take advantage of the opportunity to learn more about the personalities of their opponents. U.S. Americans tend to rush through this stage or fail to note its importance. The orientation allows each side to gain valuable information about the opponents. Relationship building is important in many cultures.

In many organizations, the salespeople are responsible for the negotiations and relationship development. In an examination of cultural issues at the national, organizational, and individual levels, it was found that culture affects a salesperson's negotiating style. Salespeople with high problem-solving orientation are likely to have a problem-solving approach that is more cooperative and leads to relationship building between two organizations. Successfully communicating interculturally is easier for people with a high cultural awareness and sensitivity to changing their actions depending on the cultural environment. How supportive or bureaucratic an organization is also empowers or disempowers an individual to use the problem-solving approach effectively. A salesperson in a bureaucratic organization loses the ability to use his or her intercultural communication competency due to the rules within the organization, although an individual from a supportive organizational culture is strengthened by the organization to use his or her intercultural communication abilities (Chaisrakeo & Speece, 2004).

Cultural Noise

Cultural noise includes anything that distracts or interferes with the message being communicated. Nonverbal messages, such as body language, space, and gift giving, can impede or expedite negotiations. For example, giving an inappropriate gift or one wrapped improperly is a form of cultural noise. In addition, what a person says can result in cultural noise, such as negotiators who criticize their competitor or make disparaging comments about their competitors' products.

National Culture

Fisher (1980) maintains that "patterns of personality do exist for groups that share a common culture" (p. 37). National character affects the negotiation process a great deal. People of the United States value time; punctuality is important. To a large degree, they also believe that they determine their own fate. The people of Latin American countries, on the other hand, are less concerned with time and stoically accept their fate. While numerous other differences exist between the values of the two cultures, these two attitudes could hamper negotiations considerably regardless of the attractiveness of the terms offered. Latin Americans ethnically are also a mixture of indigenous, European, Pacific Rim, and African heritages. Ethnic identity can be very personal in different parts of the world.

In Kenya, the Maasai leaders have been negotiating without the Magadi community members concerning adding a second soda mining plant at Magadi. The Magadi community leaders say the Maasai leaders hijacked the process. It is not unusual for patronage and bribery to take place in Magadi. Workers at the Magadi Soda Company also have problems with company management concerning harsh working conditions, poor medical coverage, lack of employment opportunities, nepotism, and lack of water, education, and security (Tiampati, 2004). This is one example of national character and indigenous people having problems.

Research on the impact of national culture on negotiation outcomes has shown that U.S.–Japanese cultural differences have limited the joint gains of the negotiation partners. The researchers attributed the negotiation shortcomings to the lack of knowledge of their counterparts' national cultural priorities and the necessity of such an understanding (Brett & Okumura, 1998). Equitable governance structure, preferences for negotiation that integrates the negotiators' interests, and the dyad's collectivism to each other have all been found as important to the success of an alliance (Cai, Wilson, & Drake, 2000; Tinsley, 1998).

Studying a national culture in preparation for negotiations will give you the central tendencies of a population, but it may not give you the within-group or individual variance you may need to negotiate successfully. It also does not tell you how many cultures may exist in the individuals with whom you are negotiating. National culture is only one of the cultures that we all carry within ourselves. Other cultures include professional, social class, ethnic, regional, gender, and organizational/corporate (Sebenius, 2002b).

Power and Authority

Power is the ability to influence others; authority is the power to give commands and make final decisions. With the ability to influence comes the responsibility of the action taken. Power can make people and companies dependent or independent. Power can be an advantage or a disadvantage, depending on how it is used, but it must be used within the bounds of moral and ethical behavior (Lewicki, Saunders, & Barry, 2011).

Negotiators use power to influence strategies. Direct influence includes questioning, offering, posturing, and persuading. Indirect influence strategies include appeals for sympathy, references to personal stakes in the negotiation, and references to status. Direct power strategies are meant to help the opponent; indirect strategies are appeals to the opponent to help you. The use of direct or indirect influence strategies is different from culture to culture. For high joint gains, information sharing should be used immediately; posturing and persuading should not be used late in the negotiations (Brett, 2007).

For power to be meaningful, it has to be accepted. **Authority** (associated with power) is how an alliance chooses to conduct decision making, strategy setting, and influence over each other. When you accept power, you are giving it the authority to exist to the extent the control is acceptable to you. The personal constructs of the receiver of the power determine the strength of the power exerted. To create a synergism between global business partners, the firms must have balanced authority. **Balanced authority** allows each partner to share the decision-making role (Bradenburger & Nalebuff, 1996). If one of the partners seeks an **authority advantage** over its partner, this is normally done by claiming to possess superior resources or a superior position in the alliance. The alliance will probably fall apart (Teegen, 1998). The incentives exist to collaborate and at the same time compete with their alliance partner both during and after negotiations (Bradenburger & Nalebuff, 1996).

The balance of authority between partners positively affects the performance of the alliance (Saxton, 1997). If each partner has authority over its areas of expertise or specialization, generally you will have a successful dyad. Many researchers have found that an unbalanced authority relationship or asymmetrical relationship is inherently unstable and tends to collapse (Anderson & Weitz, 1989; Lorange & Roos, 1991; Nooteboom, Berger, & Noorderhaven, 1997; Teegen & Doh, 2002).

An example of the use of power and authority might occur in a meeting between the Chinese, who do not believe in a time schedule for negotiations, and the time-conscious U.S. Americans. The Chinese have the power of time on their side and possibly could make the U.S. Americans feel pressured to make compromises. Japanese negotiators have observed that they can make U.S. negotiators agree to concessions because they can "outwait" the impatient Americans (Engholm, 1991) (see Figure 1).

FIGURE 1 The Negotiation Waiting Game

It is only with knowledge of the relative power of those negotiating that someone can determine if a deal is possible or not, will know whether to continue to negotiate, or if it is time to accept an offer (Brett, 2007).

Perception

Perception is the process by which individuals ascribe meaning to their environment; it is strongly affected by their culture. The stress of negotiation can cause misperception, but more often it is due to the different meanings of verbal and nonverbal cues in the cultures involved. For example, U.S. Americans might "talk" with their hands to clarify or exaggerate a particular point during negotiations with a German negotiating team. The Germans may incorrectly interpret the motions as spontaneous emotional displays that they consider impolite. Likewise, if companies were to send only one person to negotiate with the Japanese, the Japanese would assume the company was not serious about negotiating an agreement (Lewicki et al., 2011).

An example of differences in perception: A group of U.S. businessmen are visiting China exploring the possibility of building a factory in China. While the Chinese are showing them sites, the U.S. people ask about the level of the available water pressure. The Chinese are perplexed and ask why. The U.S. people say because they need to be sure the water pressure is sufficient to fight fires for insurance purposes. The Chinese answer that they have sufficient water pressure but want to know why the U.S. people are speaking of bad luck before they begin the project because that will assure bad luck. What one culture sees as planning and being necessary, another culture may perceive differently. (Ping, 2000)

Stimuli have both a physical size and a socioenvironmental meaning that can be different for each individual within and across cultures. Our experiences determine what stimuli we are sensitive or insensitive to. Although it is obvious to the Japanese and U.S. Americans that the two cultures are very different, it may not be so obvious that U.S. citizens and Canadians also have many cultural differences. Sometimes thinking we are alike can be more dangerous than knowing we are different and being careful of our verbal and nonverbal behaviors.

Perceptions of alliance negotiation objectives, particularly uncertainty avoidance, have been found to cause problems in negotiations (Schneider & De Meyer, 1991).

Interpreters and Translators

Language considerations when negotiating include the following:

- Language serves as a key to culture.
- Who should be at the table and conversing?
- What is the social identity of those at the table?
- Facilitated dialogue is a slow process. (D'Amico & Rubinstein, 1999)

Using interpreters and translators can affect the negotiation process both positively and negatively. On the positive side, you have more time to think about your next statement while your previous statement is being translated. Because of the time it takes to translate, you are also more careful to state the message succinctly. On the negative side, because language and culture are intertwined, translators may not convey the intended message due to the nuances of the languages involved.

Women as International Negotiators

Although in some countries women are not typically included on negotiation teams, in many countries they are considered as equals at the negotiation table. These countries include Denmark, England, France, India, Israel, Norway, Sweden, Switzerland, and the United States. In these countries women are welcomed additions to international negotiation teams since women are acknowledged as important contributors to a team's success because of their interpersonal skills, patience, social skills, sympathy, understanding, listening skills, and willingness to accept the values of other people. Research confirms that women actually have an advantage over men during negotiations because they are more adept than men at reading nonverbal messages and are therefore able to gain information from the body language, voice pitch, intonation, and eye movements of other team members. In addition, the fact that women are often viewed as less threatening and less competitive than men can be advantageous in problem-solving situations (Martin & Chaney, 2012; Wilen, 2000).

"Women traveling internationally report that they often receive more special treatment than their male colleagues: invitations to dine at special restaurants; additional sightseeing tours; and more courtesies, such as airport pick up and drop off." (Wilen, 2000, pp. 175–176)

To assure that they are treated professionally when negotiating in international situations, women should dress appropriately as people in many cultures are quite conscious of appearance. Dressing conservatively in dark, high-quality suits (preferably skirted suits) with leather hand-bag and dark leather medium-heeled shoes is recommended in many countries of Asia, Europe, and Latin America. Simple elegance in attire in traditional, conservative colors and styles is considered preferable to clothing in bright fashion colors and the latest styles. Further, casual attire for shopping and sightseeing should be conservative and in muted colors.

A U.S. businesswoman, who was making a presentation in Japan on Valentine's Day, wore a red dress for the occasion. She apparently did not know that red is not worn for business in Japan; it is considered too provocative. Japanese audience members were shocked; they just sat and stared. The businesswoman's attire was totally inappropriate and was viewed as an insult. (Wilen, 2000)

In addition to wearing appropriate attire, women who wish to be successful on international negotiating teams should become knowledgeable about issues to be discussed and should expand their knowledge of the language of their foreign counterparts. Women should research the customs, including attitudes toward women, of the country with which they plan to conduct business and be prepared to adjust their attitudes and behaviors to conform to expectations of the people of the country. For example, in some cultures older men are paternalistic and protective of women; thus, women should not be offended by such treatment (Hodge, 2000; Martin & Chaney, 2012).

Additional suggestions for successful experiences as female members of international negotiating teams include behaving professionally with quiet self-assurance and self-confidence, being patient and compassionate, showing respect for the host culture and their customs, recognizing the importance of humility, demonstrating a cooperative attitude, and having a good sense of humor (Axtell, Briggs, Corcoran, & Lamb, 1997).

If women establish their experience, competence, and authority prior to negotiating internationally, they will be given professional treatment by foreign executives, who are aware of the important role that women play in U.S. businesses (Hodge, 2000).

Environment

The environment in which the negotiations take place is particularly important for intercultural negotiations. If meetings are held at the office of one of the parties, then that party has control and responsibility as host to the other party. When one of the parties is at home, they have "home court" advantage—the advantage of access to information and human resources. When negotiators are on their home territory, they are likely to be more assertive than when in the host's territory. A reason for this may be conditioning. We are taught that it is rude to be impolite to someone in his or her home or office. The host negotiators may also have a feeling of superiority because the other team is coming to them (Lewicki et al., 2011). One way to avoid this competitiveness is to choose a neutral site. The neutrality of the site eliminates the psychological advantage of the home ground.

A U.S. company was negotiating with a Saudi company. The Saudi company determined all of the environmental factors: messengers were used between the negotiators, lists of questions and points were given for consideration, and the seating chart was dictated by the Saudis. The U.S. company conceded the process; however, they felt that it showed flexibility and interest rather than weakness. It depends on the two cultures. Between two hierarchical cultures it would signal weakness; between egalitarian cultures it signals flexibility. (Brett, 2007)

The actual room where the negotiations take place could play an important role if the room makes one of the negotiating teams feel comfortable and the other team uncomfortable. Cultural differences need to be considered when choosing the site. Details to consider include the physical arrangement of the room, the distance between people and teams, and the formal or informal atmosphere of the room.

The arrangement of the table and chairs can also make a difference. Some cultures ascribe a title to people according to the seating arrangement. Those same cultures also would expect the other team to have the same number of negotiators and negotiators of equal rank to theirs. The Japanese particularly have been surprised when the United States sends a younger person of a lower rank to meet with a top official of their company. Because the Japanese conduct side negotiations with their counterpart in the opposing company, it is necessary for everyone to know his or her counterparts. Two ways of arranging seating in a meeting to accomplish this purpose are shown in Figures 2 and 3 (Funakawa, 1997).

Relationship and Substantive Conflicts

Being able to identify the conflict in which you are involved is important. Issues form out of substantive and relationship-based differences. The substantive issues include use and control of resources. The relationship-based issues center on the long-term friendship or partnership. Negotiations should be conducted in such a way as to protect future relations.

The conflict may be seen from the point of view of both negotiators or may be seen from the point of view of only one negotiator. The conflict may involve a deadlock, behavior difference, lack of a common goal, communication problems, poor translators, misunderstandings, secrets, lack of feedback, or unfamiliar tactics. Some of these factors may be due to the negotiators' perceptions of reality and their unconscious ability to block out information that is inconsistent with their cultural beliefs. Negotiation breakdown or deadlock may be identified by the negotiators' repeating themselves using the same arguments. The negotiators may not be saying anything constructive but merely allowing the passage of time, or nonnegotiation tactics may be used to try to change the attitudes of the other side (Brett, 2007).

Jervis (2000) defines **cognitive dissonance** as follows: "Two elements are in a dissonant relation if, considering these two alone, the obverse of one element would follow from the other" (p. 442). A simpler definition is that cognitive dissonance is the psychological conflict or anxiety that results from inconsistencies between what one does and what one believes. Cognitive dissonance, logic, and reasoning differences normally due to cultural differences are often the focus of such conflicts because your perspectives are based on your cultural training, and your oppositions' perspectives are based on their cultural training. Cognitive dissonance may generate the following emotions and actions: frustration, regression, fixation, resignation, repression, projection, and aggression (Cohen, 1998). If you are aware of the possible cultural shocks before entering negotiations, it will be easier to adapt your negotiation style to accommodate both your own and others' ethnocentrism and maintain your patience while dealing with the differences. Part of negotiation is being able to discern what is going on mentally with the negotiators on the other side of the table. By

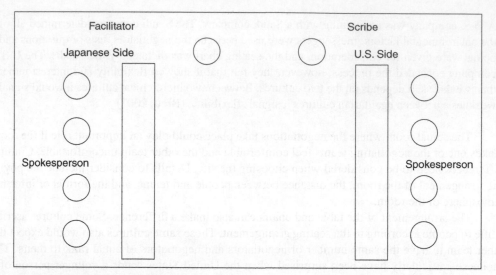

FIGURE 2 Seating Arrangement A

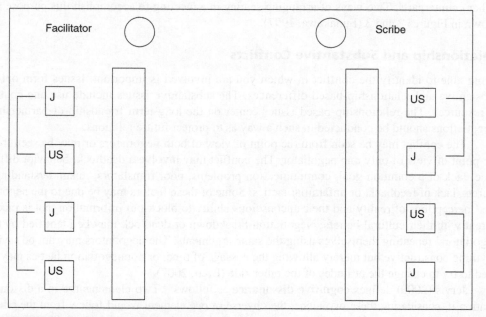

FIGURE 3 Seating Arrangement B

studying the psychological predisposition of the other culture, you will be familiar with at least some of the variations between the two cultures. Communicating adequately is difficult when the cultural programming of the negotiators differs. Within a culture, there is normally an internal consistency to the beliefs and values of that culture. In intercultural negotiation, people need to be cognizant of not projecting their cultural thinking onto the other side. Be sure to discuss every point and not attribute motives to the other side that may, in fact, be nonexistent. Cultures are different concerning how they conceptualize information, how they use information, and how they associate causes and effects.

A sales executive who worked in Vietnam had been meeting with a potential customer to gain his business. The Vietnamese person was very difficult to convince about the advantages of the product, and it did not seem as if a contract would be signed. Later the sales executive was walking with his boss to the tennis court and ran into the potential customer. The customer knew his boss and told him to come to the customer's office the next day to sign the contract. (Verluyten, 2002)

To prepare for behavioral differences, you must train yourself to perceive the differences and adjust your reasoning accordingly. Developing "an efficient and coherent mental cross-referencing system" (Fisher, 1997, p. 22) that automatically adjusts your reactions saves time and money and avoids problems. Although it is not possible in the international setting, much less in our day-to-day activities, to have a built-in response to all situations, if you build a mechanism to screen, sort, code, and store differences, you are able to respond more quickly. In other words, you develop a new mindset. This new cognitive structure allows us to share a defined culture and way of acting and thinking. Because our cognitive structures are programmed to our own cultures, reprogramming disturbs the existing system. Our mind inherently tries to make cognitive dissonance fit our current cognitive system rather than expanding our cognitive system by recognizing the difference and developing more storage cognitively (Fisher, 1997).

Lifestyles within cultures vary, and so does the vocabulary that develops to explain the culture. When cultures are different, the words that develop are also different. The subjective meaning of the translation can be very important. The United States is a very individual-oriented society. The Japanese equivalent of the word for individual has a negative connotation because the Japanese are a group-oriented culture. Education in the United States means academic achievement and is associated with school attendance. In the Spanish culture, however, education includes being polite, well bred, and sensitive as well as covering school attendance and academic achievement. The idea of "fair play" is an example of a concept that does not exist in any other language, yet is used frequently in U.S. business, sports, and other aspects of life. Because fair play is a culturally bound phrase, other cultures cannot be expected to understand its meaning. Gestures, tone of voice, and cadence further complicate the translation situation (Cohen, 1998).

A study by Planken (2005, p. 386) indicates that the areas you can talk about safely during negotiations involve:

1. The initiator—greetings, enquiry about how the other person feels, introductions, business card exchange, and personal work history
2. The business relationship—prenegotiation contract and history of existing corporate relationship
3. Future business—future cooperation and future dealings
4. The business environment—markets, target groups, competitors, and the economy
5. Product information—product characteristics, manufacturing information, product range, and delivery
6. Corporate information—management; company history; core activities such as distribution, promotion, personnel, or pricing policy
7. The invitation—lunch, drinks, coffee, and company/factory visit
8. Nonbusiness topics—travel, sports, news, culture, language, hobbies, holidays, and family

Planken (2005) also found that younger, aspiring negotiators used "you" more than the experienced negotiators did (indicates other orientedness); however, both established negotiators and aspiring negotiators used the "we," which shows inclusiveness.

STEREOTYPES THAT AFFECT INTERCULTURAL NEGOTIATIONS

The way people of a culture view themselves and the way they are actually viewed by persons of other cultures often have an impact on intercultural negotiations. Schneider and Barsoux (2002) point out the disparities that exist between the way U.S. people think of themselves and the way they are viewed by foreigners.

U.S. Persons' Views	Foreigners' Views of U.S. Persons
• Informal, friendly, casual	• Undisciplined, too personal, familiar
• Egalitarian	• Insensitive to status
• Direct, aggressive	• Blunt, rude, oppressive
• Efficient	• Obsessed with time, opportunistic
• Goal/achievement oriented	• Promise more than they deliver
• Profit oriented	• Materialistic
• Resourceful, ingenious	• Work oriented; deals are more important than people
• Individualistic, progressive	• Self-absorbed, equating the "new" with "best"
• Dynamic, find identity in work	• Driven
• Enthusiastic, prefer hard-sell	• Deceptive, fearsome
• Open	• Weak, untrustworthy

Negotiators from the United States should, therefore, take into consideration this disparity in viewpoints and make a concerted effort to change some of the negative stereotypes, such as being rude and obsessed with time, when interacting during negotiations.

COMPARATIVE NEGOTIATION STYLES

Intercultural negotiators need to be selected carefully. People who can negotiate well in their own culture may not be successful at negotiating interculturally. Intercultural negotiators need to be able to ascertain where their opposition "is coming from." The negotiator must be able to grasp the situation and be able to recognize whether the opposition's negotiators are bound by their culture or are taking on some of the opposing cultural characteristics. Being able to discern role behavior and knowing the proper deference is important in intercultural negotiations (Moran & Stripp, 1991). A brief comparison of the negotiation styles of different cultures is shown in Table 1 (Elashmawi & Harris, 1998; Ruch, 1989).

CHARACTERISTICS OF EFFECTIVE NEGOTIATORS

Effective negotiators are observant, patient, adaptable, and good listeners. They appreciate the humor in a situation but are careful to use humor only when appropriate. Good negotiators are mentally sharp. They think before they speak, and they are careful to speak in an agreeable, civil manner. Businesspeople who negotiate internationally know that negotiations are carried out consistently within a culture but that cultures have their own distinct negotiating styles (Berger, 2006). They do their homework on the countries with which they are negotiating and become

TABLE 1 Negotiation Styles of Different Cultures

Element	U.S. Americans	Japanese	Arabians	Mexicans
Group composition	Marketing oriented	Function oriented	Committee of specialists	Friendship oriented
Number involved	2–3	4–7	4–6	2–3
Space orientation	Confrontational; competitive	Display harmonious relationship	Status	Close, friendly
Establishing rapport	Short period; direct to task	Longer period; until harmony	Long period; until trusted	Longer period; discuss family
Exchange of information	Documented; step-by-step; multimedia	Extensive; concentrate on receiving side	Less emphasis on technology, more on relationship	Less emphasis on technology, more on relationship
Persuasion tools	Time pressure; loss of saving/ making money	Maintain relationship references; intergroup connections	Go-between; hospitality	Emphasis on family and on social concerns; goodwill measured in generations
Use of language	Open/direct; sense of urgency	Indirect; appreciative; cooperative	Flattery; emotional; religious	Respectful; graciousness
First offer	Fair ±5 to 10%	±10 to 20%	±20 to 50%	Fair
Second offer	Add to package; sweeten the deal	–5%	–10%	Add incentive
Final offer	Total package	Make no further concessions	–25%	Total package
Decision-making process	Top management team	Collective	Team makes recommendation	Senior manager and secretary
Decision maker	Top management team	Middle line with team consensus	Senior manager	Senior manager
Risk taking	Calculated; personal responsibility	Low group responsibility	Religion based	Personally responsible

knowledgeable about their history, customs, values, and beliefs. Effective negotiators know that in many cultures history is revered, and displaying knowledge of the country's past can do much to pave the way to smooth negotiations. Good negotiators praise what is praiseworthy and refrain from criticizing anything about the negotiators or their country. They keep their promises and always negotiate in good faith (Sebenius, 2002a).

Negotiators, however, cannot escape their own cultural mindsets. Even professional training cannot erase the deep-seated perceptions from childhood (Cohen, 1998). These perceptions must not be vocalized, however, because nothing is to be gained by denouncing the behavior or customs of others simply because they do not fit your cultural mindset. Because such factors as social skills, gender, age, experience in intercultural relations, and background may be important in a specific culture, considering these factors when selecting negotiators is recommended.

Noted negotiator Dr. Chester L. Karrass says, "In business, you don't get what you deserve; you get what you negotiate. Why take 'no' for an answer? Successful people don't. They get what they want by negotiating better deals for both parties." (Karrass, 1996)

IMPORTANCE OF PROTOCOL IN INTERCULTURAL NEGOTIATIONS

Protocol is important in understanding which negotiation strategy should be followed. Leaptrott (1996) gives three fundamental classifications of protocol: tribal, collective, and pluralist. Tribal involves the family unit, close relationships, and a connection to the past. Collectivism is an extension of tribal and includes larger groups, such as a town, nation, or race. The pluralist society has many different groups and combinations of groups, and individuals are free to join those they want to join. Most countries fit one of these three protocol classifications. Table 2 includes a comparison of the three protocol types. Parts of China, Africa, and India are examples of countries

TABLE 2 Protocol Characteristics of Tribal, Collective, and Pluralist Cultures

Area	Tribal	Collective	Pluralist
Person's responsibility	Supports family and follows rules of society	Group contribution, honor, conformity	Personal growth, achievement, independence
Expectations of others	Mutual support and absolute loyalty	Humility, respect, support	Integrity, performance, competence
Interaction with others	With strangers, aloof, formal; with friends, warm, welcoming, trusting	Does not stand out, friendly yet noncommittal to strangers; loyal, firm relationship with friends	Informal, direct communication
Traits respected	Status, strength, cunning	Strength with humility, cleverness, knowledge	Creativity, personal achievement, status
Attitude toward foreigners	Cautious, defensive, formal, distrustful	Cautious, aggressive, defensive	Open, curious, nonhostile
Reason to work	Works to live	Works to live	Lives to work
Life objective	Respect of group, contribute to family	Succeeds at work, to get opponent to concede something	Success beyond goals

(continued)

TABLE 2 Continued

Area	Tribal	Collective	Pluralist
Definition of winning	Receiving what is asked for	Zero-sum, win–lose	Zero-sum or win–win
Business environment	Strong vertical hierarchy, leaders inaccessible, open offices for lower levels, offices for managers	Shared power, no one stands out, open offices, location important	Layered hierarchy, private spaces, best spaces for top management
Conducts business	Must control, manipulative, correspondence limited	Divided responsibilities; strategy and ritual are important; correspondence open, shared	Direct, formality with strangers, correspondence to many
Learning style	Visual, data, coaching generalized; repetition helpful	Shown, learns with others best	Detailed information, verbal text, verification
Feedback	Avoids details, not accountable, subjective feedback	Within the group, consensus a must, nothing negative	Direct, specific, objective, impersonal
Decision making	Decisions at the top; pride, emotion before objectivism	Consensus, final decisions from the top	Independent, rational process, mid-management approval
Attitude toward time, schedules, plans, and change	Linear time, process oriented, changes are okay, no detailed plans	Process oriented, no definition of length of time necessary, need for changes seen as errors	Linear time, punctual, detailed plans, change expected
Approach to problem solving	Blame assessment more important than solving problems and consequences for those who are to blame	Problems are evaded; someone loses face; conflict; no problem admitted	Addressed quickly, rationally; analyzes after the fact

that are still basically tribal because they are agrarian societies. A person's word is more important to building a relationship than anything else in tribal cultures. Collectivistic cultures are also very concerned with relationships; examples can be found in Japan, Greece, Spain, and Indonesia. Examples of pluralist societies include the United States, United Kingdom, and France.

The three styles of protocol are very different in some areas and similar in others. This makes the way the variables of policy, interaction, deliberation, and outcome are used vary, depending on the two cultures involved in the negotiation. In addition, remembering to consider the situation from the other culture's viewpoint yet maintaining your own cultural viewpoint will avoid problems in many instances.

Although all cultures share the need for honesty, courage, respect for human dignity, fairness, and love, these values can have very different meanings in different cultures (Samovar, Porter, & McDaniel, 2009). Reality is difficult to assess when two cultures do not share the same definition of needs. If the expectations are not met and the perceptions are wrong, disastrous business consequences are usually the result (Ping, 2000).

GROUP VERSUS INDIVIDUAL ORIENTATION

Group orientation ideally results in a solution that is good for everyone because all points of view are supposedly considered. Negotiations with **group-oriented** negotiators are detail oriented to determine the proper solution. Your identity belongs to the group of which you are a member. The group has to reach a consensus on any and all decisions, and this probably is not done during the negotiation sessions. The individuals in the group avoid making an individual decision. Individuals who are not group oriented may feel that group-oriented negotiators appear to stall, are not interested in the negotiations, and give ambiguous statements. Group-oriented cultures tend to view contracts as flexible (Hofstede & Hofstede, 2005).

Japan is one of the most group-oriented cultures in the world, perhaps because of the number of years they were physically secluded from other cultures; however, given the number of years they have now interacted with other cultures, many Japanese have adapted very well to different negotiation strategies. Although the Japanese culture is quite different from that of the United States, Japan and the United States do have a common work ethic—both applaud hard work. Even though the original management styles were very different, as joint ventures and subsidiaries of Japanese companies become part of the U.S. economy, U.S. corporations are beginning to use some of the Japanese management concepts. Both cultures are gaining an understanding of their differences and are learning to cope. Other group-oriented cultures include the Chinese, Polynesians, Native Americans, and Africans (Hofstede & Hofstede, 2005). This group approach assumes that the action taken is conservative and well thought out and that all options were considered in the decision (Berger, 2006).

Brazilians, although very gregarious, value the group over the individual, believe in saving face, and are indirect in business affairs. Brazilians also are very flexible; they feel that to be intelligent and imaginative you have to be able to adjust to new developments (Moran et al., 2011).

If you are **individually oriented**, you will be concerned with the best contract for your company and may not be concerned about whether the agreement is good for the other company. If more than one negotiator is on your team, one person will probably control the negotiations and make the final decision concerning the various issues being discussed. Usually, much individual sparring has taken place with members of the other team before the negotiation meeting. The individually oriented person tends to interpret the contract very rigidly.

Aramco was losing money on one of its trucking operations in Saudi Arabia. Finally, an Arab was able to buy the franchise and set up his own system. Knowing his own people, he worked out a series of complex reinforcement schedules for each truck and driver. He even penalized them for every valve cap that was missing and rewarded drivers when nothing that was supposed to be there was missing. Oil levels in the crankcase, maintenance schedules, time schedules. everything was examined and recorded. The cost per ton-mile dropped to a third of what it had been under American management. (Weaver, 2000, p. 14)

The U.S. culture is probably one of the most individualistic cultures in the world. Another individualistic culture is Latin America. According to Brett (2007), a Latin negotiation is frequently an internal contest of individuals battling for position and power. Other cultures that are very individualistic include the British, French, Australians, and Canadians (Hofstede & Hofstede, 2005).

FACE-TO-FACE STRATEGIES

Face-to-face strategies are concerned with negotiating in person rather than through the mail, fax, telephone, telegraph, lawyers, or other intermediaries. People in many cultures will only negotiate on a face-to-face basis. The Japanese, in particular, do not like to make commitments over the telephone or in writing until after numerous face-to-face meetings have taken place. In many European countries, as well as in India and Japan, contracts are considered an insult to the trust of the partners. They place great importance on face-to-face encounters and oral agreements (Moran et al., 2011). Arabs also place a lot of importance on trust and relationship building; most negotiations will be broken into many different meetings (Alon & Brett, 2007).

Some of the face-to-face negotiators' behaviors include the following:

- **Irritators**—phrases that are used repeatedly, such as "generous offer."
- **Counterproposals**—immediate counterproposals made less frequently by skilled negotiators.
- **Argument dilution**—using multiple arguments when one is sufficient; a technique used less by skilled negotiators.
- **Reviewing the negotiation**—done more often by the more skilled negotiators (Moran et al., 2011).

ROLE OF THE MEDIA

Representatives of the media—television, radio, and newspapers—have a unique position in creating multicultural understanding and misunderstanding. Most of the views you have of other cultures have been gained through the media window. The media have been used in various ways, including supporting and tearing down political candidates and officeholders and defining and distorting numerous messages. Media people also represent a culture and have cultural biases. The media tend to have a stereotypical view of business. Media members have generally presented other cultures through the bias of the U.S. perceptual grid.

Advertisers make up the largest group of negotiators in the world—they all compete for consumers' dollars. Advertisers use media extensively and have learned that differences in culture necessitate different delivery and content if the ad is to successfully promote a product (Prosser, 1985).

Movies are big promoters of stereotypes. Many times, the wrong perception of a culture is gained from the subject matter presented in movies or a television series that is broadcast in foreign countries. Many of the stereotypes foreigners have of U.S. Americans (such as all carry guns) are due to movies and television series. Likewise, U.S. Americans hold views of other cultures (such as the belief that all followers of Islam do not drink alcoholic beverages) based on movie and television messages. Because perceptions of other cultures are often acquired through the media and may be brought to the negotiation table, an awareness of the role of the media is important.

An example of media influence in the world today is the CNN (Cable News Network) broadcasts during Operation Desert Storm. The antagonists and protagonists in the battle and everyone else in the world who had access to satellite television broadcasts watched the CNN coverage. Another example of media influence is the number of teenagers worldwide who wear jeans, listen to the same music, and watch the same movies. Still more examples of world coverage were the 9/11 attacks in the United States, the war in Afghanistan against the Taliban, and Operation Iraqi Freedom.

PERSONAL CONSTRUCTS

Personal constructs refer to individual belief systems and attitudes. The individual belief system, attitudes, or personal constructs differ from culture to culture and often from person to person within a given culture. What you expect to happen cognitively is based on your life experiences. No two people in the world have the same set of life experiences. Cultural stereotypes are dangerous even though they provide clues to the behavior of the "average" person in the culture.

The reason "birds of a feather flock together" is such a powerful adage is because we like to spend time with those who are like us. This is one of the reasons why people say, "They're in America; they should act like Americans." The U.S. Americans who make these statements, however, do not understand they need to reciprocate and adopt certain foreign behaviors when they visit another country. Of course, without a lot of time and willingness, it is very difficult "to do as the Romans do."

The question has been raised as to whether it is possible for a person to become a "native" of another country (Brett, 2007). Perhaps not, but it is possible to learn about the culture, customs, and traditions and to be sensitive to them. People react more positively to people who shift their communication style toward the new culture; however, the other culture may become threatened if the group distinctiveness is threatened. Moderate levels of adaptation seem to improve relations, but large levels of adaptation may have negative effects. Moderate adaptation reflects respect and sensitivity toward another culture. Those who choose strong adaptation may unintentionally be perceived as having an uncomplimentary view of the new culture, a similar view held of individuals who choose not to adapt at all (Brett, 2007).

When Brett (2007) looked at the cultural variance within cultural prototypes and allowed the distributions to overlap, the people in the area that overlapped for both cultures showed the people who were most alike from both cultures. Even though these people were in the tails of their respective cultures, these individuals were closer to each other than they were to their own cultural majorities.

Everyone is ethnocentric to a great degree. Because losing ethnocentrism means changing, it is a very powerful construct. Resistance to change is a universal construct (Hendon, Hendon, & Herbig, 1999). Negotiations take place within the political, economic, social, and cultural systems of the countries involved; these are the environmental issues of negotiation.

The cultural systems involved in the negotiation may be similar or divergent. Negotiations take place within the context of the four Cs: common interest, conflicting interests, compromise, and criteria (Moran & Stripp, 1991).

Alfonso Lopez-Vasquez has researched Hispanic work styles brought into the Anglo workplaces. One of his main findings has been that both sides, the U.S. Americans and the Hispanics, have misconceptions and apprehensions about each other. One of the mistakes

U.S. Americans have made is to treat the Hispanic workers as if there are no differences in the two cultures. To get the kind of work they want, U.S. Americans have to understand the cultural differences. (Staa, 1998)

Common interest considers that both parties in the negotiation share, have, or want something that the other party has. Without a common goal, there is no need for negotiation. Areas of **conflicting interests** include payment, distribution, profits, contractual responsibilities, and quality. **Compromise** includes areas of disagreement. Although a win–win negotiated settlement would be best for both parties, the compromises that are negotiated may not produce that result. The **criteria** include the conditions under which the negotiations take place.

Communication is plagued with misinterpretations. When perspectives, environment, the four Cs, and the negotiation situation are all considered together, the possibility of misinterpretations is magnified. When the negotiators are from different cultures, they have different mindsets or differing cognitive systems for reacting to situations. For example, ethics and ethical behavior that are always near the surface can confound negotiations if the two cultures have very different views on proper business ethics. For example, the Japanese consider a contract to be an adaptive tool rather than a rigid legal document as most U.S. Americans would interpret it. Nigerians, Mexicans, and the Chinese find that bribes placed in the proper places help business run smoothly, but such behavior is considered unethical in the United States.

During the Persian Gulf War, the soldiers from various countries were restricted to the military compounds because the Saudi Arabians were afraid that if the soldiers had contact with the Saudi civilians, it would threaten the Saudi way of life. This was the beginning of the United States' realization that everyone does not want our form of life. The Taliban and al-Qaeda also are very opposed to and feel very threatened by the U.S. way of life.

The mindsets of businesspeople have developed to give stability and are mutually compatible with other businesspeople in their field in their culture. When cognitive dissonance is acknowledged due to a different culture, peace of mind is lost, and you will strive to reestablish a new peace of mind. Realizing that you are locked into your own mindsets is important. Acknowledging that the other culture's representatives are having the same mindset difficulties is crucial. When negotiating with another culture, you will find beliefs you do not share and will have cognitive dissonance. The more abstract a subject is, the more difficult it will be to view it from your counterpart's mindset (Fisher, 1997).

The following is an example of how cognitive dissonance works and how we try to make something fit into our current mindset.

In the West, we are surrounded by right angles—rooms, windows, doors, furniture, and buildings. If someone asks you what the shape of the filing cabinet across the room is, you would say rectangular. However, unless you are looking at the object directly from above or in front, you would be seeing the object from an angle, and it would not appear to have 90° angles. Because from experience you know these things have 90° angles, you know it is a rectangular object. These are preconceived cognitives that you have learned to trust. If you are placed in a room that has been devised to elude our senses because it is not built proportionally, you will try to make objects in the room fit your cognitive model. It is almost impossible for persons to visualize reality as it is, rather than how it is in their mind. (Fisher, 1997)

If friendship and trust are important, it may be necessary to plan a number of social activities. These activities are essential in building personal relationships before negotiations begin or before a solution can be reached in the negotiations. In many cultures, business is conducted with family and friends, and personal relationships are considered important for the long run. In other cultures, friendships are not important to business relationships. The following summary of negotiating strategies of the United States and other selected countries is a beginning point for anyone doing business in these countries. As was emphasized earlier, it is important to avoid stereotyping. People who have lived and worked in another culture may alter their negotiation strategies based on firsthand knowledge of strategies that have proven effective.

Brazil

Characteristics of Brazilian negotiating style include the fact that people of Brazil have a polychronic view of time rather than a monochronic view, which means they can do several tasks simultaneously. Brazilians are rather emotional; they are a nonconfrontational and face-saving culture. Their negotiation style is indirect. Brazilians are known to be flexible, perhaps due to economic uncertainty in their country (e.g., fluctuations in interest, inflation, and exchange rates) and constantly changing Brazilian laws. Brazilians are considered a risk-averse culture; thus, encountering a play-it-safe attitude during negotiations is not unusual. Negotiators from other cultures may be surprised at the flexibility of Brazilians when it comes to solving problems. Brazilians do not readily admit defeat but constantly look for ways to reach a resolution. Brazilians are, in fact, known as "experts of improvisation" (Moran, Harris, & Moran, 2011; Morrison & Conaway, 2006).

Canada

Canada has two major groups, as well as variations throughout the provinces, when it comes to negotiation strategies. The two major groups are the French-speaking province of Quebec (including parts of New Brunswick and eastern Ontario) and the remainder of Canada.

French Canadians are less open than the remainder of the Canadians and exhibit a stronger ethnocentrism than people of the other provinces. Canadians tend to be well informed, analytical, and prefer objective information. The French Canadians are more linear in their problem-solving process, and the English Canadians are more concerned with abstract or theoretical values in their problem-solving process. Although they are not quite as direct as U.S. negotiators, they approach negotiations with a strong sense of self-determination. Canadians are closer to the British than to people of the United States when it comes to controlling their emotions and do not need to be friends to engage in business. Negotiators are selected for expertise and success in negotiating. However, gender, age, and social class are used to disqualify negotiators more by the French Canadians than the English Canadians. French Canadians are more concerned with protocol than are English Canadians. Promptness and wise use of time are important in Canada. Trust is also an important component in negotiations in Canada (Moran et al., 2011). Canadians choose the more individually oriented negotiation strategies. Most of Canada is considered tribal; some parts are pluralistic (Leaptrott, 1996).

China

When negotiating with the Chinese, remember that they believe in a win–win negotiation strategy that allows both sides to be winners to increase the strength of the relationship. The Chinese value a cooperative approach to negotiation rather than bargaining strategies. They actually believe that negotiators who use the win–lose approach to make a large profit at someone else's expense are "unscrupulous merchants." However, that does not mean that all Chinese negotiators are altruistic. Although concessive negotiation can be used, it is important that stability and harmony are in no way harmed by the negotiations. Both sides should be willing to make concessions to achieve and maintain a harmonious relationship. The environment is also important; a neutral site is recommended (Zhao, 2000). Because the Chinese will have many people on their negotiating team, the other side needs to match the number on the Chinese team. They should also have a seating arrangement worked out in advance—one that reflects the status and hierarchy of the team members.

Because verbal and nonverbal information is more important to the Chinese than formal, written, or legal documents, everything that is in writing also needs to be discussed. The Chinese establish that they want an agreement in broad terms and then work on the details, although the U.S. team wants to work from the details to an agreement. Bribery is not looked on favorably in China (Zhao, 2000). In summary, relationship building is important to the Chinese; they tend to be group oriented and prefer face-to-face negotiations. China is considered a collective culture (Leaptrott, 1996).

France

Before beginning negotiations with the French, it is important to have a good French-language interpreter who can decode high-context and nonverbal communication in addition to translating the language. The French expect the negotiator to have the correct social and educational background and have the authority to make decisions. If a relationship has not been developed first, it is not unusual for the French negotiator to have a certain distrust of members of the opposing team. Trust is earned. Because the French are Cartesian-logic oriented, presentations should be complete and detailed. Negotiators need answers for many different scenarios in addition to the one they hope to sell. French negotiators do not mind if the negotiations develop into debates.

The French are indirect in their negotiating style in contrast to U.S. negotiators, who are direct and bottom-line oriented. Quality is more important than speed; the negotiations should not be rushed but should take as much time as necessary. The French do not conduct negotiations during meals; mealtimes are meant to be enjoyed (Asselin & Mastron, 2000). The French are individualistic in their negotiation strategies; they also prefer face-to-face negotiations. The French are striving toward pluralism; however, they are more tribal in the southern part of the country (Leaptrott, 1996).

Germany

Germany's strategies during negotiations are very serious. Germans insist on permanent and stringent contracts. In the Federal Republic of Germany, the corporation, employer associations, and unions each have roles in negotiations. However, with the merging of East and West Germany, these social partnerships are changing.

The German strategy is to begin business immediately after introductions. Their strategy is very slow and methodical with no humor involved in the process. They are not impressed with "educated guesses"; it is better to acknowledge a lack of information. Although negotiating with Germans may be slow, they tend to be direct. Negotiators will know where they stand during the negotiation process (Samovar et al., 2009). The Germans are individualistic and also prefer face-to-face negotiations. Germany is considered a pluralistic country (Leaptrott, 1996).

Japan

In Japan, negotiations are carried out before the transaction gets to the negotiation table. Through conversations between numerous individuals on both sides that can take place in restaurants, bars, golf courses, and offices, persuasive appeals are made. The Japanese then meet and come to a consensus before meeting with the other side at the negotiation table. The negotiation table is a ritual rather than a place to actually change offers or minds (Sebenius, 2002a). The Japanese look for a win–win situation.

For the Japanese, negotiation is a status game with people of equal levels discussing business issues in casual settings. The power levels between the companies can be important. A larger corporation generally holds more relative power in the negotiations than a medium- or small-sized company. Showing commitment to a long-term relationship and being enthusiastic are important strategies to use. The Japanese will learn everything possible about the members of the opposing negotiation team and their corporation. To negotiate successfully with the Japanese, it is important to be well prepared with data and information and to learn a great deal about the Japanese. When disputes arise, taking a break to discuss options is recommended for members of both teams. The Japanese generally do not have authority to make concessions without discussing them with their colleagues first (Nishiyama, 2000). The Japanese are very group oriented; they often use media and prefer face-to-face negotiations. Japan is a collective culture (Leaptrott, 1996).

Mexico

Connections, introductions, and relationship building are important to doing business in Mexico. Using connections is common with favors being exchanged on both sides. While *la mordida* (a bribe) seems very unethical to U.S. negotiators, it is simply a way to get things done in Mexico. However, as salaries in Mexico increase, the practice of *la mordida* is expected to cease. Decisions tend to be made by the senior executives in all but the largest organizations rather than by committee (Hinkelman, 1994).

Mexican negotiators are selected on status, family connections, personal or political influence, and education. Protocol is quite important to Mexicans; however, they are not overly concerned about time. Being on time for appointments, however, is expected. Emotional arguments are considered to be persuasive arguments. Trust is initially assumed and then proven through interpersonal actions.

Negotiating strategies are more win–win than win–lose in Mexico. Because a friendship has developed, it is expected that each side would want both parties to profit. Mexican negotiators prefer to have the issues before them well in advance of the negotiations. A neutral site should be chosen. Patience is of the utmost importance when negotiating with Mexicans. Talks will begin after social conversation has been exchanged. Bargaining in negotiations is considered part of the game by Mexicans. Using objective facts is recommended when presenting a proposal. The best proposal should not be put on the table first; leave room to bargain. Most Mexican executives view the personal commitment to be more important than the written contract (Hinkelman, 1994). Mexicans tend to be group oriented in their negotiation style and prefer face-to-face negotiations. Mexico is a tribal culture (Leaptrott, 1996).

The Netherlands

The Netherlands have been very active in trade since the 1600s. Depending on which region (north or south) people live, they will be quiet or gregarious. Overall they are honest negotiators. There is an aversion to chaos as they are well organized. They tend to be open to ideas rather than being threatened by the new phenomena. This leads to the Dutch's being direct and pragmatic but not contentious. Problem solving is considered a group effort. Social status is measured by occupation as it is in the United States, so U.S. negotiators would not see a difference. Although negotiations may move slower than in the United States because of the Dutch belief that negotiation is a team effort, after they have made a decision based on consensus, the Dutch will move very fast and will expect the same from the other firm. The Netherlands is the most pluralistic country (Leaptrott, 1996; Morrison & Conaway, 2006).

Singapore

Age is important in Singapore. While collectivism is taught in the schools, Singapore is home to three very different cultures: Chinese, Malay, and Indian so the value systems can be very different from individual to individual. In the business world consensus of the group is important. Family is very important to Singaporeans. Social status is based on political power, wealth, and education (Morrison & Conaway, 2006).

South Korea

Because Koreans are rank and status conscious, you need to match the rank of the individuals who are attending the negotiations. Personal questions are not unusual and are used to help determine rank and status within your organization. Harmony is important in Korean society; however, Koreans can be direct, express emotion, and be a little aggressive during negotiations. Being overly direct, on the other hand, is not appreciated in Korea. Criticizing the competition is inappropriate. Using local foreign trading agency representatives to introduce members of your team is highly suggested. Because a relationship should be developed before doing business, it takes multiple trips to conduct any business with the Koreans. Their logical orientation is more cyclical in nature, allowing them to discuss items out of sequence. Negotiations will stress logic and the profit structure of the deal. Every Korean at the negotiation will need a counterpart from the other firm. South Korea is a collective culture (Leaptrott, 1996; Morrison & Conaway, 2006).

Taiwan

The Taiwanese are similar to the people of the Republic of China in their negotiations; however, they have been more active for a longer time negotiating with and manufacturing for the West. As a major exporter of textiles, electronics, machinery, metals, timber products, and high-technology items for more than three decades, they have a modern economic system with a large middle class. They do not consider themselves part of mainland China; this fact should be remembered during negotiations. A personal relationship needs to be developed before doing business. Harmony is important, and they never say "no." The logic used in negotiations is more cyclical than linear. Seating protocol is important; the team leader should be seated in the middle with other team members seated to the left and right in rank order. Humility, sincerity, honesty, and compatibility between counterparts are all important. Direct criticism is considered impolite. The Taiwanese believe in self-control and dislike anyone who is loud or boisterous. Reciprocity of goodwill gestures is essential. Taiwan is a collective culture (Leaptrott, 1996; Morrison & Conaway, 2006).

United Kingdom (England, Scotland, Wales, and Northern Ireland)

The British are very matter-of-fact about negotiations. Objective facts are listened to with interest, but emotional displays are considered improper. The British do not easily change their minds on an issue and are very analytical. They tend to understate positions during negotiations. Although they tend to be individualistic, company policy is always followed without question. Business friendships are not necessary, and the British have no difficulty saying "no" during negotiations. Like U.S. negotiators, the British tend to be very deadline-oriented (Morrison & Conaway, 2006). They are individualistic in their negotiation strategies. England is a tribal culture; Scotland and Wales are pluralistic (Leaptrott, 1996).

United States

U.S. negotiators are very focused on completing the deal. They tend to be profit oriented and direct in their negotiating strategies. Their presentations tend to be to the point. U.S. negotiators do not need a personal relationship to enter into negotiations with another party. Many U.S. persons do not even develop personal relationships with people with whom they work. They will work during meals, while playing golf, or at almost any other time. Because the United States is made up of many different cocultures, variations exist by ethnic group, region, gender, or age. U.S. negotiators can be very informal. U.S. negotiators respond well to facts and numbers. Many U.S. people have difficulty deciphering high-context nonverbal signals. U.S. negotiators like to bargain from a position of strength; this sometimes leads to bargains that represent a win position for them and a lose position for their opponent. U.S. negotiators tend to choose strategies that are individually oriented and many times use the media (Morrison & Conaway, 2006). The United States is a pluralistic society (Leaptrott, 1996).

Terms

Argument dilution	Conflicting interests	Irritators
Authority	Criteria	Perception
Authority advantage	Cultural noise	Personal constructs
Balanced authority	Face-to-face	Power
Cognitive dissonance	strategies	Protocol
Common interest	Group-oriented	Reviewing the
Compromise	Individually oriented	negotiation

Exercise 1

Instructions: Circle T for true or F for false.

1. T F National culture is the same for all citizens within a nation.
2. T F For power to be meaningful, it should be accepted.
3. T F A woman can negotiate as well in Japan, Saudi Arabia, and France as she can in the United States.
4. T F The environment of intercultural business negotiations is unimportant.
5. T F Effective negotiators are observant, patient, adaptable, and good listeners.
6. T F Different protocols can affect negotiations.
7. T F Criteria include changes the negotiators must make in contractual responsibilities.
8. T F U.S. Americans tend to choose strategies that are group oriented.
9. T F The Netherlands is a collectivistic culture.
10. T F If the United States were to send only one person to negotiate with the Japanese, they would assume the U.S. company was serious.

Questions and Cases for Discussion

1. Why is the selection of the players for the situation so important?
2. Explain how power and authority affect negotiations.
3. What roles do interpreters and translators play in the negotiation process?
4. Explain how gender can have an impact on successful negotiation. Identify cultures in which women are treated as equals at the negotiation table and cultures in which they are not.
5. How can the negotiation situation and environment affect the participants in the negotiation if it is held in the home country, the opponent's country, or a neutral country?
6. How do relationship and substantive conflict affect negotiations?
7. Stereotypes are how we learn about national culture. What are the advantages and limitations of stereotypes during negotiations?
8. Discuss differences in negotiating with people who are group oriented versus those who are individual oriented. Give examples of cultures that are group oriented and those that are individual oriented.

9. Explain how media affect intercultural communication. Give examples of media-induced stereotypes.
10. Explain what is meant by personal constructs and how they affect the negotiation process.
11. How do conflicting interests affect negotiations?
12. Describe your strategy for negotiating with people whose culture believes that being very emotional in a negotiating setting is good, that it is not important to know facts or details, and that status is important.
13. Identify three personal constructs you hold that differentiate you from most people of the macroculture in your country and explain how these personal constructs may confuse a negotiator who has a stereotype in his or her mind about your country's culture.
14. Would it be easier for U.S. Americans to negotiate with Canadians, Mexicans, or Japanese? What support can you give for your answer?
15. Give some guidelines for women who wish to be successful international negotiators.

CASES

The following procedure is recommended for analyzing the cases: (a) read the case carefully paying attention to details, (b) read the questions at the end of the case, (c) reread the case, taking notes on or highlighting the details needed for answering the questions, (d) identify relevant facts, underlying assumptions, and critical issues of the case, (e) list possible answers to the questions, and (f) select the most logical response to the question. Your professor may ask that you submit answers to the case questions in writing.

Case 1

Your instructor will separate the class into two negotiation teams. One team is from the United States; the other team is from Mexico. You are to respond from the cultural perspective of your country (either the United States or Mexico). The U.S. corporation desires to lower its cost of production and believes it can do so by manufacturing in Mexico. However, because the U.S. firm does not have experience manufacturing in Mexico, it wants to negotiate with Agua Manufacturing in Mexico. The management of Agua Manufacturing is anxious to do the production for the U.S. corporation because it has excess capacity. The negotiations will take place in Mexico so that the U.S. representatives will be able to see and evaluate the facilities. Answer the following questions from the point of view of the Mexican negotiation team and the U.S. negotiation team. You will probably need to research the cultural background of Mexico and the United States. Remember that even if you were born and reared in the United States, it is sometimes difficult to see yourself as others see you.

1. Explain the negotiation perspective, environment, and negotiation situation.
2. Where do you expect there to be common interests, conflicting interests, and compromises? What is the criterion for achievement?
3. What is your negotiation strategy? What are your tactics?
4. How important is culture in this situation?

Case 2

A U.S. American woman executive is sent to negotiate a contract with a corporation in Saudi Arabia. She dresses conservatively in a dark business suit and completes her makeup and hair as she would in the United States. She finds the Arabs to be very aloof. She is asked when her boss will be arriving and is feeling ignored. What mistakes have been made? What can be done to correct such a situation?

Case 3

Your company has chosen to use an export management company that will handle all the sales and financial transactions for your products overseas. In what way could this be an advantage, and how could it be a disadvantage? Does the size of the firm matter?

Case 4

A group of high-powered businessmen from New York City arrive in Mexico City to give a presentation. They have timed, detailed agendas, a long contract, and specific plans for a joint venture. They distribute the materials and say they are pressed for time and need to complete the meeting so they can catch their plane. The Mexicans sat very quietly during the presentation. After the presentation, the New Yorkers on their way home congratulated themselves on their success. The Mexicans, however, felt they would not be able to work with these New Yorkers. Why do the two sides view the meeting differently?

Case 5

You are on your way to negotiate a joint manufacturing agreement with a company in India. You have never met representatives of the Indian negotiating team, but you have corresponded by e-mail and telephone. How long do you anticipate you will have to stay in order to finalize the agreement? What do you know about their negotiating style? What do you know about their culture?

Activities

1. Write a paragraph on the role that holidays and religion might play when negotiating in Saudi Arabia.
2. Consult a book on cultural etiquette, such as Martin and Chaney's *Global Business Etiquette* (2012), and write a one-page summary on the role that gift giving plays when negotiating with the Japanese or Chinese.
3. Consult a book on nonverbal communication, such as Roger E. Axtell's *Gestures: The Do's and Taboos of Body Language Around the World* (1998), and prepare a one-page summary of the role that nonverbal communication plays when negotiating with persons in a South American country of your choice.
4. From recent issues of the *Wall Street Journal* or your local newspaper, find an article related to negotiations between the United States and another country. Make a short oral report summarizing the article.
5. Be prepared to discuss the role that bargaining plays when negotiating with persons in different cultures.
6. Underline unacceptable behavior in the following scenario: The ABC Corporation's negotiating team has been invited to dine with the Mexican team at a Mexican restaurant. Some of the team members do not care for Mexican food. At the restaurant, Tom is uncomfortable and very hot, so before sitting down he takes off his jacket and loosens his tie.

He now feels comfortable and starts talking with two of the Mexican team members. As Juan refers to him as Dr. Ross, Tom stops him and tells him to please call him Tom. Tom asks the Mexican team leader if there is some way by which they can compromise over an issue discussed during the day.

The first course is served, which is chicken soup with the chicken's feet in the dish. Tom winces as he sees the chicken's feet and pushes the bowl to the side.

7. The following is a self-assessment exercise you may take; the interpretation of the results follows.

Negotiation Skills Self-Assessment Exercise*

Please respond to this list of questions in terms of what you believe you do when interacting with others. Base your answers on your typical day-to-day activities. Be as frank as you can. For each statement, please enter on the score sheet the number corresponding to your choice of the five possible responses given below:

1. If you have never (or very rarely) observed yourself doing what is described in the statement.
2. If you have observed yourself doing what is described in the statement occasionally, but infrequently: that is, less often than most other people who are involved in similar situations.
3. If you have observed yourself doing what is described in the statement about an average amount: that is, about as often as most other people who are involved in similar situations.
4. If you have observed yourself doing what is described in the statement fairly frequently: that is, somewhat more often than most other people who are involved in similar situations.
5. If you have observed yourself doing what is described in the statement very frequently: that is, considerably more than most other people who are involved in similar situations.

Please answer each question.

1. I focus on the entire situation or problem.
2. I evaluate the facts according to a set of personal values.
3. I am relatively unemotional.
4. I think that the facts speak for themselves in most situations.
5. I enjoy working on new problems.
6. I focus on what is going on between people when interacting.
7. I tend to analyze things very carefully.
8. I am neutral when arguing.
9. I work in bursts of energy with slack periods in between.
10. I am sensitive to other people's needs and feelings.
11. I hurt people's feelings without knowing it.
12. I am good at keeping track of what has been said in a discussion.
13. I put two and two together quickly.
14. I look for common ground and compromise.
15. I use logic to solve problems.
16. I know most of the details when discussing an issue.
17. I follow my inspirations of the moment.
18. I take strong stands on matters of principle.
19. I am good at using a step-by-step approach.
20. I clarify information for others.
21. I get my facts a bit wrong.
22. I try to please people.
23. I am very systematic when making a point.
24. I relate facts to experience.
25. I am good at pinpointing essentials.
26. I enjoy harmony.
27. I weigh the pros and cons.
28. I am patient.
29. I project myself into the future.
30. I let my decisions be influenced by my personal likes and wishes.

*From Pierre Casse. (1981). *Training for the cross-cultural mind* (2nd ed.). Washington, DC: Sietar, Interactive Style Questionnaire Situation Management Systems, Inc.

31. I look for cause and effect.
32. I focus on what needs attention now.
33. When others become uncertain or discouraged, my enthusiasm carries them along.
34. I am sensitive to praise.
35. I make logical statements.
36. I rely on well-tested ways to solve problems.
37. I keep switching from one idea to another.
38. I offer bargains.
39. I have my ideas very well thought out.
40. I am precise in my arguments.
41. I bring others to see the exciting possibilities in a situation.
42. I appeal to emotions and feelings to reach a "fair" deal.
43. I present well-articulated arguments for the proposals I favor.
44. I do not trust inspiration.
45. I speak in a way which conveys a sense of excitement to others.
46. I communicate what I am willing to give in return for what I get.
47. I put forward proposals or suggestions that make sense even if they are unpopular.
48. I am pragmatic.
49. I am imaginative and creative in analyzing a situation.
50. I put together very well-reasoned arguments.
51. I actively solicit others' opinions and suggestions.
52. I document my statements.
53. My enthusiasm is contagious.
54. I build upon others' ideas.
55. My proposals command the attention of others.
56. I like to use the inductive method (from facts to theories).
57. I can be emotional at times.
58. I use veiled or open threats to get others to comply.

59. When I disagree with someone, I skillfully point out the flaws in the other's arguments.
60. I am low key in my reactions.
61. In trying to persuade others, I appeal to their need for sensation and novelty.
62. I make other people feel that they have something of value to contribute.
63. I put forth ideas which are incisive.
64. I face difficulties with realism.
65. I point out the positive potential in discouraging or difficult situations.
66. I show tolerance and understanding of others' feelings.
67. I use arguments relevant to the problem at hand.
68. I am perceived as a down-to-earth person.
69. I go beyond the facts.
70. I give people credit for their ideas and contributions.
71. I like to organize and plan.
72. I am skillful at bringing up pertinent facts.
73. I have a charismatic tone.
74. When disputes arise, I search for the areas of agreement.
75. I am consistent in my reactions.
76. I quickly notice what needs attention.
77. I withdraw when the excitement is over.
78. I appeal for harmony and cooperation.
79. I am cool when negotiating.
80. I work all the way through to reach a conclusion.

SCORE SHEET

Enter the score you assigned each question (1, 2, 3, 4, or 5) in the space provided. (Note: The item numbers progress across the page from left to right.) When you have recorded all your scores, add them up vertically to attain four totals. Insert a "3" in any numbered space left blank.

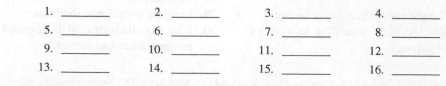

1. _____	2. _____	3. _____	4. _____
5. _____	6. _____	7. _____	8. _____
9. _____	10. _____	11. _____	12. _____
13. _____	14. _____	15. _____	16. _____

(continued)

17. _____	18. _____	19. _____	20. _____
21. _____	22. _____	23. _____	24. _____
25. _____	26. _____	27. _____	28. _____
29. _____	30. _____	31. _____	32. _____
33. _____	34. _____	35. _____	36. _____
37. _____	38. _____	39. _____	40. _____
41. _____	42. _____	43. _____	44. _____
45. _____	46. _____	47. _____	48. _____
49. _____	50. _____	51. _____	52. _____
53. _____	54. _____	55. _____	56. _____
57. _____	58. _____	59. _____	60. _____
61. _____	62. _____	63. _____	64. _____
65. _____	66. _____	67. _____	68. _____
69. _____	70. _____	71. _____	72. _____
73. _____	74. _____	75. _____	76. _____
77. _____	78. _____	79. _____	80. _____
IN: _____	NR: _____	AN: _____	FA: _____

NEGOTIATION STYLE PROFILE

Enter your four scores on the following bar chart. Construct your profile by connecting the four data points.

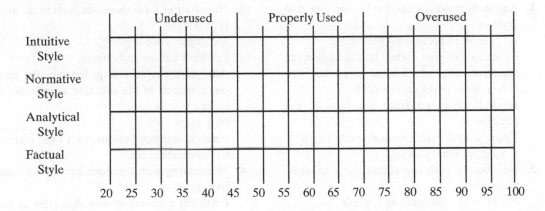

Intuitive

Basic assumption: "Imagination can solve any problem."

Behavior: making warm and enthusiastic statements, focusing on the entire situation or problem, pinpointing essentials, making projections, being imaginative and creative in analyzing the situation, switching from one subject to another, going beyond the facts, coming up with new ideas all the time, pushing and withdrawing from time to time, putting two and two together quickly, getting the facts a bit wrong sometimes, and being deductive.

Key words: Principles, essential, tomorrow, creative, idea.

Normative

Basic assumption: "Negotiating is bargaining."

Behavior: judging, assessing, and evaluating the facts according to a set of personal values, approving and disapproving, agreeing and disagreeing, using loaded words, offering bargains, proposing rewards, incentives, appealing to feelings and emotions to reach a "fair" deal, demanding, requiring, threatening, involving power, using status, authority, correlating, looking for compromise, making effective statements, focusing on people and their reactions, judging, attention to communication, and group processes.

Key words: Wrong, right, good, bad, like.

Analytical

Basic assumption: "Logic leads to the right conclusions."

Behavior: forming reasons, drawing conclusions, and applying them to the case in negotiation, arguing in favor or against one's own or others' position, directing, breaking down, dividing, analyzing each situation for cause and effect, identifying relationships of the parts, putting things into logical order, organizing, weighing the pros and cons thoroughly, making identical statements, and using linear reckoning.

Key words: Because, then, consequently, therefore, in order to.

Factual

Basic assumption: "The facts speak for themselves."

Behavior: pointing out facts in neutral way, keeping track of what has been said, reminding people of their statements, knowing most of the details of the discussed issue and sharing them with others, clarifying, relating facts to experience, being low key in their reactions, looking for proof, and documenting their statements.

Key words: Meaning, define, explain, clarify, facts.

GUIDELINES FOR NEGOTIATING WITH PEOPLE HAVING DIFFERENT STYLES

1. Negotiating with someone having a factual style—
   Be precise in presenting your facts.
   Refer to the past (what has already been tried out, what has worked, what has been shown from past experiences).
   Be indicative (go from the facts to the principles).
   Know your dossier (including the details).
   Document what you say.
2. Negotiating with someone having an intuitive style—
   Focus on the situation as a whole.
   Project yourself into the future (look for opportunities).
   Tap the imagination and creativity of your partner.
   Be quick in reacting (jump from one idea to another).
   Build upon the reaction of the other person.

3. Negotiating with someone having an analytical style—
   Use logic when arguing.
   Look for causes and effects.
   Analyze the relationships between the various elements of the situation or problem at stake.
   Be patient.
   Analyze various options with their respective pros and cons.
4. Negotiating with someone having a normative style—
   Establish a sound relationship right at the outset of the negotiation.
   Show your interest in what the other person is saying.
   Identify his or her values and adjust to them accordingly.
   Be ready to compromise.
   Appeal to your partner's feelings.

References

Alon, I., & Brett, J. M. (2007). Perceptions of time and their impact on negotiations in the Arabic-speaking Islamic world. *Negotiation Journal, 23*(1), 55–73.

Anderson, E., & Weitz, B. (1989). Determinants of continuity in conventional industrial channel dyads. *Marketing Science, 8*(4), 310–323.

Asselin, G., & Mastron, R. (2000). *Au Contraire!* Yarmouth, ME: Intercultural Press.

Axtell, R. E. (1998). *Gestures.* New York: John Wiley & Sons, Inc.

Axtell, R. E., Briggs, T., Corcoran, M., & Lamb, M. B. (1997). *Do's and taboos around the world for women in business.* New York: John Wiley.

Berger, K. P. (2006). *Private dispute resolution in international business: Negotiation, mediation, arbitration, Volume II: Handbook.* The Netherlands: Kluwer Law International.

Bradenburger, A. M., & Nalebuff, B. J. (1996). *Co-opetition.* New York: Doubleday.

Brett, J. M. (2007). *Negotiating globally: How to negotiate deals, resolve disputes, and make decisions across cultural boundaries* (2nd ed.). San Francisco, CA: Jossey-Bass.

Brett, J. M., & Okumura, T. (1998). Inter- and intracultural negotiations: U.S. and Japanese negotiators. *Academy of Management Journal, 41*(5), 495–510.

Cai, D. A., Wilson, S. R., & Drake, L. E. (2000). Culture in the context of intercultural negotiation: Individualism-collectivism and paths to integrative agreements. *Human Communication Research, 26*(4), 591–617.

Casse, P. (1981). *Training for the cross-cultural mind* (2nd ed.). Washington, DC: Sietar.

Chaisrakeo, S., & Speece, M. (2004). Culture, intercultural communication competence, and sales negotiation: A qualitative research approach. *Journal of Business & Industrial Marketing, 19*(4), 267–282. Retrieved September 6, 2004, from the Emerald.

Cohen, R. (1998). *Negotiating across cultures.* Washington, DC: United States Institute of Peace Press.

D'Amico, L. C., & Rubinstein, R. A. (1999). Cultural considerations when "setting" the negotiation table. *Negotiation Journal, 15*(4), 389–395.

Elashmawi, F., & Harris, P. (1998). *Multicultural management 2000.* Houston, TX: Butterworth-Heinemann.

Engholm, C. (1991). *When business east meets business west.* New York: John Wiley & Sons, Inc.

Fisher, G. (1980). *International negotiation.* Yarmouth, ME: Intercultural Press.

Fisher, G. (1997). *Mindsets: The role of culture and perception in international relations.* Yarmouth, ME: Intercultural Press.

Funakawa, A. (1997). *Transcultural management.* San Francisco, CA: Jossey-Bass.

Hendon, D. W., Hendon R. A., & Herbig, P. (1999). *Cross-cultural business negotiations.* Westport, CT: Praeger.

Hinkelman, E. G. (Ed.). (1994). *Mexico business: The portable encyclopedia for doing business in Mexico.* San Rafael, CA: World Trade Press.

Hodge, S. (2000). *Global smarts: The art of communicating and deal making anywhere in the world.* New York: John Wiley & Sons.

Hofstede, G., & Hofstede G. J. (2005). *Cultures and organizations* (2nd ed.). New York: McGraw-Hill.

Jervis, R. (2000). Cognitive dissonance and international relations. In G. E. Weaver (Ed.), *Culture, communication, and conflict* (pp. 442–443). Boston: Pearson Publications.

Karrass, C. L. (1996). *In business, you don't get what you deserve; you get what you negotiate.* Los Angeles, CA: Stanford Street Press.

Leaptrott, N. (1996). *Rules of the game: Global business protocol.* Cincinnati, OH: Thomson Executive Press.

Lewicki, R. J., Saunders, D. M., & Barry, B. (2011). *Essentials of negotiation* (5th ed.). New York: McGraw-Hill.

Lorange, P., & Roos, J. (1991, January/February). Why some strategic alliances succeed and others fail. *Journal of Business Strategy, 12,* 25–30.

Martin, J. S., & Chaney, L. H. (2012). *Global business etiquette: A guide to international communication and customs* (2nd ed.). Westport, CT: Praeger.

Moran, R. T., Harris, P. R., & Moran, S. V. (2011). *Managing cultural differences* (8th ed.). Burlington, MA: Butterworth-Heineman.

Moran, R. T., & Stripp, W. G. (1991). *Dynamics of successful international business negotiations.* Houston: Gulf.

Morrison, T., & Conaway, W. A. (2006). *Kiss, bow, or shake hands* (2nd ed.). Holbrook, MA: Adams Media Corporation.

Nishiyama, K. (2000). *Doing business with Japan.* Honolulu, HI: University of Hawaii Press.

Nooteboom, B., Berger, H., & Noorderhaven, N. G. (1997). Effects of trust and governance on relational risk. *Academy of Management Journal, 40*(2), 308–338.

Ping, M. D. (2000). Culture and business: Interacting effectively to achieve mutual goals. In G. R. Weaver (Ed.), *Culture, communication, and conflict* (pp. 518–526). Boston: Pearson Publishing.

Planken, B. (2005). Managing rapport in *lingua franca* sales negotiations: A comparison of professional and aspiring negotiators. *English for Specific Purposes, 24*(4), 381–400.

Prosser, M. H. (1985). *The cultural dialogue.* Washington, DC: Sietar.

Ruch, W. V. (1989*). International handbook of corporate communication.* Jefferson, NC: McFarland.

Samovar, L. A., Porter, R. E., & McDaniel, E. R. (2009). *Communication between cultures* (7th ed.). Belmont, CA: Wadsworth/Thomson Learning.

Saxton, T. (1997). The effects of partner and relationship characteristics on alliance outcomes. *Academy of Management Journal, 40,* 443–461.

Schneider, S. C., & Barsoux, J. L. (2002). *Managing across cultures* (2nd ed.). Upper Saddle River, NJ: Prentice Hall.

Schneider, S. C., & De Meyer, A. (1991). Interpreting and responding to strategic issues: The impact of national culture. *Strategic Management Journal, 12*(4), 307–320.

Sebenius, J. K. (2002a). The hidden challenge of cross-border negotiations. *Harvard Business Review, 80*(3), 76–86.

Sebenius, J. K. (2002b). In practice: Caveats for cross-border negotiators. *Negotiation Journal, 18*(2), 121–133.

Staa, D. (1998). No need for inter-American culture clash. *Management Review, 87*(1), 8.

Teegen, H. J. (1998). Authority and trust in cross border partnerships: Mexican firm perspectives. *Journal of International Management, 4*(3), 223–229.

Teegen, H. J., & Doh, J. P. (2002). U.S.–Mexican alliance negotiations: Impact of culture on authority, trust, and performance. *Thunderbird International Business Review, 44*(6), 749–775.

Tiampati, M. (2004). Soda extraction threatens Magadi Maasai. *Cultural Survival Quarterly, 28*(3). Retrieved November 18, 2004, from the ProQuest.

Tinsley, C. (1998). Models of conflict resolution in Japanese, German, and American cultures. *Journal of Applied Psychology, 83*(2), 316–323.

Verluyten, S. P. (2002, October). *Intercultural incidents and vignettes.* Distributed at the Association for Business Communication Conference, Cincinnati, OH.

Weaver, G. R. (Ed.). (2000). *Culture, communication, and conflict: Readings in intercultural relations* (2nd ed.). Boston: Pearson Publishing.

Wilen, T. (2000). *International business: A basic guide for women.* n.p.: Xlibris Corporation.

Zhao, J. J. (2000). The Chinese approach to international business negotiation. *Journal of Business Communication, 37*(3), 209–237.

Glossary

Argument dilution refers to using multiple arguments when one is sufficient; a technique used less by skilled negotiators.

Authority is the power to give commands and make decisions.

Authority advantage occurs when one partner in negotiations claims to possess superior resources or a superior position in the alliance.

Balanced authority allows each partner in negotiations to share the decision-making role.

Cognitive dissonance is the psychological conflict or anxiety that results from inconsistency between what a person does and what a person believes.

Common interest considers that both parties in the negotiation share, have, or want something that the other party has.

Compromise is settling negotiation differences by mutual concessions.

Conflicting interests are areas of possible disagreement in negotiations, such as profits, quality, and terms of payment.

Criteria are conditions under which the negotiations take place.

Cultural noise refers to anything that distracts or interferes with the message being communicated.

Face-to-face strategies are concerned with negotiating in person.

Group-oriented negotiators are detail oriented to determine the proper solution.

Individually oriented refers to negotiations that are concerned with the best contract for your company rather than what is good for the other company.

Irritators are phrases used repeatedly by negotiators, such as "generous offer."

Personal constructs are the individual belief systems and attitudes that are different for different cultures.

Power is the ability to influence others.

Reviewing the Negotiations is a face-to-face negotiation behavior that is done more often by more skilled negotiators.

Answers to Exercises

True/False

1. F
2. T
3. F
4. F
5. T

6. T
7. F
8. F
9. F
10. F

Index

Page references followed by "f" indicate illustrated figures or photographs; followed by "t" indicates a table.

293